Connecting with Consumers

Connecting with Consumers

Marketing for New Marketplace Realities

Allan J. Kimmel

OXFORD
UNIVERSITY PRESS

OXFORD
UNIVERSITY PRESS

Great Clarendon Street, Oxford OX2 6DP

Oxford University Press is a department of the University of Oxford.
It furthers the University's objective of excellence in research, scholarship,
and education by publishing worldwide in

Oxford New York

Auckland Cape Town Dar es Salaam Hong Kong Karachi
Kuala Lumpur Madrid Melbourne Mexico City Nairobi
New Delhi Shanghai Taipei Toronto

With offices in

Argentina Austria Brazil Chile Czech Republic France Greece
Guatemala Hungary Italy Japan Poland Portugal Singapore
South Korea Switzerland Thailand Turkey Ukraine Vietnam

Oxford is a registered trade mark of Oxford University Press
in the UK and in certain other countries

Published in the United States
by Oxford University Press Inc., New York

British Library Cataloguing in Publication Data

Data available

Library of Congress Cataloging in Publication Data

Data available

Typeset by SPI Publisher Services, Pondicherry, India
Printed in Great Britain
on acid-free paper by
CPI Antony Rowe, Chippenham, Wiltshire

ISBN: 978–0–19–955650–2 (Hbk)
ISBN: 978–0–19–955651–9 (Pbk)

1 3 5 7 9 10 8 6 4 2

CONTENTS

PREFACE

If you don't like change, you're going to like irrelevance even less.

General Eric Shineski, Retired Chief of Staff, US Army

It's a good bet that the retired General did not have the marketing profession in mind when he uttered this comment about change, but his implied warning could not have been more apropos for marketers in light of the transformation we are seeing in the consumer marketplace. To a great extent, consumers are far ahead of the curve in exploiting the potential of new technological and social developments that have largely defined these early years of the twenty-first century. Those marketers who tenaciously hold on to the tried-and-true methods of their trade are becoming irrelevant at a speed that can only be truly appreciated by their more forward-thinking competitors.

What we are experiencing today in marketing is something akin to a paradigm transition. The marketing concept has been turned on its head, forcing marketers to rethink their basic approaches for serving consumers that had worked so well for so many years. To some extent, it was inevitable that marketers would reach an impasse with their traditional arsenal of communication, persuasion, and selling tactics. Societal and technological changes are inevitable, but their breadth and impact seem particularly profound and accelerated with the dawn of each new century. Many of the changes that have heralded the start of the current century are linked in one way or another to a digital revolution that some social historians view as significant as the Industrial Revolution of the eighteenth century. At the heart of this era's revolution is the growing role that the personal computer and portable mobile devices play in our lives, with the Internet serving to connect consumers globally in ways that hardly could have been foreseen as recently as a few decades ago. At the same time, marketers have themselves to blame for their loosening grip on the consumer marketplace, as the proliferation of both above-the-line and below-the-line marketing tactics has led to a state of overkill that has served to drive potential customers away. The purpose of this book is to trace these various developments, consider their impact on the potential reshaping of the market-ing profession, and describe the emerging set of tools that can enable marketers to respond to new marketplace realities. To satisfy these objectives, I have divided the book into two main sections, with Part I covering the rising power of consumers and Part II surveying the connected marketing approaches and techniques that are slowly emerging as the most viable alternatives to traditional marketing methods. With the exception of the concluding chapter, I have included stand-alone boxes throughout that provide a focus on research and theory, on the one hand, and practical applications, on the other.

For some time, I wrestled with the possibility of replacing the term *Connecting With Consumers* in the book's title with *Consumers in Control*. Although I believed that both options would effectively characterize the book's content, I eventually decided to stick with my first impulse after concluding that the word "control" would set the wrong tone and serve to reinforce perceptions of the marketer/consumer relationship as an adversarial one. Dating back to Vance Packard's best-selling book, *The Hidden Persuaders* (1957), many have held the opinion that marketers and advertisers, through the adroit use of the media and psychological techniques, manipulate and brainwash consumers into desiring and purchasing products that they do not really want or need. Although marketers' primary defense against such charges has been that marketing does not create needs, but rather suggests ways that needs can best be satisfied to the mutual benefit of companies and customers, either side of the argument concerning marketing control and manipulation is today more or less moot. The top-down business-to-consumer (B-to-C) model that has reflected the modus operandi of marketing has been undercut by the recent trend toward consumer-to-consumer (C-to-C) influence. Marketing is in need of a new paradigm that acknowledges consumer connectedness and seeks to leverage the consumer conversation through *collaboration* rather than *control*. Although the balance of power has shifted to the consumer for each of the various aspects of the marketing process, collaboration is what the future of marketing likely will be all about. Marketers can indeed avoid irrelevance in the face of change, but this will require a clear commitment to connecting with consumers rather than searching for ways to reestablish control over them.

When I first heard marketing guru Don Schultz assert that there has not been a marketing book yet written that begins with the customer, my path was clear. All good books require a beginning, middle, and an end, and in my view, the consumer should be front and center not only at the start, but also in the middle and at the end. That is something I have strived to accomplish in the writing of this book, which is equally intended for marketing students and professionals and, more generally, for consumers. Nonetheless, it would be misleading to suggest that this book has a true ending, because the changes that it describes continue to unfold. As I state in the book, these are exciting times for marketers, who have a clear choice: embrace the ongoing changes as opportunities for reshaping their relationship with consumers, or cling to the past at the risk of becoming irrelevant.

I approached the writing of this book with no small amount of trepidation, given the range of content to be covered and the staggering amount of available source material to draw from. My thanks go out especially to Matthew Derbyshire, Assistant Commissioning Editor of Business and Management books at Oxford University Press, for his unflagging support and enthusiasm for this project from the start. I also thank my good friends Len Dintzer and Joel Asher, who recommended useful source material along the way, and who always seem to be at least one or two steps ahead of me when it comes to awareness and understanding of new technological developments. Finally, I owe a debt of gratitude to the graduate students at ESCP Europe who completed their theses under my tutelage, and whose work provided invaluable insight into several of the topics covered in this book, including Georges Camy, Veronica Carvallo, Laura Davies, Julie Deffontaines, and Caroline Wilsford. Finally, I want to express my appreciation to Oxford University Press for offering me this second opportunity to contribute to their impressive catalog.

Paris, France   Allan J. Kimmel
August 2009

LIST OF FIGURES

LIST OF EXHIBITS

LIST OF TABLES

LIST OF BOXES

ABBREVIATIONS

ACTIVE   Adoption, Connected, Travelers, Information-Hungry, Vocal, and Exposed
CGC   Consumer-Generated Content
CIT   Critical Incidents Technique
CPR   Cardiopulmonary Resuscitation
CRM   Customer Relationship Marketing
DIY   Do-It-Yourself
DMC   Digital Media Communications
DVR   Digital Video Recorder
EM   Electromagnetic
EMF   Electromagnetic Field
FAQs   Frequently Asked Questions
HL   Hargreaves Lansdown
ISP   Internet Service Provider
LCD   Liquid Crystal Display
LED   Light Emitting Diode
LSI   Latent Semantic Indexing
MLM   Multilevel Marketing
MMOGs   Massive Multiplayer Online Games
MOA   Motivation, Opportunity, and Ability
MROC   Market Research Online Communities
NPS   Net Promoter Score
NWOM   Negative Word of Mouth
OS   Opinion Seeking
PDA   Personal Digital Assistant
PETA   People for the Ethical Treatment of Animals
PVR   Personal Video Recorder
PWOM   Positive Word of Mouth
P2P   Peer-to-Peer
ROI   Return on Investment
RSS   Really Simple Syndication

SIMM	Simultaneous Media Usage Survey
SNCR	Society for New Communications Research
SOV	Share of Voice
SRIC-BI	SRI Consulting Business Intelligence
SUV	Sports Utility Vehicles
VALS	Values, Attitudes, and Lifestyles
VCR	Videocassette Recorder
WOMM	Word of Mouth Marketing
WOMMA	Word of Mouth Marketing Association

PART I

Consumer-to-Consumer Influence: The Rising Power of Consumers

1 Marketing in Evolution

That we are a shopping species is not exactly new news. On the heels of the industrial revolution, commercial selling and buying behavior have represented activities that firmly defined successive generations, as fully interwoven within the fabric of industrialized nations as technological, scientific, social, and political developments. Each new product innovation increasingly brings to the fore the defining mantra of modern man and woman—"I shop, therefore I am." It is not an exaggeration to say that in contemporary times, the buying and having of material goods, along with a growing array of services, have become as central to people's sense of being as family and career. In this light, it is not surprising that consumer psychologist Michael Solomon (2008) chose to subtitle his highly regarded *Consumer Behavior* textbook with the phrase *Buying, Having, and Being*.

As we enter the second decade of the twenty-first millennium, the changes that are occurring within the marketing landscape are startling. The traditional "top-down" marketing paradigm (so-called *business-to-consumer marketing*, or B-to-C) whereby consumers were content to select goods produced, distributed, and promoted by companies and advertisers who decided what customers needed and desired, has been turned on its head in an amazingly short span of time. In its place are bottom-up, grass-roots approaches (so-called *consumer-to-consumer marketing*, or C-to-C) that are shaping the business world in ways unimagined only a few decades ago. Consumers are increasingly taking control of the marketplace and are no longer merely passive participants in the wide array of activities that comprise the marketing enterprise. Whether it be the creation or modification of products, the establishment of prices, the availability of goods, or the ways in which company offerings are communicated, consumers have begun to take a more active role in each of the various marketing functions.

At the root of this newfound consumer power are the technological developments that have facilitated the means by which people connect with one another, giving rise to the influence of social networks and word-of-mouth communication. With the advent and rapid evolution of the Internet and mobile communication devices, the familiar adage, "there is power in numbers" perhaps has never had greater resonance than it does in today's marketing environment. We no longer are merely a shopping species, we are a *connected* shopping species, and it is this connectedness that goes a long way toward explaining how and why consumers have gained greater control over the marketing process. The challenges and opportunities that these and related developments pose for marketers cannot be overstated: they pervade the ongoing discussions at corporate marketing and advertising board meetings and conferences (see Box 1.1), influence

---

BOX 1.1 FROM MARKETER CONTROL TO CONSUMER CONTROL

Indicative of the growing realization among marketers that consumers are increasingly gaining power in the marketplace are some of the opinions espoused during the 2006 annual conference in the United States of the Association of National Advertisers (Elliott, 2006). Among the partici-pants at the conference were decision makers from leading consumer goods firms, including Procter & Gamble, Burger King, Wal-Mart, BMW's Mini USA, and MasterCard. The following comments reflect the shifting nature of the consumer-marketer balance of power:

> The power is with the consumer. Marketers and retailers are scrambling to keep up with her. . . . Consumers are beginning in a very real sense to own our brands and participate in their creation . . . We need to learn to begin to let go.
>
> A. G. Lafley, chief executive at Procter & Gamble

> Today, the customer is in charge, and whoever is best at putting the customer in charge makes all the money.
>
> Stephen F. Quinn, senior vice president for marketing at Wal-Mart Stores

> Content is no longer something you push out. Content is an invitation to engage with your brand.
>
> Cammie Dunaway, chief marketing officer at Yahoo!

> If you have a global brand promise, 'Have it your way,' it's about putting the customer in charge, even if they say bad things about the brand.
>
> Russ Klein, president for global marketing, strategy, and innovation at Burger King

James L. McDowell, managing director at Mini USA, revealed that nearly 60% of the estimated 40,000 Minis the company sells annually in the United States are customized by their owners. Some Mini owners, for example, go so far as to adorn their cars in provocative costumes for Halloween. Far from viewing such consumer alterations of the original product as a threat, McDowell's reaction was more deferential when he acknowledged that "It's a great thing every day to wake up and see what consumers have done to the brand, [even though] it's not a culture we necessarily would have come up with on our own."

---

organizational decision making, and have served to establish new marketing research objectives and parameters. Marketers across the globe are frantically trying to keep pace with spiraling social and technological changes that are redefining the consumer land-scape, struggling to remain relevant while faced with the growing threat of obsolescence.

It is ironic that in an age in which marketers can reach their audiences with greater facility than ever before, firms have never been less in control of their customer targets. However, the increasing connectedness of consumers provides a range of unique and promising opportunities for marketing managers, and strategies can be utilized to harness their influence in order to achieve profitable commercial outcomes—provided these strategies are appropriately researched, evaluated, and adequately implemented. In recent years, marketing managers have begun to develop a variety of strategies for leveraging

C-to-C influence, including word-of-mouth, buzz, viral, mobile, and guerilla marketing. Once labeled simply "word-of-mouth marketing," Justin Kirby and Paul Marsden, editors of *Connected Marketing: The Viral, Buzz and Word of Mouth Revolution* (2006), coined the term *connected marketing* to refer collectively to the toolbox of approaches and techniques used to leverage consumer connections and influence informal communications in order to add measurable value to a product or brand. Connected marketing techniques, which a growing number of marketing experts are advocating as an integral aspect of an overall marketing strategy, are largely evolving through trial and error. According to Hogarth-Scott and Kirby (2006, p. 94), "What is happening now . . . is similar to the early days of the Web: Marketers and practitioners are trying new approaches, reviving old ones, and bandying about catchy terms without always understanding what they mean."

What Kirby and Marsden have dubbed connected marketing techniques elsewhere have been referred to by other equally descriptive terms: *participation marketing* and *engagement marketing* are two prominent examples. Whichever term we choose to use, the essential message is the same—that marketers have to stop talking at consumers, or talking for them, and instead must connect with them by entering the ongoing consumer conversation and establishing a dialogue with their customers. The means by which this dialogue can be enacted serve as an underlying theme in the chapters that follow and are considered in-depth in Part II of this volume. But before getting to the nuts and bolts of the emerging forms of connected marketing, it is important to place current developments into historical perspective, by first considering the basic tenets, objectives, and tools of traditional B-to-C marketing. With the marketing basics in hand, we can then turn our attention to some of the developments that have led to a shift in power from marketers to consumers.

Two Marketing Philosophies: The Selling Concept Versus the Marketing Concept

Marketing is one of those terms that is used in everyday parlance, but how is it technically defined? Here are four related perspectives on the term:

> An organizational function and a set of processes for creating, communicating, and delivering value to customers and for managing customer relationships in ways that benefit the organization and the stakeholders. (American Marketing Association, 2006)

> . . . the management process that identifies, anticipates, and satisfies customer requirements profitably. (The Chartered Institute of Marketing, 1976)

> . . . a societal process by which individuals and groups obtain what they need and want through creating, offering, and freely exchanging products and services of value with others. (Kotler, 2003, p. 9)

Satisfying market needs through the commercialization of products and services in such a way that satisfies internal company needs and those of the company's investors.

(Kirby & Masden, 2006, p. xvii)

At the core of these conceptualizations is the recognition that marketing is a management process that consists of a variety of functions, all intended to facilitate an exchange relationship between companies and customers. Originally, the exchange process was guided by what has come to be known as the "selling concept," a traditional philosophy that emphasizes company profits regardless of consumer needs. That is, if a product is not selling at sufficient levels, then more aggressive marketing efforts must be initiated, such as significant price cutting, increased advertising, and more aggressive selling strategies. When people express cynical opinions about marketers as persons who will resort to any sort of manipulative tactic to sell an unneeded product, these opinions are likely rooted in a view of the marketing enterprise that is firmly aligned with the selling concept. Over the years, a philosophy known as the "marketing concept" has evolved, which promotes an orientation that is more consistent with the marketing exchange notion, emphasizing that firms must first analyze the needs of their customers and then make decisions abut how to best satisfy those needs, more efficiently than the competition. The marketing concept focuses on providing customers with what they seek, even if that entails the company's development of entirely new products or the elimination of current ones. Whereas the sales concept is oriented toward maximizing the sales of current offerings by whatever means necessary, the marketing concept emphasizes the identification of consumer needs and the efficient satisfaction of those needs.

The marketing concept is complicated by the fact that the consumer environment is dynamic and ever-changing, so that what customers want or need today—and the means by which they can satisfy their needs and desires—is not necessarily the same tomorrow. However, this complication clarifies why communication is essential to the marketing process. Marketers *must* communicate in order to inform, persuade, and remind their potential customers, as well as to differentiate their offerings from those of competitors (Kotler et al., 2002). But consumers *must* communicate with marketers so that the latter can identify who are their existing or potential customers, and the current and future needs of those customers. Whereas the selling concept implies a monologue in the sense of marketers talking *at* consumers, the marketing concept reminds us that in the contemporary environment, marketing requires a dialogue, with marketers talking *with* consumers—at the same time that consumers are talking more and more with each other. The growing dialogue between marketers and their target segments enables marketers to better understand how they can best satisfy consumer needs and why consumers would be interested in buying, having, and using their products and services.

These marketing philosophies reflect a long-standing distinction between two basic strategic approaches—push and pull. There has been a shift in marketing over the years to more of an emphasis on utilizing 'pull' strategies—spending on advertising and consumer promotion to build consumer demand. In contrast, a 'push' strategy calls for using the sales force and trade promotion to push the product through channels (producer to wholesaler to retailers, the latter of whom promote to consumers). Interestingly, there has been an exponential increase during recent years in a return to push marketing, albeit in new guises ("Push Marketing," 2006). For example, a variation of push marketing is evident in efforts by companies to encourage satisfied brand users to spread the word to others, such as friends, family members, and coworkers. It also is apparent when companies design controversial—and in some cases, shocking—advertisements in order to create marketplace buzz.

The various elements at the center of the marketing enterprise collectively are referred to as the *marketing mix*, defined as "the set of marketing tools the firm uses to pursue its marketing objectives in the target market" (Kotler, 2003, p. 15). The marketing mix concept dates back to a 1964 article written by Neil H. Borden in which he described the marketing manager as a "mixer of ingredients," involved in activities related to product planning, pricing, distribution channels, advertising, packaging, brand management, and the like. Borden's early listing of marketing elements has been simplified over the years into four basic categories, known today as the *4 P's of marketing*: product, price, place, and promotion (see Table 1.1). Traditionally, the marketing mix elements comprised the variables that were largely controlled by the marketer in order to most effectively satisfy a target group. As will become increasingly evident, this is less true today as consumers are becoming active participants in determining the nature and application of the marketing elements.

Product

A critical aspect of marketing activity involves decisions about the physical goods and services offered by the company, including features, appearance, brand name, packaging, warranty, and accessories. Product-related studies represent a common marketing research activity, with firms regularly conducting product and service tests, as well as research on product name and packaging (ARF/AMA, 1998). Because innovation can serve as a driving force for profits, the development of new products and the modification of existing ones represent ongoing concerns for most companies. Indeed, it is estimated that 30% of a company's sales come from products less than 4 years old (Trott, 2008).

One company that vividly demonstrates how innovation fuels profitability is Apple, the iconic consumer electronics firm whose initial breakthrough can be traced to the launch of its mouse-driven Macintosh computer in 1984. A key driver for Apple's subsequent success in the realm of consumer electronics has been the company's continued inventiveness, as exemplified by the enormous popularity of the iPod music player, the iPhone, iTunes Music Store online service, and the user-friendly iMac portable computers.

Table 1.1 The 4 P's of Marketing: Sample Questions

Product
What attributes or benefits are important? What brand name should be used? How should the product be styled? How should the product be packaged and shelved? Should there be product variations? Does the product have any safety issues?

Price
What pricing policies are appropriate? What is the best suggested retail price? How should price variations be established? How do consumers perceive prices? How effective are volume discounts and wholesale prices? What seasonal pricing strategies should be used?

Place (distribution)
How should the product or service be made available to consumers? What distribution channels and distribution centers should be established? How should inventory be managed? Where should company plants, factories, and warehouses be located? Should the product or service be available internationally? What transportation systems should be utilized?

Promotion
What type of advertising should be developed? Which media should be used for advertising and other promotions? What influence tactics should be used for face-to-face selling? How can good public relations for the company best be achieved? What is the relative effectiveness of different promotional methods (e.g., advertising, coupons and discounts, personal selling, or direct marketing)? How should the marketing communication budget best be managed?

Source: Kimmel (2007).

By combining technological expertise with a flair for keeping just ahead of the times, Apple has maintained its reputation as a pioneer, spawning a range of imitative offerings by competitors in efforts to mirror Apple's "digital lifestyle" concept (Redman, 2003).

Price

Pricing represents another important focus of marketing activity. Although the setting of prices is determined by a number of economic and competitive forces, companies may decide to set high prices in an effort to maximize profit over the short term or to sell at a low price (perhaps also offering free service) in order to beat the competition over the longer term. Competing on price is a common marketing approach, and marketers are well aware of consumers' sensitivity for price discounts and special offers.

Historically, Apple has utilized a "price skimming" strategy, which involves setting an initially high price for a short time for each innovative product it launches onto the market. The objective of this approach is to "skim" the greatest possible margin from consumers who are most avid about being first to adopt the latest product, without regard to price. As demand falls among the early adopters, the price then is incrementally lowered to increase sales and eventually a more stable price with an acceptable margin is established. This is the strategy Apple utilized when it introduced the iPhone, which initially bore a US$599 price tag. Soon after its introduction, Steve Jobs lowered the iPhone's price to US$299, thereby setting off a barrage of criticism among early adopters who quickly lost a certain degree of cachet in owning the product and among others who charged that Apple's initially high price was unjustified and unduly exploited the trend setters.

Perhaps as a result of this experience, Apple decided to utilize a "market penetration" pricing strategy for introducing its new 3G iPhone. Unlike skimming, penetration pricing involves setting lower prices in order to achieve a dominant market share. Success of such a strategy is dependent on price-sensitive markets, and it is important that the firm utilizing it has limited market share or is a new market entrant. Because Apple had a relatively low market share in the smartphone category, it introduced the 3G iPhone at a price equal to or lower than Apple's key competitors (Palm and RIM), but with additional features specifically intended to appeal to business users. As aptly described at the time of the impending launch, "this time Apple is setting its price low and its volume high, gunning for the common man instead of the zombie fan" (marketing-ninja.com, 2008).

Place

Another important element of marketing is related to distribution channels, which concerns how firms get their offerings to consumers and intermediaries (such as wholesalers, distributors, and retailers). Some of the most profound changes in the modern marketing environment pertain to this marketing mix element, as is apparent when one considers how new communication technologies, such as electronic retailing and interactive shopping via the Internet, have facilitated at-home shopping (Sherman & Topol, 1999). Also of growing interest is the design of retail settings so that consumers can shop more efficiently and derive greater satisfaction from the bricks-and-mortar shopping experience (e.g., Jones, 1999). This includes the strategic placement of small LED video screens throughout the store and shopping cart handles equipped with scrolling promotional information.

Another example of how marketing placement has been transformed in recent years is seen in the growing popularity of *olfactory marketing*—the development and use of scents to create shopping environments more conducive to impulsive buying. Some retailers use odors specifically designed to seduce consumers as they shop, inducing shoppers to linger longer than they had planned and buying more than they intended. This marketing ploy was used by Verizon Wireless when it launched its LG Chocolate phone in 2006 with chocolate-scented point-of-purchase store displays, accomplished by embedding plastic, scent-infused strips into the displays and by adding a scented varnish to information posters (Shapiro, 2006). Bowls of Hershey Kisses chocolates also were placed on the counter next to the phone displays. According to Verizon, the use of scents added excitement to the shopping experience, effectively associated aroma to its Chocolate brand identity, and likely contributed to the successful launch of the product.

Promotion

For many people, marketing is synonymous with advertising, and it is true that advertising continues to serve as a critical element of the marketing enterprise. Nonetheless, advertising is but one aspect of the promotional mix, which may also consist of public relations, direct marketing, personal selling, and sales promotion. Each of these tools plays a vital role in fulfilling a firm's various communication objectives by providing information to target audiences in an effort to elicit some sort of positive response, whether it be the generation of sales, enhanced awareness, favorable attitudes toward the brand, and so on.

Apple's early series of creative video advertisements for the iPod were elegantly simple in design, yet quite effective in lending an air of freshness and excitement to the mp3 player's identity. The ads depicted people in silhouette, happily dancing to music while the classic white earbud wires swung along to the tune. The advertisements likely conveyed feelings that would be difficult to arouse through a persuasive appeal delivered by a store salesperson. Similarly, the long-standing promotional campaign for Absolut vodka relies on a series of witty and artistic print ads, each of which highlights the brand's iconic clear-glass, non-labeled bottle. The combination of the readily recognizable bottle, its associations to purity, and the much-appreciated advertisements, have catapulted Absolut, which was first exported in 1979, from a Swedish domestic vodka to one of the world's leading spirit brands.

Adding "People" to the Mix

The 4 P's framework has stood the test of time as a guiding template for marketing activities, although for each marketing program, the goals, planning, and funding for each element must be integrated in a coherent manner that conforms to the firm's overall corporate culture and objectives. In recent years, some have argued that other "P's" need to be formally added to the marketing mix for more specialized marketing circumstances. For example, Booms and Bitner (1982) proposed a "7 P's of services marketing" framework, which includes three additional marketing components in addition to the four described above: *process* (i.e., the systems or processes used to assist the organization in delivering services), *physical evidence* (i.e., the organization's actual physical environment in which services are delivered, as well as tangible evidence attesting to the service quality), and *people* (i.e., the firm's employees and support staff who interact with and serve customers). Fellow customers represent another group of people who affect service experiences (such as the persons who comprise the crowd at a rock festival).

Other modifications of Borden's original conceptualization of the marketing mix have been suggested in recent years in an effort to present a framework for marketing that better conforms to the important societal and technological changes that have altered the contemporary consumer marketplace. One application of the 4 P's notion has been adapted to e-mail marketing, given this tool's rising prominence in marketing campaigns with the advent of the Internet (Eyram, 2006). The first P of e-mail marketing is *permission*, in that any e-mails that are sent without first obtaining the explicit consent of the recipient are likely to be regarded as spam—intrusive and unwanted communications that contribute to consumers' growing negative attitudes toward legitimate marketing efforts. Whereas permission consists of a request to receive personal information and an invitation to market a firm's offerings to individually-identified consumers, *privacy* pertains to the manner in which the information obtained from consumers is treated. In essence, privacy, which derives from the respect for personal autonomy, involves the extent to which an individual's attitudes, beliefs, and behavior are to be shared with or withheld from others (Ruebhausen & Brim, 1966). The implementation of a clear and concise privacy policy has important implications for a firm's reputation, given the myriad means by which consumer information has become accessible in recent years.

Another P of e-mail marketing is *profiling*, which is an activity that allows marketers to provide recipients with relevant information consistent with their consumption preferences. With specific details about the personal characteristics and interests of individual consumers in hand, marketers are in a better position to target those consumers with offers about products and services that prospects are likely to find appealing. Consumer profiles are developed from data obtained from marketing research surveys and other sources (such as order history, requests for information, and e-mail metrics) and can provide a basis for the launch of a more efficient and less wasteful marketing campaign. Not surprisingly, profiling has aroused ethical concerns among those who argue that the practice exploits the privacy rights of individuals so that firms can better achieve their marketing objectives.

Personalization represents the fourth P of e-mail marketing, and in one form or another, it is likely to become central to all forms of marketing in the future. Individualizing the content of a marketing message so that it acknowledges the uniqueness of each recipient is likely to garner more favorable responding from targets and can be a means for establishing a bond between the brand and the customer. For example, an e-mail message that includes a reference to a product that the recipient previously ordered or expressed interest in represents a simple, yet effective technique for personalizing the message, while providing a link to a cross-selling opportunity ("Now that you're experiencing the benefits of a new Xerox laser printer, we'd like you to have a look at our toner cartridges offer") (Evans, 2007). The significance of developing a marketing effort that promotes a more intimate link to the customer cannot be overstated in light of the growing tendency for consumers to turn to personal sources, such as friends, family members, neighbors, and colleagues for marketing information.

Personalization also appears as a central aspect of marketing in Idris Mootee's "new 4 P's of marketing" model (2004), which was proposed as a supplement to the original marketing mix concept in order to accommodate the emergent Web 2.0 phase of the

Internet (see Chapter 2). According to Mootee, CEO of the digital innovation company Idea Couture Inc., personalization refers to the customization of products and services through the use of the Internet. Dell.com and Amazon.com represent early examples of companies having derived huge profits from consumer personalization.

In addition to *personalization*, there is the concept of *participation*, which consists of the various means by which customers can become actively involved in the brand, helping to define what it stands for, how it is promoted, and so on. Mootee envisioned participation as the concept that leads to a true democratization of the marketing process. Another new P in Mootee's conceptualization is *peer-to-peer*, the component that acknowledges the active nature of consumers within social networks and brand communities, where market-related conversations have the capacity to lead to true engagement with products and services. The fourth new P is *predictive modeling*, which entails neural network algorithms that marketers have begun to apply to marketing-related problems.

The four marketing mix elements that comprise Mootee's contemporary twist on the traditional 4 P's framework (see Figure 1.1) are beginning to represent the focal points of marketers' efforts to respond to new marketplace realities (e.g., emerging social media); as such, we will return to them throughout the book. As will become evident in subsequent chapters, they provide links to four fundamental "C's" that are increasingly likely to be found at the root of successful marketing efforts: conversations, convenience, communities, and customer value. These ideas reflect a growing acknowledgment among marketing professionals of the need to place consumers front and center in their marketing planning. This may at first reading be a surprising point, given that the true essence of marketing, as suggested by the central notion of exchange, is to serve the needs and satisfy the desires of people. Are not people already at the center of most marketing efforts? The reality is that marketers, in more cases than not, have failed to include consumers as the focal point of their marketing efforts. This, counter to the traditional marketing mix approach, was suggested by Gareth Morgan (1988) in his book *Riding the Waves of Change*, when he argued that one of the greatest limitations of the 4 P's approach "is that it unconsciously emphasizes the inside–out view (looking from the company outwards), whereas the essence of marketing should be the outside–in approach."

In recent years, the emphasis on "people" (who have long been relegated to the "outside" of marketing efforts) as an integral component of marketing planning has become apparent in the emergence of customer relationship marketing (CRM). The concept of *relationship marketing* dates back to 1983 when Leonard Berry made the distinction between a marketing approach that is oriented toward the creation, main-tenance, and enhancement of long-term relationships with customers and *transaction marketing*, which viewed the customer in terms of short-term transaction objectives. In essence, relationship marketing is all about developing meaningful, value-laden rela-tions with customers (and other stakeholders) over the long term and being less

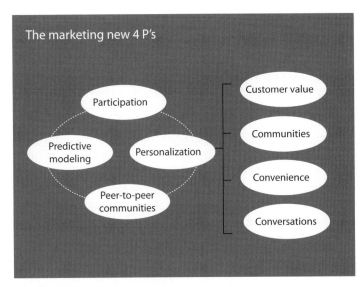

Figure 1.1 Mootee's Revised Marketing Model

concerned about the quick payoff that comes from a one-time purchase (O'Connor & Galvin, 2001). In his book on the topic, Gordon (1997, p. xx) described relationship marketing as an "ongoing process of identifying and creating new value with individual customers and then sharing the benefits from this over a lifetime of association."

The recent interest in relationship marketing has come about as an increasing number of companies have come to recognize the importance of developing strong bonds and loyalties with consumers to maximize customer retention. As opposed to the "leaky bucket" theory of business, which holds that new customers will always be available to replace defecting current ones, it now is understood that retaining customers is a more efficient and cost-effective approach for assuring a company's success in the competitive contemporary marketplace (see Box 1.2). Indeed, long-term, loyal customers are profitable for a variety of reasons, including the fact that they tend to buy more and they sometimes pay more premium prices than other customers. In addition, they represent a source of referrals for new customers; they make it difficult for competitors to increase their market share; and having a happy and loyal customer base creates visibility and awareness for the brand, which enable the company to attract new customers (Aaker, 1991; O'Connor & Galvin, 2001).

Perhaps most importantly, current customers are cheaper and easier to hold onto when compared with the costs and efforts to recruit new ones, especially when existing customers are satisfied or loyal. This is because new customers not only will be expensive to contact, but they will need a substantial reason to risk leaving a company or brand that they already are happy with, and that reason will be costly for the firm that attempts to attract them.

BOX 1.2 FOCUS ON RESEARCH: THE PROFITABILITY OF CUSTOMER RETENTION

Financial evidence attesting to the greater profitability of long-term customers has been demonstrated by Reichheld and Sasser (1990), who analyzed the actual lifetime value of customers across a variety of different industries. Their findings revealed that a 5% increase in customer retention resulted in 25–85% profit increases, depending on the industry considered. Nonetheless, customers are more difficult to retain than the preceding discussion might suggest. Reichheld (1996) later reported that American companies lose up to half of their customers in 5 years. Indeed, customers *will* leave, no matter how loyal they might be, if their problems, concerns, or complaints are not seriously addressed, their favored brands become too difficult to obtain through local channels, or when their preferred firm breaks certain unwritten relationship rules (such as a breach of trust, failure to keep a promise, and neglect) (Fournier, 1998). As the reader might have surmised, this is where relationship marketing becomes of interest to a business. The overriding objective in using this marketing approach is to deliver added value to customers in order to influence long-term satisfaction, which hopefully will translate into high levels of customer loyalty.

Although there are no hard and fast guidelines as to how to develop stronger relationships with consumers or how to build true loyalty, a variety of marketing tactics can be employed with these goals in mind. Typically, however, a company that takes relationship marketing seriously is apt to devise a broad, all-encompassing program that is truly customer-centered, such that each organizational decision focuses on how the experiences and satisfaction of the customer can be enhanced (O'Connor & Galvin, 2001). Several recommendations have been offered by marketing professionals as to what components should comprise such a program. For example, Kotler et al. (2002) suggest that a business can utilize any of three "customer value-building" approaches to create stronger customer relationships: (*a*) add financial benefits and loyalty rewards, such as frequent shopper programs, patronage refunds, and upgrades to frequent customers; (*b*) add social benefits, by individualizing and personalizing the company's products and services to better satisfy customer needs and wants; and (*c*) add structural ties, by providing customers with special equipment or computer linkages that help them manage their orders or inventories.

In the contemporary marketing context, where competition has never been more intense due to a proliferation of brands and a convergence in quality among those brands, relationship marketing has become one way for a firm to provide added value in order to appeal to target customers and emerge as the winner. However, even with the development of successful CRM programs, marketers now must face a growing challenge imposed by a new marketing reality—that consumers may not need to develop relationships with companies anymore because of the benefits accrued from their relationships with each other.

Generation C: Consumers' Growing Control Over the 4 P's

Recent trends in consumer behavior have begun to significantly shift control over various facets of the marketing process from the marketer to the consumer, although this shift has been promulgated to a certain degree from both sides of the marketing equation. From the marketer's perspective, there is a growing recognition that much can be gained from inviting consumers into the creation process and tapping into their creative skills, experiences, and instincts. For decades, consumers have kept their insights into and preferences about the things they consume largely to themselves because they lacked adequate opportunities and means to interact with companies. With greater access to professional hardware, software, and online distribution channels enabling them to share content with companies, that situation has begun to change, and consumers are proving to be more than willing to accept the invitation to enter into a collaborative dialogue with firms. However, on the other side of the equation, some of the same developments that have brought customers and marketers closer together have served to connect consumers with each other with greater facility than ever before; consequently, consumers are finding it more economical and personally gratifying to bypass professional marketing efforts altogether by collaborating directly with each other to satisfy mutual needs.

Both developments—marketers joining forces with consumers and consumers serving one another as non-professional marketing surrogates—are offshoots of an emerging marketplace trend that has been dubbed "Generation C," where "C" stands for "Content." Generation C pertains to the proliferation of consumer-generated content (CGC) that has rapidly been accumulating on the Internet, including text, images, video, and audio content. This content can be attributed on the one hand to the creative talents of consumers and, on the other, to the manufacturing of content-creating and publishing tools that facilitate the production and sharing of consumers' creations. Generation C is all about the transformation of consumers from individuals who have long been content to passively consume what marketers place in front of them, to *prosumers*—members of extensive networks who actively create, produce, and participate in marketing-related functions.

The collaborative interaction between marketers and consumers is especially evident with regard to one fundamental element of the marketing function—product. For many years, new product managers preferred to work in rather closed and secretive ways, fiercely protective of their intellectual property, insulated from external input, and content to rely on the findings of their own new concept research. Many companies still operate in this way when it comes to new product development although sooner or later, they are likely to be left in the dust by more forward-thinking competitors. The new business environment is one in which companies have become more openly collaborative, not only with consumers, but with other companies. Don Tapscott and Anthony D. Williams (2006) famously coined the term *wikinomics* to describe how an increasing number of twenty-first-century companies are relying on a combination of mass collaboration and open-source technologies to fundamentally alter the face of marketing innovation. At the heart of wikinomics (and business success) are four principles—openness, peering, sharing, and acting globally—which, according to Tapscott and Williams (2006, p. 30), effectively serve to "tap the torrent of human knowledge and translate it into new and useful applications." The authors explain:

> People, knowledge, objects, devices, and intelligent agents are converging in many-to-many networks where new innovations and social trends spread with viral intensity. Organizations that have scrambled to come up with responses to new phenomena like Napster or the blogosphere should expect much more of the same—at an increasing rate—in the future. (p. 31)

Another term that increasingly comes up in discussions of consumer-firm collaboration in the new-product development process is *customer-made*, which describes "the phenomenon of corporations creating goods, services and experiences in close cooperation with experienced and creative consumers, tapping into their intellectual capital, and in exchange giving them a direct say in (and rewarding them for) what actually gets produced, manufactured, developed, designed, serviced, or processed" ("Customer Made," 2006). The customer-made trend is given impetus thanks to some of the benefits consumers can accrue from their participation in the collaborative process, including the status that is derived from showing off their creative skills; the guarantee that goods, services, and experiences will be tailored to their needs; monetary rewards and possible job employment for assisting companies in the development of successful innovations; and the pleasure and satisfaction that come from cocreating with preferred brands. Some examples of the emerging customer-made trend are included in Box 1.3.

The customer-made trend in part offsets the ethical concern that many products in the consumer marketplace have been developed primarily to provide value to the manufacturer and retailer, without regard to the satisfaction of essential customer needs. In fact, in most industrialized nations one can observe a proliferation of products that offer little real value to consumers, such as mascara for babies, salted bandages, silicon thigh implants, and a growing range of pet products and services, the latter ranging from Halloween costumes and limousine services for cats and dogs to pet spas, fitness centers, vacation resorts, and retirement homes (Tanikawa, 2004). Although such ostensibly useless products may provide a certain degree of novelty to the purchaser, one may argue that they merely serve to encourage consumers to "buy and have" regardless of the need-satisfying properties of the acquisitions. Additionally, it is argued that many products merely add to the creation of false wants and the encouragement of materialistic values and aspirations, thereby influencing consumers to value material objects more than personal development and socially-oriented causes. General Motors' Chevrolet division found out the hard way that times have changed with regard to the marketing of products that many consumers find objectionable, like fuel inefficient sports utility vehicles (SUVs). When Chevy created a Web site enabling prospective

BOX 1.3 FOCUS ON APPLICATION: CUSTOMER-MADE, WIKINOMICS, AND THE NEW FACE OF CONSUMER–FIRM INTERACTION

''Customer-made'' and ''wikinomics'' are overlapping terms that lie at the heart of new approaches that companies are using to connect with consumers. A number of applications will be discussed in greater detail in subsequent chapters with regard to how connections are created and used in practice, including those of Dell's Ideastorm, My Starbucks, and P&G's InnoCentive network, to name a few. At this juncture, however, a few examples should suffice to whet one's appetite for more to follow.

- In what has rapidly become a well-known advertising tactic, more and more brands are inviting consumers to contribute to their next advertising campaign. The typical approach usually takes the form of a competition, whereby one or more consumer-created ads are selected by the brand for public dissemination. Some examples include L'Oréal's ''You Make the Commercial,'' McDonald's ''Global Casting,'' and MasterCard's ''Write a Priceless Ad.'' Another example involved Dorito's, a snack food offered by Pepsico's Frito-Lay division, which challenged consumers to create an ad that would run during the 2007 Super Bowl, the annual US National Football League's championship game that is one of the most widely viewed television broadcasts worldwide. The promotion was cosponsored by Yahoo!Video, whose video tools were made available to aspiring consumer-advertisers for producing their creations. Dorito's selected five of the best user-generated videos and then uploaded them to Yahoo's video site, where people could view them and vote for their favorite (''Doritos: You Create,'' 2006)

- A good example of how companies can exploit the customer-made trend is to announce product or service development contests, open to consumers from around the world. One company that successfully employed this approach was Nokia, which created the Nokia Concept Lounge during the summer of 2005. For this campaign, Nokia invited designers from the Benelux countries to share ideas and design the next new cool phone. As it turned out, entries were submitted from around the world. The winning concept was a flexible wristband style phone, the ''Nokia 888,'' created by a Turkish designer, Tamer Nakisci. In 2005, Nespresso launched a similar design competition, aimed at imagining the future of coffee rituals. Some of the novel submissions included the Nespresso InCar coffee machine and the Nespresso Chipcard. The Chipcard was a device that stores coffee preferences for registered consumers and communicates with a central database to produce a personalized cup of coffee for registered consumers.

- Some companies offer co-creators a percentage of a brand's earnings as a result of a product development based on their input, suggestions, or design idea. The toy manufacturer LEGO utilized this create-and-sell strategy through its LEGO Factory Web site, which invited children and other building enthusiasts to design models, using free downloadable software. Participants were given the opportunity to win LEGO prizes. During one short-term competition, winners were entitled to have their model mass-produced and sold at Shop@Home, receiving a 5% royalty on each set sold.

- Another increasingly commonplace customer-made approach is for companies to systematically engage in true ongoing conversations with consumers, typically by generating online dialogues through the sharing of relevant knowledge. This is something Honda UK implemented when it became the first sponsor of the 2TalkAbout Honda blog network, which provides

(cont.)

> **Box 1.3** (*Continued*)
>
> site visitors the opportunity to post their opinions about the well-known Japanese brand and respond to others' views. The blog is part of the 2TalkAbout content network, which allows consumers to communicate with each other about their favorite brands. The Honda blog is intended for anyone in the online community with an interest in Honda vehicles. Although completely independent from the Honda company, brand engineers and representatives regularly log onto and contribute to the 2TalkAbout Honda site (which eventually migrated to the Woyano platform), where they respond to (often critical) feedback and provide users with direct access to the brand. This sort of Internet-based open dialogue between consumers and companies is consistent with the tenets put forth in the groundbreaking book, *The Cluetrain Manifesto* (Levine et al., 2000).

customers to "Make Your Own Tahoe Commercial," the resulting CGC was hardly what the car company had anticipated. Numerous derogatory videos were created by consumers, casting Chevy and its new Tahoe SUV in an extremely negative light, including a commercial created by US politician and environmental guru Al Gore, emphasizing how such vehicles contribute to global warming (Jaffe, 2007).

Despite the growing collaborative openness that is serving to bring consumers and companies together as never before, Generation C also has served as a springboard for C-to-C marketing activities, such that consumers are increasingly taking advantage of opportunities to avoid any engagement with companies and their formal marketing efforts. Tapscott and Williams (2006) were not exaggerating when they proclaimed that "Millions of people already join forces in self-organized collaborations that produce dynamic new goods and services that rival those of the world's largest and best-financed enterprises." The authors use the term "peering" to refer to this new mode of innovation and value creation, which provides consumers with greater autonomy over each of the traditional 4 P's of the marketing process. This is seen in the enormous success of eBay, the online auction and shopping Web site that enables consumers to bypass marketing mediators in the establishment of prices (which are sometimes negotiated between sellers and buyers) and distribution of goods (which do not require a visit to a bricks-and-mortar store). Other examples of C-to-C peer production have evolved into well-known fixtures of the digital era, such as the social networking communities of MySpace and Facebook, the content-sharing Web sites YouTube (for videos) and Flickr (for photos), the open-source computer operating system Linux, virtual worlds like Second Life and Haboo, and the online, free encyclopedia Wikipedia (which is collaboratively maintained by readers).

Another manifestation of Generation C that has emanated from the consumer side of the marketing equation is apparent in the growing trend for customers to modify or maintain manufactured goods beyond their intended nature or use. For example, "IKEA Hackers" are consumers who regard the well-known Swedish furniture company IKEA's final products merely as starting points for creations that can be put to alternative uses (Green, 2007). Some actual examples of consumer-generated IKEA product reinventions include music speakers made from IKEA salad bowls, children's clothes produced from IKEA quilt covers and pillow cases, a blond electric guitar body created from an IKEA pine tabletop, a cat litter box simultaneously used as a living room end table, and a waterproof dress produced by a consumer who altered an inexpensive IKEA shower curtain.

Much to the chagrin of loyal owners of the Newton, Apple's early line of personal digital assistants (PDAs), the company decided to take the product off the market in 1998. However, long after it was abandoned by Apple, thousands of Newton enthusiasts essentially took over the product and continue to use it. Consumers have upgraded the device over the years through the development of new software, enabling it to perform functions it was never meant to perform. It now can connect to Macs, PCs, and Unix machines, as well as a variety of networks (from wireless Wi-Fi networks to the always-on GPS mobile phone networks); it streams mp3 files off the Internet; and it can audibly read headlines that have been automatically fetched from online news sites. According to brand community experts Albert Muñiz and Thomas O'Guinn (2001, p. 420), "Newton users fulfill the role advertising and branding would normally play. They've taken possession of the product and the brand away from Apple, and when you talk to them you get the sense that it's *their* brand."

How Marketing Works

Now that we have had a look at some of the basic elements of the marketing enterprise, we can turn our focus to the dynamics that underlie the means by which it functions. More specifically, as consumers have begun to occupy a more dominant position in modern marketing paradigms, what does this imply for our understanding of how the marketing process actually works? To answer that question, let us first have a look at how marketing traditionally has been understood to work.

The Traditional Model

Traditionally, there have been two schools of thought on what it means to say that marketing works. The *sales orientation* places an emphasis on purely sales-related marketing objectives and measures. In this view, the only reason an organization spends money on marketing activities such as advertising and sales promotion is to sell its products or services. Marketing "works" in the sense of the firm's efforts meeting or exceeding sales-related objectives, such as increases in market share, return on investment, sales volume increases, and so on. Because such measures may vary for a variety of other reasons (e.g., competitor actions), they rarely, in and of themselves, provide a sufficient test of the success of the firm's marketing activities.

Because of the limitations of the sales approach, the *sequential approach* (sometimes also referred to as the *communications approach*) is often preferred as a means of setting marketing objectives and assessing a marketing effort's success. This approach is based on the assumption that marketing activities are capable of producing a series of prior (or intermediary) effects which precede sales, but ultimately lead to profit. These effects could include the creation of consumer awareness, providing knowledge about the benefits of a product or service, developing more favorable customer attitudes, and so on. Dating back to Edward K. Strong's AIDA model (1925)—AIDA representing an acronym for "attention–interest–desire–action"—various sequential frameworks subsequently have been proposed to suggest the process by which marketing efforts, such as advertising and personal selling, are supposed to move a prospect from awareness to actual purchase. These so-called *response hierarchies* or *hierarchies of effect* (e.g., Lavidge & Steiner; McGuire, 1978) regard purchase behavior as the end result of a sequence (or process) of consumer decision making, with marketing first having effects on the beliefs of targets, then their feelings, and finally their intentions or behaviors (see Figure 1.2). Advertising and other marketing activities thus are viewed as having their impact on customer targets in a rather straightforward, linear manner, moving them along to higher states of readiness to buy. The key is to determine where along the hierarchy consumer target groups are located (e.g., they may be aware of a brand but not know much about it) and which kinds of methods and appeals are likely to have the greatest impact in moving potential customers closer to a purchasing response.

The sequential approach operates on the assumption that consumers are rational decision makers. This is a reasonable assumption for many of the purchase decisions we make that are important enough for us to give serious thought and consideration. For example, imagine that a consumer has developed an interest in flat-screen, high-definition

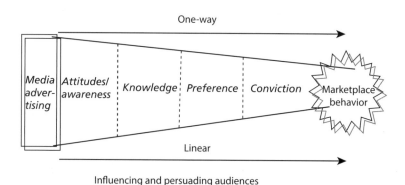

Figure 1.2 The Traditional Linear Model of Marketing Communication

televisions, perhaps as a result of exposure to one or more marketing communications, such as a magazine advertisement, a flyer received in the mail, a prominent store display, etc. We might expect this consumer initially to take steps to gain knowledge about the product—its features, advantages and disadvantages over his current TV, the prices of various brands, and so on. As a result of this information search, certain brands might emerge as the more intriguing possibilities, whereas other brands are likely to be eliminated from further consideration. It may be that an ad for a Sony LCD flat-screen TV initially sparked interest in the product, but after perusing the performance details presented in various brochures, the consumer may have developed a stronger preference for Panasonic's line of Plasma TVs. Eventually, one model is likely to emerge as the consumer's top choice, and assuming the opportunity presents itself—his current TV begins to have reception problems or a terrific deal is offered for the Panasonic at a local shop—a purchase of a Panasonic Plasma HD TV might then be made. Although overly simplistic, this example demonstrates how a rational consumer would move from a state of awareness to a purchase, by following a sequence of decision making that spans the stages of comprehension, attitude, and conviction.

Over the years, the sequential approach has proven rather useful for firms in setting marketing communication objectives and developing a promotional plan; however, certain limitations with this approach have become apparent, giving rise to questions about its utility that never really have been sufficiently resolved (cf. Fill, 1999). For example, there is a degree of vagueness about how it can be determined that a majority of consumers in the target group are adequately aware or have a suitable level of comprehension so that efforts can be devised to move them to the next stage of the hierarchy. Additionally, as the reader may already have surmised, consumers do not approach many purchase situations in a logical, rational fashion, but instead act out of impulse or an overwhelming emotional response to a product. These difficulties notwithstanding, a new set of criticisms of these traditional ideas about how marketing works have been voiced with increasing frequency in recent years. One statement effectively summarizes the essence of the complaints: as marketplace realities have evolved, the traditional marketing models, and their applications, have not.

A Model for the New Marketing Landscape

During his keynote address at the thirteenth International Conference on Corporate and Marketing Communications in Slovenia, Don E. Schultz (2008) shared a very simple observation that nonetheless resonated throughout his audience: "Marketing communication used to be so easy." Schultz is a noted researcher and writer who has spent the better part of his academic career establishing the foundations of the traditional linear approach to marketing communication that is found in nearly all of the textbooks devoted to the subject matter. But in his keynote address, Schultz presented a quite different message, one that has begun to be voiced independently by other prominent marketing figures. The crux of this message is that the traditional marketing models no longer work because the marketing landscape—and the consumer targets who inhabit it—has undergone such fundamental changes. To clarify why this is so, it is helpful to have a closer look at the prototypical approach to marketing communication, which arguably is the standard by which most companies operate at the present time.

As illustrated in Figure 1.3, traditional communicators essentially have employed similar methods in their attempts to appeal to their intended consumer audiences. When Schultz asserted that marketing communication used to be so easy, he was referring to the unidirectional (communicator → receivers) approach depicted in Figure 1.3, which begins with marketers first identifying an issue or need, making the required product, developing a communication theme and creating the ads and incentives, identifying some appropriate media channels through which to transmit the communication(s), and then waiting for the desired audience responses to occur. It should be apparent that this approach is consistent with traditional assumptions about the sequential nature of consumer decision making. It also represents a straightforward application of the original 4 P's, with the assumption being that if the marketer does these things—develops a good product, offers it at an attractive price, makes it accessible to target customers—then consumers will respond accordingly. But bear in mind that Schultz was speaking in the past tense when he reflected on the clear-cut and uncomplicated nature of this approach, suggesting that this model is no longer tenable in the contemporary marketplace. A starting point for understanding why this is the case is apparent in Idris Mootee's assertion (2004) that marketing's historical problem is that it attempts to impose a brand onto the customer. For example, a television ad pushes out a carefully designed idea of what the brand is without engaging the audience members to whom the message is directed. In other words, the marketing efforts are directed to a largely passive consumer base without any attempt to involve them in a more active way.

Figure 1.3 The Marketing Communication Shouting Match
Source: Schultz (2008).

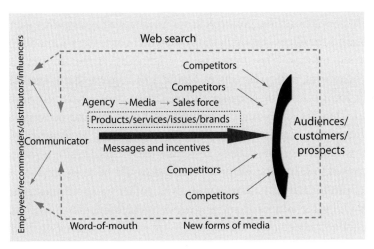

Figure 1.4 Consumers Blocking Out Traditional Marketing Communication
Source: Schultz (2008).

But there is much more to the story than this. Because competition has grown in nearly all consumer goods and services sectors, many competitors are vying to have an impact on audiences in similar ways, imposing their messages and incentives onto increasingly overwhelmed audiences. Thus, the challenge for each firm becomes one of creating the most original ad, designing a product with the most desirable added features, offering the best money-off offer—whatever it takes to rise above the myriad offers associated with other brands. In short, by treating consumer audiences as passive recipients of marketing offers, companies end up getting into a shouting match, bombarding their targets with so many appeals that those targets simply stop listening. This outcome is suggested in Figure 1.4 where, in contrast to the traditional model, a barrier is situated between the multiple competitors and their target audience. What this implies is that it has become progressively more difficult for the traditional communication process to work because the excessive bombardment of promotional messages has led to advertising clutter. In the context of television, *advertising clutter* is defined as the "proliferation of advertising that produces excessive competition for viewer attention, to the point that individual messages lose impact and viewers abandon the ads (via fast-forwarding, changing channels, quitting viewing, etc.)" (Lowrey, Shrum, & McCarty, 2005, p. 121). The problem of clutter, described in more detail in Chapter 2, clearly extends beyond television; indeed, it also characterizes consumers' rising aversion to other marketing formats, including outdoor signage, e-mail spamming, Internet pop-up messages, and SMS messaging.

Because of the sheer volume of marketing, audiences would find it next to impossible to process everything, even if they so desired. Moreover, with the aid of new technologies, such as TiVo and other personal video recorders, filters, and pop-up blockers that enable audiences to bypass advertising, consumers are finding it progressively easier to avoid the many promotional messages and marketing offers that come their way and for which they have little or no interest. The dotted lines originating at the communication target (audiences, consumers, and prospects in Figure 1.4) suggest that consumers no longer wait passively for a marketing message of interest to come their way because they no longer have to. They are now equipped with the technologies and networks that facilitate the rapid and extensive acquisition of information of interest. To illustrate, if we return to the consumer who had become serious about the idea of purchasing a flat-screen TV, we might be surprised to learn that his only reactions would be to sit in front of his current television and wait for relevant ads to appear or to gather up some magazines in the hope that he would find some articles about new television technologies and offers. Instead, the consumer might actively engage in a variety of information-seeking methods, such as an extensive search of Internet forums, SMS messaging to friends and relatives who know more about the product than he does, visits to virtual online stores, e-mails to a friend in Thailand who works for Panasonic (but whom he has never met in person). Our hypothetical shopper is then likely to integrate all the information he has gathered about the product and brands to arrive at a purchase decision. This approach is a far cry from the traditional linear marketing model, in which the firm independently develops and communicates an offer and then waits for the consumer target to respond.

Conclusion

Developments in the consumer marketplace present fundamental challenges for companies to recognize the limitations of the traditional marketing approach and to reorient their thinking about how best to meet their objectives. If audiences are bypassing traditional marketing efforts, then firms need to put those audiences front and center in seeking new ways to reach and engage them. This point was effectively summarized on Mootee's blog (http://mootee.typepad.com), in his analysis of new marketing realities:

> The first generation of marketing took a pure functional view and was entirely tactical in nature, dominated by the 4P's ... focusing on pushing mass market product messages and driving store promotions. The next generation of marketing takes a "customer" view: uncovering unmet needs, facilitating conversations, realizing, and delivering real customer value through "customer engagement." Many of those popular tricks in the marketer's toolkit are now obsolete. It's time for a new one.

2 The Twenty-First Century Consumer Landscape: New Realities

The contemporary consumer landscape is undergoing a dramatic evolution. This evolution is marked by three significant new realities that have served, either directly or indirectly, to shift the balance of control in the marketing equation from marketers to consumers. In Chapter 1, I suggested how consumers have steadily begun to usurp control over the traditional 4 P's of marketing. Three additional new realities, which in turn serve as the focus of this chapter, can be summarized as follows:

1. Media and audience fragmentation
2. Targets tuning out formal marketing efforts
3. Consumer connectedness

Together, these new realities are fundamentally shaping the economic, social, political, and ethical environments in which commercial business unfolds. Although for many firms it is business-as-usual when it comes to marketing activities, these changes in the marketplace are requiring new marketing efforts for sheer competitive survival. As marketers increasingly adopt new strategies and tactics for responding to the evolving marketing landscape, we might imagine one more new reality to fully emerge in coming years, that of marketers' deep engagement with their consumer targets.

Media and Audience Fragmentation

By now, it is common knowledge that both the means of communicating with consumers and the methods by which consumers obtain information have undergone dramatic changes in recent years. These changes represent various forms of *fragmentation*, a term that perhaps better than any other gets at the root of why marketing communication is no longer as simple as it once was. With regard to media, fragmentation describes a media landscape that includes increasing options for the reception of content. These options have evolved from the development of multiple forms of traditional "above-the-line" media—television, newspapers and magazines, radio, outdoor, and cinema—largely as a result of the growing availability of a wide range of online and electronic devices. These technological options, which provide more choices and channels for consumers to receive media content than ever before, have begun to shape what may be considered as a global digital revolution—a revolution as profound as the Industrial Revolution of the eighteenth century.

One of the early indications of media fragmentation was seen with the arrival of cable and satellite television when, seemingly overnight, a limited number of channel offerings suddenly proliferated into hundreds, broadcast from many countries, in different languages, and with nonstop availability. Whereas the average US household received only a handful of channels during the early decades of television, that figure had risen to 27 by 1994 and over 100 by 2000 (Nielsen Media Research 2008). What initially proved to be a boon for viewers turned into something of a nightmare for advertisers, because the added choices essentially served to divide the media audience among the increased number of outlets, thereby making media planning and buying a more difficult process (see Figure 2.1). The proliferation of relatively inexpensive digital devices such as mobile phones, laptop computers, and wireless handheld devices (such as the Blackberry and PDAs), with features that allow for e-mails, text messaging, Web browsing, and other wireless information services, have emerged as common media devices for the transmission and sharing of marketing messages.

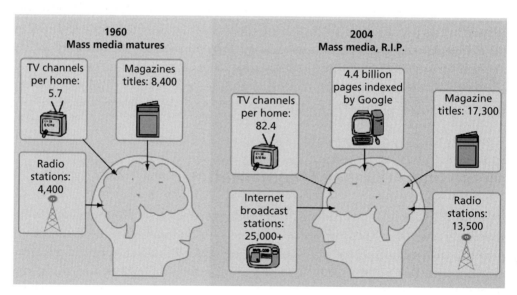

Figure 2.1 Digital Technology Opens a Pandora's Box of Media Outlets

Source: Schmitt (2004). *Left brain marketing*. Forrester Research, Inc. Available: http://www.forrester.com/Research/Document/Excerpt/0,7211,33961,00.html

Unlike traditional media, these new technologies allow for bidirectional communication between consumers and marketers, thereby adding the variable of interactivity to the marketing communications mix. These developments have provided consumers with a greater degree of control over how they choose to receive information, what information they are willing to receive, the means by which they may gain direct access to marketing communication sources, and the outlets through which marketing messages are shared with other consumers.

An inevitable by-product of the technological developments that have given rise to the variety of media now available to consumers is *audience fragmentation*, a term that refers to the increasingly diversified nature of media usage habits and patterns. At one time, marketers were content to rely on mass marketing techniques, sending out their messages to as many people as possible in their attempts to maximize corporate profits. The traditional broadcast media—television and radio, in particular—were especially conducive to this so-called *marketing aggregation strategy*. This was a reasonable marketing communication approach given media usage habits at the time, when reaching large audiences of consumers was far easier than it is today. For example, in 1965 advertisers could reach 80% of Americans aged 18–49 years with ads run on the three major broadcast television networks. By 2004, they could only reach 31% through those same networks (Bianco, 2004). According to some estimates, today an ad would have to be aired on 100 channels to reach 80% of adult Americans ("The Mass Market," 2004).

Before the arrival of cable TV, the personal computer, and the Internet, it was pretty predictable that the majority of adult members of the population would be spending their evenings sitting next to their radios or, later, their TV sets, attending to a limited number of broadcasts. Today, of course, this is far from the case because the media options have expanded, thereby fragmenting the audience into a myriad of diverse media usage targets (see Box 2.1). Prime-time TV viewing hours now may be used to surf the Internet, read an e-magazine, trade SMS messages with friends, stream music on a portable handheld device, watch a movie on a portable DVD player, upload photos to a social networking site, and so on. Eric Schmitt of Forrester Research, Inc. adroitly summarized this development when he stated that "Monolithic blocks of eyeballs are gone. In their place is a perpetually shifting mosaic of audience microsegments that forces marketers to play an endless game of audience hide-and-seek" (Schmitt, 2004, p. 3). This description is indicative of the ongoing shift among marketers away from a broadcasting mentality to one that can properly be referred to as "narrowcasting"— attempting to reach the desired consumer segment, cluster, or niche, at the right time, through the appropriate media channels, with a message that is likely to strike a personal chord. As Procter & Gamble's (P&G) Chief Marketing Officer Jim Stengel noted during a 2004 advertising agencies conference, "We must accept the fact that there is no 'mass' in 'mass media' anymore and leverage more targeted approaches" (cf. Schmitt, 2004).

BOX 2.1 FOCUS ON RESEARCH: MEDIA FRAGMENTATION

During their presentation at the 2004 Australian Marketing Institute National Conference in Melbourne, two directors from the international research company Roy Morgan, Michele Levine and Simon Pownall, provided some informative data from Australia to illustrate ongoing changes in the ways people are using media (Levine & Pownall, 2004). At the outset, they pointed out that until recently it would have been possible to introduce a new product or brand to 90% of the Australian population simply via a Sunday night "roadblock"; that is, by running an advertisement on the three major Australian TV networks at the same time during the airing of the Sunday night movie. Today, that is no longer possible now that the Internet and Pay TV have emerged as significant new alternatives for media consumption. Their data revealed a steady rise in Internet usage among Australians aged 14 years and older, from 10% having accessed the Internet at least monthly in 1996 to 65% in 2003, while across the same time period more traditional media usage had gradually declined. The percentage of persons viewing commercial TV over the past 7 days dropped from 75% in 1996 to 68% in 2003, compared with the viewing of Pay TV during the past 7 days, which rose from 5% in 1996 to nearly 20% in 2003.

Levine and Pownall's analysis did not reveal much of a change since the early 1990s in Australian newspapers and magazine readership figures, with the percentage of people using either medium varying only slightly between 80% and 90% over the 10-year period, 1994–2003. In fact, globally, print circulation rates have proven to be predictably unpredictable. One analysis of daily newspaper circulation rates revealed a decline in twenty-six out of the forty countries studied during the period 1993–7, although an increase was evident in thirteen of the other countries. The survival of both newspapers and magazines is highly dependent on advertising revenues, and advertisers are apt to reduce their ad spending on those media outlets if they have reason to believe that readership rates are declining. Some newspaper publishers are quick to point out that daily circulation rates significantly understate actual newspaper readership now that we have entered a period during which newspapers may be read online. A recent *The New York Times* analysis supported this view when figures were gathered for seven of the most widely read American newspapers, including *USA Today, The Wall Street Journal*, and *The Washington Post*. For each newspaper, average weekday circulation rates were significantly lower than Web-unique daily audiences in 2005. For example, the average weekday circulation figures for *The Washington Post* showed that 0.8 million people had purchased the newspaper, whereas the average daily readership of the newspaper online was pegged at 7.8 million.

Another recent study compared how newspaper readers are differentially reached by advertisers depending on the context in which the newspaper is read. The study, conducted by the Asahi Shimbun Company, compared the readership habits of business persons at home, while commuting, and at work. Overall, the results suggest that business professionals are more likely to read newspaper ads when the newspaper is read at home. More than half (50.8%) of business people who read the morning edition of a newspaper at home answered "I look at ads about interesting products or services," as opposed to 34.2% while commuting. More than one-fifth of the respondents who read the morning edition of a newspaper while commuting (21%) or at the office (20.4%) reply "I never look at ads," compared with only 9.1% at home.

Although classified advertising for automobiles, real estate, and employment opportunities represent the bread and butter of newspaper revenues, mainstream consumer goods firms continue to place ads in that medium. Despite the growing problem of media fragmentation, to date newspapers still turn a profit and represent an attractive channel for reaching a mass audience; in fact, many newspapers garner higher profit margins than the average Fortune 500 company. The fact that a growing number of readers are shifting from print to online publications represents an interesting opportunity for both newspapers and magazines, the latter in the form of e-zines. One newspaper association assessment found that 57 million Americans visited a newspaper Web site during the third quarter of 2006, an increase of 24% over the preceding year, and online advertising revenues continue to grow (Seelye, 2006).

Finally, new digital devices are on the way that stand to revitalize the newspaper industry. One new technology allows for the creation of so-called *electronic paper*, which provides a high quality electronic facsimile of ordinary paper, as exemplified by Amazon.com's wireless book reading device, the Kindle. As of this writing seven French publications had joined France Télécom to test a new electronic paper device that allows users to download the content of newspapers over a wireless network, an approach that is also being considered by other companies elsewhere (Pfanner, 2008). The innovation takes the form of a black plastic rectangular box with a screen that is half the size of a sheet of notebook paper and provides images that appear like ink on newsprint, which can be read in total darkness or bright sunlight. Because the device is portable, it has a distinct advantage over electronic versions of newspapers that already are available online.

The Internet

The actual extent of fragmentation in the contemporary marketing landscape can be illustrated with a few specific examples of new media. A logical starting point is the Internet, which has seen a phenomenal spurt of users globally since the turn of the millennium. Specifically, the number of Internet users tripled from 384 million in 2000 to 1.7 billion in 2007. Geographically, the largest segment of Internet users are Asians (41.2%), followed by Europeans (24.6%), North Americans (15.7%), Latin Americans/Caribbeans (10.9%), Africans (3.4%), Middle Easterns (2.9%), and Australians/Oceanics (1.3%) (World Internet Users, 2009).

Early attempts to gauge the impact of the Internet on television viewing initially revealed little if any influence. One study of more than 22,000 adult Americans found that in 2002 respondents were watching on average between 4.2 and 4.9 hours of TV per day, regardless of how much time they spent using the Internet per week (which ranged from less than 1 hour to more than 20 hours). However, this situation appears to be changing as more households acquire a broadband Internet connection and spend more time online engaged in a variety of activities. Broadband connections, which allow Internet users to remain online however long they choose without additional cost (versus Internet dial-up service), showed a steady rise in North American households, from 29 million (23.1% of households) in 2003 to 69.4 million in 2008 (56.3%), and is projected to steadily increase to 89.9 million (69.3%) by 2011. Broadband figures are even higher in some European countries; for example, by 2008, nearly 80% of French Internet users had broadband connections. By the end of 2006, there were approximately 251 million broadband households worldwide, with the United States and China representing the two largest broadband markets in the world, and estimates are that this figure will rise to 640 million by 2013 ("Broadband Households," 2007; Gardner, 2009). Early indications are that broadband households in the United States tend to watch 2 hours less TV per day than those without Internet access, although the impact on consumers' traditional media usage has not yet evolved in some European countries, such as France and Germany (Le Quoc & Favier, 2008).

Digital Video Recorders

Another innovation that has begun to have a significant impact on consumers' traditional media usage habits is the digital video recorder (DVR; also referred to as personal video recorder, PVR), which enables digital recording of video content to a hard drive or other memory format for later viewing. Two of the best known and widely adopted examples of DVR are TiVo in North America and Australia (first available to the public in 1999) and Sky Plus in the United Kingdom (introduced in 2001), the latter of which is now being marketed globally. Nearly half of American households and one-fourth of British households were equipped with DVRs by 2009 (Forrester Research). The eventual widespread diffusion of DVRs is a troublesome development for marketers, given that the devices include ad-skipping features that enable viewers to fast-forward through commercials. The concern that television viewers are screening out marketing messages with their digital recording devices, which similarly greeted the appearance of the videocassette recorder (VCR, or video recorder) in the 1970s, has prompted advertisers to adopt strategies that enable a more complete integration of commercial content with noncommercial programming. This is especially evident in the growing ad spending on product placements, which weave products into television programs as a means of gaining greater brand exposure among viewing audiences (see Box 2.2).

BOX 2.2 FOCUS ON APPLICATION: PRODUCT PLACEMENTS

Back in the early days of television, it was a rare event to see a known brand name appearing on the label of a product used by the TV program's characters. A large bottle of ketchup on the kitchen table was far more likely to bear a label marked "Ketchup" than "Heinz." In today's branded marketing landscape, the converse is true, now that product placement has become a common marketing tactic to counter TV viewers' growing ability and inclination to screen out non-program content. *Product placement* refers to the inclusion of products, services, and brand names in films, TV programs, games, etc. for deliberate promotional exposure, usually in return for an agreed financial sum. Companies may choose to pay a fixed price to have their products woven into program content (a "paid placement") or instead may opt to offer products or services in exchange for appearance or mention in the program (a "barter placement"), such as an airline company providing free tickets to producers of a TV series.

In addition to providing marketers with a means to circumvent the ad screening problem in order to build brand awareness, product placement has other strengths that make the approach particularly appealing to commercial firms. Among these are the potential to reinforce brand image, develop stronger emotional connections with viewers by better associating the product with relevant non-commercial content, and reach specifically targeted audiences likely to be viewing the specific program. It also appears that product placements—whether used in movies, TV shows, computer games, or at social and sporting events—can serve to generate informal word-of-mouth conversations among like-minded consumers. A famous example of this occurred after The Hershey Company agreed to have its Reese's Pieces peanut butter cups placed in the 1982 film, *E.T. the Extra-Terrestrial*, after Mars declined to have its flagship M&M's candies appear, when approached by director Steven Spielberg. During the film, the endearing space alien E.T. is lured out of hiding by a boy who scatters Reese's Pieces in his path. Mars' miscalculation proved to be a boon for Hershey's when sales of Reese's Pieces increased by 65% soon after the film's release and eventually soared to US$35 million in sales after one year ("How Sweet," 1982). The enormously successful film was a common topic of conversation among its most avid admirers—young people, the very consumer segment that was a prime target for Hershey—and it is likely that Reese's Pieces was a commonly mentioned element during those conversations. In this example, Universal, the company that made the film, did not directly receive money from Hershey's for the product placement, but instead agreed to a tie-in between E.T. and Reese's Pieces after the film's release. Hershey's spent more than US$1 million on advertising that included the E.T. character, and E.T. stickers were offered free with Reese's Pieces packaging for redemption of E.T. T-shirts and movie posters.

Three methods of product placement are commonly used by firms to weave consumer brands into noncommercial programming (Clifford, 2008). The simplest and most direct form of placement involves having a product used by cast members, as is often seen in reality TV shows like *American Idol* and *Lost*. The American TV series *24* regularly included scenes of the program's heroes using Apple's iMac portable computers. (A 2006 report by Nielsen Media Research found that Apple's products were mentioned or viewed 250 times over a 4-month period on major American TV channels.) A second method is to integrate a product or company into a program's plot line, sometimes with marketers acting as consultants on the script. Fans of the popular American TV series *Friends* likely recall the episode in which one of the characters purchases Pottery Barn furniture and then tries to convince another character that the furniture is antique. A third approach to product placement is to associate a product with the values or aspirations of a character, a technique that was evident in the 2007 miniseries *The Starter Wife*, which was sponsored solely by Pond's, makers of a variety of skin-care products. The 6-hour series concerned a female character in her forties who, after being abandoned by her husband, attempts to start a new life. This theme was perfectly consistent with the Pond's marketing strategy at the time, which was to promote its "age-defying" skin-care remedies for older women. As part of the agreement with the network, Pond's served as an active creative partner in shaping the storyline and character development; the emissions included some standard product placements, such as scenes showing Pond's creams in a character's bathroom; and a few key "signature moments" occurred during the program, including an on-screen interaction with the Pond's brand that explicitly triggers a thought or motivation in a character (Stevenson, 2007).

Product placement represents a cost-effective means for marketers to reach target audiences. If we consider the aforementioned example from *Friends*, it likely would have cost Pottery Barn upward of US$250,000 to air a 15-second advertising spot during such a widely viewed prime-time TV program. By contrast, a 15-second product placement exposure of the Pottery Barn brand woven into the plotline of the program could be negotiated for less than US$10,000, depending on

(cont.)

Box 2.2 (*Continued*)

the agency–client agreement. One drawback to placing products in filmed content is that it can often take many months to negotiate a deal. As a result, more firms are opting to utilize some form of *virtual advertising*, which is a type of digital technology that inserts electronic images of signs, brand logos, and product packages into live (e.g., as a sporting match is played) or previously taped TV programs and movies. Unlike non-virtual product placements, virtual ads can be negotiated morequickly after production of a program is completed. Virtual advertising also provides different sponsors an opportunity to better target audiences geographically or by lifestyle preferences. In this way, a consumer watching the Olympics on television in Mexico City might be exposed to a placement on a stadium perimeter board for Danone's Bonafont mineral water, while the same coverage in Madrid might show the logo for Danone's Fontvella mineral water. Product placements and virtual advertising are likely to be the wave of the future in advertising, where the brand and the non-commercial programming are integrated more flawlessly than previously could have been imagined.

Mobile Devices

Along with the personal computer and Internet, among the most important new media technologies to have emerged in recent years are those that enable greater portability and mobility. Consumers are now able to access virtually any kind of information and connect with marketers and fellow consumers with greater facility than ever before, anywhere, and anytime. The mobile phone is a device most people now take for granted, perhaps in part because of its remarkable growth and rapid technological evolution. It is difficult to believe that in the recent past, this device did not even exist. Yet, over the span of less than 20 years, the mobile phone industry has reached subscription rates that took well over a century for the fixed telecommunications industry to attain. Consider some of the figures:

- According to market research and consultation company Informa, by July 2007, the total number of mobile phone owners was estimated at 2.3 billion, and is forecast to grow to 4 billion by the end of 2009.

- In some countries, such as Italy, Sweden, and the United Kingdom, the penetration rate of mobile phones exceeds 100% per capita, with significant numbers of consumers using multiple phones. For example, in 2006, Germany reached a penetration rate of 92.6%, with roughly 76% of Germans owning one phone and 16% having two phones. Similarly, with a penetration rate of 114.8% in the United Kingdom, approximately 87% of the British have one phone, and 27% have two phones.

- Regionally, by the end of 2007, penetration reached 100% in western Europe, with a total of 402 million mobile phone subscriptions. Worldwide, the total of mobile phone subscriptions reached 3 billion by mid-2007, with one in four owners having two or more subscriptions ("3 Billion," 2007).

- In some markets, ring tones, the mobile phone jingles that signal that one has received a call, generate more revenues than traditional music singles.

New applications are dramatically expanding the potential of mobile telephones at the same time that consumers worldwide are demanding engaging content and useful services from their portable devices. Among the more compelling developments is the emergence of 3G ("Third Generation") wireless mobile phone technology, which is capable of supporting full-motion video, videoconferencing, and high-speed full Internet access. Although relatively slow in fully grasping the advantages of 3G mobile handsets, such as always-on data access, high data speeds, and greater voice capacity, consumers are increasingly recognizing how these enhanced services allow for more interactivity and a wider range of applications ("American Consumers," 2006). The emerging services typically are classified either as mobile commerce (such as electronic banking, downloading money-off coupons, and location services) or mobile entertainment (including mobile TV and music, sports scores updates, and the downloading of entertainment content). By the end of 2007, there were approximately 614 million 3G subscribers, and this number is forecast to increase at an annual growth rate of 34% in the near future ("RNCOS Releases," 2008). This trend is expected to spearhead consumer adoption of 3G-based mobile TV, with an annual subscriber growth rate forecast at nearly 48% by 2012.

Another new development that has converged with mobile phone technology is the application of PC-based flash technology, which enables manufacturers to provide customizable user interfaces and a greater variety of options for mobilizing Web applications. Although Japan and other Far Eastern countries have led the way in flash-enhanced handsets, the number of such devices already had reached 200 million globally by the end of 2006.

One of the more intriguing offshoots of these various developments in mobile phone applications is the emergence of what is likely to become a third major service category of handset devices, mobile social networking. We'll have much to say about the burgeoning phenomenon of online social networking throughout this book, but at this juncture it is important to recognize that what had largely been limited to the personal computer is now spreading to handheld media devices. Two of the most successful online social networking sites, MySpace and Facebook, have developed mobile applications. In the first 6 months since its launch, MySpace recorded over 7 million unique visitors to MySpace Mobile, and Facebook recorded 4 million unique registrations soon after its mobile launch. Additionally, a variety of mobile-only social networking players, such as airG, Mocospace, myGamma, and itsmy.com, have recorded early successes ("Everyone Is Talking," 2008). By early 2008, a groundswell of local mobile phone companies had added their own social networking applications, including offers that allow users to upload videos and live broadcasts directly to the Internet, and others that incorporate blogging, pictures or voice-to-text in the mobile network. In summarizing the impact of these various developments, Publicis Groupe executives Maurice Lévy and Dan O'Donoghue (2005, p. 14) asserted that the mobile phone is rapidly becoming the dominant means by which the world is being recreated by and for consumers: "Indeed, the Internet is a fascinating medium, but the mobile phone allows *you* to be the center of *your* universe."

There is some debate as to what the future of mobile social networking holds for marketers, who are attracted to the possibilities of this emerging form of consumer-to-consumer communication as a new channel for promoting their goods and services. Unlike Internet-based advertising to date, which has the potential to benefit from banner ads and search engine algorithms, among other options, mobile advertising is more limited and early indications are that consumers are averse to current marketing practices on their handheld devices (Viscarolasaga, 2008). This poses a challenge for marketers who will have to be more creative in developing new approaches for reaching consumers in order to become active and welcome participants in the consumer handheld conversation.

Video Games

Another development that has contributed in a major way in leading the consumer migration away from traditional mass media content is the phenomenal success of the commercial entertainment medium of video games. In the United States, video game sales represent a multibillion dollar industry, generating more annual revenue than the domestic movie box office. Gaming consoles are rapidly becoming as prevalent as televisions, exceeding 100 million units in American households alone, and the soaring consumer adoption of handheld gaming devices and game-enabled mobile phones continues unabated. By 2007, sales of video game software reached US$15 billion annually in the United States, while online video game revenue exceeded US$1 billion by 2006. As for the European market, a 2008 study led by Forrester Research revealed that 72% of the 14,000 European Internet users surveyed play a video game while online ("Technographics Insight," 2008). Although the variety of game platforms has continued to grow, it appears that the personal computer represents the platform of choice for European game players, with 60% of respondents saying they regularly play games on their computer, whereas 33% indicated they regularly play games on a console and 27% on their mobile phone. The study also found that consumers tend to be more invested in video game consoles, spending more money on game titles and devoting more time to play individual games.

As an example of the success of video games in capturing consumers' limited attention and dollars, Microsoft's computer game *Halo 2* garnered over US$125 million in worldwide sales in its first weekend and *Halo 3* earned US$300 million during its first week. Microsoft CEO Bill Gates may have effectively been referring to the entire video game industry when he dubbed the success of *Halo 3* a cultural phenomenon "that embodies our vision for the future of entertainment, where some of the world's greatest creative minds will deliver a new generation of interactive storytelling" ("MS Celebrates," 2007).

At the same time that gaming is drawing valued consumer attention away from traditional mass media, it provides enormous opportunities for marketers. According to the President of Pod Digital, Steve Curran (2007), the new generations of video games have certain distinctive characteristics that set them apart from other media: (*a*) they are interactive in nature, and thus provide an engaging and involving means of getting messages across to consumers; (*b*) they provide an ideal opportunity for social networking, in that players recommend games to friends and compete with their peers and with strangers; (*c*) they represent a compelling medium to inform, educate, and entertain, because they are capable of capturing the focused attention of players; (*d*) they can be used on every major digital platform, including televisions, mobile phones, personal computers, game consoles, handheld devices, and PDAs; and (*e*) their appeal for consumers crosses demographic and gender boundaries. As a result of aggressive marketing tactics, video games are no longer the sole province of young males; indeed, recent studies reveal that more than 50% of game players are 35 years or older and female (Digital Marketing Services, 2004). Many gamers are high-income, educated, and professional persons who utilize the Internet for social networking, information searches, and e-commerce. In recent years, seniors residing in nursing homes have taken to multiple player games, such as Nintendo's Wii bowling game, as a much appreciated form of recreation and social interaction (Baig, 2009).

Given the growing success of video games, it is not surprising that marketers regard *advergaming*—that is, the use of video games as a channel for advertising a product, brand, or viewpoint—as a key mechanism for reaching consumer targets who no longer are accessible via traditional media channels. Advergaming provides marketers with an excellent opportunity for acquiring invaluable consumer data by offering players in-game product-related choices, and the games are likely to be shared with others. For example, Honda's 3D online racing advergame, which included in-game cars modeled after actual Honda cars, was largely designed as a market research tool enabling Honda to create elaborate psychographic profiles of customers. By offering consumers the opportunity to win a Honda CR-V, registrants willingly provided a range of personal data, including their age, address, occupation, hobbies, their car preferences, and details about their currently owned vehicles. Overall, the game yielded a 30% registration rate among users, who on average played the game for about 5 minutes (Curran, 2007).

Interactive Outdoor Media

Outdoor billboards (and other signage) represent one of the earliest and most prevalent forms of marketing communication, traditionally used as a local medium to reinforce advertising campaigns primarily run through television and print media channels. Traditional billboards are cost effective, provide marketers with the capability of reaching specific targets repeatedly, and can have strong visual appeal. These qualities lie behind advertisers' steadily increasing outdoor expenditures, especially in the consumer sectors of local services and entertainment, communications, retail, and real estate. In the United States, outdoor spending grew from US$2.87 billion in 1993 to US$5.50 billion in 2003, but currently represents only about a 2.5% share of total domestic advertising revenues ("US Advertising Spending," 2008). By contrast, outdoor advertising comprises 12% of total advertising spending in France, 10% in the United Kingdom, and 8% in Spain ("Advertising Spending Worldwide," 2008). Now that digital technology has come to outdoor and in-store communications, conventionally passive outdoor marketing efforts are making way for increasingly interactive ones. One of the first examples of this new approach was applied by the lingerie brand Pretty Polly, which publicly displayed posters that asked for the "pressing" of a button under the model's bust. This then resulted in the display of information about the range of the brand's underwear (Beer, 2002).

One of the new trends that is beginning to change the face (both literally and figuratively) of outdoor signage is the transformation from "paper and paste" signs to electronic screens. The digital ink billboard represents one of the more promising new developments for outdoor advertising, and has been spreading rapidly throughout North America and Europe since 2007. Originally designed by the Israeli company Magink, the digital ink billboard utilizes a technology that produces full-color, print-quality displays. In addition to the high quality of the billboard imagery, the digital displays are low on energy consumption, requiring energy only to swap between images. A distinct advantage of this new type of billboard over the old-fashioned variety is that it allows billboard companies to control the digital advertisements and their content from an off-site computer according to the needs of advertisers. The technology also improves on existing electronic billboards that make use of light emitting diode (LED) screens, which provide grainier images that sometimes fade in strong sunlight.

Another new electronic outdoor advertising medium involves the use of liquid crystal display (LCD) screens. These devices, which resemble small television screens, are mounted in various public settings to reach highly selective audiences that are particularly valued by advertisers. The LCD screens are used both to provide information and advertising presentations and have been displayed in supermarkets, pharmacies, subway stations, elevators, hotels, public areas, and commuter transportation vehicles. For example, a small LCD screen can be mounted on the shelf in a pharmacy to present a video promotion describing the health benefits of taking vitamins that are sold in the shop.

An increasing number of electronic advertising displays are exploiting their potential for active engagement by encouraging consumers to interact with them via their mobile phones. This is accomplished by embedding within the advertising medium battery-powered tags equipped with built-in Bluetooth or infrared signals, which enable passersby to point and click their phones at a billboard or some other display to access additional information and services from the Internet. One of the innovators of this technology is

Hypertag, which promotes its "point–click–receive" service as follows: "Imagine walking down the street and seeing a poster advertising an airline; you point and click your phone at the tag, download flight times and make a booking." Like other new out-of-home media, the battery-powered hypertag technology has a great degree of flexibility and offers a wider range of potential applications when compared with non-electronic displays (see Box 2.3).

BOX 2.3 FOCUS ON APPLICATION: ENGAGING CONSUMERS THROUGH DIGITAL OUTDOOR MEDIA

Interactive outdoor media can serve as platforms for unique advertising efforts that can effectively engage consumer attention and have a strong impact on persons who otherwise might not be exposed to a traditional marketing campaign. A variety of creative applications of the hypertag technology have been employed with outdoor advertising. In the typical case, passersby interact with an outdoor billboard or display using their mobile phone or PDA. Digital content electronically stored in the hypertag is activated by Bluetooth or infrared signals and then delivered directly to the user's phone. In one application in New York City, Yahoo! collaborated with the interactive shop R/GA to promote Yahoo!'s automotive Web site. The companies created a digital billboard that enabled pedestrians to play a video game broadcast on a large section of the twenty-three-stories-tall Reuters sign in Times Square via their mobile phones.

In another example, the Ogilvy advertising agency designed an interactive billboard campaign to promote the Ford Fiesta automobile in Belgium. The campaign involved inviting each passerby with a mobile phone to participate in a game that offered a chance to win a free Ford Fiesta. The passerby was first asked to send an SMS using a code electronically provided by the billboard. The billboard would then respond by sending a return message to the phone posing a particular question. The response to the question, also sent by SMS, activated the billboard to respond like a pinball machine, with a correct answer awarded an "extra ball" (i.e., entry into the drawing for the Fiesta) and an incorrect answer causing the billboard to "tilt." Another interactive mobile marketing operation was launched by the Unilever brand Dove in 2004 as an element of the brand's "Campaign for Real Beauty," a global marketing effort intended to promote women's natural beauty and self esteem ("First Interactive," 2004). With the aid of SMS codes, consumers were invited to participate in the campaign by voting on the beauty of graphically displayed faces of various women appearing on mobile digital billboards driven throughout New York City and Los Angeles. The graphics ranged from supermodels to a 96-year-old woman bearing the tagline "Wrinkled?" or "Wonderful?" Real-time voting results were fed to a large LED billboard in Times Square, and participants received instant feedback on their mobile phones after casting their votes. This involvement encouraged people to visit the Dove Web site for further details about the campaign and to participate in discussion groups on the topic of natural beauty. Overall, more than 1 million votes were cast by mobile phone and approximately 10,000 consumers posted messages on the Dove Web site.

Pepsi's Miller Beer launched a campaign that included Bluetooth-enhanced posters at bus shelters in six American cities. The posters provided a free music download to persons with Bluetooth-enabled phones as they waited for a bus. In a variation of this campaign, in order to promote the 2009 season of the HBO series *Big Love*, the cable TV network installed in several American cities street-level billboards that included several audio jacks. Passersby were encouraged to plug in their headphones to hear recordings of secrets about the various characters depicted in

(cont.)

Box 2.3 (*Continued*)

the billboards. Similarly, BBDO Canada created interactive poster displays that were mounted in subway cars. Each poster had a fully functional headphone jack embedded in it, which allowed riders to listen to samples of various exclusive tracks available at pepsiaccess.ca.

As the latter example suggests, there are potential applications of these digital innovations that extend beyond their use in outdoor billboards for engaging consumers. The hypertag technology currently is being applied to other media channels, such as print and television. In the near future, it will be possible for phone users to point their mobile handsets at a magazine page or television screen to be linked to a content-relevant web page ("Billboards Are Talking," 2003).

Finally, in what may be the ultimate example of engaging consumers with newly designed outdoor media technology, it is now possible to bring advertising content directly to target consumers in public settings rather than waiting for people to come to a specific outdoor display. The Irish company Adwalker designed a digital media platform that is worn as a compact body pack, fully equipped with an LCD screen, wearable PC, handheld touch screen, and printer (see images below). Representatives of the company don the patented Xybernaut Wearable Computer and engage with consumers in various public settings (shopping malls, convention centers, and various busy urban settings) to enable portable brand advertisements and point-of-sale functions.

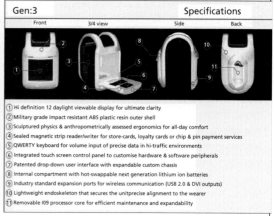

Source: www.adwalker.com

Launched in 2004, the interactive media platform is capable of delivering a unique suite of highly targeted media and marketing applications, including point-of-sale, ticketing, and digital coupons via credit card and smart card transactions; interactive games and competitions; real-time information updates which are downloaded via the Internet; multimedia messaging allowing mobile phone interaction with passersby; and consumer data collection, which can be uploaded to a database for analysis. Adwalker's list of clients for promotional campaigns has included Sears, Ford, Microsoft, Panasonic, Castrol, Paramount, and Diageo. In one campaign, Castrol, a major sponsor of the Euro 2008 Football Championships, mobilized Adwalker in cities across Austria and Switzerland, where the sporting event was hosted.

A simpler, but more lightweight version of the Adwalker device consists of an LCD screen that is integrated in a T-shirt and limited to displaying videos. Developed by BrandMarketers, one of the initial successful applications of the T-shirt TV involved a promotion for the film *I, Robot*. A trailer for the film was literally brought to potential moviegoers to stimulate interest in and buzz about the film prior to its official opening in movie theaters. At least for the time being, such "walking advertise-ment" technologies are extremely effective in stopping people in the street and, assuming that audiences are strategically reached, capable of engaging them with relevant marketing content.

As traditional static advertising displays are being converted to digital ones, they are paying off for outdoor advertisers. Digital posters and displays allow advertisers to rotate messages so as to present communications from several different marketing sources throughout the day. In industry parlance, this is referred to as "day-parting," a method that is distinctively advantageous to leaving the same paper or vinyl ads on display for extended periods before having to manually replace them. Additionally, digital tags in outdoor advertising allow companies to monitor the effectiveness of their campaigns by providing a record of the number of mobile phone interactions from each site.

These various innovations in outdoor marketing are effective ways of drawing crowds of consumers and generating buzz, and they rapidly are becoming obligatory for firms in their efforts to get their messages noticed. As David Lubars, the chairman and chief creative officer of BBDO North America, explained, "It used to be, you were creative within a template. Now you have to not only be highly creative in the content, but the delivery has to be creative" (Clifford, 2009).

Fragmentation in Perspective

This overview of some of the more compelling new media developments, which have served to fragment a consumer population that once was capable of being treated as a mass market, would appear to complicate the marketing process, compounding the problem of knowing how, when, and where to reach specific consumers. Although there is much truth to this new marketing reality, despite the greater simplicity and success of the aggregate marketing approach during earlier times, to a great extent the consumer population has always been fragmented—if not in terms of media usage patterns, surely in terms of individual differences in lifestyle, personality, interests, and background characteristics. In this light, the fragmentation of media and audiences during the ongoing digital revolution should serve as a wake-up call to marketers that their traditional tools for targeting consumers are no longer sufficient. The differential targeting of consumer segments through media where those segments are most likely to be present represents an enormous opportunity for contemporary marketers. Per-sonalized messages that are transmitted through appropriate media are more likely to capture the attention of consumer targets, arouse their interest, engage them, and stimulate an interaction, while at the same time minimizing the misuse of company resources. For some examples of how marketing communications can be effectively personalized for different types of consumers, see Box 2.4.

BOX 2.4 FROM MASS MARKETING TO MICROMARKETING: TAKING A MORE TARGETED APPROACH TO REACHING CONSUMERS

The one-size-fits-all mass marketing approach once so prevalent among firms is waning as audiences increasingly fragment across a wide range of media platforms—narrowcast cable TV channels and radio stations, specialized magazines, computer terminals, game consoles, PDAs, and mobile phones. A global brand like McDonald's until recently devoted two-thirds of its marketing budget to television advertising, whereas today that figure is closer to one-third (Bianco, 2004). Instead of investing major expenditures of money on 30-second network TV advertising spots, McDonald's now utilizes a more precisely targeted approach to reach its prime target audiences. The restaurant chain advertised on Foot Locker Inc.'s in-store video network in an effort to appeal to young males; paid for closed-circuit sports programming in Hispanic bars to capture Latino consumers; placed ads in the custom-published magazine *Upscale*, which is distributed to barber shops in order to reach African-American customers; and advertised in women's magazines (*O:The Oprah Magazine*) and on specific Web sites (Yahoo! and iVillage, Inc.) to reach mothers. Thus, it should come as no surprise when McDonald's chief marketing officer, M. Lawrence Light, proclaimed, "We are not a mass marketer."

Reaching and communicating with audiences even through the same media platform can be a challenge, given the diversity of types of persons likely to be making use of it. For example, Internet users comprise a myriad of consumer segments who are likely to be visiting different kinds of Web sites for very different purposes. This might require an advertiser to design different kinds of promotional appeals for different sites or to customize certain aspects of a message intended for similar sites depending on the varying characteristics of visitors to those sites. Digitas, a unit of the global advertising firm Publicis Groupe, has developed a system consistent with the latter approach that links a database of consumer information with its online advertisements. The system can deliver hundreds of custom ads, each aimed at particular consumers based on their Web habits, demographics, and past interactions with the advertiser.

In one example of this approach, Digitas created three versions of the same relatively simple General Motors online ad for its new Acadia crossover utility vehicle (Karp, 2007). The three ads, whose layout included a relatively small image of the vehicle with accompanying text, are likely to look identical at first glance, but more careful scrutiny will point out certain key differences. The first two versions were intended to serve as initial appeals for persons just beginning to shop for a car. Both versions include a tagline (i.e., a clever phrase that is intended to summarize the essence of the appeal) that reads, "It's every bit as flexible as you," followed by additional copy that elaborates on a key attribute of the car. This is where the two versions differ: one includes the technical statement, "With GM-exclusive Smartslide Seating System and a re-configurable interior" to encourage people who do product research to visit the GM site to obtain further information about the feature-named seating system. By contrast, the second version includes the non-technical statement, "With a re-configurable interior and the most interior space in the class," and excludes the Smartslide Seating System feature name. This version is then targeted to Web users who may be turned off by technical names. The third version of the Acadia ad is shown to people who are known to already have seen one of the earlier ads with the tagline. In place of the tagline is the statement, "With the most accommodating 3rd row seats in the class." Rather than the general promise about more interior space, the phrase "3rd row" is likely to be noticed by car buyers with large families, and the superlative "most" is used when data show that a consumer has begun online comparison shopping. An additional modification from earlier ads is the positioning of the image of the car, which is placed higher for people who want a closer look after already having seen the ad earlier.

The Digitas approach to customizing ads clearly is in line with the sorts of personalized marketing approaches that are likely to progressively overtake any vestiges of the mass marketing strategies of the past. Some companies are currently running nearly 4,000 versions of an ad for a single brand, and that number of iterations is apt to grow along with further technological innovations (Karp, 2007).

From the perspective of the media industry, fragmentation necessitates new models for doing business. A series of articles published in *The Financial Times* under the rubric "The End of the Mass Market" highlighted three alternative strategies utilized by the media industry in response to the new marketing environment: horizontal integration, vertical integration, and the search for new sources of revenue. As summarized by Tim Burt and Simon London (2004) of the global business consulting firm Bain & Company, *horizontal integration* is an approach that involves the building or acquiring of media properties across a broad range of platforms. This strategy has some of the same objectives as the market aggregation approach, but acknowledges that media companies are no longer capable of reaching a mass audience through a single outlet, such as a magazine or TV channel. Instead, capturing large audiences requires the building of a portfolio of media properties, with each targeting a different group across a range of media platforms. Examples of companies that utilize this approach include HBO, the Chicago Tribune Group, Fox News, and the BBC, each of which manages an array of offerings beyond their core product, such as Web sites, TV assets, and radio stations.

Vertical integration is an alternative strategy that involves the marriage of a media content provider with a media distribution company. This strategy was evident in 2004 when the national cable TV network Comcast Corp. made an unsolicited offer to buy the Walt Disney Company for US$54 billion. Such an approach provides media distributors with market power, the assumption being that they can strike better deals with content providers by having content of their own to offer in return. However, the aforementioned problem of fragmentation can pose a risk for industries that attempt to own distribution channels, as is apparent with the challenges that the Internet has posed for the contemporary music industry, including artists selling their music directly from their Web sites.

The third emerging strategy is that of media companies attempting to create alternative sources of revenue. At present, this is being accomplished through the subscription model promoted by music and film retailers or via the pay-per-download system pioneered by Apple. These methods, used by digital radio stations (e.g., Sirius and XM), personal video recording services (e.g., TiVo and Sky Plus), and music downloading services (e.g., Apple's iTunes) typically require customers to pay a monthly or per-download fixed fee to obtain media content. According to Burt and London, such subscription services are especially conducive to precision marketing, in the sense that service providers can exploit their detailed knowledge of consumer media usage habits to deliver targeted advertising. As of this writing, TiVo had begun to present its service as a platform for building interactive advertisements.

Consumers Tuning Out Formal Marketing Efforts

The changes in the nature and variety of marketing technologies and media have given rise to a number of emerging concerns and challenges for advertisers and other marketing communicators. The fact that the methods for communicating messages continue to expand means that today's consumers in industrialized parts of the world are bombarded with an ever growing number of marketing stimuli, to the point where marketing has become virtually inescapable.

Marketing Clutter and Its Consequences

According to some estimates, the average American is exposed to at least 3,000 to 5,000 marketing messages daily, ranging from television, radio, and billboard ads to logos on clothing and Internet banners (Vollmer, 2008). This estimate (translating to about three ads per minute) represents a significant increase from the roughly 2,000 ads the same individual might have been exposed to during the mid-1970s. As the competition for consumers' attention rises, and as consumers increasingly learn to employ technologies that screen out traditional advertising, marketers are frantically exploiting each and every previously untapped channel for getting their messages across to target audiences. These include, but are not limited to, innovations that extend beyond what already are becoming familiar marketing tactics that utilize branded clothing, scents (e.g., the aroma of freshly baked bread emanating from the entrance of a supermarket), interruptive online ads, unsolicited mobile phone clips, and trademarked sounds. Consider the following examples:

- The advertising agency TBWA\Chiat\Day has placed ads on gas pump handles, dry cleaner hangars, napkins, swizzle sticks, bathroom stalls, and banana skins.
- The corporate logo for Snapple beverages was pressed into the sand by beach cleaners as they traversed the beaches of New Jersey, USA.
- Video screens airing short promotional videos interspersed with noncommercial content have begun to appear with increasing frequency on the front seatbacks in taxis.
- Ads for the over-the-counter children's cold relief medication Tylenol were printed on the disposable paper covering on pediatricians' examination tables.
- To promote its 2006 fall lineup of programming, CBS stamped laser imprints onto 35 million eggs distributed throughout the United States in order to promote its fall lineup. Along with the company's trademark eye insignia, the stamps highlighted upcoming television programs with humorous slogans like "Funny Side Up," "Leave the Yolks to Us," "Hard Boiled Drama," and "Crack the Case on CBS." This so-called

"egg-vertising" medium also has been used by Schick to promote its new Quattro Titanium razor for men, with Styrofoam egg cartons containing eggs with clean-shaven faces printed onto their shells and a promotional flyer for the razor.

- Healthquest Technologies Inc. developed the Wizmark Interactive Urinal Communicator, a urinal cake that serves as a medium for advertising. The Wizmark is capable of presenting electronic displays with moving or flashing images, as well as providing voice messages and music. Liquid activated and sensitive to changes in lighting, the device has been placed inside the men's rooms of bars, restaurants, theaters, office buildings, and sporting complexes to promote a range of products (e.g., beer products, sporting events, radio shows) and social causes (e.g., safe sex, alcohol, and drug abuse) to captive audiences.

- Some airlines have begun to make use of advertising space on motion sickness bags, and it is no longer unusual to see promotions inside the trays used for airport baggage screening or seatback dining trays inside airplanes. In the Salzburg, Austria airport, a sushi restaurant effectively captured travelers' attention by placing giant pieces of fake sushi on the baggage carousels.

Although some of these approaches are likely to sound bizarre, it is probably also true that consumers are becoming increasingly desensitized to even the most outrageous promotional tactics. Nonetheless, many marketers are left with no choice than to attempt to capture attention through whatever unique means they can devise. According to marketing consultant and author Al Ries, "The simple fact is that traditional advertising isn't working well. If it were, you wouldn't see so many advertisers looking for new ways to spend their money." Gary Ruskin, executive director of the watchdog group Commercial Alert, noted that "Corporations are trying to lay claim to every micrometer of space for commercial advertising. They don't view anything as sacred anymore." Indeed, some marketing agencies have gone so far as to consider putting ads on condoms and stickers that bartenders can attach to currency when they make change (Johnson, 2001).

These creative innovations in reaching consumers notwithstanding, some traditional forms of advertising, such as television, cinema, and outdoor, show no immediate signs of abating. The number of promotional messages on American television alone has increased more than 250% since the mid-1960s, from 2,600 advertisements per week to more than 6,000 per week by the end of the 1990s, resulting in a 39% rise in total television content devoted to advertising (Schmitt, 2004; Solomon, 2008). This growing clutter of TV advertising is largely attributable to two factors: (*a*) an increase in number of ad minutes per program hour and (*b*) the use of shorter commercials (Lowrey, Shrum, & McCarty, 2005). For example, US network advertising minutes per prime time hour steadily rose from 9.70 minutes in 1991 to 12.05 minutes in 2001; a similar increase occurred across all other day parts (network news hour, early morning, daytime, and late night programming). Total US network advertising break time for

3 hours of prime time increased from 38.73 minutes in 1991 to 52.72 minutes in 2003, while average break length rose from 1.77 minutes to 3.16 minutes over the same time span. (Total break time includes commercials, sponsorship announcements, promotions, teasers, and public service announcements.) Since 1996, the amount of advertising clutter has steadily increased on both broadcast and cable TV, to the point where an "hour-long" program is likely to comprise only about 40 minutes of original noncommercial programming (not accounting for product placements).

The fact that similar increases have not been seen on European television is largely attributable to more stringent regulations about on-air advertising time. In France, for many years government-funded channels could carry up to 12 minutes of commercials per hour, with only one or two breaks during movies. With the Trautmann law, the number of advertising minutes per hour for public broadcasters was cut to 8 minutes per hour by 2001. (Similar regulations in the United States were eliminated during the mid-1980s when they were ruled to violate antitrust laws.) Beginning in January 2009, a new law served to ban all advertising on the French state-funded TV channels from 8:00 p.m. to 6:00 a.m. The average number of minutes of advertising per hour on the top networks from 1996 to 2006 remained relatively stable in France (4.79 minutes in 1996; 4.96 minutes in 2006), Great Britain (7.0; 7.0), and Germany (7.33; 8.40), although proposed European Union regulations allowing for 12 minutes of commercials per hour may serve to raise those numbers by 2010 (Lowrey, Shrum, & McCarty, 2005).

One of the underlying causes of advertising clutter is the increase in fragmentation, which has compelled many marketers to adopt a "scorched earth" mindset consistent with earlier market aggregation strategies. In other words, it is thought that saturating the marketplace with marketing messages through a variety of channels will somehow compensate for fragmentation. This strategy, however, tends to be both inefficient and costly because certain messages inevitably will reach some members of the intended audience more than desired, whereas other audience members will not receive the communications at all (Schmitt, 2004). Moreover, clutter is likely to impede message recall, especially when one considers that a majority of consumers engage in other activities, such as using their PC or mobile phone while watching television (see Box 2.5).

The ability for any one promotional message to break through marketing clutter to capture attention, arouse interest, and have its intended effects has become exceedingly difficult. As the number of marketing message exposures continues to grow, consumers' ability (and desire) to differentiate among the various messages has diminished. This has become an unanticipated negative consequence of firms' increasing use of celebrities to endorse their products in advertisements. For example, Levi's gambled €7.7 million to have the popular Japanese pop star Takuya Kimura promote its Engineered Jeans in Asia. The company soon learned that consumers felt the pop star was everywhere. At the time, Mr. Kimura was also endorsing Kirin beer, Toyota cars, Suntory whiskey, credit cards, phone services, and his own films and TV shows. According to one Levi's

---

BOX 2.5 FOCUS ON RESEARCH: MULTITASKING DILUTES MEDIA ATTENTION

Advances in digital technology and the emergence of innovative communication devices have transformed the consumer environment into one that has spawned an emerging trend toward *multitasking*—the tendency for individuals to engage in multiple tasks at the same time. People are surfing the Internet while watching TV, chatting on their mobile phones while driving, and reading their e-mails on PDAs during meetings.

Various studies simply confirm what most marketers already assumed, which is that a majority of consumers tend to utilize different forms of communications media simultaneously. A 2003 analysis by the Media Center at the American Press Institute and BIGresearch reported that 70% of consumers in general are apt to engage in media multitasking, and the Mobium Creative Group found that as many as 83% of business professionals are apt to do so as they carry out their work-related tasks (Greenspan, 2004). Multitasking tends to involve a combination of new and old media, as when individuals check their text messages on their mobile phone while watching television. According to the Media Center and BIGresearch 2003 Simultaneous Media Usage Survey (SIMM), television appears to be the medium that is most likely to entail multitasking activities, with 66% of the more than 13,000 respondents indicating that they regularly or occasionally go online while watching television; 66% regularly or occasionally read their mail; and 74% regularly or occasionally read the newspaper (The Media Center, 2004). SIMM studies, which survey participants drawn from an online interactive base of 60 million Americans, provide highly accurate measurements of how audiences use and consume media.

On the surface, it may appear that simultaneous media use is a positive development for marketers who fear that new media are undercutting the potential to reach consumer targets through traditional channels. However, results from the Mobium Creative Group study suggest otherwise—it appears that rather than reinforcing consumer reach through multiple channels, media multitasking tends to dilute the impact of marketing messages. Fully 80% of business professionals surveyed claimed to pay more attention to one medium as opposed to others when they multitask. Specifically, when inquired about the last time they used media simultaneously, business professionals revealed that they paid the most attention to the Internet (41%), newspapers (20%), and television (18%), with all other media scoring 5% or less (i.e., trade journals, general business publications, radio, direct mail, and sales literature).

What these findings seem to suggest is that broad, multichannel marketing campaigns not only exacerbate the growing problem of advertising clutter, but they also appear to be surprisingly ineffective for capturing consumer attention. For instance, if a target consumer group is comprised of television/personal computer multitaskers, an expensive television campaign may escape the attention of viewers whose heads are down during advertising breaks. Unless a media mix is strategically developed and carefully targeted, increased ad spending is likely to continue to reap diminishing returns.

---

representative, "He's diluting our brand because people are confused." Results of a 2006 study conducted by the NPD Group market research firm provided additional evidence of how consumers have difficulties correctly identifying which products some celebrities endorsed. One finding revealed that 17% correctly recalled that Donald Trump had appeared in commercials for Visa credit cards, but another 14% thought that he had endorsed American Express. In general, consumers were aware that the famous American business magnate and TV personality was endorsing a financial services company, but were unclear as to which one. If consumers have difficulty linking celebrity endorsers to the appropriate brands, imagine the confusion they have recalling which brands are advertised at all amidst all the clutter.

Marketers also are well aware that a majority of messages are screened out entirely by their intended audiences, who may be bored, irritated, apathetic, or simply overwhelmed by excessive marketing exposure. This screening process has become much easier for consumers with the development of technologies that allow them to avoid the intrusions of unwanted promotional messages (e.g., by "zipping" or "zapping" through recorded messages, installing Internet pop-up blockers on their computers, and the like). By September 2007, there were 2.5 million users of Adblock Plus, a Firefox Internet browser free extension that deletes all advertisements from Web sites, with numbers of new users rising by 400,000 each month (Cohen, 2007). A 2003 Forrester research analysis found that consumers who owned digital video recorders admitted to skipping 20% of all televised ads (Jennings & Jackson, 2003). The results of a Neilson Media Research study published in June 2007 revealed an even higher percentage of ad-skipping among DVR owners. In the latter study, the proportion of viewers who claimed to attend to TV commercials was 69.9% among 18- to 49-year-olds in households with DVRs, a figure 24% lower than it was for real-time viewers in that age bracket in all households. For example, the real-time airing of the popular prime-time TV show, *The Office*, showed a 6.2% viewer decline during commercials, whereas a 50.9% drop-off was noted in households that owned a DVR (including real-time and playback viewing).

Consumer Attitudes Toward Marketing and Advertising

Along with the proclivity of target audiences to ignore the many marketing messages that are directed their way, there has been a rise in skepticism regarding the veracity and purpose of the messages that consumers do attend to. The rise in skepticism about marketing tactics is consistent with a growing trend among consumers to be less trusting of business enterprises than in the past. According to a USA Today/CNN/Gallup survey, nearly 50% of adults surveyed said that corporations can be trusted only a little or not at all to look out for the interests of their employees as opposed to only 10% who think that corporations can be trusted a great deal in this regard (Armour, 2002). In the United Kingdom, a significant decline in consumer respect for corporations was noted during the period spanning 1997 to 2003 (TGI Premier), consistent with opinions in other European countries. An overall average of 58% of the adult respondents surveyed in a large-scale 2003 European Union study claimed that they "do not trust" big companies, ranging from 51% in Spain to 64% in the United Kingdom, and 65% in Sweden (Eurobarometer 60, 2003).

BOX 2.6 MARKETING SCAMS, SWINDLES, AND FRAUDS
_____

Recent statistics attest to the claim that consumers are frequently duped by dishonest and deceitful marketers and con artists, resulting in the lowering of the reputation of legitimate marketing professionals. Typical of marketing scams are those that offer consumers promises of money, prizes, or wealth. Once the incentive is proposed, confidence is gained, the target is enticed to participate and pay, and then never receives the promised reward. Recent estimates suggest that scams cost consumers globally many billions of dollars each year, with online fraud currently showing the most dramatic rise among the various forms of unsavory marketing activities. Typical of online scams appearing in e-mail spam messages are claims of lottery winnings, work schemes that guarantee success, cheap loans, and free gifts. Not surprisingly, research reveals that elderly consumers are most likely to be victimized by marketing scam artists (Langenderfer & Shimp, 2001).

In one variation of a prize promotion scam, illegitimate marketers pose as custom representatives who telephone potential victims in the United States and inform them that they have won a prize from a Canadian company. The targets are led to believe they only have to send money to pay customs duties before their winnings can be released. Through a convoluted explanation of international customs laws, the prospective victims are enticed to send certified funds via an overnight delivery company to a fictitious address. With the use of the airbill number provided by the victim, the packages are redirected to the scammer in another location and the swindlers then disappear without a trace.

The rising levels of consumer distrust no doubt can be attributed to a variety of factors, including the prevalence of major scandals involving previously reputable companies; disapproval of multinational corporations and their aggressive marketing tactics; the prevalence of business scams, swindles, and unethical marketing practices (see Box 2.6); and the growing presence of large, anonymous companies (cf. Aditya, 2001; Dery, 1999; Klein, 1999; Langenderfer & Shimp, 2001; Schlosser, 2001).

Opinions about advertising have not fared much better. The results of a widely cited survey of American attitudes toward advertising revealed that while 44% of adult respondents claimed to like advertising in general, 52% believed that advertisements could not be trusted and 69% felt that they had been misled by advertising at least some of the time (Shavitt, Lowrey, & Haefner, 1998). A more recent assessment of American attitudes conducted by Yankelovich Partners, a leading marketing services consultancy firm, reported that 56% of survey respondents said they "avoid buying products that overwhelm them with advertising and marketing," 60% said their opinion of advertising "is much more negative than just a few years ago," 65% said they believed that they are "constantly bombarded with too much" advertising, and 69% said they are "interested in products and services that would help them skip or block marketing" (Yankelovich Partners, Inc., 2005). As an indication of the extent to which many consumers now hold marketing efforts in disregard, another 33% of the Yankelovich survey participants said they would be "willing to have a slightly lower standard of living to live in a society without marketing and advertising."

Similar findings regarding attitudes toward advertising have been reported among European consumers (e.g., Feick & Gierl, 1996), with a steadily declining percentage of Europeans who consider advertising as enjoyable as TV programs (from 29.8% in 1989 to 18.0% in 2003) corresponding to a clear increase in those who find TV ads annoying (from 23.2% in 1996 to 31.4% in 2003) (cf. Kemp, 2008). These findings are bad news for marketers, especially in light of research evidence supporting the presumed relationship between attitudes toward advertising and consumer purchasing behavior; that is, a negative attitude toward advertising has been found to result in an unwillingness to purchase advertised brands (e.g., Bush, Smith, & Martin, 1999).

The news is not all bad for advertisers. For each of the advertising attitude surveys cited above, the researchers noted that consumers' feelings tend to be rather conflicted and they hold a love/hate relationship with advertising. For example, 52% of Shavitt et al.'s (1998) respondents admitted that they like to look at ads, 61% believed that ads are informative, and 68% revealed that they sometimes used ad information in making a purchase decision. Similarly, 55% of the respondents in the Yankelovich study claimed to enjoy advertising. Thus, it would be misleading to posit a blanket statement that consumer attitudes about advertising are completely negative. As the proliferation of ad sharing online (e.g., at YouTube.com and the growing number of consumer-generated blogs about advertising) attests, consumers appreciate ads that they find enjoyable, informative, and creative, and they desire advertising that respects their time and attention. Nonetheless, attitudes about advertising have clearly declined in recent years, a trend that the Yankelovich researchers attributed to the saturation and intrusiveness resulting from marketers' efforts to maintain control over audiences. As J. Walker Smith, President of Yankelovich Partners, concluded, "This is not about new versus traditional media. New media, like digital and wireless technologies, will never solve the ongoing decline in marketing productivity. The most resistant consumers are still waiting for better marketing practices, no matter what media is thrown at them" ("Marketers Must Change," 2005). Smith's comments appear prescient in light of a subsequent study of consumers' opinions about the acceptability of various forms of mobile advertising ("Acceptable Types," 2007). At least 74% of the more than 3,500 mobile phone users surveyed viewed each type of new mobile media advertising as "totally unacceptable," ranging from "a sponsored text link that appears as a result of an Internet search I did on my mobile phone" (74% totally unacceptable) to "a video clip appearing on my cellphone from a retail store I am currently in the vicinity of" (84% totally unacceptable).

As consumers increasingly tune out traditional advertising, marketers must rise to the challenge and tailor advertising so that it appeals to targeted consumer segments and reaches them through appropriate alternative outlets. For example, according to a recent comScore survey, consumers aged 18–34-years-old have shown a marked preference for receiving advertising about "high fun" products (i.e., music, movies, food, apparel, and entertainment) from user-generated content Web sites, whereas for "high trust" items (i.e., health care, financial services) they prefer advertising that appears on general media and news Web sites ("Where Do Social Media," 2007). When asked as part of the Yankelovich study about the marketing practices that they would prefer, consumers responded most favorably to the following: (*a*) marketing that is short and to the point; (*b*) marketing that they can personally choose to see when it is convenient for them; and (*c*) marketing that is personally communicated to them by friends or experts they trust. It has become increasingly evident that consumers are less willing to support the traditional marketing approach whereby companies thrust their products and promotions onto a passive customer base. Consumers want involvement and they increasingly want to be in control of when, how, and where they receive marketing messages.

Consumer Connectedness

It already is old news that consumers are connected with each other as never before; nonetheless, consumer connectedness is discussed here as a new marketplace reality because most marketers have yet to fully come to grips with the profound impact that this development is having in the business environment. As a new marketplace reality, it can be said that consumer connectedness subsumes most, if not all, of the other marketplace developments previously discussed in this chapter.

To a great extent, the new technologies of the digital age have served more than anything else to bring people together. An obvious point of fact is that people have always willingly sought out others for sharing or for assistance in numerous consumption situations—think Tupperware parties, teens congregating at the local mall (so-called mall rats), birthday celebrations with friends at a local restaurant, shopping for a wedding dress with mom, enjoying a baseball game with a best friend, sharing your favorite bottle of single-malt whiskey with a business client, and so on. With the emergence of the Internet and mobile phone, however, consumers now can connect with virtually anyone, anywhere, and anytime. As Larry Weber (2007) pointed out in the opening pages of his book, *Marketing to the Social Web*, the Internet should not be thought of as a channel, but rather as an *aggregator*—a tool for bringing ideas, information, and people together. Internet search engines such as Google, Bing, Yahoo!, and Ask act as *reputation aggregators* that gather Web sites with the best product or service offer, usually in order of reputation or Internet traffic. But it is the *social web*, including networks like Facebook and LinkedIn, that best serves to illustrate the profound power of technology in connecting consumers. As Weber (p. 4) defines it, the social web is "the online place where people with a common interest can gather to share thoughts, comments, and opinions." As the social web (also referred to as Web 2.0; see Chapter 3) is central to marketers' potential for leveraging consumer-to-consumer influence, we will return to it in more detail throughout this book. But for now, a cursory overview of some of the social web's manifestations can help provide an answer to the question, "Just how connected are consumers in the contemporary marketing context?"

The short answer to the question is "very." Traditional *mass* media outlets broadcast their communications in a one-way fashion, with information disseminated to large (and largely, anonymous) publics. *Social* media operate according to complex networks of interpersonal exchange typically involving multithreaded conversations. The term "social web" is especially apropos to the nature of the relationships created by the Internet and other new digital tools. Later in this book, when we focus on the means by which marketing information is exchanged via the word-of-mouth process, the impact of web-like networks on the ways consumers navigate the marketplace will become especially apparent. At one time, consumer influence typically spread slowly as a function of face-to-face interactions with neighbors, friends, family members, and work colleagues. A brief exchange between next-door neighbors about a terrific new film that just opened in town might have set off a linear chain reaction of influence that ended up creating a buzz throughout the neighborhood by the end of the week, assuming the circumstances were right and enough physical contacts, in person or by telephone, were made. The situation is quite different today, with consumers capable of interacting with people halfway around the globe, with nothing more than Internet access. It might take a day or two, but buzz could be generated nationwide about a new film by a connected, informed few who happen to get the message disseminated through the appropriate online social circles.

Social Networks

Consumer connectedness is most fully realized through social networks—primarily Web-based places where people come together to share content, questions, and advice related to mutual interests. Such networks are manifest in various formats that facilitate interactions and connections between users, such as discussion groups, message boards and forums, file-sharing, video, and voice chat. Social network users are able to set up personal profiles and explore the interests and activities of other users' profiles, thus enabling the identification of persons with similar interests and the possibility of connecting with them. Among the best known social networking sites are MySpace, Facebook, LinkedIn, Twitter, Friendster, Bebo, Stumbleupon, iVillage, Xanga, Hi5, Flickr, Orkut, and Last.fm (see Box 2.7). Branded Web destinations, such as Amazon, Netflix, and eBay may also be considered examples of social networking sites (Weber, 2007). The worldwide embrace of social networks has been rapid and impressive, and

BOX 2.7 SOCIAL NETWORKING SITES

At the time of this writing, the online, user-generated encyclopedia Wikipedia listed more than eighty social networking sites. Whether the growing number of such sites is likely to yield diminishing returns in the future is not yet clear; nonetheless, some social network sites are experiencing growth in online visitors that shows no current signs of abating. The fact that major social networks, like MySpace, Facebook, Friendster, LinkedIn, Twitter, and Bebo are garnering an enormous amount of Internet traffic should come as no surprise to the readers of this book, who are likely to have already created a personal profile on one or more social networking sites. A July 2007 comScore study revealed that the established sites experienced substantial growth from 2006 to 2007, with MySpace showing a 72% increase in worldwide traffic, attracting more than 114 million global visitors aged 15 and older, while Facebook grew by 270% over the same period to 52.2 million visitors. By August 2008 Facebook had overtaken MySpace as the world's most visited social networking site with 113 million visitors (San Miguel, 2008). Among the other social networking sites that showed similar magnitudes of growth were Bebo (up 172% to 18.2 million visitors), Tagged (up 774% to 13.2 million visitors), and Twitter (752% growth in 2008 to 4.43 million visitors). The comScore study also found that MySpace and Facebook were likely to draw visitors based in North America (62.1% and 68.4%, respectively), whereas a majority of Bebo visitors (62.5%) are based in Europe. Orkut has more of a foothold with Latin American (49%) and Asia-Pacific (43%) audiences, with Friendster more firmly entrenched in the Asia-Pacific region (89%).

Created in 2004, MySpace, one of the original and most successful of the social network sites, had obtained more than 250 million registered users, 115 million monthly unique visitors, and 50 billion page views over the span of its first 4 years in operation. Although largely drawing visitors from North America, like other social networks, MySpace has progressively served to link a global community; indeed, by 2008, the creators of MySpace had developed thirty localized versions in fifteen different languages. On the horizon for MySpace, and likely other social networking sites, are the following trends: (a) friend categorization (i.e., a personal profile can consist of separate pages specifically designed for work, friends, and family); (b) increased personalization (i.e., users can customize their MySpace homepage to reflect their usage habits, with an expanded set of skins and themes to select from); (c) portability (i.e., the ability to access and post to MySpace on one's portable phone at any time; (d) collaboration (i.e., providing MySpace users with a greater opportunity to expand the site's platform); (e) community building (i.e., providing support services, such as MySpace user content monitoring, that assist companies in their efforts to build brand communities); and (f) hypertargeting (i.e., combining demographic data obtained during registration with MySpace profile preference to segment users according to their passions) (Stevens, 2008).

Facebook, one of the most rapidly expanding social networks at the time of this writing, opened up the site to outside companies in an effort to incorporate more profitable features for the network. Within the first 15 months 400,000 developers worked on tools to enhance the Facebook platform, although not without posing some problems. For example, numerous trivial applications clogged the site, and some companies used tricks to spread themselves among Facebook users. As a consequence, Facebook began to put greater emphasis on trustworthy and secure applications (e.g., by setting up additional levels of verification) and the development of tools that protect the privacy of Facebook users. During a presentation at

(cont.)

Box 2.7 (*Continued*)

his company's annual F8 conference for developers, Facebook's youthful chief executive Mark Zuckerberg predicted that there would soon be a new wave of social networking sites that build on top of the information provided by network users (Stone, 2008). According to Zuckerberg, "We are going to see the big social networks start to decentralize into a series of social applications across the Web." All told, it looks like the near future holds much in store for expanding the applicability and utility of social networks.

recent analyses of Internet usage activity attest to their soaring popularity. In fact, there is evidence that social networks are driving Internet usage in the European Union: as the general online Internet audience has begun to plateau, social network audiences have steadily increased since the beginning of 2007.

The Pew Internet & American Life Project, the nonprofit Pew Research Center's initiative that conducts research on the Internet's impact on communities, reported that by the end of 2007, participation in social media represented a fundamental element of the American teenager's life. An increasing number of young people—the first generation to have grown up online—have embraced the conversational nature of interactive online media. According to the findings of Pew's "Teens and Social Media" report (Lenhart et al., 2007), 93% of teenagers aged 12- to 17-years-old use the Internet, a majority of whom are treating it as a venue for some form of social interaction, including the sharing of creative content, telling stories, and interacting with others who share common interests. As MySpace Vice President Jay Stevens pointed out at the 2008 Web 2.0 conference in Paris, young people have a deep desire to express themselves creatively, and the social network technology now allows them to share their creations as never before. Overall, 55% of online teens have created a profile on a social networking site. Some 64% of the teen Internet users engage in some type of content creation, a 7% increase since 2004. Girls (54%) were more likely to post photos online compared with boys (40%), although boys were nearly twice as likely to post videos where they could be seen by others (19% vs. 10%). The sharing of creative content nearly always fueled online conversations; for example 89% of the teens who posted photos revealed that people comment at least "some of the time" on the images.

Another extensive analysis of social networking was published in 2007 by Fox Interactive Network, Inc. (2007), and its findings provide an even more compelling picture of how this new form of online activity has fundamentally changed the ways people interact with each other and with other media (see Figure 2.2). Overall, the Fox report (p. 4) concluded that "we learned that social networking is a quantum change in how we interact—with each other, with bands and brands, and with the entire media landscape." Among the key findings of the study, which incorporated both quantitative and qualitative feedback from more than 3,000 American Internet users, were the following:

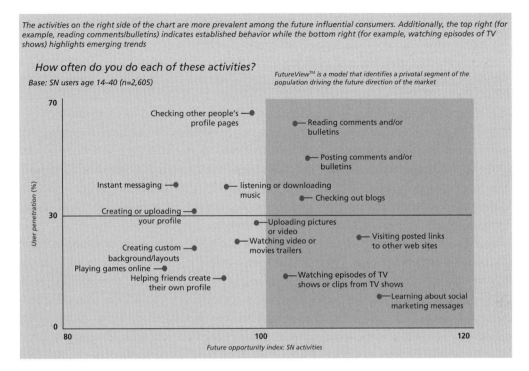

The activities on the right side of the chart are more prevalent among the future influential consumers. Additionally, the top right (for example, reading comments/bulletins) indicates established behavior while the bottom right (for example, watching episodes of TV shows) highlights emerging trends

Figure 2.2 Social Networker Activities

Source: Fox Interactive Media, Inc. (2007).

- More than 70% of Americans aged 15- to 34-years-old actively participate in online social networks, on average more than 7 hours per week; although they are likely to connect at all hours of the day and night, usage peaks during early evening prime-time hours.

- Participants tend to prefer social networks over other forms of communication and entertainment; when asked which free-time activity they would choose, social networkers selected "checking out social network sites" (17%) as their favorite activity online or off-line, on par with cell phone usage, and ahead of television viewing (14%), surfing the Web generally (10%), playing a video game (9%), and listening to an mp3 player (7%) or radio (1%).

- More than 31% of online social networkers claim to spend more time on the Internet in general after they began to use a social network site.

- Participation in social networks enriches existing relationships with family and friends; 69% say they use social networks to connect with existing friends and 41% to connect with family members.

- Social networking plays a role in initiating meaningful brand connections; 40% of participants claim to use social networking sites to learn more about brands or products that they like, and 28% say a friend has recommended a brand or product to them through such sites.

In conjunction with the Fox study, Marketing Evolution, a return on investment (ROI) measurement and consulting firm for leading global brands, investigated the impact of social interaction on marketing campaigns within MySpace. Based on in-depth case studies of MySpace clients, the research found that brands such as Adidas and Electronic Arts attributed more than 70% of their marketing ROI to the "Momentum Effect," a Marketing Evolution metric that quantifies the impact of a brand within a social network in terms of its "pass along" power among consumers.

Social networks appear to be more than a passing fad, and they are projected to show exponential expansion over the next decade, especially in conjunction with growth experienced by mobile service providers. Juniper Research, a firm that specializes in the identification and appraisal of high-growth opportunities across the telecommunications and media sectors, estimates that end-user generated revenues from social networking, dating, and personal content delivery services will increase globally from US$576 million in 2007 to US$5.74 billion by 2012, with social networking accounting for 50% of the total by the end of the forecast period (Holden, 2007). Juniper also predicts a rise in active users of mobile social networking sites from 14 million in 2007 to nearly 600 million in 2012. The sheer amount of content accumulating on social network sites is likely to provoke fundamental changes in traditional search models and in the ways businesses conduct research on consumers and collect data on customers ("Top Trends," 2008). Three future trends in social networking were forecast by the Fox Interactive Network study: (*a*) watching television within social network sites, (*b*) visiting outbound links, and (*c*) learning more about social marketing messages.

Before leaving this section on social networks, it is important to mention another variation of social connectivity that is manifest in the development of *brand communities*, which are loosely defined, non-geographically determined collectives of consumers who share deep commitments to particular brands. Unlike the social networking sites described above, brand communities tend to emerge spontaneously as certain brands begin to attract contingents of brand adorers who typically connect with each other online, although at times they may meet at organized off-line events. Brand communities are based on the concept of the urban (or neo-)tribe, a notion first postulated by French sociologist Michel Maffesoli and later developed by geographer Kevin Hetherington. According to Hetherington (1998), personal identity is rooted in the desire to belong, and is derived in large part through participation in neo-tribes—"communities of feelings" where empathy, emotion, and like-mindedness form the basis for the construction of intentional communities. Extending these ideas to brand communities, consumers can be understood as forming connections with others as a result of shared consumption-related emotions, passions, and experiences, thereby developing a stronger sense of self through their social networking activities. The implications of brand communities for marketers are discussed in greater detail in subsequent chapters.

Blogs

Another way that the Internet has come to occupy a central role in connecting consumers is evidenced by the phenomenal spread of online blogs (also called *web logs* or *weblogs*); that is, personal Web sites in the form of journals or online diaries often limited to a particular subject. People can create and manage as many blogs on virtually any topic of human interest as they have time and the interest to maintain, through the periodic posting of ideas, images, and links to other blogs or Web sites. Technorati, a specialized Internet search engine for blogs, found that the *blogosphere*—the "community" of all blogs on the Internet—is expanding at an exponential rate, doubling in size nearly every 6 months. Established by the end of 2004 as a key aspect of online culture, by mid-2005, the number of blogs in existence exceeded 50 million worldwide. Approximately 175,000 new blogs are created each day, and 1.6 million legitimate new messages are posted daily on those blogs (Sifry, 2005). As of this writing, Technorati had identified 133 million blogs since it began tracking them in 2002.

The blogosphere connects like-minded people in a way that heretofore was not possible and has rapidly evolved as a primary conduit for the informal spread of marketplace information. Estimates vary regarding the percentages of people who create and read blogs (see Box 2.8), but one consistent finding is that these figures are rapidly increasing worldwide. A Universal McCann survey reported that by mid-2008, 10% of American adults had published a blog, whereas a 2008 Pew Internet study found that 12% of adult Internet users (9% of all United States adults) had created or worked on their own online blog (Smith, 2008). Younger Americans engage in blog publishing at more than twice the rate of adults ("Half of Adults," 2008). The previously mentioned 2007 Pew Internet & American Life Project found that 35% of all teenage girls and 20% of teenage boys engage in blogging activity. Blog readership has skyrocketed over an incredibly short period of time. For example, when the media agency Interpublic Group conducted their first survey of blog readership in 2006, they reported that 50% of their respondents claimed to read blogs, a figure that climbed to 70% in their survey conducted 2 years later. The Universal McCann report estimated that more than 70% of Internet users create blogs in South Korea and that 90% of South Koreans read blogs.

There are several reasons why blogs have struck a chord with Internet users. Even the novice Internet user is likely to find the blog creation process to be relatively painless and easy, with a variety of blogging services and online tutorials providing useful

---

BOX 2.8 FOCUS ON RESEARCH: MEASURING BLOG READERSHIP

Estimates of blog readership have been found to vary according to how people are asked about that form of online activity. The Pew Internet & American Life Project investigated this systematically by comparing the results of two measurements of blog reading, each of which is intended to capture a somewhat different set of behaviors (Smith, 2008). The first measure asks the present-tense question, "*Do you ever read* someone else's online journal or blog?" The results of a 2008 study resulted in 33% of American Internet users (24% of all adult Americans) answering this question affirmatively, with 11% claiming to do so on a typical day.

The second blog readership question is phrased in the past tense, "*Have you ever read* someone else's online journal or blog?" This question resulted in higher estimates of blog readership, with 42% of American Internet users (32% of all adults) affirming that they had read a blog. It is not surprising that the second (past tense) question resulted in a higher estimate, because it captures people who may have read blogs at one time, but for some reason are not doing so currently. The second question also resulted in a higher proportion of men than women reporting that they *have* read other people's blogs, a finding that the study's authors suggest is attributed to males' tendency to be heavily represented among early adopters for new technologies, with women catching up over time. Thus, the second question is likely to include men who read blogs initially, but who likely would have answered in the negative to the question posed in the present tense.

---

insights into the process (see, for example, "Blog tutorial" at http://www.photoshop-support.com). Although I hardly would consider myself a high-tech whiz, I was able to set up and publish my blog (http://parisrestaurantreviewsandbeyond.blogspot.com) in less than 30 minutes. Blogs also are appealing because they allow bloggers the opportunity to share their opinions and establish conversations with virtually anyone with similar interests, at virtually no cost. Blog content tends to have higher credibility than content disseminated through traditional broadcast outlets because blogs typically are perceived by readers as independent and unaffiliated, with blog authors (considered by some as "citizen journalists") expressing their honest viewpoints untarnished by any apparent ulterior motives. This latter point is one reason that company blogs are rapidly becoming a fixture of the corporate online landscape. Such blogs represent a key means by which companies can effectively communicate and engage with current and prospective customers, and posted blog content is less likely to be seen as a formal selling effort than if it were to appear through more traditional communication channels. An additional benefit derived from incorporating blogs within a brand's Web site is that the blogs use tags that enable them to be tracked through specialized blog search engines, such as Technorati. A *tag*, which is a relevant keyword, phrase, or label assigned to a blog entry, tends to increase the visibility of the blog and its capacity for drawing Internet traffic. For a more technical explanation as to how tags work, see Rainie (2007).

The future of blogging in terms of content and impact remains to be seen. In its 2008 "state of the blogosphere" study, Technorati reported that at least 94% of the blogs it tracks had gone dormant, with only 7.4 million blogs having had any new postings during the previous 120 days, and only 1.5 million with postings in the last 7 days (Technorati, 2008). These are still sizable numbers, but the indications are that at present, many individual bloggers do not view the effort as justified by the potential rewards (Carr, 2008). Nonetheless, blogging now represents an established Internet utility, and will likely continue to be a major focus of corporate marketing communication and emerging consumer applications.

Other Social Web Activities

In addition to social networking sites and blogs, there are other popular trends in social media that are serving to increase the repertoire of activities that connect consumers. One important social web trend is that of online video viewing, exemplified by Google's Internet site YouTube, which was launched in 2005. Sites like YouTube are public platforms for viewing and sharing video clips, which are uploaded by users for free broadcast. As with other social media activity, it is difficult to obtain precise figures regarding the number of videos and degree of viewership on YouTube and related video sites; however, the estimates to date are somewhat staggering. Drawing again from com-Score, Inc.'s real-time measurements of Internet activity, YouTube apparently reached 74.5 million unique visitors by November 2007, with 2.9 billion on-demand videos streamed each month ("Google Sites' Share," 2008). Other popular online video sites include Fox Interactive Media with 419 million videos viewed, followed by Yahoo! with 328 million, and Viacom Digital with 304 million. The Pew Internet & American Life Project's findings revealed that 19% of all American adult Internet users view at least one video per day, and that 57% have viewed at least one video online. Video sites remain most popular among younger users, with 31% of 18- to 29-year-olds claiming to watch videos online daily. What these figures clearly suggest is that online video viewing sites, along with sites that specialize in music sharing and streaming (e.g., Last.fm and Pandora) and the sharing of photographs (e.g., Flickr), are rapidly replacing traditional broadcast media, such as television, as a primary source of media entertainment for people.

Another source of consumer connectivity comes from the increasing popularity of online multiplayer games and virtual worlds. Massive multiplayer online games (MMOGs) such as *World of Warcraft*, along with virtual social worlds like Second Life, Habbo Hotel, There, Kaneva, and Cybertown allow the consumer to participate in games or simply interact socially with thousands of people simultaneously (cf. Good, 2007). The multiplayer fantasy game *World of Warcraft* was created in 1994, and by July 2007 it boasted a worldwide base of 9 million subscribers, and up to 200,000 simultaneous connections. Second Life, the ground-breaking three-dimensional virtual world, was developed by Linden Research, Inc. in 2003 and, like subsequent online fantasy worlds, provides users with a place to socialize and connect with other players through the use of voice and text chat. These online developments also assist consumers in realizing deep-seated desires to experience what it would be like to be someone else, because players assume the role of a fictional character or *avatar* (a digital representation of the player within the virtual world). In this way, consumers can reinvent themselves by creating and living out their personally constructed stories, dreams, and fantasies online. Some consumers have become so attached to their virtual lives that they have gone so far as to bequeath their avatars to loved ones in the event of their real-life death.

Like social networking sites and online brand communities, immersive online spaces provide a means for active consumers to satisfy their desire for community. A 2003 Pew Internet & American Life survey of American university students found that one in five respondents (20%) felt that gaming helped them to make new friends as well as improve existing friendships (Jones, 2003). Although the student gamers generally agreed that online games enabled them to spend more time with friends, 60% admitted that gaming sometimes plays a surrogate role when friends are unavailable.

Conclusion

The developments described in this chapter are not intended to serve as a static representation of the contemporary marketplace; rather, they can be seen as a snapshot of an environment in evolutionary flux (albeit with some short-term projections). As Don E. Schultz (2008) noted, it is rather ironic that marketers have given consumers a variety of new media and technologies, and now those gifts are being used to tune marketers out or bypass marketing efforts altogether. As traditional media move into a digital age for which marketers were ill-prepared, one thing is certain: there is much more to come and the challenges that marketers are facing today are only likely to expand in the future. As David Hiller, senior vice president of the television and publishing group, the Tribune Company, predicted, "An endless multiplication of bandwidth and channels" is on the horizon (Burt & London, 2004). And who knows what else. Notwithstanding the sea change of technological developments that have served to transform the marketplace as we once knew it, it is safe to say we haven't seen anything yet.

3 Targeting Consumers in the Era of Web 2.0

As recent developments in the consumer marketplace have shifted increasing levels of influence to consumers, the basic marketing tasks of identifying, targeting, and understanding consumers have become more of a challenge than ever. The interruptive, top-down marketing approaches of the past now seem archaic in light of the new era of consumer conversation, content, collaboration, and community. But one thing that has not changed for marketers in the Web 2.0 era is the need to define audiences and identify appropriate means for targeting them. Indeed, a critical initial step in attempts to capture attention and engage with target audiences lies in discovering where and how to find them and grasping how best they can be reached.

In Chapter 1, I described the growing awareness and corresponding concerns of marketers about the increasing power of consumers, as reflected in some of the comments presented at the 2006 annual conference of the Association of National Advertisers (see Box 1.1). At that same conference 1 year later, speaker after speaker addressed the theme of "behavioral targeting," which involves more precisely aiming marketing communication at consumers based on their behavior, as opposed to their attitudes or perceptions (Elliott, 2006). For example, the Microsoft Corporation has aggressively invested in "well-targeted advertising," using both traditional and new media to monitor what consumers are doing, such as by keeping track of which Web sites they visit and how long people remain at those sites. In an all-too familiar refrain among advertisers these days, Microsoft CEO Steven A. Ballmer asserted that "the more we know about customer behavior, the more every ad is relevant," because relevance enhances the likelihood that a consumer will pay attention to an ad.

This chapter expands on these ideas about reaching relevant targets by first providing an overview of Web 2.0 and some of the traditional marketing concepts related to communication, targeting, and consumer segmentation. Next, the focus shifts to a concentration on consumers themselves, with an eye toward the behavior of especially influential (such as teens) and emerging (such as seniors and minorities) segments, the opinion leadership process, and consumer relationships with brands and each other.

Welcome to Web 2.0

It is now commonplace to hear talk of consumers inhabiting a rapidly evolving but relatively amorphous universe popularly referred to as Web 2.0. Although many pundits are likely to laud the merits and potentialities of the brave new social world of Web 2.0, few have been successful in pinning down what the term actually refers to. In a very general sense, as mentioned in Chapter 2, Web 2.0 is roughly synonymous with the term "social web." However, if Wikipedia, the online user-generated encyclopedia, is indeed a fundamental and illustrative component of this new marketing environment, then the Wikipedia (http://en.wikipedia.org) definition of Web 2.0 is probably a good starting point for clarifying the term:

> The term "Web 2.0" describes the changing trends in the use of World Wide Web technology and web design that aim to enhance creativity, communications, secure information sharing, collaboration, and functionality of the Web. Web 2.0 concepts have led to the development and evolution of Web culture communities and hosted services, such as social-networking sites, video-sharing sites, wikis, blogs, and folksonomies.

It is widely agreed that the origin of the term Web 2.0 can be traced back to a brainstorming session led by Tim O'Reilly (2005), founder and president of O'Reilly Media, that took place at the 2004 MediaLive International, Inc. conference, which is held for producers of technology tradeshows and conferences. It was there that some of the significant changes that the Internet was undergoing at the time were discussed, along with attempts to discern why certain Internet sites had survived the 2001 burst of the dot.com bubble and what those successful sites had in common (see Box 3.1)

Web 2.0 can be seen as an evolution of the World Wide Web that applies various new types of Web-based applications, including blogs, social software, and peer production. However, from a marketing perspective, it is perhaps most constructive to envisage Web 2.0 not as a technology (e.g., AJAX or XML), a place (the Internet), or a set of applications (e.g., Google, Facebook, BitTorrent), but as a philosophy that is firmly rooted in the recognition of consumer's increasing connectedness, participation, and control over marketing functions. This conceptualization of Web 2.0 as reflecting "a common vision of its user community" is exemplified by Hoegg et al.'s description of Web 2.0 (2006, pp. 31–2) as a "philosophy of mutually maximizing collective intelligence and added value for each participant by formalized and dynamic information sharing and creation." Although acknowledging that Web 2.0 in the broadest sense represents a philosophy or common vision, it is clear that as a new business model perspective, it is beholden to certain sets of tools. According to Hoegg et al., Web 2.0 services are offered in three forms: (*a*) platforms or content-creating tools that enable users to create, store, manage, and share content (e.g., in the form of blogs) and facilitate navigation tasks (e.g., in the form of directory services); (*b*) online collaboration tools in

BOX 3.1 SOME DIFFERENCES BETWEEN WEB 1.0 AND WEB 2.0

The following list of illustrative differences between the original World Wide Web and the new Web 2.0 eras was generated by Tim O'Reilly and his associates as a starting point for formulating their sense of the Web 2.0 concept. By further comparing the distinctions in the list (see O'Reilly, 2005), the team was able to identify some essential elements of difference, three of which are elaborated below in the form of Web 2.0 lessons for corporate success in the evolving marketing environment.

Web 1.0	Web 2.0
DoubleClick	Google AdSense
Ofoto	Flickr
Akamai	BitTorrent
mp3.com	Napster
Britannica Online	Wikipedia
personal Web sites	blogging
evite	upcoming.org and EVDB
Domain name speculation	Search engine optimization
Page views	Cost per click
Screen scraping	Web services
Publishing	Participation
Content management systems	wikis
Directories (taxonomy)	Tagging ("folksonomy")
Stickiness	Syndication

Lesson 1: "Leverage customer-self service and algorithmic data management to reach out to the entire web, to the edges and not just the center, to the long tail and not just the head."

This lesson is apparent through a comparison of the pioneering Internet advertising approach DoubleClick and the more recent Google advertising application known as AdSense. DoubleClick is based on a very traditional advertising approach that relies on selling technology products and services primarily to advertising agencies and media companies in order to allow their clients to target, deliver, and report on their online ad campaigns. This approach relies heavily on tracking Internet users' surfing behavior through the use of browser cookies to determine access and response to online ads, an approach that has aroused concerns over consumer privacy. According to O'Reilly, DoubleClick was ultimately limited by its service business model, which emphasized publishing rather than participation, putting all of the decision-making responsibilities in the hands of advertisers rather than consumers, and focusing only on the most frequently visited Web sites.

By contrast, Google's AdSense, like the similarly modeled Yahoo! Search Marketing (formerly Overture), relies on Google's Internet search technology, which enables the placement of ads on Web sites based on Web site content, users' geographical location, and so on. Unlike DoubleClick's cost-per-action-based service, AdSense invites Web site owners to enroll in the Google program to have text, image, and video ads placed on their Web sites. The ads then generate revenue on the basis of a per-click or per-impression basis. This approach has the advantage of placing ads that are less intrusive than traditional Internet banner ads and pop-ups, with consumer-friendly ad content typically relevant to the Web site. For example, an Internet server who visits the Paris Chamber of Commerce Web site is likely to be exposed to unobtrusive ads for hotels and restaurants in Paris, business schools in the area (such as ESCP Europe), and the like.

The AdSense approach is in line with Chris Anderson's insightful notion of the "the long tail" (2006), which in part refers to the collective power of the small sites that comprise the bulk of

(cont.)

Box 3.1 (*Continued*)

Internet content. More generally, the long tail, derived from statistics' right-skewed distribution curve, signifies the totality of lower demand or lower sales markets and products. Unlike Double-Click's emphasis on servicing only a few thousand of the largest and most successful Web sites, the AdSense approach provides the opportunity for an ad to be placed on virtually any web page.

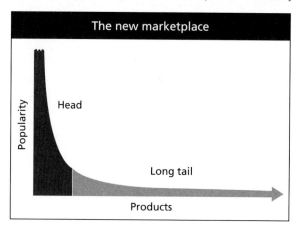

The Long Tail (Anderson, 2006)

Source: http://www.thelongtail.com/about.html.

Lesson 2: ''The service automatically gets better the more people use it.''

Anyone who has utilized the BitTorrent downloading application is probably already familiar with this second lesson. As a peer-to-peer (P2P) file-sharing communications protocol, every user participates as a server. For example, if a music file is downloaded by some users, that file is provided in fragments that are served from multiple locations. As a result, popular files can be downloaded more quickly because of the greater number of users who provide bandwidth and fragments of the complete file. O'Reilly contrasts the BitTorrent application with the Web 1.0 Akamai platform for Internet content and application delivery. Akamai essentially bypasses any consumer participation by mirroring the content from customer servers, which tend to be large Internet, media, and computer companies. To improve service, Akamai must add additional servers. The spirit of Web 2.0, as exemplified by the BitTorrent approach, is descriptively summarized by O'Reilly thusly:

> . . . every BitTorrent consumer brings his own resources to the party. There's an implicit ''architecture of participation,'' a built-in ethic of cooperation, in which the service acts primarily as an intelligent broker, connecting the edges to each other and harnessing the power of the users themselves.

Lesson 3: ''Network effects from user contributions are the key to market dominance in the Web 2.0 era.''

A central principle that accounts for the enormous success of some companies that have survived the Web 1.0 era and emerged as leaders of the Web 2.0 era—Yahoo!, Google, eBay, and Amazon, to name a few—is seen in their ability to exploit the potential of the Internet to harness collective intelligence. As O'Reilly points out, eBay's basis for existence as a central online auction and selling site is the fact that its product is comprised of the collective activity of all its users who serve as buyers and sellers of new and used consumer goods. The role of the company is to facilitate a context that enables the site to grow organically from a continually evolving degree of user activity. As the largest

US e-commerce retailer, Amazon incorporates a number of practices to encourage and enhance user engagement, including user reviews, recommendations tailored to each visitor to the site, and the use of user activity to produce more efficient search results. Unlike many other online retailers whose search results more likely than not lead to the company's own products, Amazon uses a real–time computational system that leads search results with "most popular" items.

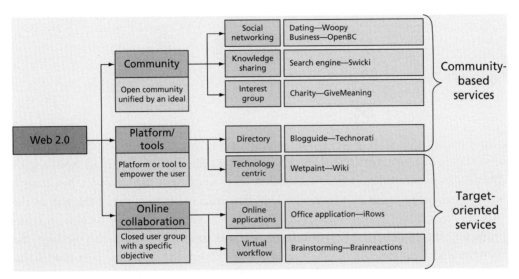

Figure 3.1 Overview of Web 2.0 Applications

Source: Hoegg et al. (2006).

the form of applications that map a process to an online environment, thereby providing greater efficiency for collaborators to work together (e.g., by increasing the accessibility of "to-do" lists and agenda); and (*c*) community services, which unify users who share similar objectives (e.g., by providing services that allow for the social creation of content) (see Figure 3.1). These features of Web 2.0 have implications for the approaches used by contemporary marketers to define targets and are also critical for the emergence of Web 2.0 communities, the latter of which are discussed later in this chapter.

How Information Spreads

Traditional models of communication originally placed the mass media in a predominant role in terms of the way information was thought to disseminate to an aggregate of consumers (see Figure 3.2a). This linear view, the so-called "one-step flow of

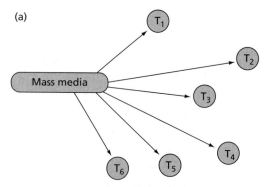

Figure 3.2a The One-Step Flow of Communication Model
T_n is a member of the target audience. From Fill (1999).

communication model," posited that information is directed from a source (such as a broadcaster or journalist) to prospective audiences like bullets propelled from a gun. The decision of each member of the audience as to whether or not to act on the message was viewed as the result of a passive role in the process—if they got in the way of the "bullet," they would be hit. Accordingly, companies were thought to be able to communicate efficiently with different target audiences simply by varying the message and the type and frequency of channels used for conveying the message. This model was soon recognized as an oversimplification of the communication process for two basic reasons: (*a*) it ignores the possibility that through personal influence consumers can have an impact on each other and (*b*) it does not take into account the fact that some consumers, for a variety of reasons, may not receive the intended message.

The one-step flow model was eventually supplanted by another view which was widely held until somewhat recently. The "two-step flow of communication model" gained prominence on the heels of a famous study of voting behavior conducted by Paul Lazarsfeld and his survey research team during the 1940 US presidential campaign (Lazarsfeld, Berelson, & Gaudet, 1944). Initially carried out as a test of the one-step flow of influence from the media, the researchers found that campaign advertisements transmitted through radio and print channels had negligible effects on actual voting behavior and only minor effects on changes in candidate preference. Instead, people were very selective in terms of attending only to aspects of the messages that conformed to their preexisting opinions. (This observation is consistent with what is today referred to in marketing as the "weak theory of advertising.") Importantly, the study revealed that the main factor in determining voting decisions was the informal social group to which an individual belonged and, more specifically, the influence of someone in the group who was more tuned in to the media than the others. This "opinion leader" (or "influential") was better informed than other members of the group and more likely to pass on information (either solicited or unsolicited) to the others.

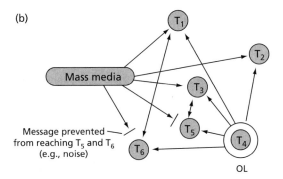

Figure 3.2b The Two-Step Flow of Communication Model
T_n is a member of the target audience. T_4 is an opinion leader. From Fill (1999).

Returning to our consideration of the two-step flow model of communication, we see that opinion leaders are recognized as playing a critical role in the flow of information from mass media sources to other consumer targets (see Figure 3.2b). The original version of this model posited that information flows in two steps to a mass audience: in the first step, the message passes from the media source to the opinion leader, and in the second step, from the opinion leader to the rest of the group. Later versions of this model added that information originating from the mass media does not only reach opinion leaders but others as well who may not be influenced until they check with their group's opinion leader(s). Thus, in Figure 3.2b we see that consumer T4, who represents an opinion leader for a consumer group, serves as the original source of information for persons T5 and T6, who were not reached by the original transmission of the message, and as a message reinforcer for targets T1, T2, and T3. In short, the two-step flow model rejected the notion that the mass media alone influence product purchase, brand selection, and the transmission of ideas and other information to a mass audience. Rather, the personal influence attributed to influential members of the group also plays an important mediating role in the communication process.

The currently accepted "multistep flow of communication model" goes beyond the two-step model by proposing multiple, often complex patterns of influence within the group (see Figure 3.2c). It is understood that the mass media is more efficient than ever before in reaching most people directly, including opinion leaders and information receivers. However, the emergence of alternative media, along with the significant role of interpersonal relations in the flow of information, has undermined the image of a passive audience at the mercy of omnipotent traditional media. Although the opinion leader is given an important role in this model, it is thought that opinion leaders and members of the target audience all influence each other through a complex pattern of two-way communication. The bidirectional nature of the interpersonal interactions is suggested in the figure by double-headed arrows, thereby adding the feedback notion that was missing in earlier communication models.

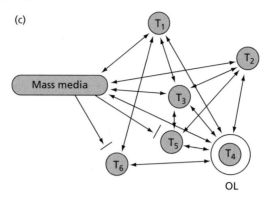

Figure 3.2c The Multistep Flow of Communication Model
T_n is a member of the target audience. T_4 is an opinion leader. From Fill (1999).

Another interesting aspect implied by the multistep model is that an individual consumer may receive the same information from more than one source. For example, in the figure, we see that person T3 could have received the original message directly from the media (e.g., a television program), the group's opinion leader T4 (e.g., as posted on a popular blog), and another group member T2 (e.g., an SMS message on one's mobile phone), and then discussed the story face-to-face with targets T1 and T5. This multiple source element is significant because it is likely that the more times a person receives the same information, the more apt he or she is to believe it (Allport & Lepkin, 1945; Kimmel & Keefer, 1991).

This more complex multistep model of communication, when applied to a consideration of consumer networks, is useful for identifying the nature of referral relations (i.e., connections depicting "who-told-what-to-whom" pathways) among consumer audiences, whether the message that is passed from person to person is a product or service recommendation, a description of a new product, a suggestion about product usage, or a commercial rumor (Reingen & Kernan, 1986). An example of a word-of-mouth (WOM) network appears in Figure 3.3, depicting referral connections along which information about a new service might be spread (Mowen, 1995). In such networks, it is important to understand that a social tie between two individuals may be strong (e.g., two close friends who get together on a regular basis) or weak (e.g., neighbors who infrequently meet in passing, but who one day happen to have a brief discussion about the new service). In Figure 3.3, we see that an individual may pass a message on to persons with whom one has strong ties or weak ties, and the fact that one has strong ties with someone does not necessarily mean the message will be shared with that person. Additionally, within the WOM network, smaller clusterings of interconnected consumers who share strong ties with one another may exist (e.g., in Figure 3.3 persons B, C, and D form one such group, while F, G, and H form another). The more tightly knit such groups are, the more likely it is that a message will spread rapidly among

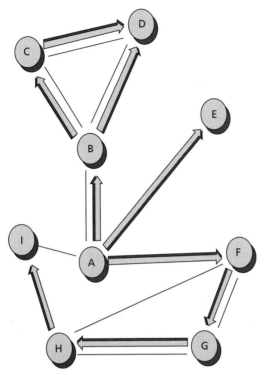

Figure 3.3 A Word-of-Mouth Referral Network
Lines with arrows represent referrals.
Lines without arrows represent strong ties. From Mowen (1995).

group members. In recent years, technological advances have expanded researchers' ability to "map out" consumer networks and referral chains (e.g., Fieseler, Fleck, & Stanoevska-Slabeva, 2008).

The communication models described above help us better understand how thinking about consumer connections have evolved during the last half century and what a revised communication model for the Web 2.0 era should look like (see Figure 3.4). The one-step flow model implied that marketers could simply contact as many consumers as possible by broadcasting messages through mass media channels. This conceptualization no longer holds sway in a consumer environment progressively dominated by connectivity to multiple devices, social networking, multitasking, and the like, where people have access to so many media channels and can communicate with each other with such ease. And while it still is true that certain individuals are likely to serve as central hubs of influence, it also now is the case that nearly anyone can serve as a significant conduit of information or catalyst of marketing trends, provided those persons have sufficient ties with others and that certain contextual forces are in place.

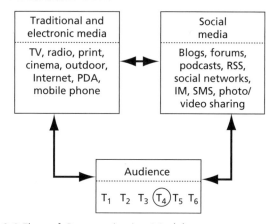

Figure 3.4 The Web 2.0 Flow of Communication Model
(Members of target audience (T_n) communicate with each other, with opinion leader (T_4) most socially connected.)

Market Segmentation and Targeting

When deciding which consumers to target, most marketers continue to follow the traditional market segmentation approach originally proposed by Wendell Smith in a groundbreaking 1956 *Journal of Marketing* article. Smith described market segmentation as a marketing strategy that involves analyzing the demand side of the market to gain insight into consumers and the various "wants" they bring to the marketplace. In so doing, marketers can satisfy basic marketing objectives consistent with the marketing concept by matching the correct offer to individuals whose life and work experiences presupposed certain sets of needs.

Since Smith's early conceptualization, *segmentation* has come to represent "any analysis that attempts to identify groups of individuals who are similar in attitudes, response to marketplace offerings, where they live, or how they are described," for a wide range of marketing-related tasks (Fennell & Allenby, 2004, pp. 29–30). The assumption is that the marketplace is composed of widely diverse sets of consumers, some of whom are more like each other in certain regards, and more different from others in those same respects. In short, the typical market segmentation approach is to divide a market into subsets of prospective customers who share certain commonalities, such as similarities in the ways they behave, similar wants and desires, shared characteristics that somehow relate to purchase behavior, or some combination of these things (Bearden, Ingram, & DeForge, 2007). Firms then are in a better position to tailor their offers or develop products and services so that they conform to the preferences and needs of specific customer groups, which then serve as target markets (or groups of consumers) for which marketing exchanges can be nurtured. Together, a market for a particular product or service will be comprised of different customer segments that vary in terms of their

---

BOX 3.2 STAGES IN THE DEVELOPMENT OF A MARKET SEGMENTATION AND FIVE CRITERIA FOR SUCCESS

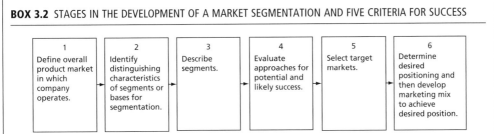

Source: Bearden et al. (2007). Reproduced with permission of The McGraw-Hill Companies.

1. Market segments must present measurable purchasing power and size; that is, marketers must identify segments sufficiently large to give them good profit potential.
2. Consumers within a segment must be markedly unique and distinguishable in their reactions from members of other consumer groups.
3. Marketers must find a way to effectively promote to and serve the market segment, free of organizational or other constraints.
4. The firm must target segments that match its marketing capabilities. Targeting a large number of niche markets can produce an expensive, complex, and inefficient strategy.
5. Market segments must be stable so that consumer behavior can be predicted with an adequate degree of confidence and so that customer satisfaction and loyalty can be maintained over the long term.

---

response to different marketing mix offerings (i.e., price, promotional appeal, product characteristics), although not all of the segments would likely prove profitable for a company to target.

Targeting involves the challenging task of selecting those segments that are especially predisposed to respond favorably to the firm's offerings, assuming that the firm has the capabilities of reaching them and that the segments offer reasonable profit potential, among other considerations (Perera, 2006; see Box 3.2). Given the diversity of consumer needs and preferences, many companies have shifted their marketing efforts from a mass marketing approach to one of mass customization. Products and services are customized and personalized for individual customers, manufactured by automated systems, and offered at a mass production price (Bearden, Ingram, & DeForge, 2007; Pine & Gilmore, 2000). Mass customization is another by-product of the new interactive technologies described in Chapter 2, which enable consumers to interact with companies so as to specify their unique requirements and needs.

Consumers now play a more active role in determining the nature and design of the company's offer, with firms gaining stronger insight into potentially profitable segments to target. With the advent of the Internet, businesses can now customize product development and distribution, as well as advertising messages, to better conform to the specific characteristics and needs of their customers (Barnhardt, Liu, & Serfes, 2007). Dell Computers is an example of a growing number of companies that have successfully demonstrated how complex manufactured products can be customized to satisfy diverse needs and provide unique value for customers. Similarly, the Web sites of Nike and Converse offer a customization option to consumers, enabling shoppers to create their preferred pair of athletic shoes according to desired style, colors, and fit. Amazon.com personalizes its page displays on the basis of customer purchasing and browsing behavior, offering customized recommendations and links for future purchases.

Target Segments and Influencers

Sometimes the decision about which consumer groups to target is fairly straightforward (see Box 3.3). For example, Peugeot likely would select adult consumers, especially middle-class parents—as its primary target market for a new family sedan. Nonetheless, its marketing campaign may also focus on children as a secondary communication target because of the strong influence they may have on their parents' decision about what family car to purchase. It may seem odd to suggest that major carmakers would spend significant amounts of money to target children in ad campaigns, although this is exactly what Daimler-Benz, General Motors, and other major companies have done. According to one estimate, children influenced more than US$9 billion worth of American car sales in 1994 (Stanley, 1995). As one car dealer explained, "Sometimes,

Exhibit 3.1 Daimler-Benz Targets Children

BOX 3.3 FOCUS ON APPLICATION: ACTIMEL AND CONSUMER TARGETING

A good example of successful targeting is illustrated by Danone's marketing activities for its health drinking dairy product, Actimel (known as DanActive in North America). Packaged in small 62.5 ml bottles, the product is a fermented dairy drink that has the effect of strengthening the body's natural defenses. Initially introduced in France in 1997, Actimel's enormous success in the country—220 million bottles consumed in 2002—in large part can be attributed to skillfully targeted marketing efforts and an increasingly more concise selling proposition (San-Galli, Krouglikoff, & Kimmel, 2005). The advertising positioning at the launch emphasized a ''healthy start to the morning'' to anchor the product in consumer's habits, with breakfast traditionally being a very ritualized meal. The initial target for this campaign consisted of adults who live active, professional lives. Over the years, however, Danone targeted other groups, including mothers, children, and, most recently, seniors, as the message became increasingly stronger and more precise (from ''the morning gesture'' to ''builds your resistance by helping your natural defenses''). Although the leading health drinking product in France, by 2005 nearly 85% of French households still had not yet tried the product; thus, each target group represented an interesting opportunity for penetration and profitability.

Actimel is not a health product per se, yet its health claim also required Danone to communicate with consumer influencers, including pharmacists and doctors. These groups are positioned at the top of Danone's so-called pyramid of influence, followed by opinion leaders, and then the media (press, etc.). The pyramid lists marketing targets according to the degree of influence by that group on ultimate buyers of the product, who are situated at the base of the pyramid. The higher in the pyramid, the greater the presumed influence on consumers, the end users of the product. Actimel's brand managers were wary that skeptical consumers would consult their doctors or pharmacists to inquire about the efficacy of the Actimel health claim. Danone made sure to provide those potential influencers with specific details about the results of scientific studies supporting the health claim so that the medical experts could give their informed judgment to consumers, rather than a response along the lines of ''Actimel won't do anything for your health—it's just a lot of marketing nonsense!''

Over the past decade, the French marketing campaigns for Actimel generally relied on traditional marketing communication tools—television advertising to appeal to adults in general and moms, promotions (e.g., free Actimel bottles in McDonald's Happy Meals, promotional game CDs for children, money-off offers), and product testimonials for targeting seniors. Nonetheless, as an innovative product with a distinctive marketing positioning, along with its appeal for various consumer segments, it is clear that there is much opportunity for Danone to build on Actimel's success by stimulating C-to-C influence through emerging media and social networking efforts.

the child literally is our customer. I have watched the child pick out the car.'' Also, when a company like Daimler-Benz creates print ads depicting a young child thoughtfully examining an exact toy replica of a Mercedes, it is clear that the firm hopes to strike a chord with youngsters who represent future buyers of the car sometime in the not too distant future (see Exhibit 3.1).

That children may serve as potentially strategic targets for a wide range of products and services suggests that demographic characteristics—in this case, age—can provide marketers with one rudimentary way of segmenting a market. Other demographic characteristics—such as gender, race, marital status, income level, occupation, religion, and life cycle stage—along with geographic delineation, traditionally have served as basic criteria for determining consumer segments. What was sufficient in the past, however, is hardly applicable for the contemporary marketing environment, and most marketing professionals would agree that such criteria are rarely sufficient in and of themselves for specifying targets. In fact, according to some critics, strong brands are those that have appeal across demographic and geographic lines, so that when firms rely on such basic segmentation approaches, it is a sure sign that they have a weak brand. This view is not shared by all marketers; indeed, it can be argued that no brand reasonably can be expected to be responsive to all the diverse demand-creating conditions that underlie a product purchase (Fennell & Allenby, 2004). Even within the same target segment, such as young suburban married women, there are likely to be differences in what members of that segment desire from the same offering: consistent quality, low price, brand image, convenience, practicality in use, and so on. As a result, once a market has been segmented and segments to target have been determined, the offering must be positioned through appropriate marketing strategies (Bagozzi et al., 1998; see Box 3.2). By positioning, it is meant that an effort is made to capitalize on the diversity of customers by achieving an appropriate image of the brand in their minds that is likely to provide a competitive advantage for the firm.

Contemporary segmentation approaches are more likely to combine demographic and geographical variables with psychological, attitudinal, and behavioral characteristics. For example, psychographic segmentation groups consumers together according to similarities in lifestyles (i.e., characteristic ways of living) and personality traits (i.e., personal characteristics like sociability, open-mindedness, materialism). In this way, marketers can elaborate descriptive profiles of the prototypical member of a target segment to better visualize the sorts of individuals they are trying to reach. This is evidenced by a creative brief that was developed by a major UK tobacco company for marketing one of its low-tar cigarette brands to young women (Hastings, 2001, personal communication), who were described psychographically as follows:

> The core low-tar smoker is female (though males are by no means to be ignored), upmarket, aged 25 +, a smart health conscious professional, who feels guilty about smoking but either does not want to give up or cannot. Although racked with guilt, they feel reassured that in smoking low tar they are making a smart choice and will jump at any chance to make themselves feel better about their habit.

Certain companies now provide commercial customer segmentation services to firms through the use of systematic approaches that are based on an array of segmentation variables. Two long-standing and widely known examples are represented by PRIZM, which relies on demographic and geographic variables and the VALS system, which is built from attitudinal variables (see Box 3.4).

As mentioned at the outset of this chapter, behavioral targeting is rapidly supplementing, if not supplanting, more traditional approaches to segmentation. Previously, when marketers attempted to behaviorally segment consumers, they did so by relying on

BOX 3.4 FOCUS ON RESEARCH: SYSTEMATIC APPROACHES TO CONSUMER SEGMENTATION

Two research-based, proprietary segmentation approaches—PRIZM, which was developed by the Claritas (now Nielsen Claritas) marketing research firm, and the VALS system (for "Values, Attitudes, and Lifestyles"), created by SRI Consulting Business Intelligence (SRIC-BI)—have been utilized by a considerable number of firms for targeting marketing campaigns. Typical of such comprehensive systems, PRIZM and VALS divide a vastly diverse population—the United States—into a manageable number of segments and then analyze which segments would provide the most value potential for businesses utilizing the services.

Although largely based on demographic and residential cluster analyses of the US population, PRIZM also incorporates behavioral information (including product and brand usage) to develop rich descriptions of diverse American types. Dating back to the early 1970s and periodically updated on the heels of new census data, the PRIZM system works from the assumption that relatively similar households tend to group together naturally in a geographical sense. Until recently, drawing from the 1990 US census database, PRIZM divided the American marketplace into sixty-two neighborhood lifestyle clusters on the basis of social rank (income, education, etc.), household composition (age, gender, family type, etc.), mobility (length of residency, auto ownership, etc.), ethnicity (race, ancestry, language, etc.), urbanization (urban, rural, housing density, etc.), and housing (owner/renter status, size, etc.). The neighborhood types were determined through the application of a statistical technique known as *cluster analysis*, which groups similar objects into respective categories on the basis of a set of relevant identifying factors. The clusters then are refined on the basis of actual consumer purchase data records taken from multiple sources.

The most recent version of the system, PRIZM-NE (for "The New Evolution"), which followed the 2000 US census, groups American consumers into fourteen cluster groupings comprised of sixty-six different segments (http://www.claritas.com). For example, the segment known as "Young Digirati" (included within the "Urban Uptown" grouping) includes "tech-savvy singles and couples living in fashionable neighborhoods on the urban fringe," who are "affluent, highly educated and ethnically mixed." These individuals live within communities that are made up of trendy apartments and condos, fitness clubs, clothing boutiques, casual restaurants, cafés, and bars. Like other Urban Uptowners, the Young Digirati share an urban perspective that is reflected in their marketplace behavior, including heavy spending on computer and wireless technology, traveling abroad, shopping at exclusive retailers, frequenting the arts, listening to jazz/indie rock radio, and subscribing to fashion/music/electronics magazines. Another segment, "Blue Blood Estates" (included within the "Elite Suburbs" grouping) consists of very wealthy, university-educated married couples with children. These are successful suburbanites who own million dollar homes, purchase expensive clothing and cars, and have country-club memberships. "Shotguns & Pickups" (a segment within the "Middle America" grouping) consists of young, working-class couples with large families, who live in small or mobile homes. They own hunting rifles and pickup trucks, listen to country music radio, drink Canadian whiskey, and read hunting/car and truck magazines.

For marketing applications, Claritas analyzes which segments should be targeted for particular consumer goods, based on lifestyle characteristics and behavioral patterns. For example, relative to the three segments described above, an analysis might reveal that for expensive, midsize imported sedans, consumers within the Blue Blood Estates are considerably more likely than other segments to purchase, whereas individuals who comprise the Shotguns & Pickups segment would be considerably less likely to purchase. Members of the Young Digirati segment might fall along the average in terms of likelihood of purchasing this type of automobile.

(cont.)

Box 3.4 (*Continued*)

In contrast to the PRIZM approach, the VALS system is based on the premise that consumers with similar attitudes or psychographic characteristics will tend to exhibit similar types of consumer behavior (http://www.sric-bi.com). Consumers are classified into eight different lifestyle segments on the basis of their responses to a battery of questions about their attitudes toward risk, status, and other indicators. Revised most recently in 2003, the segments are now determined according to where a person falls along two dimensions: (*a*) "primary motivations" (i.e., persons whose choices are motivated by either beliefs, need for approval, or a desire for physical or social activity) and (*b*) "resources and innovation," which reflects the ability of people to achieve their dominant motivation, consistent with their income, education, health, energy level, self-confidence, and the like. The eight VALS types consist of four high resources/innovation groups (Innovators, Thinkers, Achievers, and Experiencers) and four low resources/innovation groups (Believers, Strivers, Makers, and Survivors). Consumer segments have been compared in terms of specific lifestyle-related activities and media-usage habits.

SRIC-BI's research reveals, for example, that Innovators (i.e., persons who are motivated by achievement-oriented goals) tend to be status-oriented consumers with abundant resources who are successful, sophisticated, active, and independent. They are on the leading edge of change; accordingly, they are drawn to top-of-the-line products and brands, as well as new products and services (such as high-tech innovations). By contrast, Believers (i.e., persons who are motivated by ideals) are more apt to be conservative and conventional consumers with limited resources, having strong beliefs and attachments to traditional institutions (church, community), and a tendency to purchase domestic products.

In terms of specific comparisons of consumer behavior for these two VALS types, it has been determined that Innovators are more likely than Believers to engage in gourmet cooking, drink imported beer, participate in cultural activities, read business and literary magazines, and engage in risky sports. Believers, on the other hand, are more likely to drink coffee daily, and read *Reader's Digest* and fish and game magazines. American readers interested in determining their VALS type can complete the SRIC-BI presurvey, available online at http://www.sric-bi.com/VALS/presurvey.shtml.

In recent years, SRIC-BI developed a VALS segmentation system for the Japanese marketplace, which classifies consumers according to life orientation and attitudes toward change (see http://www.sric-bi.com). Other segmentation systems are available for use in the United States and other countries (e.g., the ACORN lifestyle classification in the United Kingdom), some of which are based on customer transactional data (i.e., they rely on records of customer purchase information). Although transaction-based segmentations tend to be more predictive of the likelihood of households to respond to a given offer, they provide little insight as to who consumers actually are or what motivates their behavior. As a result, marketers are less apt to have access to the sorts of personal details that would enable them to tailor relevant messages and select appropriate communication channels (Schroeder, 2000).

classifications that grouped people according to buyer groups (in terms of loyalty to a brand or company) or adopter groups (in terms of readiness to purchase or use a new product or service). More recently, behavioral targeting is increasingly likely to be accomplished with an eye toward the evolving Web 2.0 environment. Of specific interest to marketers is how consumers use the Internet for connecting with companies and with each other, and by extension, how they relate to other new media technologies (such as the mobile phone and PDA; see section on "Web Communities").

Emerging Consumer Target Groups

As the connected marketing era continues to evolve, marketers are finding it essential to focus their targeting efforts on previously neglected consumer groups, or to rethink how they best can contact the groups they have traditionally targeted with communication campaigns. For example, although young adult, White males have long represented a key consumer target for marketers because of their spending power, the recognition that members of this demographic segment spend a lot of time online has begun to be exploited by firms. Thus, in 2006, when Heineken USA introduced its first premium light beer in the American market, it did so by first launching a barrage of ads on Internet sites most likely to be visited by their core beer drinking market—men aged 25- to 29-years-old. In addition to running video ads on sites like espn.com, foxsports.com, maxim.com, msm.com, yahoo.com, and stuffmagazine.com, the company also created a separate site, heinekenlight.com, to complement its already-existing sites for its Amstel and Heineken brands.

The decision to commence the Heineken Premium Light campaign with Internet ads was attributed to the recognition that the target market is tech-savvy and very likely to be reached in the online space. Among adults aged 18 years or older, men between the ages of 21 and 34 tend to engage in the highest Internet usage (http://www.pewinternet.org/trends.asp). Interestingly, prior to the emergence of the Internet, it was always the case that educated young men and professionals were lighter TV viewers, whereas older and less-educated people were heavier TV viewers. To date, the presence of the Internet has not changed these TV usage patterns.

The Youth Market: Children and Teens

The growing tendency for marketers to target youthful consumer audiences was briefly mentioned above. Children and teens have become interesting targets for marketers not only because of their significant influence on household purchases, but also because of their steadily rising spending power. Additionally, as discussed in Chapter 2, young people are increasingly connected to new technologies and are key players within the universe of social media.

In terms of "pester power," estimates reveal that children's influence on household consumer purchases has risen exponentially since the 1960s. In the United States, children aged 2 to 14 influenced approximately US$5 billion in parental purchases during the 1960s, a figure that had grown to between US$200 and US$260 billion by the early years of the twenty-first century (McNeal, 1992, 2007). In France, it is estimated that children currently influence approximately €25 billion in household purchases annually.

Among the purchase categories most likely to show the impact of youthful influence are clothing, groceries, vacations, and technology-related purchases (Taylor, 2007).

At the same time that young people's influence on parental spending has risen, so too has their purchasing power. In the United States, children aged 3 to 11 represent a population subgroup of 36 million, with a collective US$18 billion in purchasing power in 2005, a figure that is projected to reach US$21 billion in discretionary spending by 2010 (Brown & Washton, 2006). Estimates are that children's aggregate spending doubled during each decade of the 1960s, 1970s, and 1980s, and tripled in the 1990s. In fact, some experts refer to the 1980s as the "decade of the child consumer," a period during which it became likely that both parents would be spending more time out of the home at work (McNeal, 1992). Feeling guilty about devoting less attention to their children, parents started spending more money on them. Marketers have followed in kind. Prior to the 1980s, only a narrow range of companies were likely to direct their marketing efforts toward children, such as candy makers, breakfast cereal manufacturers, and fast food restaurant chains. Today, children are targeted by hundreds of different companies, including phone companies, carmakers, clothing stores, and so on.

The purchasing habits of young people are likely to look oddly familiar wherever they are observed in industrialized regions of the world. Accessories such as sneakers, backpacks (for carrying schoolbooks and laptops), videogame consoles, portable music players, mobile phones, and acne cream are apt to be part and parcel of the typical adolescent's list of must-have acquisitions. Young people worldwide have more discretionary income than in the past in part because many are delaying the responsibilities of adulthood until a later age. In France, for example, it has been said that children become adolescents earlier, but adults later; that is, while the average age of the onset of puberty has declined from 13 to 11 years of age during the last 60 years, schooling has lengthened and it now takes longer for the typical French youth to receive a diploma and first employment (Mermet, 1998). Adulthood is now more likely to be regarded by young people in terms of financial independence, as opposed to having children and raising a family; thus, the responsibilities of adulthood have been delayed. A similar trend has been observed in India, where young people under the age of 25 represent more than 50% of the country's population (Bansal, 2004) and what it means to be considered a "youth" has expanded well beyond the age range that traditionally characterized the term.

The rise in spending in recent years among young people also has a lot to do with the desire to be connected through new technologies. Along these lines, Wharton marketing professor Stephen Hoch observed that children today "need more stuff," particularly in the area of technology ("Hot Today," 2008). Not surprisingly, approximately half of all 11- to 14-year-olds currently own a portable phone, with 57% having one by the age of 13. The likelihood that teenagers will acquire a cell phone steadily increases with age for boys and girls; by 2007, 91% of all 17-year-old American girls and 78% of 17-year-old American boys had their own cell phone (Mindlin, 2008). One reason for the rapid diffusion of portable phones among young people is that it provides a sense of identity and self-esteem by virtue of enabling acceptance by one's peers. As ownership has increased, mobile phones have become essential for young people to gain membership into peer groups, where members organize their social lives on the move (Charlton & Bates, 2000).

The Internet provides another obvious means by which young people stay connected with each other and with the marketplace. Although estimates vary and continue to rise, it is clear that a majority of young people are Internet users. For example, eMarketer.com figures for 2008 revealed that 42.3% of American children aged 3 to 11 used the Internet at least once a month. A total of 15.4 million children went online in 2008, a figure that is expected to increase to an estimated 16.6 million by 2011. Among US teens aged 12 to 17, 79% went online at least once a month in 2008 and is expected to rise to an estimated 87.1% by 2011. In the United Kingdom, 4.2 million young persons aged 8 to 15 (65%) were found to have Internet access at home in 2007. A large proportion of these young Internet users engages in social networking activities (see Chapter 2) and often participates in virtual worlds. Approximately one-fourth of child and teen Internet users in the United States visited virtual playgrounds (such as Club Penguin, Webkinz, and Stardoll) or virtual worlds (such as Habbo.co.uk and Second Life) at least once a month in 2006, estimated to rise to 53% by 2011 (eMarketer.com). Virtual visits are often prompted by recommendations received from friends and acquaintances (Barnes, 2007*b*).

In essence, most young people in the contemporary marketplace, from the United States to Japan, are attached—almost literally—to their mobile phones and laptops, chatting online with friends as well as strangers, sending SMS text messages, and uploading photos and other personal content. The trend toward multitasking, discussed in Chapter 2 (see Box 2.5), also clearly applies to the media-usage habits of children and teens. For example, teens represent the most likely demographic to have simultaneous TV and Internet usage ("TV Viewing and Internet," 2008), and younger children and teens regularly engage in a variety of communication activities, including playing videogames, watching DVDs, reading magazines/comics/newspapers, listening to the radio or mp3 player, and using a mobile phone. Consistent with these points, eMarketer senior analyst Karin von Abrams, following a 2008 assessment of British youth, concluded: "In order to reach these new media consumers, marketers can no longer rely on simple, old-style media plans and traditional platforms" ("UK Kids and Teens," 2008).

Senior Consumers

Now that we have briefly considered some of the consuming habits of younger members of the population, we can turn our attention to the upper end of the age spectrum. Marketers are increasingly coming to grasps with the realization that advancing age does not imply a disconnection from the marketplace or lack of involvement with new communication technologies. Many of the product usage and purchase patterns acquired during our youth, as well as company and brand loyalties, persist as we age. Add to this the fact that the senior consumer segment is growing faster than any other segment globally, it is understandable that identifying effective strategies for connecting with this segment has become a new marketing priority.

A total of 12.6% of the 305 million Americans who comprised the US population in 2008 were aged 65 or older, a percentage that is forecast to double by 2030, four times the growth rate of the 18 to 59 age group for the same period. In Europe, the growth of the senior market is even more pronounced: the median age of Europeans at the time of this writing was 37.7 years, but predicted to rise to 50.3 by 2050. One-fourth of all Austrians and one-third of all Germans are expected to be 60 or older by 2015 (dataranking.com). It is not surprising that the Adeg Aktiv Markt 50 + supermarket chain, launched in Austria in 2003 to specifically cater to older customers, has met with such great success. Each Aktiv Markt is designed with the needs of older shoppers in mind, including signage in large type, magnifying glasses available on store shelves, wide aisles, nonskid floors, plenty of places to sit, lower shelves with more accessible items, and wider parking spaces (Everitt, 2004). Similar changes to turn several of its stores into senior-friendly environments recently have been made by the Lawson convenience store chain in Japan, a country in which 21% of the population is over the age of 65 (Onishi, 2006).

In terms of media usage, it has long been known that seniors represent the age segment that has the highest rates of TV viewing (e.g., between 4 and 5 hours daily in countries such as the United States and Australia). Compared with other age groups, reaching elderly consumers with marketing messages typically requires heavier components of daytime TV, direct mail, and magazines. In the United Kingdom, several successful seniors-oriented magazines have emerged in recent years, including *Active Life, Saga,* and *The Oldie.* Targeted to British seniors within the 60- to 70-years age range and distributed by the post office, each magazine focuses on issues likely to be of interest to its readers—gardening, health, holidays, finance, and legal matters.

It also is the case that seniors are very much active online, with 72% of 50- to 64-year-old Americans and 41% of those over the age of 65 claiming to use the Internet by December 2008 (pewinternet.org). The Pew Internet & American Life Project, discussed in Chapter 2, reported that the number of seniors who go online increased by 47% between 2000 and 2004. Elderly consumers in the United States control approximately 70% of all disposable income in the country and spend more than US$7 billion online annually (Bloch, 2005). In the United Kingdom, the share of the Internet population comprised of persons over the age of 55 is still small but growing, having increased from 16% to 19% during 2006–7, a relative increase of 22% (nielsen-online.com).

Studies of elderly consumers' online behavior have revealed that seniors tend to perceive themselves as 15 to 20 years younger than their biological age; accordingly, their online purchasing does not tend to diverge much from younger segments, with some predictable exceptions (e.g., higher purchasing of medications and health-care products and minimal buying of youth-oriented products, such as teen fashion). Nonetheless, according to online marketing consultant Michael Bloch (2005), there are certain recommendations that should be taken into account when attempting to communicate with seniors on e-commerce sites:

- Provide a readily noticeable link to a "seniors" section with discounts on your site (e.g., "Special offer for Seniors!"), as elderly shoppers tend to look for special deals and like to be singled out for special treatment.
- Establish your credibility, for example, by ensuring that the privacy policy is clear and the site is secure, by providing clearly written terms and conditions, and by prominently displaying guarantees, industry affiliations, and security seals.
- Provide appropriate consumer images on your site. Elderly consumers tend to be turned off by promotional copy that attempts to target them through images of twenty-something models or with infirmed elderly persons in wheelchairs. Instead, they are likely to respond more positively when consumers in ads are shown as healthy and vibrant mature individuals in their mid-30s to mid-40s. (Costs for artwork can be reduced by relying on a number of useful Web site imagery and stock photography resources that are now available online.)
- Utilize off-line media to drive seniors to your online sites and offers. As suggested above, seniors are very comfortable with print media, including magazines that specifically target their age group. It is important to visibly display your web address in print material or promotions so that it will be noticed.

Bloch also points out that although seniors may not have the "scan, click, and buy" mentality of younger Internet users, they can be very loyal once their trust has been gained. Thus, heavier investments in serving the seniors segment at the outset are likely to pay off over the longer term.

One topic that has not yet been addressed with regard to senior consumers is the extent to which they participate in social networking activities via their mobile phones or computers. To date, the evidence suggests a relatively low involvement in such activities. A recent demographic analysis of online social network users in the United States (conducted as part of the Pew Internet & American Life Project) revealed that the share of adults with profiles on online social networking sites rose from 8% in 2005 to 35% by 2009; however, younger online adults were far more likely than their older counterparts to use social networks, with 75% of 18- to 24-year-olds doing so compared with only 7% of Internet users aged 65 and older ("Social Network," 2009). It will be interesting to see what the future holds as the younger population that grew up with online social networking start to grow into middle age and beyond.

Minorities

As ethnic and minority populations have grown in recent decades, marketers have concluded that they cannot ignore these potential targets in their campaigns. For example, in the United States, census data reveal that the number of Caribbean Americans (more than 22 million) is growing at a faster rate than that of Black Americans and represents one of the most economically viable minority communities in the country. To a large extent, the process of marketing to ethnic groups and minorities does not vary to a great extent from that of mainstream marketing. However, marketers need to be sensitive to the unique identities and needs of such communities, keeping in mind that minorities do not represent a single, homogeneous group. Also essential is the need to gain insight into the media these diverse groups are likely to access and the ways in which these media are used. Overall, the most important ideal is to consider all the possible cultural nuances of each minority target audience.

Recent statistics regarding Internet usage reveal that ethnic groups are increasingly connected. For example, the results of a recent terra.com syndicated survey of Hispanic households in the United States found that 43.2% of those households possessed either a dial-up or broadband Internet connection by 2008, and 30% of those who claim to use the Internet spend 13 or more hours weekly online ("Terra Briefs," 2008). Overall, US Hispanic Internet users spend more time weekly surfing the Internet than they spend watching TV, listening to the radio, or reading magazines and newspapers. Internet usage is higher than TV for younger Hispanics, but the difference is reversed for those aged 35 or more. Another finding revealed that 48% of US Hispanic Internet users who also watch TV use some combination of DVR/VOD, which enables them to avoid advertisements run solely on TV.

As an indication of how US Hispanic Internet users differ from the general US population, a recent Yahoo! study indicated that the former spend significantly more hours per day than the latter with technology (i.e., portable phones, SMS, PDAs, blogs, video games, e-mail, portable music, movies; 14.0 versus 8.0 hours) and media (i.e., Internet, TV, newspapers, magazines, radio; 13.5 versus 9.0 hours) (Madansky & Alban, 2007). Overall, it was reported that US Hispanics spend more than half of each day engaged with Internet and technology devices, and that these devices provide an important means for connecting with family, friends, and community in the United States and their country of origin.

When marketers fail to take into account the special characteristics and behaviors of ethnic groups and other minorities, they are likely to find that their marketing efforts come up well short of their objectives. In fact, there are some common mistakes that often are made when targeting such groups (Murphy, 2005). These are summarized below, along with corresponding recommendations that stem from these lessons:

- *Considering that ethnic or minority groups represent a single, homogeneous group and will respond similarly to a particular marketing campaign.* Whether attempting to communicate with Maghreb immigrants in France or Caribbean inhabitants in North America, or some other group, it is necessary to recognize that none of these populations are homogeneous. For example, although a majority of Caribbeans are Jamaican or Haitian, other islands should not be neglected. Each community is diverse and each subgroup represents a niche. Similarly, ethnic groups are often inappropriately grouped together with other minority groups in the country. For example, it is usually a big mistake for marketers to classify Caribbeans with Black Americans in the United States, or Maghreb with West Africans in France, and expect a marketing campaign to translate well across these groups. This strategy is likely to cause resentment among those persons who do not identify with the other groups.
- *Neglecting the ethnic or minority media.* People of different heritages identify with their culture and outlets that promote their culture, so the local media that target such communities are very important. Every major city that has a high percentage of people representing an ethnic or minority culture is likely to have targeted media outlets and Web sites for that market. Additionally, their audiences are often responsive to content in the language of their country of origin.
- *Foregoing community involvement.* Each ethnic or minority community is likely to host many types of yearly events (carnivals, music festivals, theatrical plays, celebrations of each country's independence day, etc.). All these events represent opportunities for companies to get involved with the community and increase awareness. Advertising is not enough.

Finally, as is the case for marketing to seniors, it is also true that persons from minority communities can become very brand loyal. A firm that offers high quality, reliable service and is supportive of the community is in a good position to build a long-term relationship with customers from that community.

Movers and Shakers: Opinion Leaders, Brand Advocates, and Innovators

It goes without saying that some people are more influential than others. Sociologists and communication theorists have long contended that there are individuals within any social group or community who are more likely to be leaders of opinion or trend setters whom others tend to rely on as role models or for decision-making guidance. The most common term to describe these influential persons is "opinion leader," a concept derived from Lazarsfeld and Katz's two-step flow of communication model (see above).

According to this initial characterization, an opinion leader is an active media user who serves to convey mass-mediated content to others. Over the years, the opinion leader notion has been applied by marketers to obtain a better understanding as to how new product innovations diffuse across a community or population. In contemporary marketing parlance, opinion leaders are more likely to be conceptualized as consumers who are knowledgeable about one or more product or service category and who offer advice and have influence over others within a social system.

Opinion Leaders

In typical interpersonal interactions, the opinion leader plays a significant role in informally offering guidance to other consumers by providing information about a specific product or product category, product acquisition and usage, brand attributes, and perhaps a wide range of other consumption-related topics. What this suggests is that at one time or another, most of us act as opinion leaders, offering advice about a product to friends, family members, neighbors, acquaintances, and business colleagues. More typically than not, this advice is limited to a specific category: you may know a lot about business schools and feel pretty confident advising friends who are in the process of deciding where to apply for entry into an MBA program; however, that might be where your opinion leadership capabilities end. Because of your limited range of expertise and the likelihood that not many opportunities arise for you to extend your influence to other consumers, others may not perceive you as an opinion leader, and you may not perceive yourself as one either, despite the fact that at times you do serve as one. Some people play a more significant role as influencers and are more likely to be designated by others (including marketers) as opinion leaders. They are very knowledgeable about one or more product or service category and their influence extends across a broader array of people and is wielded on a more frequent basis. It is these sorts of influentials who are likely to capture the interest of marketers, for obvious reasons. Conventional wisdom suggests that if you can connect with opinion leaders, they will do the rest of the work by influencing everyone else.

Marketers have learned quite a bit about opinion leaders and the opinion leadership process since the early work of Katz and Lazarsfeld (cf. Rogers & Shoemaker, 1971; Venkatraman, 1989). For example, it is understood that opinion leaders should not be thought of as absolute leaders who tell everyone else what to think and are blindly followed by those in their social group; rather, they are persons from whom others informally solicit or passively receive information or advice about products and services. Opinion leaders typically are considered to be highly credible sources of consumer-related information because they are perceived as neutral and objective (unlike company representatives or advertisers) and as apt to convey unfavorable information about a product or brand as favorable. Because the credibility of formal marketing efforts often is in doubt, given the rise in consumer skepticism, perhaps coupled with a lack of basis for trusting the source, an opinion leader is likely to be chosen as an essential contact for verification or advice about a product, service, brand, company, price, and the like.

Although it has proven somewhat difficult to draw a profile of characteristics of the typical opinion leader—in large part because opinion leadership tends to be product-category specific—there is evidence that such individuals are likely to be high in innovativeness (i.e., they are more likely than others to try new products and services), self-confidence, and gregariousness, and are also heavy users of special interest media (Schiffman & Kanuk, 2006; Summers, 1970). It has been observed that financial opinion leaders are more likely to be regular readers of such publications as *Money, Barron's, Financial Times,* or *The Wall Street Journal* and frequent viewers of business-oriented TV programs (Stern & Gould, 1988). It also appears that opinion leaders tend to influence others who are very much like themselves, in terms of age, socioeconomic status, and educational background. The fact that opinion leaders tend to be very similar to those whom they influence makes it rather difficult to identify the opinion leaders in a particular community or social group; nonetheless, a variety of methods have been developed by marketing researchers to overcome this problem (see Chapter 5).

A special type of opinion leader is signified by professional expertise. So-called *professional opinion leaders* are persons such as doctors, pharmacists, car mechanics, and computer service technicians who are paid to give their expert opinions to the persons whom they serve. Their expertise stems from their specialized training and experience, and their advice—assuming it is not perceived as being linked to some self-serving ulterior motive—is likely to be viewed as highly credible by recipients. The doctor who is approached by a patient who has questions about the legitimacy of Actimel's health claim (see Box 3.3) is essentially pushed by that patient into the role of professional opinion leader. Professional opinion leaders may go a step beyond simply influencing their customers or clients; indeed, their influence may extend to their peers, in which case the influentials would be referred to as *key opinion leaders* (KOLs), a term that is more commonly applied to physicians. KOLs often belong to a specific area of expertise, such as doctors who specialize in cardiology, and some are engaged by firms during the prelaunch product testing stage for advocacy activity or marketing feedback (Moynihan, 2008).

Some marketing experts believe that the term "opinion leader" is misleading in that it suggests that there are leaders of opinion in the consumer marketplace who tell everyone else what to do and think and are then blindly followed by the masses (see Box 3.5). As a result, some marketing experts prefer to use other terminologies, such as "influentials" (Berry & Keller, 2003; Blackwell, Miniard & Engel, 2005), "leveraged influencers" (Silverman, 2005), "network hubs" (Rosen, 2002), and "customer evangelists" (McConnell & Huba, 2002)

BOX 3.5 MTV INFORMS ADVERTISERS OF AUDIENCE OPINION LEADERS

The headline of an early 1990s' MTV print advertisement depicting a cool-looking Gen-Xer proclaimed, "Buy This 24-Year-Old and Get All His Friends Absolutely Free." Intended to inform prospective advertisers of the potential influence on the consumption behavior of others wielded by MTV's audience members, the ad clearly exaggerates the true power of the typical opinion leader.

In the ad, MTV's prototypical 24-year-old influencer is characterized as someone who "knows what car to drive, what clothes to wear, and what credit card to buy them with. And he's no loner. He heads up a pack. What he eats, his friends eat. What he wears, they wear. What he likes, they like. And what he's never heard of ... well ... you get the idea." Consumer researchers are well aware that opinion leaders can serve as powerful conveyers of product- and service-related information and advice for their peers. Nonetheless, opinion leaders should not be thought of as all-powerful leaders of opinion who others follow without question.

---

to refer to consumers who play a more substantial role in imparting marketplace information and advice to others. Other terms might be used to better reflect the nature of influence an individual tends to impart in social interactions, such as skeptic, adviser, or trendsetter.

In his best-selling book, *The Tipping Point*, author Malcolm Gladwell (2000) argued that opinion leaders vary in kind, and he identified three types of persons who are especially influential in getting certain products, services, or ideas to spread quickly across a population: connectors, salespeople, and mavens. These influentials are at the heart of Gladwell's key principle explaining how social epidemics or trends spread. "The law of the few" is the idea that social epidemics are a function of the relatively small number of people who transmit "infectious" agents (see Chapter 4). *Connectors* have extensive webs of social connections—they seem to know everyone. If you have ever walked around town with a friend and found that your friend was bumping into people she knew on virtually every corner, chances are your friend would qualify as a connector. *Salespeople* are individuals who are naturally able to transmit a message effectively. They are characterized by personalities that enable them to be especially persuasive in the context of others—their messages are especially "sticky" (i.e., they stay in the minds of those who receive them and are easily remembered) and convincing (i.e., they are capable of motivating people to action). *Mavens*—a Yiddish term meaning "one who accumulates knowledge"—are people who gather enormous amounts of information of all types. They are very much attuned to what is going on in the marketplace, and know the details about many products and services they themselves may never acquire or use. What makes market mavens especially interesting as potential influencers is that in most cases they do not keep their knowledge to themselves; rather, they love to share it with others. Say you were to ask an acquaintance if he knew where you could buy a special Italian bowl that you would like to give to your grandmother on her next birthday. If that acquaintance happened to be a market maven, chances are he would not stop at "Galeries Lafayette in Paris," but would add more specifics, such as which metro line to take to get there, which store entrance to use, the floor where you can find the bowl, which direction to take once you reach the floor and exit the elevator, and the name of the salesperson who is likely to offer you the best service. Mavens are a lot like that.

Of course, given how much there is to know these days, it is understandable that market mavens are very rare. Most of us tend to fall under the heading of *monomorphic* opinion leaders; that is, we are experts in a limited field. Fewer of us would be characterized as *polymorphic* opinion leaders; that is, we are experts in several fields, some of which may be unrelated. Consumers having enough generalized market-related knowledge and information to be considered as market mavens are far less common—it is unlikely that there would be more than one or two in a social network (Feick & Price, 1987).

All of us, however, are likely to find ourselves engaging in the opinion leadership process as *opinion receivers* (i.e., we receive unsolicited suggestions or advice from opinion leaders) or *opinion seekers* (i.e., we actively approach opinion leaders for advice and guidance). It is important to recognize that the opinion leadership process is not static; indeed, there are occasions when opinion leaders also are likely to be opinion seekers. This is because opinion leaders are actively involved in one or more product categories and are desirous to talk about them with others, to solicit feedback and opinions, or simply to learn more.

Although I will have much more to say about the opinion leadership process in Chapter 4, it is interesting to consider at this point some of the motivations that prompt people to act as opinion leaders within their social milieu. Several motives have been suggested (e.g., Schiffman & Kanuk, 2006), including the following:

- self-enhancement (e.g., to achieve status by appearing to be "in the know" and demonstrating one's expertise; to reduce post-purchase uncertainty);
- to gain attention and show off or to experience the power of influencing others;
- product involvement (i.e., when one has a very good experience with a product or service, there often is a strong desire to share this with others);
- altruism (i.e., to assist a friend, relative, coworker, etc. by providing advice); and
- message involvement (i.e., to express one's reaction to a stimulating advertisement or marketing campaign by conveying it to others).

The motivations of opinion seekers tend to be more self-evident, and to some extent mirror the motives of opinion leaders. For example, opinion seekers may seek self-enhancement via their attempts to reduce the risk of a purchase or search time. Product involvement needs can be satisfied by learning how to best use a product or to get a better idea of the brands and product options that are available in the market. Finally, opinion seekers can learn which products are most likely to gain the approval of others.

Innovators

If one considers the process by which new products or services (i.e., "innovations") spread over time among the members of a social system, it should become apparent that the diffusion follows a predictable course not unlike a normal distribution. What this means is that a predictable proportion of all ultimate adopters will acquire the product right away, and other adopters will follow in due course. The initial adopters of an innovation are referred to as "innovators," and typically comprise a rather small percentage (roughly 2.5%) of all eventual adopters. Innovators are likely to be venturesome consumers who like to take risks; they are relatively young, well-educated, and higher in financial well-being than others in their social group. At the other end of the distribution are the "laggards," approximately 16% of adopters who are the last to acquire an innovation. Laggards are very traditional consumers who tend to be suspicious of innovations and innovators; they are older, less educated, and lower in socioeconomic status than persons within the other adopter groups. Between these extremes one finds more typical consumers, the early (34%) and late (34%) majority, who are apt to be deliberate and somewhat more skeptical adopters.

A final group of adopters known as "early adopters," tend to adopt on the heels of innovators. Like innovators, early adopters (roughly 13.5% of all adopters) are younger and better educated than the adopters who follow them. As the adopter group that is comprised of the respectable members of a social system who are highly connected with others, a majority of opinion leaders tend to be found among the ranks of the early adopters. Innovators, by contrast, are very atypical consumers who tend not to be very integrated with other members of their social system. As mentioned, they are risk-takers; after all, innovations tend to highly priced when they first appear in the marketplace (recall Apple's iPhone) and, no matter how much product testing they may undergo prior to launch, are likely to be perceived as unproven by most consumers. Because of their venturesome consuming tendencies, innovators tend not to be regarded by others as opinion leaders. Although early adopters often look to innovators to decide whether or not to adopt a new product, early adopters must be independently convinced. They do tend to be innovative, in the sense that they acquire new products or use new services before the majority of other consumers, but because they are not ranked among the initial consumers to adopt, they are not classified as *innovators* per se.

Despite these points, it would be foolish to suggest that innovators are not influential in determining the fate of innovations; to the contrary, firms are especially attuned to how innovators respond to their new offerings. Should innovators respond unfavorably, it is a good sign that the product is unlikely to succeed among the general consuming public. On the other hand, if innovators, and, in turn, opinion leaders are observed by others to adopt an innovation, that innovation can begin to spread throughout the population. Moreover, there are those who contend that most successful marketplace trends ultimately can be traced back to the initial actions of a tiny number of super-influential types (e.g., innovators, trendsetters, especially cool people). This argument brings us back to Gladwell's law of the few principle, a concept I will discuss in greater detail in Chapter 4.

Brand Loyals and Brand Advocates

When people think about brand loyalty, what usually comes to mind is consumer purchasing support; that is, a consumer who is loyal to a brand is likely to buy it repeatedly over time. Although it is true that a pattern of repeat purchasing is an important aspect to what we think of as brand loyalty, that turns out to be only part of the story. True loyalty consists of another important ingredient, best characterized as an underlying positive attitude (i.e., a strong liking) or commitment to the brand. In fact, consumers can be distinguished on the basis of their loyalty to a specific brand according to whether their repeat purchasing (i.e., brand support) and positive brand attitude (i.e., brand commitment) are high or low (Knox & Walker, 1995). When both components are low, consumers are not at all loyal to the brand; instead, they would be characterized as *switchers*—shoppers who assume that most brands are essentially the same in terms of quality and thus select a brand largely on the basis of purchase price. *Habituals* are consumers who tend to buy a brand within a specific category repeatedly (i.e., brand support is high), but do so mainly out of habit rather than a strong liking for the brand (i.e., commitment is low). Such consumers do not give much thought to brand selection and, because they do not have a strong attachment to their regular brand, are quite vulnerable to competing offers. *Variety seekers* (low purchase support, high commitment) like to play the field. They may have a strong commitment to a preferred brand, but like to try alternative brands from time to time, particularly for different use occasions. Finally, *loyals* are high on both support and commitment; that is, they tend to purchase the same brand repeatedly, and do so out of a strong, favorable evaluation of the brand that follows an active and engaged decision-making analysis. These are persons who believe that they would incur a variety of costs if they switched to another brand (e.g., loss of money and time, dissatisfaction). They may imbue their preferred brands with human qualities and actually consider the brand as they would a good friend (Fournier, 1998).

For some consumers, loyalty to a specific brand may reach an intensity level that borders on the extreme. Truly committed loyals are completely devoted to a brand and take pride in using it; the brand is so important to their self-concept that it influences how they feel about or perceive themselves and who they are to others; and they are likely to recommend the brand to other consumers. Take, for instance, this description of Heather, a committed Pepsi loyal (McLaren, 1998):

...[she] drinks 14 cans a day, paints her fingernails with Pepsi logos, chooses her dates based on whether they drink Pepsi or Coke, and surrounds herself with Pepsi paraphernalia.

Some brand enthusiasts go so far as to have themselves tattooed with the logo of their preferred brand, such as Sam, an Apple Macintosh brand consultant from Canada (www.bmezine.com):

> I thought it was cool and decided an Apple tattoo would be the natural choice given that it'd been a part of my life for almost twenty years. I always felt that Apple was to the computer industry what Harley Davidson was to the motorcycle industry—the definition of perfection. Besides, bikers have Harley tats and not Kawasaki, so why not an Apple tat for me?

And another example from Paul, a graphic designer from Chicago:

> I wanted to show my loyalty to Apple. I use Macs all day long and I couldn't be happier. People really think it is impressive to care about something so much.

The fact that loyal consumers are likely to recommend their favored brand to others helps us understand why firms devote so much time and effort to nurture customer relationships and build brand loyalty. The more committed loyal consumers are to a brand, the more we can presume that they would be willing to put forth a concerted effort to spread the word by acting as brand evangelists. This is precisely what brand advocates do. *Brand advocates* are loyal customers who appreciate a product or service so much that they are willing to serve as ambassadors for the brand, enthusiastically recommending it to others. In Figure 3.5, we see that advocates are found at the pinnacle of a conceptual pyramid that represents varying degrees of loyalty relationships consumers may develop toward liked brands (Rusticus, 2006). Brand adopters—those consumers who are satisfied enough with the brand to become regular users—are situated at the base of the pyramid. The middle tier is comprised of brand adorers, those current buyers who are especially satisfied with the brand and who have a strong

Figure 3.5 The Brand Advocacy Pyramid

Source: Rusticus (2006).

connection and loyalty to it. The key challenge for many brand managers in an era where C-to-C influence has never been stronger is to develop means to convert brand adorers into brand advocates, customers who are so satisfied with the brand experience that they are prepared to proselytize about it (i.e., spread the word to others via WOM). A number of strategies have been developed to accomplish this conversion, such as the use of ice cards. (See Chapter 7 for a discussion of ice cards and other brand advocacy approaches.)

Brand Community Members

Many loyal consumers feel compelled to connect not only with the brand to which they are committed and the company that produces it, but with other consumers who share a similar loyalty. As pointed out in Chapter 2, brand communities often spontaneously evolve to connect non-geographically bound collectives of brand admirers. Brand communities consist of members who not only feel an important connection to a brand, but toward one another, even if they have never met in person. Such communities have emerged over time for far-reaching varieties of brands, such as toys (Barbie, American Girl), computers (Apple's iMac), mp3 players (iRiver), movies (*Star Wars, Harry Potter*), rock bands (Slipknot, Phish), cars (Saab, Ford Bronco, Jeep), motorcycles (Harley-Davidson), and TV shows (*Star Trek, Xena Warrior Princess*), and often continue to thrive long after the firm has discarded the brand (as was the case for the Apple Newton, an early example of a PDA).

According to Muñiz and O'Guinn (2001), two researchers who have extensively studied brand communities, collectivities of brand admirers are identified by three important characteristics: *(a) shared consciousness*: a collective sense of identity or consciousness of kind, whereby members feel connected to each other and distinguished from users of other brands (e.g., Macintosh members communicate with each other through Web sites, co-opting Apple's old slogan, "For the rest of us"); *(b) rituals and traditions*: members engage in a variety of ritualistic social processes through which the meaning of the community is reproduced and transmitted, including celebrating the history of the brand, sharing brand stories and myths, and the use of special lexicon and ritualistic communication behaviors (e.g., Saab owners acknowledge each other on the road by waving, honking, or flashing their headlights); and *(c) moral responsibility*: a sense of duty to the community as a whole, and to individual members of the community (e.g., Saab owners will pull over to help another Saab owner in distress).

Given these characteristics, it is interesting to conjecture as to where brand community members would be situated in the brand advocacy pyramid depicted in Figure 3.5. One aspect of the moral responsibility to the community is that members often feel obliged to recruit new people into the community, but only if those persons fit the group's norms and standards. In other words, true brand loyalists are likely to believe that some people either are not worthy of the brand or would somehow undermine its cachet. After all, if everyone adopted the brand, it could very well lose a large part of whatever it is that makes it so special. Thus, although brand community members are likely to serve as advocates of the brand to which they are committed, we might expect that advocacy to have its limits.

Web Communities

In Chapter 2, we focused on another type of community that has become prominent during the Web 2.0 era as a result of the ways in which the Internet serves to link people. Now widely referred to as a *Web 2.0 community*, the term typically encompasses any sort of virtual collectivity of individuals, whether it be a social network, an Internet forum, a social software web application, or a group of blogs. Hoegg et al. (2006) identified five specific categories into which Web 2.0 communities can be classified depending on the type of content and functionalities their services offer: (*a*) blogs and blogospheres (e.g., Technorati), (*b*) wikis (e.g., Wikipedia); (*c*) podcasts (e.g., Loomia), (*d*) social networks (e.g., MySpace or Friendster), and (*e*) social bookmarking or folksonomies (e.g., del. icio.us). Among the most popular Web communities at the time of this writing are YouTube, Digg, Facebook, Wikipedia, StumbleUpon, and Last.fm. Other community-powered Web sites are quickly emerging, such as *instructables*, where people construct Web sites as do-it-yourself (DIY) guides in order to share and discuss what they do and how they do it; *Scribd*, a Web site that operates as a kind of YouTube for documents, where users can upload, search, rate, and share all kinds of documents; online "how-to" manuals like *eHow* and *wikiHow*; and video sites (e.g., Howcast), which detail ways of making repairs or fixing any number of things, including computers and mp3 players, as well as providing financial and health tips; *SideReel*, which is intended as an ultimate, user-generated directory for movies and TV shows, including reviews, personalized recommendations, and information about impending releases; and *work.com*, a community-powered resource for small business owners and entrepreneurs ("6 Unique," 2007).

As these examples suggest, Web 2.0 communities reflect the increasing online role of peer production, and grow from common interests related to information, communication, and interaction. Like brand communities, Web 2.0 communities typically develop norms based on shared values and meanings. Although some brand communities, such as Harley-Davidson's, were around long before the Internet, a majority of brand communities today exist largely as virtual communities and, in this sense, can be classified as a variant of Web 2.0 communities.

Because of their increasing impact on businesses, marketers are finding it essential to include Web 2.0 communities within their new business models. What is important from a business model perspective is not so much the resulting community itself, but the services that can potentially result in a Web 2.0 community (see Figure 3.1). Based on their analysis of forty Web 2.0 applications, Hoegg et al. (2006) identified three components of services that enable Web 2.0 community-building:

- The main focus pertains to content and services for collaborative creating, management, updating, and content sharing; depending on the specific content, the services can take the form of text, videos, or images.
- The services provide automatic update procedures that evaluate user input and enable a new common state of knowledge to emerge.
- Trust-building services are provided, such as ratings, voting, and feedback.

Whatever form a Web 2.0 community's services ultimately take, in one way or another they will offer a variety of participation possibilities for users. Whether or not a Web 2.0 community is viewed as a successful one in offering valued services often comes down to a question of numbers; that is, success is often considered in terms of user traffic ("6 Unique," 2007). Practically speaking, potential consumers of Web 2.0 communities basically consist of any Internet users, and those who ultimately engage with an online community may do so in a manner that varies along a continuum of involvement ranging from passive to active. It is this sort of online behavior that has become the focus of recent segmentation efforts that rely on the behavioral targeting approach that was mentioned at the outset of this chapter.

For example, through the use of extensive consumer surveys of social network users, Forrester Research, Inc. utilizes a "social technographics" segmentation approach, which classifies people hierarchically according to how they use social technologies (based on consumers participating in at least one social technology-related activity per month). In a recent analysis of European online adults (see Li & Bernoff, 2008), 11% of respondents were classified at the top of the social participation ladder as "creators." Creators are social technology users who are most active in terms of the production of content. They may publish a blog, create personal web pages, upload videos or music they have created, or post articles or other documents that they have written. At the next level are "critics" (21%), people who respond to the content of others by posting reviews, commenting on blogs, posting ratings or reviews of products, contributing to online forums, and editing wiki articles. "Collectors" (14%) are organizers of content, either for themselves or others, by using RSS feeds, adding "tags" to web pages or photos, and voting for Web sites online (e.g., at digg.com). The next classification is that of "joiners" (11%) who maintain a profile or visit social networking sites like MySpace and Facebook. At the bottom of the ladder are "spectators" (40%), people who merely consume social content, by reading blogs, viewing photos or videos, listening to podcasts, and reading online forums and customer ratings and reviews. Among the online adults surveyed, 50% were classified as "inactives" who

---

BOX 3.6 FOCUS ON RESEARCH: WHAT KIND OF SOCIAL NETWORKER ARE YOU?

The results of a study of 1,000 social network users (aged 18 to 24) commissioned by MySpace and conducted by Future Laboratories identified six social network personality types (Martin, 2008; Stevens, 2008). To carry out their interviews, Future Laboratories set up a "virtual hide" in MySpace and spent 6 months asking participants how they define themselves as MySpace users. The six types are briefly described below, along with the corresponding percentage of participants who fell within each classification. Which are you?

1. *Essentialist* (38%)—An Internet user who primarily visits social networking sites to keep in touch with friends and family, but does not bother with any other options on offer.
2. *Transumer* (28%)—A social network user who follows new trends rather than making them. Transumers regularly search for content created by others, and readily follow others' suggestions and join groups of interest to them. These individuals are not unlike Forrester's "spectators" (see text) in that their online participation is likely to be of a passive nature.
3. *Connector* (10%)—This social network type specializes in identifying new trends and linking to cool content, and who then actively share information and links with others. Connectors regularly link people with other people, sites, and groups they feel others should know about and can enjoy.
4. *Collaborator* (5%)—This type of user creates ideas, events, activities, and projects online by teaming up with other users. In a sense, collaborators act as facilitators, bringing people together for satisfying creative objectives.
5. *Scene-Breaker* (5%)—This person is a kind of early adopter who is constantly on the lookout for whatever scene, trend, or movement is new online. Scene-breakers act as self-appointed talent scouts and then share their newly discovered online talent (e.g., a previously undiscovered indie rock band) on social networking sites.
6. *Netrepreneurs* (4%)—This is the sort of person who uses social networks to make money. Netrepreneurs represent the business brains of social networking, but represent the least common type of social networker. (The remaining 10% of the study participants were not classified into any of these six types.)

---

neither create nor consume social content of any kind. Another segmentation of social networker personality types was developed by researchers on behalf of MySpace (see Box 3.6). Either segmentation approach could prove invaluable to firms in their efforts to reach the most responsive type of online networkers for a connected marketing campaign. This could be done by first determining the proportion of each type of social networker within subgroups of consumer targets and then selecting the appropriate social strategies to deploy first, perhaps with the intent to move consumers up the participation ladder by increasing their level of engagement.

Conclusion

We have now considered a wide range of consumer targets and influencers (see Table 3.1) that comprise the contemporary marketplace in the Web 2.0 era—a

Table 3.1 Types and Characteristics of Consumer Influencers

Influencer type	Basis for expertise	Characteristics
Opinion leader	Enduring involvement in product category, heavy user of special-interest media for involvement category	Integrated into social group, greater interest in product category, higher status, sociable, early adopter, similar to those he or she influences
Product innovator	Purchase/use of innovative product/service; trade shows; interactions with personal sellers; likely to seek out new trends, products, etc. online	Younger, well-educated, higher income than peers, risk-takers, less integrated into social groups than opinion leaders
Professional opinion leader	Professional training, expertise, and experience	Paid professional, respected, trusted, implicit power to influence
Market maven	General market knowledge, heavy usage of wide range of information sources	Highly motivated to share knowledge and information
Committed brand loyal	High level of direct experience with the brand through purchase support and product usage	Strong attachment to brand, recommend brand to others, self-concept extended by brand
Brand advocates	High satisfaction with adopted brand, incentives offered by producer of the brand	Brand evangelists, enthusiastic endorsers, highly loyal to brand
Brand community member	Enduring involvement with the brand, links to other brand-involved consumers, greater access to firms	High level of commitment to the brand and to the community, sense of shared identity and moral responsibility

Source: Based, in part, on Mowen (1995).

marketplace that is more complex and technologically savvy than in the past. The dramatic rise in consumer engagement with marketing and the extent and depth of consumers' connections with each other provides a fertile environment for marketers in their efforts to develop new means to get in on the discussion and connect with their targets. Before considering the specific ways by which this might be achieved, it is first important to dissect the nature of C-to-C communication and the role of WOM, which are covered in depth in Chapter 4.

4 Word-of-Mouth Influence

"The power of word of mouth" is perhaps one of the most familiar phrases to anyone who has engaged in even the most cursory reading of material related to the topic of connected marketing and other recent marketing trends. This is for good reason— marketers are finding that as many consumers turn off to traditional promotional messages, the power of interpersonal influence continues to grow. In recent years, an impressive body of evidence has accumulated demonstrating how word of mouth (WOM) represents a primary source of information for consumer buying decisions, whereas the influence of traditional marketing campaigns, such as mass media advertising, has diminished. Consumers are likely to try a brand recommended by a previous user and often are more apt to believe product endorsements received from friends and acquaintances than advertising appeals (e.g., Rusticus, 2006). Nonetheless, some of the assertions about the marketing potential of strategies that enable firms to leverage consumer WOM border on "puffery," an advertising term used to refer to the exaggerated subjective claims about products that often appear in advertising messages (e.g., "Bayer—the world's best aspirin!"). A quick survey of some of the key resource articles and books on the topic provides some representative examples of WOM hyperbole:

- "WOM is more powerful than all of the other marketing methods... put together." (Silverman, 2005)
- "Because of the sheer ubiquity of marketing efforts these days, WOM appeals have become the only kind of persuasion that most of us respond to anymore." (Gladwell, 2000)
- Product buzz and viral marketing are some of the most powerful and most effective marketing vehicles ever discovered. (Steve Jurvetson, venture capitalist of Hotmail fame)
- "The greatest advertising medium of them all is the human voice." (Al Ries, review of Emmanuel Rosen's *The Anatomy of Buzz Revisited*, 2009)
- "[Word of mouth is] the greatest of all brand messages." (Dobele & Ward, 2003)
- "Word of mouth is the most important marketing element that exists." (Gordon Weaver, as quoted in Lau and Ng, 2001)

Whether or not the hype exceeds the true promise of WOM marketing remains to be seen, but in contrast to advertising puffery, where the claims are impossible to substantiate, there are methods for estimating the extent of WOM and its impact. In this chapter, we focus on the nature of WOM consumer influence, factors leading to its occurrence, and its potential effects. In the final section of the chapter, we will scrutinize some widespread misconceptions related to this most talked-about marketing topic. Our consideration of WOM continues in Chapter 5 with an emphasis on measurement and research issues.

The Nature of WOM

WOM communication and opinion leadership represent the two key processes that underlie how personal influence takes place in consumer-related situations. By "personal influence," it is meant that consumers have the capacity to affect each other's attitudes and behaviors relative to something in the marketplace (e.g., a brand, a store sale, an advertisement) through their informal exchanges. Widely acknowledged as the core mechanism fueling C-to-C influence is WOM—the informal communication between consumers about products, brands, services, stores, promotions, and companies. The opinion leadership process serves as a basic mechanism by which WOM is transmitted. Although often treated as synonymous with WOM, the expression "marketing buzz" has emerged to refer to the totality of what people are saying about a product or service at any particular time (Rosen, 2002).

The term "word-of-mouth" was originally coined by William H. Whyte, Jr. in a 1954 *Fortune* magazine article entitled "The Web of Word of Mouth." In his article, Whyte reported an interesting phenomenon regarding room air conditioners, which at that time had just been introduced into the American consumer market. He observed that if one passed through urban neighborhoods (where the air conditioners typically were mounted in a front window), the appliance appeared to be distributed in clusters of homes rather than in a random fashion (see Exhibit 4.1). That is, six houses in a row might have had an air conditioner, while three on either side would not. A similar patterning was apparent with the distribution of televisions, as indicated by antennas on rooftops around the same time. Whyte concluded that the ownership of such consumer goods reflected patterns of social communication within the neighborhoods. The people who talked together about products and services showed similar purchase and usage behaviors.

Whyte's observations seem to conform very well to how many consumers are influenced by their personal interactions with others. We might imagine one innovative family daring enough to take a chance with an expensive new product and thus becomes the first in the neighborhood to purchase an air conditioner. The family members then talk about their recent purchase to their next-door neighbors, who then tell their next-door neighbor, and so on, down the block, until a family is reached that is isolated from others or decides that the neighbor's purchase is not very talkworthy. This is not to

Row houses in the city of Philadelphia. The houses marked with an X are those with air conditioners. Notice the clusters.

Exhibit 4.1 Word of Mouth (WOM) and Personal Influence

Source: Whyte (1954).

suggest that WOM spreads in a perfect linear pattern, although it is more probable that one will encounter one's next-door neighbors more frequently than a neighbor who lives several houses away and thus be more likely to discuss a recent purchase with the former. Of course, communication tools were much more limited than they are today, so it is understandable that this pattern of communication prevailed in analyses of interpersonal exchange during the early 1950s. As Whyte described it, interpersonal exchanges were most likely to occur in informal exchanges, "over the clothesline" and "across backyard fences."

One year after the appearance of Whyte's influential article, Katz and Lazarsfeld (1955) published their landmark book, *Personal Influence*, which elaborated on the role of WOM in the mass communication process. Their "two-step flow" model of communication postulated that certain people among close personal friends and family members—so-called opinion leaders—can exert personal influence on the decision making of others by passing on through informal WOM conversations information they received from the media. As explained in Chapter 3, in recent years the two-step model of communication has been supplanted by a multistep model that acknowledges the existence of multiple, often complex patterns of influence between consumers. Nonetheless, the early publications acknowledged how consumers have the capacity to affect each other's attitudes and behaviors relative to something in the marketplace (e.g., a brand, a store sale, an advertisement), and were influential in undermining the image of a passive audience at the mercy of all-persuasive mass media (Weimann, 1982). Reflecting the early origins of the term that has now entered everyday parlance, Silverman (2005) adroitly characterized WOM as the "oldest, newest marketing medium."

However novel Whyte's ideas about consumer influence must have seemed a half century ago, the power of WOM is today understood as a given in the contemporary marketplace. As recently as 1994, Ivan Misner referred to WOM in the title of his book on the topic as "the world's best known marketing secret." Fifteen years later, a Google search of the term "word of mouth" alone results in over 28.2 million hits, with "marketing buzz" turning up close to 33.4 million hits. No longer marketing secrets, these forms of consumer influence are now household terms. Not surprisingly, the Internet and other new technologies have come to occupy a central role in the transmission of WOM and the spread of marketing buzz, an impact that has shown phenomenal growth over the past decade with the emergence of blogs, Internet forums and discussion groups, text messaging, e-mail, and the like. By no means limited to face-to-face encounters over the clothesline or across backyard fences, WOM today can spread with lightning speed to reach countless numbers of consumers.

Characteristics of WOM

WOM has been technically defined in various ways in the marketing literature (e.g., Arndt, 1967; Bone, 1992; Dichter, 1966; Fornell & Bookstein, 1982; Richins, 1984; Westbrook, 1987). In what may reflect the most commonly accepted definition in contemporary practice, Silverman (2005, p. 193) viewed WOM as "positive or negative communication of products, services, and ideas via personal communication of people who have no commercial vested interest in making that recommendation." Although most definitions adhere rather closely to Silverman's conceptualization of WOM as a (*a*) personal communication that (*b*) pertains to a product, brand, service, or (marketing-related) idea (*c*) involving persons having no connections to a commercial entity or marketing source, some limitations to this view have been noted. For example, the target of WOM discussions may be an organization (in addition to a product, brand, or service). Given that WOM can be conveyed in a rather impersonal, electronically mediated way (e.g., through an anonymous posting on a chat forum) (Buttle, 1998), some instances of WOM transmission may lack a certain degree of the personal component by which it generally is identified. Additionally, as discussed in Chapter 6, an increasing number of companies have begun to offer incentives or rewards to consumers for spreading WOM or making referrals. Although some would claim that the latter case represents more of a formal marketing effort than informal WOM per se, the communications are likely to be perceived as WOM by recipients who remain unaware of any sort of corporate involvement. Thus, Buttle (1998, p. 243) chose to characterize WOM as that which is "uttered by sources who are assumed by receivers to be independent of corporate influence."

Returning to Silverman's definition, we recognize that consumers may transmit positive or negative information about a firm and its offerings. Positive word of mouth (PWOM) consists of interpersonal communication among consumers concerning a marketing organization or product/service, and may take the form of recommendations to others, conspicuous display, or interpersonal discussions relating pleasant, vivid, or novel experiences (Richins, 1983). An example of PWOM would be apparent when a friend conveys details about the terrific gourmet experience she had while dining at a new Italian restaurant in town. Because consumer recommendations (e.g., "You should buy the same ASUS gaming laptop that I bought last month—it's really great") represent a common form of PWOM, one way of assessing incidence of PWOM would be to ask consumers questions such as "In the last six months, how many times have you recommended any X?" (East et al., 2007). By contrast, negative word of mouth (NWOM) is comprised of consumer communications that denigrate or advise against an organization or offering, relate unpleasant experiences, or involve private complaining (Anderson, 1998). A neighbor who tells you about the terrible service she received at a local appliance shop will have transmitted NWOM. Various investigations have underlined the damage that NWOM can entail for retailers and manufacturers (Charlett, Garland, & Marr, 1995; Decarlo et al., 2007; Audrain-Pontevia & Kimmel, 2008; Knowledge@Wharton 2006). Incidence of NWOM can be gauged by asking consumers "In the last six months, how many times have you advised against X?"

Most everyday WOM is based on evidence or personal experience, which imbues its content with a high degree of credibility and potency for influence. It is with regards to its presumed verifiability that WOM can be distinguished from rumor, a related and sometimes overlapping form of informal, interpersonal exchange among consumers. Generally speaking, *rumor* represents a story or statement in general circulation without confirmation or certainty as to the facts (Allport & Postman, 1947; Knapp, 1994). According to the American Psychological Association's *Encyclopedia of Psychology,* a rumor is "an unverified proposition for belief that bears topical relevance for persons actively involved in its dissemination" (Rosnow & Kimmel, 2000, p. 122). If a friend tells you that he heard that the local cinema was going to be converted into a real estate agency before the end of the year, that comment—assuming there is uncertainty as to its truthfulness—would qualify as a rumor.

WOM primarily differs from rumors on its evidential basis; that is, it is presumed to be founded on evidence, whereas the veracity of rumors is unknown at the time of its spread (see Box 4.1). Further, WOM is perceived as having a more reliable, credible, and trustworthy source of information than rumors (Kamins, Folkes, & Perner, 1997). These differentiating points are essentially attributed to the fact that the content of WOM typically involves comments about product performance, service quality, and trustworthiness passed from one person to another (Charlett, Garland, & Marr, 1995). Indeed, WOM often takes the form of a piece of advice that is offered by one consumer

BOX 4.1 IS IT WOM OR IS IT RUMOR?

In the text, I pointed out how the differences between WOM and rumor generally come down to whether the message in question is based on evidence (such as the personal experience of the communicator) and the degree of credibility of the source, which are two factors that are likely to be related. Continuing with the text's example, imagine that instead of learning from a close friend that he heard from an unnamed source that the local cinema was going to shut down in the near future, he informs you that the cinema owner, who is a family friend, told him personally that because of financial difficulties, the cinema was being sold to a realtor. Let us say your friend also recommended that the two of you should go see a film at the cinema before it closes. Although there still might be some question about the veracity of your friend's comments (e.g., perhaps the cinema owner conveyed misleading information, however unlikely), in this case your friend's comments would constitute WOM. This is because you trust your friend, do not believe he is being paid to recommend the cinema, and it appears that the information is credible.

Whether or not a communication constitutes WOM depends on the extent to which it possesses certain identifying properties, the foremost of which involve (a) whether the communication deals with something in the marketplace (e.g., a product, service, brand, or company) and (b) the degree to which the message is supported by evidence. By considering three additional properties—(c) whether the communication deals with people, (d) the significance or interest of the message content, and (e) whether the message is positive or negative—it is possible to more clearly identify WOM and to differentiate it from related forms of communication, such as rumor, gossip, and news (see the table below).

Properties of Word of Mouth (WOM) and Related Forms of Communication

Property	WOM	Rumor	Gossip	News
Product/service/firm-oriented	Yes	Yes/no	No	Yes/no
People-oriented	No	Yes/no	Yes	Yes/no
Significant	Yes/no	Yes	No	Yes
Evidential basis	Yes	No	Yes/no	Yes
Connotation	$+/-$	$+/-$	$-$	$+/-$
Example:	You really should try Actimel – it's tasty and very healthy.	I heard that Actimel's health claims are false.	I saw our new neighbor in the supermarket shopping with her boyfriend.	I read in the Wall Street Journal that Danone raised the price of Actimel last week.

To summarize some of the distinctions depicted in the table, we can say that WOM represents a form of personal communication about a marketplace offering or firm that is supported by evidence. Although it is likely to be viewed as significant, this may not be the case in certain instances, such as when the receiver is presented with unsolicited information that is of little interest or relevance to him or her personally. The focus of WOM content does not pertain to people and, as discussed in the text, it may or may not be positive. The table reveals that the basic way that WOM differs from marketplace rumors lies in its confirmatory evidence. The distinctions identified in the table underscore why WOM, rumor, gossip, and news frequently seem to blend and be confused with one another, yet they also help us recognize that the three types of exchange clearly are not identical forms of communication.

(cont.)

Box 4.1 (*Continued*)

As recent cases have revealed, the Internet and other emerging communication technologies are particularly well suited to serve as conduits for the spread of unverified information to a global audience. As a result, rumors have come to represent an imposing competitor in the marketplace of information exchange, and may increasingly blur with credible WOM. In a study I recently completed with Anne-Françoise Audrain-Pontevia, we examined commercial rumors from the perspective of 133 American and French marketing managers (Kimmel & Audrain-Pontevia, 2010), who completed a questionnaire intended to assess the prevalence and types of commercial rumors that reach their ear, the severity of rumor effects, and the effectiveness of rumor control tactics that they used to counter rumors.

Respondents reported that they regularly receive rumors, primarily through informal communication channels, and that the content of these rumors tends to be negative, reflective of the anxieties associated with the anticipation of future events, and focused on external matters of concern to customers, the media, and stockholders (e.g., deaths caused by cell phones, baby food containing a risky beef ingredient, diapers causing sterility, competitor promotion). Our findings also indicated that marketplace rumors pose significant threats to a variety of company stakeholders, undermining trust among customers, lowering employee morale, and increasing stress among the workforce. As rumors have been found to be strongly linked to the anxieties of a public craving information about matters of personal relevance and timeliness, it was not surprising to find that the tactics evaluated as most effective in countering their potentially harmful effects included attempts to increase trust and provide requested information to those who seek it.

to another. Persons who convey WOM often have had personal experience with products or services from a particular organization and tend to be regarded as fairly objective sources of information by receivers. By contrast, the original source of rumor content typically is undefined or vague (e.g., "a friend of a friend") (Kimmel, 2004).

WOM Frequency

Think for a moment about some of the consumer-related decisions you make on a fairly regular basis in your everyday life: which films to see at the cinema and which TV shows to watch at home; where to shop; which restaurants to frequent; which bank, travel agency, airline, car mechanic, or dentist to use; what computer software to use; which books to read or music to listen to. If you next ask yourself in how many cases was your decision influenced by someone else, your answer should provide a pretty good idea as to the frequency and influence that WOM has in your life. A market research study conducted by the Keller Faye Group determined that consumers discuss approximately twelve brands per day ("On the Tips," 2006). At the top of the list of topics that serve as the focus of consumer discussions are media and entertainment (with consumers mentioning this category an average of 12 times per week and a specific brand 8.2 times per week), food and dining (10; 7.5), beverages (8; 7.4), telecommunications

(8; 5.2), travel services (7, 6.6), and technology (7; 5.3). The study also revealed that people are more apt to say positive things about personal care and household products, whereas financial services firms and telecommunication companies are most likely to provide the fodder for negative comments. Overall, the Keller Faye Group estimated that the average person will have 56 WOM conversations per week, with more than 15% of one's social conversations concerning a product or service.

The results of other WOM surveys consistently reveal that consumers are most likely to transmit WOM messages to those with whom they are most intimately related or familiar with. For example, NOP World reported that of US consumers who responded to their 2005 survey, a majority claimed that they are likely to pass along product or service recommendations to their friends (88%) and family members (87%), followed by people who share the same interests (66%), colleagues (61%), neighbors (42%), and other consumers (35%). Similar results were observed for Canadian consumers ("Why Word of Mouth Rules!," 2008).

Not surprisingly, certain types of consumers have been found to be more active in the spread of WOM than others, such as market mavens and opinion leaders (see Box 4.2). Keller and Berry (2005) reported that compared with the general public, influentials (defined as people who are socially and politically active in their local communities) are twice as likely to recommend products and services and to be solicited for information

---

BOX 4.2 NETWORK HUBS

Given their central role in communicating with large numbers of other consumers about products, services, and companies, it is not surprising that opinion leaders have also been referred to by consumer industry insiders as "influencers," "power users," "lead users," and "influentials." In his informative book on the creation of WOM marketing, Emanuel Rosen (2002) chose the term "network hubs" to speak about connected individuals who are in a central position to further the buzz about a product, to change a message, or perhaps to block a message from spreading. In Rosen's view, four types of network hubs can be distinguished:

1. *Regular hubs.* These are average people who represent sources of information for only a few other consumers or a few dozen, but who nevertheless can serve to influence a product category.

2. *Mega-hubs.* These are professional opinion leaders such as journalists, celebrities, analysts, and politicians who, like regular hubs, have many two-way links to others, but also have thousands of one-way links with people who receive their messages through the mass media. The American television personality Oprah Winfrey is considered to be such a hub because of her ability to reach and influence millions of people.

3. *Expert hubs.* These are specialized opinion leaders who have demonstrated significant knowledge of a certain area and thus represent authorities on the subject for other consumers. A friend who you go to for advice and information about cars because you know that person will be extremely knowledgeable about the product category represents this kind of hub. In short, expert hubs are identified on the basis of what they know.

(cont.)

Box 4.2 (*Continued*)

4. *Social Hubs*. These are individuals who are particularly central within their group because of their charisma, trustworthiness, and high level of social activity. It is usually possible to identify at least one person like this in a wide range of social groupings, including one's neighborhood, company, town, etc.

What these different varieties of network hubs have in common is that they communicate more information about particular product categories, with greater frequency, than do other people. In fact, as Rosen (2002, p. 46) points out, it is probably appropriate to speak about an individual's *degree* of influence: "If an average Palm user tells twenty other people a year about the device, and another user tells eighty people about it, that second person is clearly a hub." Through the use of questionnaires and careful observation, Rosen identified certain characteristics shared by network hubs, summarized by the acronym ACTIVE: they are ahead in adoption, connected, travelers, information-hungry, vocal, and exposed more than others to the media.

Just how influential is the network hub in the consumer marketplace? Rosen offers some statistics:

- 58% of young people rely to some extent on others when selecting a car
- 53% of moviegoers follow the recommendations of friends
- 65% of the people who bought a Palm organizer did so on the basis of recommendations from others
- 43% of travelers cited friends and family as the basic sources of information in deciding places to visit and which airlines, hotels, and rental cars to use
- 70% of Americans rely on the advice of others in selecting a new doctor

---

BOX 4.3 FOCUS ON APPLICATION: BLOGGERS AND THE FASHION INDUSTRY

Some of the most powerful opinion leaders in the contemporary marketplace are teenagers whose online Web sites provide advice, recommendations, and unbiased critiques about products or services. For example, the new "movers and shakers" in the fashion and beauty care industries are not high-paid Madison Avenue professionals, but young female consumers, via their Web sites and online blogs, such as shoewawa.com, beautyaddict.blogspot.com, and jackandhill.net. Blogger Kristen Kelly created the Beauty Addict blog in September 2005 when she was in her early twenties to share her beauty products obsession with like-minded consumers. By early 2006, her site was drawing nearly 1,000 readers per day and rapidly becoming the best-known beauty site in the blogosphere (Jaret, 2006). While she and other bloggers regularly receive free samples from the cosmetics industry and additional "swag" (a term used by beauty editors to refer to luxurious gifts bestowed on influentials to shape favorable attitudes toward the firm), they do not accept compensation for promoting brands online.

---

and advice by others seeking their recommendations. Although WOM is not restricted by consumer age, there is evidence that young consumers—whose discretionary income and influence on family purchases have grown significantly in recent years—are especially active in generating marketing buzz. Once young consumers are made aware of a product, they are likely to tell their friends and family about it. Forrester Research

(2005) found that about 50% of 12- to 21-year-olds get purchasing advice from friends and family, and 65% let others know what products they like (see Box 4.3).

Despite the proliferation and growing popularity of blogs and other online channels for the transmission of WOM, some analyses have revealed that the frequency of off-line WOM far exceeds that which occurs online. A Northeastern University study estimated that nearly four out of five WOM occasions (77%) involve face-to-face conversations, 17% occur by phone, and 6% take place online. Similarly, a Keller Faye Group analysis found that 92% of WOM conversations occur off-line (with 71% face-to-face and 21% by phone). Despite these compelling figures, there is some debate about the relative frequencies of online and off-line occurrences of WOM, with some experts pointing out that the specific nature of the WOM must be considered before accurate estimates can be made. One argument is that online WOM is simply a proxy for off-line WOM; that is, off-line WOM is picked up by influencers and early adopters who create a larger audience for the message content by spreading it online, taking advantage of the potential of search engines like Google ("Blogspotting," 2006).

Perhaps most helpful in teasing out the true story of online and off-line WOM frequencies is the distinction between intimate and incidental WOM, which was first suggested by marketing author Pete Blackshaw, who serves as executive VP of Nielsen Online Digital Strategic Services. In Blackshaw's view (2006), *intimate WOM* is that which takes place primarily among familiars and typically takes the form of a trusted recommendation. The familiarity between the parties in an intimate WOM exchange lends a high degree of credibility to the recommendation. When marketers utilize proactive strategies to encourage consumer enthusiasts or influentials to advocate particular brands to others within their personal trusted network, they are in essence attempting to stimulate intimate WOM. *Incidental WOM*, by contrast, is a more indirect form of interpersonal influence that is not based on an existing, trusted relationship. This type of message exchange is more likely to occur online, such as when a consumer creates a message (e.g., on a blog or community forum) that has no specific intended target within a trusted network of social relationships. As a permanent (i.e., archived) example of consumer-generated content, incidental WOM can have a lasting impact on other consumers and its overall "reach" may far surpass that of an intimate off-line recommendation. In fact, as Blackshaw points out, much of the discussion of brands and services within the blogosphere is posted by consumers with little deliberate intention to evangelize or persuade others, but is simply embedded within the tapestry of their ongoing narratives. Many readers of blogs seek targeted knowledge and arrive at blog sites as a result of an online search for a product, brand, or company.

The intimate versus incidental distinction implies that estimates suggesting that an overwhelming percentage of WOM exchanges occurs off-line may be somewhat misleading, especially if consumers are asked to report the frequency with which they have recommended a marketplace offering to others or have received such a recommendation during exchanges with others. A new car buyer may have a few conversations with relatives or close acquaintances who recently purchased a car, but during an online search, may also read countless postings by consumers who have recounted their car experiences on any number of blogs, forums, and customer review sites. When asked about the WOM exchanges that occurred prior to arriving at a buying decision, that consumer is probably going to recall the pointed and involved conversations with a few intimates more vividly than the blur of online discussion that may also have had a profound impact on the overall decision. Nonetheless, it is likely that a majority of *personal* instances of WOM do occur off-line, either in face-to-face interactions or telephone conversations with intimates within our social networks. The distinction between intimate and incidental WOM has also entered discussions of the relative frequency of positive versus negative WOM, an issue I address later in this chapter.

WOM Antecedents

As I pointed out in the discussion of opinion leaders in Chapter 3, there are certain underlying needs that motivate a person to talk about a product or service, including a desire to achieve status by appearing to be knowledgeable or expert in front of one's peers and an altruistic inclination to assist others. One early view of the motivations that compel people to transmit PWOM was offered in an influential paper by Ernst Dichter (1966), in which he identified factors such as involvement with the product and the desire to express oneself and relate to others through the transfer of information. In some cases, consumers who have recently made an important purchase are compelled to convey positive messages about the product and the company to others. This tendency is linked to the fact that a common side effect of the purchase, especially if it is an expensive one, is the psychological discomfort or tension that stems from having second thoughts about whether one has made a correct decision. One way that consumers can overcome this phenomenon, known as "cognitive dissonance" or "buyer's remorse," is to talk to others about the product's advantages. In this way, consumers can reduce the post-decisional dissonance they are experiencing and convince themselves that they made the right choice. At the same time, recipients of WOM save time and effort in their search for marketplace offerings and gain more confidence in their ability to make a purchase decision.

Given these points, we can recognize that WOM may serve various beneficial functions for the participants involved in its exchange. However, as it turns out, this is only one part of a more complex story. As East, Vanhuele, and Wright (2008) noted, much of the focus on the production of WOM has focused on *why* people engage in the process (i.e., their motivations), without acknowledging that people also often engage in WOM because they have the opportunity and *can* do so. The merit of this point is apparent in the results of a study by Mangold, Miller, and Brockway (1999), who identified high levels of WOM when circumstances provided the opportunity to give it (e.g., when two friends spontaneously decide to go to a restaurant and their conversation includes some of the possible venues in the area, or when you bump into a neighbor at the supermarket and he asks your advice about a product; see "Misconception 1" section). Further, Mangold et al.'s results indicated that only 3.4% of face-to-face WOM conversations were stimulated by marketing efforts, a finding that further emphasizes how much WOM is naturally embedded in and stimulated by everyday conversation.

In their review of the WOM literature, De Bruyn and Lilien (2008) identified three streams of research that have emerged to explain the antecedents of WOM. The first stream focuses on factors that compel consumers to proactively spread the word about marketplace offerings that they have directly experienced. Among the factors that have been linked to such behavior are (*1*) extreme satisfaction or dissatisfaction (Anderson, 1998; Bowman & Narayandas, 2001; Maxham & Netemeyer, 2002), (*2*) novelty of the product (Bone, 1992), and (*3*) consumers' commitment to the firm (Dick & Basu, 1994; Wangenheim & Bayon, 2004). Let us consider each of these factors in turn.

1. *Extreme satisfaction or dissatisfaction.* Because people seem to have a natural tendency to convey their experiences—particularly good and bad ones—about products and firms to others, it has long been assumed that customer satisfaction or dissatisfaction is an essential catalyst of WOM. In part, this assumption is derived from research showing higher frequencies of WOM when satisfaction or dissatisfaction are at their highest levels; that is, when consumers are extremely satisfied or dissatisfied (e.g., Anderson, 1998; Herr, Kardes, & Kim, 1991; Yale, 1987). Just imagine having seen a new film at the cinema that you thoroughly enjoyed, perhaps to the point that you would rate it as one of the best films you have ever seen. It would not be surprising to find that you could not wait to recommend it to a close friend. In this case, your extreme satisfaction would have acted as a force that compelled you to engage in the WOM process. In one widely reported study, Anderson (1998) obtained data pertaining to a large number of industries through use of the Swedish Customer Satisfaction Barometer and the American Customer Satisfaction Index. His results revealed a U-shaped curve for both American and Swedish participants when he studied the relationship between degree of satisfaction (ranging from highly dissatisfied to highly satisfied) and average amount of WOM (see Figure 4.1). In addition to finding that highly satisfied and highly dissatisfied consumers engage in more WOM, NWOM was found to increase at a greater rate than PWOM. (The relative prevalence of PWOM and NWOM is discussed below.)

2. *Novelty of the product.* In addition to satisfaction level, several authors have pointed to the importance of novelty of the product as an important element in

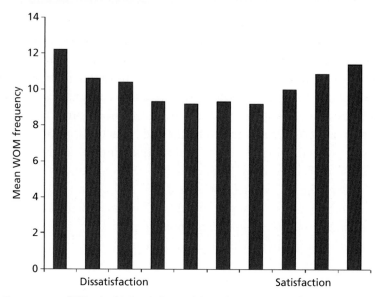

Figure 4.1 Frequency of Word of Mouth (WOM) in Relation to Satisfaction and Dissatisfaction

Source: Anderson (1998; Swedish data).

stimulating WOM. A novel or unusual product is one that offers consumers something new or different from current products or expectations and thus can serve to attract the attention of innovators and early adopters. The attention-getting aspect will generally consist of something that will be talkworthy and have informative value for others. Along these lines, Silverman (2005) argued that when people are talking about a product directly (as opposed to embedded talk about a company's offering that occurs when people are discussing something else of interest), it is because there is something so unusual about it that they want to share that information with others. An example is seen in the success of the Japanese stationary product Kadokeshi, an eraser comprised of ten connected cubes that result in twenty-eight edges. The odd-looking product is the creation of Hideo Kanbara, who recognized that school children do not like having the sharp edges of their erasers turn into round shapes. Expecting to sell 40,000 pieces per year, the Kokuyo Co., which manufactures Kadokeshi, received orders for 100,000 from stationery stores in 1 month as the new product's popularity soared among children who spread the word via WOM ("Brain Bread," 2006). The novel Japanese eraser's uniqueness was likely a key driver for stimulating WOM among students, but its functional attributes no doubt determined the positive nature of the WOM content. If a unique product lacks any apparent utility for consumers, people may be stimulated to talk about it with others, but what they say is likely to be negative and potentially devastating for the survival of the product.

3. *Consumers' commitment to the firm.* In Chapter 2, I pointed out how brand loyals are likely to serve as influentials for a firm by talking about their favored brand with others. Thus, commitment represents another antecedent of WOM, which for loyal consumers is very likely to be positive in nature. However, because of their passionate ties to certain brands, committed consumers can be expected to respond with vehemence if they believe a company has done something to undermine what they believe makes a favored brand so special.

When WOM emanates from sources whose credibility is in doubt, we might expect that committed consumers would have greater confidence in the truthfulness of positive messages about their favored brand/firm than negative messages, and thus be more likely to pass on the former. This assumption is consistent with research identifying credibility or confidence in message content as a key determinant of whether a rumor is disseminated to others (e.g., Kimmel & Keefer, 1991; Pezzo & Beckstead, 2006; Rosnow, Yost, and Esposito 1986).

Another research stream pertinent to the occurrence of WOM concerns consumer information-seeking behaviors, focusing on the circumstances that lead consumers to rely more heavily on WOM communications than formal information sources to arrive at purchase decisions. The research evidence to date suggests that consumers are more likely to seek out the opinions of others when they have little expertise in the product category (Furse, Punj, & Stewart, 1984; Gilly et al., 1998) or when the purchase decision is characterized by high perceived risk (Bansal & Voyer, 2000; Kiel & Layton, 1981) and high involvement (Beatty & Smith, 1987). What these factors highlight is that the transmission of WOM is often stimulated by an opportunity provided by the recipient, such as a consumer who plays the role of an opinion seeker. According to James Engel and his colleagues (1990), from the perspective of the consumer who actively solicits information, advice, or guidance from an opinion leader, one or more of the following conditions must be present if opinion leadership is to occur:

1. The consumer lacks sufficient information to be able to make an adequately informed choice.
2. The product is complex and difficult to evaluate using objective criteria.
3. A consumer lacks the ability to evaluate the product or service, regardless of how the information is disseminated and presented.
4. Other sources of product- or service-related information (e.g., salespeople or advertisers) are perceived as having low credibility.
5. An opinion leader is more accessible than other sources and thus can be more easily consulted.
6. Strong social ties exist between the consumer and the opinion leader (e.g., the opinion leader is liked and respected).
7. The consumer has a high need for social approval (i.e., cares about what others think).

The third research stream reflects efforts to explain the greater influence on consumers of personal information sources when compared with other sources. Factors such as source expertise (Bansal & Voyer 2000; Gilly et al. 1998), strength of social ties (Brown & Reingen 1987; Frenzen & Nakamoto 1993), and demographic similarity (Brown & Reingen 1987) have emerged as important antecedents underlying WOM influence. Some of these points were alluded to in our discussion about opinion leaders and other influentials in Chapter 3, and also conform to statistics indicating diminishing consumer trust in formal marketing messages via traditional channels (see Chapter 2).

One view of how these various factors operate to generate WOM production is suggested by the conceptual framework depicted in Figure 4.2. The model was created on the basis of a systematic program of research carried out by Robert East and his colleagues at Kingston University (United Kingdom), including studies on communicator characteristics associated with product/service recommendations. The researchers obtained evidence that rate of recommendation is often related to such factors as relative attitude to the brand (i.e., the rating of a brand compared with other available brands in terms of satisfaction), the referral status of the communicator (i.e., whether the person was recruited by recommendation or not); whether the communicator recommended other product categories, and customer tenure (i.e., duration as a customer of the brand). It is important to note, however, that a blanket statement suggesting that these factors always will produce WOM appears to be unwarranted. For example, relative attitude was found to be a strong, but not statistically significant, predictor in only five of

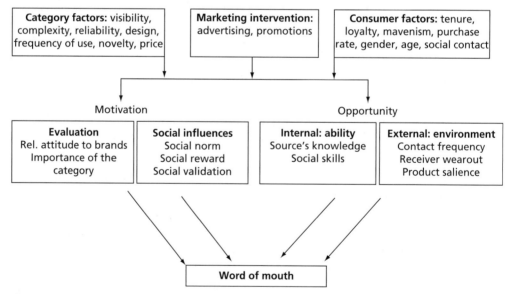

Figure 4.2 Model Explaining the Production of Word of Mouth (WOM)

Source: East, Vanhuele, and Wright (2008*b*).

twenty-three studies. Customer tenure was observed to be negatively related to recommendation for some categories (e.g., credit cards, bank accounts, supermarkets) and positively related to others (e.g., car servicing), apparently depending on the character of the service (its stability, complexity, frequency of visit, and so on).

East et al.'s WOM production model (2008*b*) is based on the assumption that behavior stems from three sources of influence—motivation, opportunity, and ability (MOA). This perspective underlines how the transmission of WOM becomes more likely when people have the desire to engage in it (e.g., to show one's expertise) and when they have the relevant skills and opportunity to do so. The top level of the framework identifies category, marketing, and consumer factors at the root of WOM production, suggesting that the process can begin with talkworthy products (e.g., those that are unusual or exceptionally functional), marketing interventions (e.g., a buzz marketing campaign), and characteristics of consumers that make them more likely to engage in WOM (e.g., mavenism, loyalty).

The framework's second level includes motivation and opportunity influences. Motivation is described by both personal aspects (e.g., relative liking for brands, satisfaction, category involvement) and social aspects (e.g., social rewards). Social influences could compel communicators to make recommendations on the basis of what they think others should do (i.e., social norm), what they would like them to do (i.e., social reward), and what is usually done (i.e., social validation). Opportunity is divided into internal influences associated with the communicator's ability and external influences tied to the physical and social contexts that enable the performance of an action. As East et al. (2008*b*) explain, some products are readily observable and frequently utilized, such as mobile phones; their "salience" thus could be expected to generate conversation and advice, especially when one has a wide circle of friends and associates. By contrast, WOM would be expected to diminish when receivers begin to tire of hearing about a service (so-called receiver wearout), as when the service is one that is dull and unchanging (such as a neighborhood's cable TV service).

To summarize, it should now be evident that there is no simple answer to the question of what factor (or set of factors) stimulates WOM. The research literature points to a multiplicity of personal, product/purchase-related, marketing-related, and situational factors that tend to serve as catalysts for the onset of WOM exchanges among consumers. Thus, it is useful to bear in mind that although offering consumers an incentive to recommend a product to others can be an effective tactic for stimulating WOM, such rewards may not be necessary in certain cases, especially for strong brands, which people will talk about anyway (see Box 4.4). Finally, many marketing pundits have keyed in on customer satisfaction/dissatisfaction as the primary WOM stimulant and choose to believe that the story largely ends there. However, this belief is short-sighted and represents one of the key misconceptions concerning WOM that I will address in the final section of this chapter.

BOX 4.4 FOCUS ON RESEARCH: A PENNY FOR YOUR THOUGHTS

As a growing number of business practitioners have come to recognize the critical role of word of mouth (WOM) in the marketing process, firms have begun to introduce referral programs designed to encourage product recommendations from existing customers in efforts to gain new ones (see Chapter 7). Various types of rewards are offered when a referral attracts a new customer or leads to a purchase, such as vouchers, gifts, free minutes, or miles. In a series of experiments conducted by marketing professors Gangseog Ryu and Lawrence Feick (2007) to study how rewards influence referral likelihood, some interesting findings were obtained. First, it was discovered that offering a reward indeed does increase referral likelihood, but that the size of the reward does not seem to make much of a difference, at least within the parameters of the rewards used in the research, which consisted of vouchers for store credit. Second, it was found that the success of the reward differs according to the nature of the social relationship between the recommender and the recipient of the referral. Rewards made little difference among close friends, but increased the chance of a referral among mere acquaintances from 56.2% to 81.1%.

Finally, the researchers observed that the strength of the brand plays a role in determining the impact of a reward on referral. When research participants were told to imagine that they had purchased a cheaper, poor-quality mp3 player from an obscure company, they were more than twice as motivated by the reward to recommend the product than participants asked to imagine a better-made, more expensive mp3 player. Thus, rewards appear to be more useful for increasing referral likelihood for consumers of weaker than stronger brands. As Feick explained, "People talk about strong brands anyway. But for weak brands, rewards lift you over the line."

The Impact of WOM

I began this chapter with reference to the familiar phrase "the power of WOM." If this phrase refers to anything, it is that WOM—whatever its cause—can have significant consequences in the marketplace. There is evidence that WOM can shape consumer expectations (Anderson & Salisbury, 2003; Zeithaml & Bitner, 1996), pre-usage attitudes (Herr, Kardes, & Kim, 1991), and post-usage perceptions of a product or service (Bone, 1995; Burzynski & Bayer, 1977). Perhaps most importantly, WOM represents a primary source of information for consumer buying decisions and thus can have an impact on a firm's bottom line (Chevalier & Mayzlin, 2006; Dichter, 1966; East, Hammond, & Wright 2007; Liu, 2006; Mangold, Miller, & Brockway 1999). Dating back to the early 1950s, researchers have reported how WOM referrals play a significant role in consumers' choices for such products and services as:

- physicians (Coleman, Katz & Menzel 1957; Feldman & Spencer 1965),
- razor blades (Sheth, 1971),
- automobile diagnostic centers (Engel, Kegerreis & Blackwell, 1969),
- automobiles (Newman & Staelin, 1972),
- farming practices (Katz, 1961),

- household goods and food products (Katz & Lazarsfeld, 1955),
- fabrics and supermarkets (Beal & Rogers, 1957),
- movies (Liu, 2006),
- Web sites (Jupiter Communications, 1999), and
- electronic purchases (cf. McConnell & Huba, 2002).

Although some of these studies are more related to category adoption than brand switching, a preponderance of evidence has begun to emerge that WOM can have stronger consequences on consumer behavior than formal marketing efforts. As discussed in previous chapters, the influence of traditional marketing campaigns, such as mass media advertising, has diminished for consumer buying decisions. For example, a 2002 study by Euro RSCG Worldwide found that consumers were more likely to get information about technology products from WOM as opposed to advertising (TV, print, and outdoor) and company Web sites, and cited referrals by work colleagues, friends, and family members as most likely to generate excitement about a technology product or service. A 2003 study by the management consulting firm Cap Gemini Ernst & Young revealed that only 17% of the 700 recent car buyers surveyed claimed that TV ads influenced their car-buying decisions. Although ads on Internet search engines (26%) and direct mail from car dealers (48%) fared better, WOM had the greatest impact on which car was ultimately purchased, cited by 71% of those surveyed. Similarly, a December 2005 study by BIGresearch found that WOM represented the most influential medium for 18- to 24-year-old American consumers when making electronic purchases, ahead of TV, magazines, Internet, in-store promotions, e-mail advertising, and direct mail.

WOM serves as a useful commodity for consumer decision making for some very basic reasons: it is quick, convenient, cost-free, and it saves time and effort. Before considering more closely how the effects of WOM vary according to the nature of the product or service category, it is important to clarify how "impact" has been conceptualized by researchers. In a straightforward application of multistage consumer decision-making models, De Bruyn and Lilien (2008) suggest that the influence of WOM can occur at three sequential stages: awareness, interest, and final decision. This view posits that WOM can have its impact via the flow of information as well as the flow of influence on its recipients, with WOM capable of affecting the transition probability at each stage (i.e., probability of becoming aware, probability of arousing interest, and probability of moving a person to positive action). De Bruyn and Lilien applied these ideas in their research on how WOM influences consumers through electronic referrals stimulated by viral marketing campaigns. At the awareness stage, recipients of an unsolicited, electronic referral first must decide whether to open the e-mail and thus become aware of its content. This decision typically is based on available cues, such as relevance of the subject line, familiarity of the sender's name, and nature of the relationship between the receiver and sender. During the interest stage, once recipients understand the purpose of the e-mail message (e.g., to encourage them to spread the word about a product or service), they may develop greater interest in learning more, depending on whether they decide that it is worth their time to investigate further. Finally, with sufficient information about the product or service in hand, the recipient may decide to buy or adopt the offer and perhaps continue the referral chain by disseminating the e-mail communication to others.

The impact of WOM has been operationalized by researchers according to how brand purchase probability is affected by the relative incidence or impact of PWOM and NWOM. Another way is to consider the effect of WOM on the adoption of new products or the choice of new brands in mature categories (East, Hammond, & Lomax, 2008). It is logical to assume that WOM will have a greater impact in some categories than others. One reason for this is that certain categories offer more alternative sources of relevant information, such as promotional materials and sales staff, whereas other categories do not. For example, the choice of a veterinarian for your new pet is likely to be limited to other pet owners whom you associate with and trust.

In their research on brand/provider choice among various product and service categories, East et al. (2005) compared the influence of recommendation with personal search, advertising, and "other" (such as editorial advice in the mass media and situations where people had no choice due to contracts or gifts). The results pointed to recommendation as the main source of information in approximately one-third of respondents' self-reported choices, with several services emerging as more responsive to WOM than consumer goods. For example, dentists (59% of respondents) were chosen on recommendation significantly more often than cars (13%), not surprisingly given greater exposure to car advertising and the opportunities that are available to test out cars before making a choice. Other categories in which recommendation had a strong impact included choice of educational institution (48%), bank (43%), car servicing (56%), coffee shop (65%), and outdoor clothing (52%). In other categories, respondents were more likely to cite other sources of information (advertising, etc.) as the main choice of information underlying their decision, such as mobile phone brand (21%), dry cleaning (14%), supermarket (10%), fashion store (13%), and hair coloring (11%).

It is difficult to draw any general conclusions based on these findings, as the relative impact of WOM on category decisions is likely to be moderated by a variety of conditions, including country context, characteristics of the recommendation source, demographic characteristics of the communicator and receiver, the nature of the sender–receiver relationship, clarity of the recommendation, intensity of expression (i.e., strength of the recommendation), and the approaches used by receivers to combine information received from different sources when deciding to adopt a product or switch to another brand. We will return to the category issue below by considering the relative impact of PWOM and NWOM on consumer choice.

The Consequences of False WOM

When WOM is negative in nature and widespread, the consequences can be severe. It has been shown that NWOM tends to decrease purchase probability and thus can be financially damaging for a company (East et al., 2008; Lau & Ng, 2001). NWOM also may affect product or service evaluations (Herr, Kardes, & Kim, 1991). These consequences can be compounded when the content of NWOM takes the form of a rumor that is baseless or outright false. Aside from purposeful actions taken by consumer groups to intentionally undermine a firm's profit margin through organized boycotts and related activities, perhaps the most serious consequence of a negative rumor can be seen in its potential for influencing how consumers think and feel about a company's brands. This influence is best understood through a consideration of the marketing concept known as *brand equity*, a term used to refer to the value added to a brand by its name and symbol. More specifically, David Aaker (1991, p. 15), who has studied the concept extensively, defines brand equity as "a set of brand assets and liabilities linked to a brand by its name and symbol, that add to or subtract from the value provided by a product or service to a firm and/or to that firm's customers." In Aaker's view, the assets underlying brand equity consist of brand loyalty, name awareness, perceived quality, brand associations, and other proprietary brand assets (such as patents and trademarks). Brand equity can provide value both to the firm (e.g., by enhancing competitive advantage, prices and margins, and trade leverage) and to the firm's customers (e.g., by enhancing confidence in the purchase decision, use satisfaction, and the process of brand decision making).

The world's top brands, such as Coca-Cola, McDonald's, Sony, Kodak, and Mercedes-Benz are characterized by high levels of brand equity because they successfully provide the assets that Aaker has identified. Compared to many of their competitors, these brands are well known and readily identified by consumers (i.e., brand awareness), they are characterized by high levels of customer loyalty (i.e., they are purchased repeatedly by consumers who feel a strong sense of commitment to the brand), they are perceived as having a high level of overall quality, and so on. Each of these brand names also conveys a ready set of associations in the consumer's mind. For example, the Mercedes name is linked to a variety of positive associations in memory for many consumers, such as well-engineered, durable, safe, and high in prestige level. The same can be said about the McDonald's name, which may conjure up in one's mind images of Ronald McDonald, the golden arches, cleanliness, speedy and efficient service, and the like. Regardless of whether a person views these associations as positive or negative, the point is that they add depth to the brand represented by the company name.

With these points about brand equity in mind, we can better understand how unfounded WOM in the form of rumors can cause serious harm to a brand as well as to a company's overall image in the marketplace. Negative rumors about the company and its products and services, when believed, can clearly undermine consumer loyalties. The trust that is inherent in loyalty to a firm can be shattered when rumors appear

BOX 4.5 WOM AND TRUST

One of the essential components that underlies the potential for WOM to be such a powerful force in the contemporary marketplace is trust. Marketing research on business relationships has revealed that trust between partners can result in substantial benefits for the parties involved: it contributes to the level of commitment to the relationship, it serves to reduce perceived risks in an exchange situation (such as a purchase), it positively influences willingness to continue in the relationship and cooperate more closely, it can facilitate conflict resolution, and so on (e.g., Anderson & Weitz, 1989; Ganesan, 1994; Morgan & Hunt, 1994). An additional benefit that is particularly relevant to the impact of WOM on consumer behavior is the reduction of uncertainty. Indeed, when it comes to relationships involving services (which are distinguished by their intangible nature), trust is essential in reducing uncertainty and vulnerability among users and potential users.

In terms of its relevance to business relationships, trust has been defined as "a willingness to rely on an exchange partner in whom one has confidence" (Moorman, Zaltman, & Deshpandé, 1992, p. 314). As implied by this definition, trustworthy business exchange partners are characterized by confidence, honesty, and competence (Donney & Cannon, 1997; Ganesan, 1994). The element of confidence suggests that trust, which is based on the expectation that the partner will not behave opportunistically, is comprised of a cognitive component (i.e., confidence or belief in the reliability of the partner) as well as a behavioral component, reflecting confidence in the intentions, motivations, honesty, and benevolence of the partner (Ring & Van De Van, 1992). The degree of willingness to rely on another lies at the heart of the trust concept.

Recent surveys pertaining to trust that consumers have in diverse sources of marketplace information corroborate these conceptual points and help us understand why WOM is so compelling in today's marketing context. Consumers are likely to use a brand recommended by a previous user, and are more apt to trust product endorsements received from friends and acquaintances than advertising appeals (Rusticus, 2006). According to a 2006 Forrester online survey, North American respondents rated the opinions of friends and acquaintances as significantly more trustworthy than reviews in a newspaper, magazine, or on television, and 60% claimed to trust consumer reviews on a retailer's Web site (Li, 2007). Similarly, a 2007 Edelman survey of adult consumers revealed that 60% of respondents considered "a person like themselves" as a credible source of information about a company, more so than a regular employee of the company (43%) or a company CEO (23%) (Edelman, 2008). As consumers worldwide are turned off by the steady bombardment of traditionally mass-mediated marketing messages, they are turning to each other for insight into brands, products, and services, in large part because of the greater trustworthiness of the advice they receive from personal relations.

These findings suggest that if marketers want to attract consumers back to their formal marketing messages, one primary task will be to regain the trust that has gradually eroded over recent decades. Although there is not consensus about the specific antecedent and outcome factors, experts suggest that a number of elements have the potential to build trust in business settings, including experience with the partner, shared values, honesty, explicit guarantees, openness in communication, desire to continue the relationship, responsiveness, clarifying exchange parameters, and the like (e.g., Geyskens et al. 1996; Morgan & Hunt, 1994). In more practical terms, marketing managers can enhance trust through truth in advertising, ethical and fair selling practices, and by ensuring the integrity of product promotions, guarantees, and promises. A variety of outcomes of trust may be anticipated, including commitment/loyalty, expansion of the relationship, cooperation, reduced uncertainty, interdependence, and higher levels of trust.

Table 4.1 Suggested McDonald's Associations Before and After the Worms-in-the-Burgers False Rumor

Before	After
Pure 100% beef	Juicy red earthworms
Big Mac	Big worms
Reliable and friendly service	Unreliable and secretive
Clean and efficient	Unclean, dirty
Nice place to take your kids for a meal	Place to avoid

Source: Kimmel (2004).

because the rumors would suggest to consumers that the company has something to hide (see Box 4.5). As in human relationships, this sort of basis for mistrust could undermine a loyal consumer's relationship with a favored brand (Fournier, 1998). This outcome would prevail whether the rumor claims that the company is involved in an alleged conspiracy (because conspiracies are by nature based on secrecy) or that its product offerings are contaminated in some way (e.g., by using cheaper and unhealthy substitute ingredients without the consumer's knowledge to cut costs).

Perhaps even more damaging is that negative rumors can influence brand associations by serving to replace positive associations in the consumer's mind (developed through direct experience with the brand, positive WOM, or the company's marketing campaigns) with negative ones (suggested by the rumor content). This possibility is consistent with the notions about how rumors work from an information processing perspective (see Kimmel, 2004). Thus, an association for McDonald's in a consumer's memory prior to having heard the (false) 1978 rumor that their burgers contain red worms to boost their protein levels might have been "big juicy burgers"; after hearing the rumor the association would be more along the lines of "juicy red worms" (see Table 4.1).

The brand equity perspective also helps us recognize that strong brand awareness can actually represent a liability for a company when it comes to rumors because rumors tend to attach themselves to better known and more successful firms. The implications for fighting false NWOM that can be derived from brand equity notions highlight the necessity to initiate public relations campaigns that reinforce the original brand image and corresponding associations (i.e., prior to the onset of the rumors), without strengthening the new associations attributed to the rumors. This is exactly what McDonald's accomplished when they launched an anti-rumor campaign emphasizing that their burgers contained "100% pure beef," without ever mentioning the word "worms."

Separating Fact From Fallacy About WOM

As the term "word of mouth" has entered widespread parlance, various misconceptions and fallacies have emerged about the concept and its functioning. Firms that rely on promotional campaigns and other tactics intended to leverage WOM often ignore or misinterpret the scientific evidence and fail to consider the limitations of a strategy, applicability to other business sectors or geographical regions, or future behavioral and attitudinal trends. A cursory reading of the WOM literature reveals several claims that do not conform to the growing body of empirical research on the topic. An examination of some of these misconceptions provides a context within which we can reconsider the role of satisfaction as a catalyst of WOM and address some additional considerations pertaining to the characteristics and consequences of WOM that were not discussed in the preceding chapter sections, such as the relative occurrence and impact of PWOM and NWOM, the extent to which people discuss their current brand or an unused brand, and whether PWOM and NWOM tend to be transmitted by the same or different people. Based on a review of the academic and mainstream literature, it is possible to identify four key misconceptions about WOM. These are described, in turn, below.

Misconception 1: WOM Is Always Driven by Satisfaction and Dissatisfaction

As mentioned in the "WOM Antecedents" section, it is widely assumed that customer satisfaction/dissatisfaction serves as a primary catalyst for WOM. Although research studies (e.g., Anderson, 1998; Herr, Kardes, & Kim, 1991) have indeed identified higher rates of WOM when satisfaction or dissatisfaction are at their highest levels, they do not support the contention that WOM is *always* (or *nearly always*) related to extreme satisfaction or dissatisfaction.

A closer analysis of the results of the relevant research studies reveals that when the satisfaction and dissatisfaction of the communicator and receiver are combined, the total only accounts for a relatively small percentage of overall WOM. In fact, research suggests that only a small part of WOM is driven primarily by customer satisfaction or dissatisfaction (East et al., 2007; cf. Heath, 1996). This is apparent if you take a closer look at the results of Anderson's study presented in Figure 4.1. The results, which take the form of a U-shaped distribution, clearly show that there is more WOM when satisfaction and dissatisfaction are at their highest levels (at the extremes of the distribution); however, we also see that WOM is still produced at about 80% of the maximum when people are neutral about an issue (i.e., around the midpoint of the distribution). Thus, it appears that satisfaction and dissatisfaction are relevant stimuli for the production of WOM, but that other factors also must prevail, particularly in situations where consumers are more or less neutral about the focal topic of discussion.

So what are the catalysts of WOM when people are not especially satisfied or dissatisfied about something in the marketplace? An answer to this question comes in part from an investigation in which consumers were asked to describe the circumstances surrounding the last time they received positive or negative advice about a service (see Table 4.2). Mangold, Miller, and Brockway (1999) found that the communicator's satisfaction or dissatisfaction accounted for only a small percentage of WOM instances (9%) reported by respondents. By contrast, "felt need" of the recipient (usually stimulated by an implicit or explicit request for information or advice) (50%) and "coincidental communication" (i.e., WOM arising out of a conversation) (18%) were revealed as more likely to provide the impetus for WOM. Also, WOM was found to arise following the receiver's comment related to a service (7%), an effort to make a joint decision (6%), and as a result of a marketing promotion (3%). Thus, customer satisfaction/dissatisfaction may serve as an underlying condition for the production of WOM but, at least according to Mangold et al.'s study on services, appears to be less important than other factors in prompting informal consumer conversations.

An interesting aspect of Mangold et al.'s results has to do with the catalysts that stimulate PWOM and NWOM. What is apparent in Table 4.2 is the high degree of similarity between the catalyst frequencies for both types of WOM, which statistically were found to be nearly perfectly correlated ($r = .96$). Although PWOM increases the likelihood of brand choice and NWOM decreases that likelihood, the research results suggest that there is not much of a difference in terms of the antecedents underlying positive and negative advice. Both types of WOM are constructive for consumer decision making.

Table 4.2 Focus on Research: Catalysts That Stimulate Word of Mouth (WOM)

WOM stimulus	Positive communication (%)	Negative communication (%)	Total (%)
Receiver's felt need (either implicit in the situation or made explicit by a request for advice)	54	47	50
Coincidental communication (when a conversation led to advice; e.g., a discussion of weekend plans led to a restaurant recommendation)	16	21	18
Communicator's dis/satisfaction (as judged by the receiver)	5	13	9
Receiver's comment about the effect of service (e.g., about the communicator's hair, which led the communicator to recommend a hairdresser)	9	4	7
Joint decision on service (e.g., which restaurant to go to)	6	6	6
Marketing organization's promotion (e.g., reference to a humorous ad prompts a comment about the firm's product)	2	5	3
Receiver's dissatisfaction/satisfaction	3	3	3
Another's comment about the effect of service	4	1	2
Media exposure (not marketing organization)	1	1	1
Unsolicited comment	1	0	1

Source: Adapted from Mangold, Miller, and Brockway (1999).

In order to determine the extent to which business professionals adhere to the belief concerning satisfaction and WOM (as well as the other misconceptions discussed below), I had 210 business students (94 university students and 116 advanced students enrolled in doctoral, advanced degree, or full-time MBA programs) and 207 business professionals complete a questionnaire intended to assess their acceptance of common misconceptions concerning WOM (Kimmel, 2009). Overall, the questionnaire responses revealed a relatively high degree of agreement with the belief that WOM is always related to the satisfaction or dissatisfaction of the person who transmits it, with 61.3% of respondents having agreed with that belief (including 25.1% who strongly agreed) as opposed to 27.3% who disagreed with it. A high degree of adherence (77.6%) to the (accurate) belief that consumers engage in more WOM if they are extremely satisfied or dissatisfied was apparent, with a majority of respondents either agreeing (32.8%) or strongly agreeing (53.8%); only 6.7% indicated disagreement with the belief. Overall, in contrast to extant research on the factors most likely to generate WOM, these findings suggest that a majority of the business respondents studied tend to associate WOM primarily with customer satisfaction and dissatisfaction.

Misconception 2: NWOM Is More Common Than PWOM

A frequent assertion among marketers is that the incidence of NWOM far exceeds that of PWOM. For example, in his book *The Secrets of Word-of-Mouth Marketing*, Silverman (2001, p. 134) claimed that "Most word of mouth, studies have shown, is negative." Similarly, Naylor and Kleiser (2000), upon finding that PWOM exceeded NWOM in their research, chose to title their paper "Negative Versus Positive Word of Mouth: An Exception to the Rule." Several research studies have indeed demonstrated the prevalence of negative WOM following unpleasant experiences in the consumer marketplace. One study revealed that up to 90% of disgruntled customers choose not to do business again with the offending company and, on average, each discussed their negative experience with at least nine other people. Further, 13% of the unhappy customers told more than thirty people (Whiteley & Hessan, 1996). In another widely cited study conducted during the late 1970s, the market research firm TARP (now e-Satisfy) surveyed 1,700 Coca-Cola customers who had complained or made an inquiry to the soft drink company for one reason or another. Customers who were satisfied with the way the company handled their complaint told an average of five other persons about their positive experiences. However, those who complained to Coca-Cola and were dissatisfied with the response told on average nine to ten people about their negative experiences, and in 12% of the cases, they told more than twenty other people. Further, 30% of the dissatisfied consumers said they stopped buying Coca-Cola products and another 45% said they would buy less in the future (TARP, 1981).

There are probably several reasons people would be induced to communicate negative information about a product, service, or company to others. Some of the motives linked to the spread of NWOM are similar to those that compel people to recommend marketplace offerings to others, such as to appear in the know, to express one's brand loyalty by attempting to steer people away from the favored brand's competitors, and an altruistic desire to assist those with whom one has close personal ties. Another compelling motive is that the spread of NWOM provides an outlet for venting any frustrations or anger one may experience in a consumer-related situation, such as rude treatment by a service representative or the purchase of a product that does not function as advertised (Halstead, 2002). By enabling consumers to express their dissatisfaction following an unpleasant experience, NWOM also provides a means for the consumer to exact a measure of revenge, especially when the grievance is not dealt with seriously by company representatives (see Box 4.6). Because the teller is likely to be perceived as having nothing to gain by talking poorly about a company, negative WOM can serve to reduce the credibility of a firm's advertising and have an influence on consumer attitudes and purchase intentions (Bone, 1995; Smith & Vogt, 1995).

The logic behind the assumption concerning the relative prevalence of PWOM and NWOM has led several authors to conclude that when satisfied and dissatisfied customers are compared, NWOM exceeds PWOM by a ratio of 2 or 3 to 1 (Hanna &

BOX 4.6 THIS COMPANY SUCKS!

In the Web 2.0 era, when consumers believe they have been seriously wronged or mistreated by a firm, they may not be content merely to share their negative experiences with a few close friends; instead, they may create a corporate complaint Web site to shout their grievances to the world. More familiarly known as "this company sucks" Web sites, this outlet provides a relatively quick and inexpensive means of exacting revenge, providing a forum for dissatisfied customers to vent their anger by fomenting negative communications about a company, warning other consumers to avoid the company at all costs, offering alternatives to the firm, and perhaps subjecting the company to ridicule. For example, one American consumer who was dissatisfied with the customer service he received after purchasing a defective coffeemaker from Starbucks established a Web site (www.starbucked.com) which is devoted to sharing disparaging information about the hugely successful chain of coffee shops. Visitors to the site are invited to e-mail descriptions of their own negative experiences involving poor customer service and to participate in a discussion board about Starbucks and other companies. The site also provides recommendations for noncorporate alternatives to Starbucks coffee shops.

Other examples of Web sites that exist to put the spotlight on what are perceived by current and potential customers to be poor or unfair corporate practices include aolsucks.org, paypalsucks.com, farmersinsurancegroupsucks.com, and anti-apple.com. Since 1997, links to 160 anti-Microsoft Web sites and nearly two dozen Usenet groups have been compiled as an MSBC Superlist (see www.msboycott.com/super). The Anti-Microsoft Webring (www.webring.com)

(cont.)

Box 4.6 (*Continued*)

also has emerged to provide a list of Web sites and resources that recommend alternatives to Microsoft Windows.

Starbucked.com welcome page.

As these examples illustrate, the Internet provides unhappy consumers with the ability to convey negative word of mouth (NWOM) almost immediately to a vast audience, and complaint sites can have an impact. For example, the creators of the pepsibloodbath.com Web site voluntarily closed itself down and declared victory after the Pepsi-Cola Company agreed to stop advertising at bullfights. The role of a ''this company sucks'' blog in moving Dell Computer to evolve its customer engagement strategy is discussed in Chapter 6.

According to one survey intended to assess consumer knowledge of and responses to corporate complaint Web sites, awareness among consumers is moderate; however, when consumers are aware of such sites, they are likely to visit them, especially when encouraged by friends and acquaintances (Bailey, 2004). Further, consumers who have a positive attitude toward complaining are more likely than others to actively participate in those sites.

Although the free speech regulations in many countries allow leeway for customers to air their corporate complaints online, there are certain ethical and legal boundaries that cannot be exceeded. For example, it generally is considered unfair practices for a competing firm to create a complaint site against another firm, especially when it is done under the false guise of a poorly treated customer (see Cisneros, 2000, for legal tips concerning complaint sites). What makes matters so troublesome for businesses is that it is exceedingly difficult to exercise influence or control over the negative WOM that is communicated online because of its informal nature and the wide varieties of forums through which it can be communicated. Nonetheless, it is abundantly clear that it is in the best interest of commercial enterprises to develop and apply mechanisms for managing this connected consumer environment.

Wosniak, 2001; Heskett, Sasser, Schlesinger, 1997), with the ratio varying according to category. However, as pointed out by East, Vanhuele, and Wright (2008), people may confuse the WOM produced by satisfied and dissatisfied customers with WOM in general. Because products that cause dissatisfaction in competitive markets are not likely to survive, most product experiences tend to be satisfactory for consumers. In other words, there just is not as much to complain about. This argument finds some support in a comprehensive review of satisfaction studies carried out by Peterson and Wilson (1992), who found that, on average, about 83% of American consumers were satisfied with their purchases, with the rest evenly divided between neutral and dissatisfied.

Following a series of more recent investigations, a picture has emerged that clearly challenges the traditional assumptions concerning the relative frequencies of PWOM and NWOM. In their systematic program of fifteen studies, East et al. (2007) reported a greater incidence of PWOM than NWOM, with an average ratio of 3:1. Further, the studies indicated that categories with high levels of NWOM also tend to have high levels of PWOM. These findings are consistent with independent studies on volume of positive and negative advice conducted by Chevalier and Mayzlin (2006) (online consumer book reviews), Godes and Mayzlin (2004) (online comments about TV shows), Naylor and Kleiser (2000) (WOM about health and fitness resorts), Holmes and Lett (1977) (coffee), and Swan and Oliver (1989) (car dealerships). Similarly, findings obtained via the Keller Fay Group's "TalkTrack" methodology, which has consumer respondents provide detailed reports on marketing-relevant conversations they engaged in during the prior day (see Chapter 5), revealed that nearly two-thirds (62%) of brand-related discussions portray products favorably, as opposed to less than 10% that feature products negatively—a 6:1 ratio in favor of PWOM (Siegel, 2006). Overall, PWOM appears to be much more common than NWOM, to a large extent because most consumers tend to be satisfied with their purchases and thus have more opportunities to give PWOM (Mittal & Lassar 1998). People no doubt lack negative examples that they could talk about. For example, you would probably recommend your current dentist, because if you continue to see him or her it is likely that you are satisfied with the treatment provided. Most people would simply not know a dentist that they would recommend against, unless they recently switched from one who was particularly unsatisfying. On average, a greater percentage of WOM instances is likely to concern the consumer's main brand, as opposed to a never-owned or previously owned brand, and PWOM is more frequent for the main brand. Research has shown that consumers rarely recommend a previously owned or never-owned brand, but often advise against them (East et al. 2007; Wangenheim 2005).

In my questionnaire study of business professionals and business students, the results were mixed with regard to adherence to the misconception concerning the relative proportions of PWOM and NWOM. Responses were approximately normally distributed with regard to the belief that NWOM is more common than PWOM; overall, however, nearly half (45.2%) of the respondents agreed with that belief as opposed to 30.6% who disagreed with it. The results revealed a low level of agreement for the assertion that most WOM pertains to non-owned brands, rather than the brand used by the consumer, with only 20.8% of the respondents agreeing. Thus, although there was a moderate degree of belief in the misconception that NWOM is more prevalent than PWOM, it appears that many respondents were aware that a greater proportion of interpersonal discussions about marketplace offerings pertains to currently owned brands, and that informal comments about those brands are more likely to be positive than negative.

With the emergence of the Internet in recent years, the PWOM versus NWOM prevalence issue has been further muddled. Alluding to the incidental/intimate WOM distinction described above, Northeastern University professor Walter Carl (2006a) suggested that the findings showing that PWOM exceeds NWOM may be limited to off-line personal conversations (i.e., intimate WOM), and that the relative frequencies might be reversed when WOM occurs online among persons who are not personally known to each other (i.e., incidental WOM). The argument is that online consumer discussions about product and service experiences are more apt to be negative than positive, such as when Internet users conduct searches concerning purchase decisions. There is some evidence suggesting this to be the case for certain higher involvement product categories, such as electronic goods and automobiles, but not for items like books and TV shows. According to one estimate, dissatisfied customers for electronic products were found to be nearly four times more likely than satisfied customers to share their story with online chat groups (cf. Rosen, 2002). As Rosen and others have pointed out, the Internet provides unhappy consumers with the ability to convey negative WOM almost immediately to an incredibly vast audience, and this can be done anonymously. Contrast this with the fact that many companies provide only limited opportunities for consumers to air their complaints or engage with company representatives; additionally, there is evidence that only a minority of shoppers who experience a problem with a retailer actually choose to contact the company directly (Knowledge@Wharton, 2006).

Whether or not the prevalence of NWOM is limited to online searches remains to be further examined; however, it probably is likely that when searching for information about a purchase online, negative evaluations can be extremely helpful. As brands have proliferated in most categories in recent decades, there has been a corresponding convergence in quality. This is not to say that there are no bad brands in the market-place, but that the lower quality brands are less bad than in the past. With so many high quality brands to select from, purchase decisions often come down to what is sometimes referred to as "the search for negative information." In other words, a single negative consumer evaluation online may be enough to eliminate the brand from further consideration, thereby narrowing the list of choices for the shopper. Evidence for this possibility was obtained in Chevalier and Mayzlin's study of the effect of consumer reviews (2006) for books on the Amazon.com and Barnesandnoble.com Web sites, where reviews were found to be overwhelmingly positive at both sites. Overall, however, the effect of one-star reviews was found to have a greater impact on sales than five-star reviews. As Carl (2006a) speculates, from the complainer's point of view, the Internet provides a forum where angry customers can air their grievances to a receptive and global audience and thus receive a validation of their negative experience—a kind of "me-too" phenomenon that is less likely to occur in personal (off-line) interactions. These are important considerations from the perspective of firms in their attempts to track ongoing buzz about their offerings. If it does turn out that there is a difference in relative prevalence of PWOM and NWOM depending on whether the WOM is intimate or incidental, then monitoring only online or off-line WOM would provide a skewed picture of the evaluative nature of what consumers in general are discussing.

Misconception 3: NWOM Has a Greater Impact on Consumer Choice Than PWOM

In addition to considerations regarding the prevalence of PWOM and NWOM is the issue of their relative impact on consumer behavior. Another widely held belief about WOM is that NWOM from dissatisfied customers has a much stronger effect on recipients than PWOM received from satisfied customers. Assael's assertion (1995, p. 639) that "negative word of mouth tends to be more powerful than positive information" is typical of this belief. There does appear to be some research support for this claim; however, there are certain considerations that limit the applicability of the experimental results to naturalistic situations in which WOM about familiar brands occurs, and the greater influence of NWOM does not appear to extend to shifts in brand purchase probability, except in certain specified circumstances (East et al., 2008). It is logical to assume that the greater rarity of negative information increases its usefulness or value of its diagnostic information (Feldman & Lynch, 1988; Lynch, Marmorstein, & Weigold, 1988) and may draw more attention because its infrequency makes NWOM instances more surprising (Laczniak, DeCarlo, & Ramaswami, 2001; Mizerksi, 1982). Nonetheless, psychological research in support of these contentions has predominantly focused on the impact of advice on recipients' attitudes, rather than the more appropriate consumer measure of change in purchase probability (which operationalizes the impact of WOM on choice).

In perhaps the most extensive analysis to date, using various measures and covering a large number of categories, East et al. (2008, p. 215) found that for familiar brands, "the impact of PWOM is generally greater than NWOM" on brand purchase probability.

Their results revealed that the pre-WOM probability of purchase typically falls below the .50 level, which means that PWOM has more latitude in increasing purchase probability than NWOM stands to decrease it. Additionally, the impact of WOM was found to be related to whether the WOM pertained to the recipient's preferred brand. Consistent with the latter finding, recipients were found to resist NWOM on brands they are likely to choose, and resist PWOM on brands they are unlikely to choose. Similarly, other studies have found evidence of a so-called reactance effect, whereby people become more committed to a favored brand in the face of negative advice (Fitzsimons & Lehmann, 2004; Wilson & Peterson, 1989). In sum, the question of the relative impact of PWOM and NWOM on consumer behavior is complex and depends on a variety of mediating factors; however, the unqualified assumption that NWOM has greater impact than PWOM cannot be supported.

The results of my WOM questionnaire study revealed a high level of agreement with the assumption concerning the relative impact of NWOM and PWOM on choice, with 76.3% of the respondents agreeing that NWOM has a greater impact (including 23.7% strongly agreeing), as opposed to 13.5% indicating disagreement. Nonetheless, when asked to consider the impact of the last instance of received WOM that affected their brand choice decision, the results presented a quite different picture. A majority of respondents reported that *both* NWOM and PWOM had an impact on their brand decision making. A total of 83.8% of respondents were in agreement that the last instance of received PWOM affected their brand choice decision and 68.6% agreed that the last instance of received NWOM affected their decision. Responses to the items about WOM impact statements were found to be related, such that persons who reported that PWOM had an impact on their brand choice decisions were apt to report that NWOM influenced their choices as well.

The tendency for a higher percentage of participants to attest to the influence of PWOM when compared with NWOM could be attributed in part to the greater frequency and salience of PWOM instances. This possibility is given credence when one considers the product/service category that served as the focus of the last instance of received PWOM and NWOM. Overall, nearly twice as many people were unable to recall the specific category pertaining to the NWOM instance than those who could not recall the category linked to the PWOM instance. In general, it may be that PWOM instances are easier to recall because they pertain to the respondents' main brand, and people are less apt to recall negative examples because they are less frequent.

With regard to the specific categories involved in the last instance of received WOM, the results revealed that WOM was most likely to have an impact on brand choices related to technology devices, dining (e.g., restaurant, cafe), clothing, services (e.g., airline, tour operators, hotels, hairdressers, banks), and entertainment (e.g., cinema, music, club) for both PWOM and NWOM, consistent with previous research (e.g., East et al., 2007; Keller & Fay, 2006) (see Table 4.3).

Table 4.3 Categories Influenced by Positive Word of Mouth (PWOM) and Negative Word of Mouth (NWOM) in the Study of Business Professionals and Business Students

Category	PWOM[a]		NWOM[b]	
	Frequency	Percentage	Frequency	Percentage
Technology devices	97	28.4	70	25.6
Dining	84	24.6	54	19.8
Clothing	52	15.2	44	16.1
Services	47	13.8	40	14.7
Entertainment	31	9.1	37	13.6
Food and beverages	14	4.1	16	5.9
Retailer	15	4.4	12	4.4
Luxury goods	1	0.3	0	0.0

[a] $N = 341$

[b] $N = 273$

Source: From Kimmel (2009).

Misconception 4: PWOM and NWOM Typically Are Transmitted by Different People

Marketers are well aware that some consumers are harder to please than others; thus, it is logical to assume that typically dissatisfied consumers tend to be more critical of products and services in their advice to others than consumers who are easier to please and more commonly satisfied. However, the belief that satisfied customers always produce PWOM and dissatisfied customers always produce NWOM appears to be unfounded (e.g., Mangold et al., 1999). Under certain conditions, people may communicate both positive and negative advice about the same product or service to different persons, depending upon the characteristics of the recipients. For example, an urban vacation destination may be recommended for someone who appreciates city life, but advised against for a person who prefers pastoral getaways. Research on whether PWOM and NWOM come from different groups of people suggests the contrary: in ten of fifteen studies across a broad range of categories, significant correlations were obtained between PWOM and NWOM at the individual level (East et al. 2007). Overall, it was found that consumers who advised against a brand are 3.5 times more likely to also recommend a brand (although not necessarily the same one).

The results of my own research revealed little agreement with the belief that different persons are involved in the transmission of PWOM and NWOM. Slightly more than half (51.2%) of the respondents agreed that most of the people who transmit NWOM are generally the same people who transmit PWOM, compared with 27.5% who disagreed with that belief. These results reflect an apparently accurate understanding, consistent with extant research, that the same consumers may convey both types of WOM according to the nature of the situation, category, and participants involved in the exchange.

Conclusion

With so much interest and attention devoted to WOM in the contemporary marketing environment, and with a rapidly growing number of articles and books appearing on the topic, it perhaps goes without saying that one should cast a critical eye on many of the assertions about the nature and dynamics of WOM that have entered mainstream coverage. As discussions about this nontraditional marketing concept proliferate in the popular media and trade literature, it is not surprising that its power as a potential marketing application is often oversold and assertions about its antecedents, consequences, and dynamics often simplified or misstated. As Andrea Wojnicki (2006) noted in an article she posted on the Word of Mouth Marketing Association (WOMMA) Web site in reference to inaccurate claims about the prevalence of PWOM and NWOM, "…popular press and trade articles have generalized and exaggerated this claim about the propensity for dissatisfied consumers to talk, and vaguely credit the statistics to 'research has shown.'"

Unfortunately, Wojnicki's point seems to apply to many other claims about WOM as well. If, as my research appears to demonstrate, business professionals tend to accept some common misconceptions about WOM, then we might conjecture that their efforts at launching WOM and buzz marketing campaigns may be based, at least in part, on a tenuous foundation. For example, without negating the potentially important impact that customer satisfaction can have in generating positive buzz that can attract significant numbers of new customers to a brand, when WOM is only considered in relation to satisfaction/dissatisfaction, a large part of the overall WOM produced in everyday personal conversations is likely to be missed. As a result, marketing practitioners will stand to lose the opportunity to leverage WOM among consumers who frequently talk about products, services, and brands but who are neither satisfied nor dissatisfied with those offerings. Thus, prior to applying word of mouth marketing (WOMM) techniques, it is in the best interest of practitioners to first consider the validity of some of their assumptions about how WOM actually works in practice (e.g., by remaining attentive to published research on the topic).

Although marketers and researchers have unraveled much of the mystery concerning this amorphous form of C-to-C communication, there remains much to be learned about WOM. The phrase "the power of WOM" clearly has a high degree of legitimacy, but it is not the be-all and end-all of the marketing process; rather, WOM marketing efforts should be seen as an important component of the overall marketing arsenal. Numerous practical applications have been tried and tested in recent years to leverage WOM among consumer targets, and our consideration of these efforts serves as the focus for Part II of this book.

PART II

Connected Marketing: Measurement, Approaches, and Techniques

5 Word of Mouth and Social Media Research and Measurement

According to a 2008 report issued by the Society for New Communications Research (SNCR), an increasing number of companies are adopting social media as a key element of their marketing communications strategy, but are struggling to find effective measuring systems, or so-called "metrics" to evaluate them. The report, *New Media, New Influencers, and Implications for the Public Relations Profession*, was based on a survey of nearly 300 advertising, marketing, public relations, and corporate communications professionals ("Social Media Marketing," 2008). Another study, jointly sponsored by Osterman Research and BoldMouth.com, reported that 51.2% of the firms that utilize word of mouth marketing (WOMM) are unable to track the performance of their marketing efforts and 67.4% lack faith in the data they gather for measuring WOM performance in terms of value or meaningfulness ("Study Reveals," 2006). Only 28.6% of the firms studied were found to have a WOMM plan in place, and lack of metrics to evaluate effectiveness was identified as the single largest reason (cited by 36.8% of the 112 WOMM respondents) for not establishing a formal WOMM plan. Not surprisingly, the results of such studies have prompted a growing number of marketing experts to conclude that marketers lack the measures necessary for launching WOM and other connected marketing campaigns.

Perhaps we should not be surprised that companies have struggled with the measurement of C-to-C communication and influence. Marketing buzz is as amorphous as the air we breathe. From a purely scientific perspective, how can it be determined what prompts people to talk about firms and their marketplace offerings, the social networks pathways that information tends to follow, and the consequences of C-to-C communication? From a practical perspective, how does one monitor and dissect the ongoing chatter that takes place in consumer contexts? How can the impact of WOMM campaigns be evaluated? According to some, most products, services, brands, and companies simply are not worth talking about, and so they are not. Thus, another question becomes one of deciphering what is important to measure in the first place; that is, what is truly meaningful and substantive from a marketing point of view, and what are the basic units of analysis?

The primary objective of this chapter is to consider some of the methodologies borrowed from a diverse array of disciplines that have been applied to the measurement of WOM and related concepts, as well as some innovative approaches that are currently being honed by connected marketing researchers and practitioners. Specifically, we will examine how WOM and C-to-C influence can be studied and tracked; measures for evaluating the impact of C-to-C influence, and some applications of WOM research (e.g., to identify influentials, to evaluate the merit of the widely used net promoter score (NPS), and to evaluate the utility of text mining). It is important in assessing these approaches to consider both their strengths and weaknesses, in addition to ways they can be applied and integrated as aspects of fledgling or ongoing marketing campaigns.

WOM Research Terminology

Perhaps a good starting point prior to surveying research methodologies is to consider some accepted terminology for WOM measurement. Before 2005, despite the already vast interest in WOM, there did not exist a common terminology for the basic units or "objects" of WOM that could be used to formulate a measurement framework. This was finally accomplished during the July 2005 Word of Mouth Marketing Association's (WOMMA) first Metrics Conference, which focused in part on the introduction of WOM metrics terminology. The objectives of the conference were threefold: (*a*) develop a common WOM terminology, (*b*) determine methods for measuring and tracking WOM, and (*c*) study how to integrate WOM with other forms of marketing media. The results of this effort are summarized in the WOMMA (2005) document, *WOMMA Terminology Framework*. In that document, WOM is defined as "the act of a consumer creating and/or distributing marketing-relevant information to another consumer." A *WOM episode* represents "a single occurrence of word-of-mouth communication," and is comprised of five *objects*:

- *Participants—creator, sender, receiver*: Individuals whose actions make up a WOM episode, and who may serve multiple roles. Participants can be described in terms of *propensity* (likelihood to take an action), *demographics* (age, locations, etc.), *credibility* (ability to influence the behavior or opinion of others), and *reach* (a consumer's potential audience size).
- *Action*—What participants do to create, pass along, or respond to a WOM-Unit. Actions are described in terms of *velocity* (the speed at which a WOMUnit moves), *distribution spread* (the number of receivers contacted by a sender), and *source diversity* (the number of different senders that transmit a WOM-Unit to a receiver).

- *WOMUnit*—A single unit of marketing-relevant information shared by a consumer. As the basic unit of a WOM episode, WOMUnits can be described according to *topicality* (degree that the marketing message is contained in the unit), *timeliness* (whether the unit reaches the receiver in time to be relevant to a campaign), *polarity* (whether the message content is positive or negative), *clarity* (whether the message is understood by the receiver), and *depth* (the characteristics of the unit that increase persuasiveness).

- *Venue*—The medium or physical location where the communication takes place. This WOM object is described in terms of *population* (total possible audience for a WOMUnit in a venue), *audience* (number of persons who actually receive the WOMUnit), and *rules* (whether a WOMUnit complies with policies set by a venue).

- *Outcomes*—The actions that are taken by a participant on a WOMUnit, consisting of five types: *(a) Consumptions* (the receiver directly consumes the WOMUnit, but takes no further action); *(b) Inquiries* (the receiver seeks more information after consuming the WOMUnit); *(c) Conversions* (the receiver completes a desired action after consuming the WOMUnit); *(d) Relays* (the receiver redistributes the WOMUnit); and *(e) Re-creations* (the receiver creates a new WOMUnit after consuming the WOMUnit).

The various WOM components are summarized in Table 5.1. The table illustrates the events that occur in a WOM episode, in the sense that a Participant takes an Action on a received WOMUnit within a specified Venue, resulting in some measurable Outcome(s). Several sample usages of the framework are provided in the WOMMA (2005) document; an example pertaining to an actual product launch appears in Box 5.1.

Table 5.1 WOMMA Terminology Framework

WOM episode	Who	How	What	Where	Result
Objects ⟶	Participant	Action	WOMUnit	Venue	Outcome
Qualities ⟶	Propensity Demographics Credibility Reach	Velocity Distribution spread Source diversity	Topicality Timeliness Polarity Clarity Depth	Population Audience Rules	

Notes: This chart illustrates what happens during a *WOM episode*.

A *Participant* takes an *Action* on a *WOMUnit* in a *Venue*, resulting in an *Outcome*. Each of these objects can be further described by several *Qualities*.

Source: WOMMA (2005).

BOX 5.1 FOCUS ON APPLICATION: BREWTOPIA AND THE WOMMA TERMINOLOGY FRAMEWORK

As an application of the WOMMA terminology framework (see Table 5.1), consider the 13-week viral marketing campaign that was launched in 2002 by the Australian start-up beer company Brewtopia (Mulhall, 2006). The objectives of the campaign were to generate demand for a custom-built boutique beer among consumers who were given the opportunity to vote on each aspect of the beer development and marketing. The firm's founder, Liam Mulhall, and his staff served as both creators and senders (i.e., participants serving multiple roles) of a viral e-mail (the WOMUnit) that was distributed to 140 of their close friends and family (the receivers). The message content invited recipients to register as members of a new beer Web site in exchange for the opportunity to vote on a variety of choices related to Brewtopia's as-yet nonexistent benchmark beer—its name, style and taste of the beer, logo, type of bottle and packaging, pricing, where it would be sold, and so on. If the company succeeded with the launch, participants would receive a single share of stock for each vote they cast, carton of beer they purchased, and registered friend they referred.

With this description in mind, we can say that credibility (a characteristic of the participants) was very high because the receivers of the viral e-mail knew the senders personally. The message had high Topicality for both the senders (whose product development depended on receivers' responses) and for the receivers (who were empowered by the opportunity to participate in the product creation and launch and obtain part stock ownership). The Venue consisted of the online medium (e-mail), with the initial campaign limited to a relatively small audience of specifically identified recipients. We can conclude that the Propensity for the e-mail recipients to Relay (another possible outcome) the e-mail message to others was low because there was no encouragement for them to redistribute the WOMUnit. Each registration and subsequent vote cast by a receiver represented Conversion outcomes.

Although the campaign was limited in scope, the e-mail medium enabled the senders to imbue the WOMUnit with a high degree of Timeliness. For example, on two occasions in which the voters' decisions could not be honored due to unforeseen expenses, the company quickly e-mailed a personal apology and honest explanation. Decisions regarding the product and its marketing were enacted immediately after votes were cast, and the details, along with a picture of the product, were immediately made known to receivers. All registered members then were invited to a launch party in Sydney, where they could purchase the beer via mail order directly from Brewtopia.

It should be noted that Brewtopia's prelaunch viral campaign was followed up by postlaunch actions in the form of a variety of sales growth campaigns, which included a focus on feedback from influentials, the employment of third parties to accelerate the buzz (tactics were used to stimulate press coverage), and continued incentives to encourage the spread of WOM. These marketing activities were essential to maintain and exploit the initial consumer excitement for the product, Blowfly Beer. Although the company is still in the process of developing additional metrics to assess the impact of its connected marketing efforts, the WOMMA framework is helpful in discerning the main components of the viral campaign that effectively put the successful, customized brewing company on the beverage industry map.

WOM Research: Traditional Scientific Approaches

In their WOM literature survey that led to the development of their multistage viral marketing model, De Bruyn and Lilien (2008) concluded that there remains a great deal of uncertainty about how WOM works. In their view, this uncertainty can be attributed to four key methodological factors: (*a*) prior research has largely focused on WOM communications that have successfully influenced the decision maker; (*b*) studies have emphasized WOM situations in which recipients were actively seeking information and already interested in the product category; (*c*) data typically are collected retrospectively, sometimes long after the WOM conversations have taken place; and (*d*) WOM surveys tend to emphasize buying behavior, while ignoring possible effects on intermediate stages of consumer decision making. A fifth factor can be added to this list, drawing from our discussion in Chapter 4, that much of research has only studied the relatively small proportion of WOM that is linked to satisfaction and dissatisfaction. These observations are useful in reminding us that the scope of WOM research should not be overly limited. For example, situations in which WOM recommendations fall on deaf ears and fail to have an impact on recipients can prove insightful in teasing out the intricacies of the C-to-C influence process, and are just as relevant for study as cases of successful WOM campaigns.

It has been suggested that one reason that WOM is so difficult to observe and its consequences so problematic to monitor is that the occurrence of WOM is too infrequent, whereas its consequences may be delayed (East & Lomax, 2007). Even though research has suggested that consumer conversations about product categories and brands are common—recall the finding that consumers discuss an average of twelve brands per day—it would be difficult to predict when those conversations would be likely to occur and how to track them via direct observation. Thus, the challenges for WOM researchers are formidable. However, despite their potential methodological limitations, several research approaches can be utilized to shed light on C-to-C influence. The survey below begins with a focus on research methods commonly used in the behavioral and social sciences. Following that discussion, we will turn our attention to some emerging approaches developed by marketing practitioners.

Behavioral Observations

In the most straightforward sense, occurrences of WOM can be assessed in terms of content and estimated frequency simply by monitoring C-to-C conversations as they occur in everyday situations. This can be done either by listening in on consumer discussions in public places, such as cafés, parks, or shopping malls, for any references to products, services, and brands. The most practical application of this approach is to observe face-to-face interactions, although overheard mobile phone conversations—albeit only half of those conversations—might be considered as well. Behavioral monitoring also can be carried out online, an approach that is considered in the "Text Mining" section below.

In scientific jargon, this activity is more apt to be referred to as *simple observation*, a research approach that generally has as its goal the careful mapping out (i.e., the description) of what happens behaviorally. As a means of describing behavioral occurrences, simple observation may be casual or systematic in nature. In casual observation, the researcher conducts the observations without prearranged categories or a formal coding or scoring system. For example, the researcher may simply choose to observe people in a particular setting and note anything that occurs of interest. This is the research approach that most closely approximates everyday, informal people watching.

Systematic observations consist of a more formalized approach to observation and measurement, necessitating that the researcher develop and employ a scoring system with a set of prearranged categories. Typically, this approach requires some sort of a checklist in which information is recorded or tabulated under appropriate headings, such as the evaluative nature of the WOMUnit (positive, negative, neutral), the product/service categories that comprise the focus of the WOM (clothing, food, technology products, airline, etc.), and the nature of the antecedent that prompted the comment (e.g., apparent satisfaction/dissatisfaction, receiver's apparent need). Categories descriptive of the participants (number of persons involved in the discussion, their gender, estimated age range) and venue (i.e., location where the conversation took place) also should be included.

One can find a number of examples of conversation studies in the behavioral science literature, dating back to H. T. Moore's early investigation (1922) of sex differences in conversation. Moore was convinced that there was a clear mental differentiation between men and women, and so he sought to obtain evidence of this by analyzing the content of their "easy conversations." For several weeks, Moore walked along a twenty-two-block area in midtown Manhattan during the early evening hours and jotted down every bit of audible conversation he could overhear. He eventually recorded 174 conversation fragments, which were coded in terms of the gender of the speaker and whether the participants in the conversation were of the same or mixed sex. Moore reported some interesting gender differences, such as the finding that female conversations included many more references to the opposite sex than did male conversations, and his study triggered a number of other hidden-observer language studies (see Box 5.2).

Although the observational approach can be a useful means for shedding light on the nature of WOM, its limitations should be apparent. There is the aforementioned problem concerning the frequency of WOM and the high degree of unpredictability as to when it is likely to occur. When WOM is observed, without further questioning of the persons involved in the exchange, a true picture of the catalysts that prompted it is likely to remain fuzzy. Nonetheless, a short interview with willing volunteers immediately following the observation would overcome the frequent problem in WOM research concerning the inherent fallibility of memory when consumers are asked to recall discussions that took place in the recent past. Another problem with this approach has to do with the selection of consumer exchanges—which likely will be limited due to time and cost issues—in terms of nature of participants and venues. Questions of generalizability to other types of consumers, locations, and situations are inevitable.

BOX 5.2 FOCUS ON RESEARCH: CONVERSATION-SAMPLING RESEARCH IN THE BEHAVIORAL SCIENCES

Behavioral scientists have long recognized the potential for the understanding of language and individual differences that comes from analyzing samples of naturally occurring speech. Around the turn of the twentieth century, the French sociologist Gabriel de Tarde (1901) recommended that conversation analysis could serve as a useful technique for studying cross-cultural and social-class differences, and since H. T. Moore's nonreactive conversation study two decades later (see text) researchers have been intrigued by the possibilities of this form of naturalistic research.

Moore's observations were restricted to a small area of New York City and thus the conversation fragments he obtained can be questioned in terms of the representativeness of the participants and their conversations. Other researchers have attempted to overcome such sampling rigidity by obtaining samples of conversation from a wider variety of places and situations. For example, Landis and Burtt (1924) unobtrusively sampled conversations in a broad range of settings, including railroad stations, campuses, parties, department stores, restaurants, theater and hotel lobbies, and streets in both residential and commercial areas. Cameron (1969) had his students listen in on the conversations of more than 3,000 persons in different settings to investigate their usage of profanity. Among those most likely to use profane words were factory and construction workers and college students; secretaries tended to swear less often than people in other professions. Carlson, Cook, and Stromberg (1936) studied sex differences in lobby conversations overheard during the intermissions of Minnesota symphony concerts. The fact that Carlson et al.'s subjects were observed in a setting in which they nearly had to shout to be heard reduced the potential for whispered speech (which may contain significantly different speech content).

Several conversation-sampling studies have been restricted to university campuses, with trained students serving as unobtrusive observers. Stoke and West (1931) studied undergraduate college students' random "bull sessions" held at night in campus residence halls. In a more recent analysis of sex differences in gossip, Levin and Arluke (1985) had students at Northeastern University eavesdrop on the conversations of other students in the campus student union. For each instance of overheard gossip (defined as small talk about other persons), the student observers recorded the gender of the gossipers, and the tone (positive or negative) and focus (i.e., who and what the gossip was about) of the gossip fragments. Levin and Arluke's analysis revealed that the two genders were equally positive and negative in tone, with females devoting only a slightly higher proportion of their conversations to gossip about a third party. The most interesting finding, however, was in content differences: female students were most likely to gossip about close friends, relatives, and their coursework (teachers and classmates), whereas male gossips were most likely to discuss celebrities and distant acquaintances.

As is typically the case in such observations of public behavior, Levin and Arluke's gossip study was carried out as a systematic observation. The student-observers were armed with a coding sheet that simply required them to check appropriate categories for describing the nature of the overheard gossip fragments. The observers did not record verbatim the actual content of what was said and the identities of the gossipers never were revealed.

Finally, there are ethical issues involving the invasion of privacy that are associated with observing personal exchanges between persons without their awareness.

Simple observations of public behavior typically are innocuous and rarely raise ethical problems. It generally is agreed that such behavioral observations are not much different than the sort of informal people watching that regularly occurs in public places where people eat, drink, meet with friends, shop, and so on. The observations are not likely to present risks to the participants, do not infringe upon their rights, and the data are recorded anonymously and in aggregate form. In such settings, people come to expect that they may at times be subject to the roving eyes and ears of others, so the research observations can be said to fall within the range of experiences of everyday life. However, in some situations, simple observations may be viewed as more invasive and, as a result, more problematic from an ethical point of view. It is one thing to observe common nonverbal behavior (e.g., gestures, postures, seating arrangements) in public settings, but another to listen in to the conversations of strangers. Most of us, of course, frequently engage in "people listening" in addition to simply watching people; in fact, with the proliferation of portable phones, we often do not have a choice whether to listen. However, unlike researchers, casual listeners are not apt to take notes or keep careful records of that which they overhear.

In evaluating the propriety of conversation research in terms of invasions of subjects' privacy and other ethical concerns, one must bear in mind that each of the cases described in Box 5.2 took place in public settings where the participants were aware that what they were saying could have been overheard by strangers in relatively close proximity. We might assume that when people have something very private and personal to discuss, they either choose a more isolated setting for their conversation or else lower their voices so that they cannot be overheard. Thus, most observation studies of this type can be justified on ethical grounds by the public (and anonymous) nature of the observations, and by the corresponding fact that the risks posed (in this case, having information of a private nature revealed to others) are no greater than those one encounters in daily experience (Kimmel, 2007).

Netnography: Text Mining on the Internet

In recent years, Internet chat groups, bulletin boards, user groups, and listservs have been studied through the emerging methodology of *netnography*, a research approach derived from ethnography (i.e., "ethnography on the Internet"), with the potential to provide researchers with a rich source of qualitative information about online communities (Kozinets, 1998). Netnography uses information that is publicly available from Internet forums to identify and understand the needs and decision influences of relevant online groups. This approach often utilizes a methodology known as *text mining*, which involves the extraction of information and heretofore unknown facts, patterns, and relationships from natural written language sources (Hearst, 2003). Consumer-generated online content offers an especially rich source of insight, and can be assessed at minimal costs (Godes & Mayzlin, 2004). The benefits of mining consumer online content (e.g., in the form of grievances, recommendations, opinions, desires, and expectations that accumulate on blogs, wikis, social networking sites, and folksonomies) can be considerable. For example, a text-mining analysis of teen fashion blogs might reveal that 80% of the bloggers who recommend shoes also discuss fashion magazines. Online opinions can be mined for identifying product features (so-called "opinion features") that have been commented on by customers and opinion statements can be analyzed to compare the relative proportions of positive and negative comments (see Box 5.3).

BOX 5.3 FOCUS ON RESEARCH: TEXT MINING ON THE INTERNET

To illustrate how text mining can be conducted for marketing purposes, consider the following example suggested by Bing Liu, author of *Web Data Mining* (Springer, 2007). To gain insight into consumer reactions toward various brands, customer reviews posted on a Web site like amazon.com can be quite informative. An example of a favorable review posted for a particular digital camera may look something like this:

GREAT Camera. June 3, 2004
Reviewer: jprice174 from Atlanta, GA

I did a lot of research last year before I bought this camera. . . . It kinda hurt to leave behind my beloved Nikon 35mm SLR, but I was going to Italy, and I needed something smaller and digital.

The pictures coming out of this camera are amazing. The 'auto' feature takes great pictures most of the time. And with digital, you're not wasting film if the picture doesn't come out. . . .

A text mining analysis of this and other reviews posted for the same product might then be carried out to summarize the positive and negative evaluations of the product's different features (along with the corresponding number of comments for each), from the perspective of customers.

SUMMARY

Feature 1: Picture quality

Positive: 12

- The pictures coming out of this camera are amazing.
- Overall this is a good camera with a really good picture quality.
- [etc.]

Negative: 2

- The pictures come out hazy if your hands shake even for a moment during the entire process of taking a picture.
- Focusing on a display rack about twenty feet away in a brightly lit room during daytime, picture produced by this camera were blurry and in a shade of orange.

Feature 2: Battery life

Once the text mining is completed in this fashion, a following step might be to graphically compare the overall results for competing brands. This allows a ready visual comparison for determining the relative strengths and weaknesses of competing brands.

(*cont.*)

Box 5.3 (*Continued*)

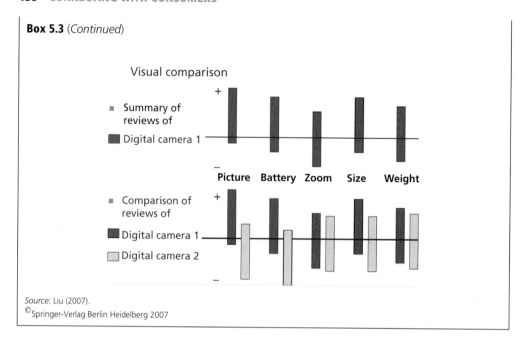

Source: Liu (2007).
©Springer-Verlag Berlin Heidelberg 2007

Online content has been exploited for investigative purposes by researchers in such fields as sociology, cultural studies, and consumer research and is likely to serve as a focus of research for many years to come. For example, netnography has been used by marketing researchers to obtain information on the symbolism, meanings, and consumption patterns of consumer groups. One type of online consumer group that has been the focus of growing interest is the brand community, which I described in previous chapters as a non-geographically bound collective of brand admirers. In recent years, brand communities have evolved for such products as motor vehicles (e.g., Saab, Jeep, Harley-Davidson), TV programs and films (e.g., *Star Trek, Star Wars*), beverages (e.g., Pepsi-Cola, Starbucks), and toys (e.g., Barbie). The Internet has been integral in the development of brand communities, largely because it facilitates the means by which community members—who typically have never met—can communicate and develop strong connections to one another. Thus, the Internet has proven to be an ideal milieu for researchers to study the brand community phenomenon.

In their studies of online brand community exchanges, Muñiz and O'Guinn (2005) have found that members possess very well-developed ideas about what the brand to which they are committed means (i.e., its true essence) and how it should be evolved by the company that owns it. These ideas, combined with members' passionate commitment, educe especially strong opinions about marketing efforts and other public activity involving the brand, such as advertising campaigns and press reports, much of which tends to be interpreted collectively by the community. Thus, when an ad's message or execution is at odds with members' conceptualization of the brand, the online discussion is likely to reflect a strong displeasure within the community, as well as an effort to defend their conceptualization of the brand or else create a new one more in line with the community's ideals. Consider the following examples of some comments from online forums following ad campaigns that ran against the brand concept possessed by committed adherents:

> "[These ads]" stink outloud. Obviously, they reflect VWoA's [Volkswagen of America] attempt to take their cars upmarket, and in the process have lost any of the flair and humor which has been a trademark of their ads for years. I personally think it is an extension of how VW has lost its way and is going to end up alienating the very people they need to touch to buy their cars.

> They've been running a 'stealth' [GM Pontiac] Vibe commercial in central Indiana...the voice-over goes on about a great financing or leasing deal on a Grand Am! No actual mention of the Vibe models, features, or financing. What the h-e-l-l is GM thinking?

These representative comments reflect the belief of the brand adherents who posted them that a manufacturer has taken the wrong direction in promoting and developing its brand's meaning. The comments typically are communally explored and debated by community members, current brand users, and prospective users (Muñiz & O'Guinn, 2005), and this content also can be content analyzed according to netnography methodologies (see Beckmann & Langer, 2005). Rich content also tends to appear online when a company engages in a marketing activity that is consistent with the meaning of the brand as understood by the community. The company's actions (e.g., a new launch or a revitalized ad campaign) are apt to be embraced and celebrated online, and they may be incorporated into consumer brand stories and narratives as well as posted on members' personal Web sites.

One intriguing new development for online research is the emergence of *market research online communities* (MROC), targeted groups of consumers who are brought together online to participate in research activities over an extended period of time (Fitzgerald, 2009; Li & Bernoff, 2008). MROCs, which can vary in size from around fifty to thousands of members, represent a variation of the more traditional off-line consumer panels, long used by marketers to gauge changes over time in customer reactions to brands and marketing campaigns. However, consistent with the emergence of online social networking, in addition to discussions related to topics initiated by the researchers, MROC participants also have the opportunity to post photos and videos, create blogs, and start new discussions. MROCs bring consumers together who share a common interest, characteristic, or disposition toward a brand, and they are encouraged to interact with one another while data are systematically gathered relative to short- or long-term research objectives. Unlike traditional focus groups, the typical MROC is available as a resource at any time and involves a far greater number of participants, whose interactions can be monitored to assess how they communicate with each other as well as with brands.

Despite the growing potential of text mining and the rapid expansion of online consumer-generated content, this research approach is not without some apparent drawbacks. As pointed out in Chapter 4, it has been suggested that online ("incidental") discussions may encourage more negative WOM (NWOM) than positive WOM (PWOM), especially for higher involvement product categories (Rosen, 2002), and that much online WOM may consist of comments solely linked to satisfaction and dissatisfaction. Additionally, persons who give positive advice in face-to-face ("intimate") conversations may not be the same as those who make recommendations on the Internet. Together, these points underline how much of the marketing-relevant discussion that occurs online may be nonrepresentative of that which occurs off-line. In other words, the analysis of online conversations can be enormously enlightening, but only represents part of a much larger overall picture of consumer exchange.

Another shortcoming of assessing consumer content online—and to some extent this is true of all the other methodologies described in this chapter—is that there typically are limits in terms of how the findings may be used to predict future consumer actions (Godes & Mayzlin, 2004). Although such predictions about future behavior are likely to be of great interest to firms engaged in the systematic measure of WOM and other C-to-C interactions, the fact is that it often is unclear whether the WOM content is an outcome of past behavior (e.g., past sales) or a potential precursor to subsequent action (e.g., future purchases).

As with behavioral observations, there are ethical concerns relevant to the investigation of online content, the most salient of which has to do with the determination of what is public and what is private (King, 1996; Kozinets, 2002). Many people consider the typical chat room or online forum to be public behavior because it is typically open to anyone who chooses to participate. A related concern pertains to how researchers present themselves online. Although it would be relatively easy to pass oneself off as just another participant, the general consensus among netnographers appears to be that researchers should disclose their identities honestly. In research on brand communities, for example, it has been found that such online groups are quite exclusive and will not admit participants who do not appear to be genuinely committed to the focal brand (Muñiz & O'Guinn, 2005). This would argue against the researcher pretending to be a brand admirer, which in this case would represent a clear case of active deception likely to be perceived as unacceptable by the participants. Brand community members, on the other hand, are apt to respond favorably to receiving attention from a researcher, given that the scientific interest could bring added prestige to the brand.

As an increasing number of behavioral scientists begin to exploit the potential of the Internet and other emerging technologies for research purposes, it is likely that new ethical dilemmas will be encountered and some familiar ones will be recast in a different light (Birnbaum, 2003). In their analysis of issues pertaining to Internet-based research, Nosek,

Banaji, and Greenwald (2002) identified three key differences between Internet research and standard laboratory research: (*a*) the physical absence of a researcher, (*b*) the questionable adequacy of informed consent and debriefing procedures, and (*c*) the potential loss of participant anonymity or confidentiality (see Box 5.4).

BOX 5.4 ETHICAL GUIDELINES FOR ONLINE RESEARCH

Although an increasing number of professional and legislative codes for marketing on the Internet have appeared in recent years—the former promoted by such organizations as the American Marketing Association, the Internet Industry Association, and the Internet Society—guidelines for the conduct of online research or netnography remain few. However, Mathy, Kerr, and Haydin (2003) have offered some useful recommendations for Internet-mediated research. In their view, at a minimum, the Internet researcher must carefully adhere to the basic ethical principles of respect for autonomy and nonmaleficence (i.e., protection from harm). This can be accomplished in large part through the development of appropriate protocols for obtaining the informed consent of participants, such as the following:

1. Individuals who are willing to participate in a survey investigation could be required to first submit an e-mail request for a copy of the instrument, along with a statement that the study's purpose, risks and benefits, intensity, and duration are clearly understood. This e-mail could then be accepted as an indication of informed consent.

2. It now is possible to have research instruments hosted on a web page, thereby enabling researchers to download responses directly to a database. With cybersurveys of this sort, informed consent is provided on the first web page, which can be designed so that authorized participants must enter a unique password acknowledging that they have read and understood the informed consent protocol. Authorized participants can obtain the password from designated professionals affiliated with the study.

3. The Web page address containing the research instrument could be restricted to persons who have specifically been selected to participate in the study. The Web page can be designed to include a box that must be checked, indicating that participants have given their informed consent. Only then would it be possible to access the measurement items. However, this approach would be possible only when the location of the Web page is specifically protected and the host page is not accessible by an Internet search engine.

According to Mathy et al., one of the keys to protecting participants from harm is the guarantee that they are using a computer and Internet access with proper physical safeguards and password protection locks. These are necessary to prevent unauthorized disclosure of confidential information that can be disseminated via the Internet.

   The physical absence of an investigator during Internet-based research means that the researcher likely will be unable to respond to participant concerns or adverse reactions once a study is underway. Moreover, should the participant choose to withdraw early from a study, this will undermine the possibility that an adequate debriefing can be conducted. Thus, special care must be taken to assure that the informed consent process is thorough and includes clear instructions that will enable debriefing for those persons who leave the study early. (It is during the debriefing that the purpose of the study is explained to participants and questions or concerns are addressed.) To protect against the possibilities that data may be intercepted by a third party or accessed once

(cont.)

Box 5.4 (*Continued*)

stored in files on an Internet-connected server, researchers should take all steps necessary to secure data so as to protect respondent anonymity (Sharf, 1999).

Nosek, Banaji, and Greenwald (2002) recommended several options for debriefing Internet participants, even in situations where they drop out before the completion of a study:

1. Debriefing statements could be forwarded later to an e-mail address provided by participants at the outset of the study (assuming the research does not require full anonymity).

2. The researcher could include a "leave the study" button on each page, which would direct participants to a debriefing page prior to their dropping out.

3. The computer program could automatically present a debriefing page if the participant prematurely closes the browser window.

In addition to these strategies, Nosek et al. suggested that additional debriefing components could be added that vary across persons, including the provision of a list of frequently asked questions (FAQs) that address concerns, clarify that such concerns are common, and emphasize the importance of the research; an e-mail address for contacting the researcher at a later time; and arranging to have the researcher available in an online chat room to respond interactively to participants' subsequent questions and concerns.

Together, these various recommendations for protecting the rights of participants in online research represent novel strategies for overcoming some of the barriers to informed consent, debriefing, and protection of privacy and confidentiality of data that are imposed by Internet technology (Kimmel, 2007). It is essential that researchers continue to search for advanced solutions to these ethical challenges as the technology evolves in years to come.

Laboratory Experimentation

Less frequently utilized to date in the investigation of WOM and consumer influence (for notable exceptions, see Ahluwalia, 2002; Ahluwalia, Burnkrant, & Unnava, 2000), experimental research methodologies represent a potentially fruitful direction for marketing researchers. The experimental approach often involves the observation of human participants in the controlled environment of a research laboratory, an artificial setting devised for the sole purpose of studying behavior. In the laboratory context, variables of interest to researchers typically can be more carefully manipulated, and behavioral responses more precisely measured, than in non-laboratory (or "natural") settings. For example, researchers could systematically introduce either PWOM or NWOM into the setting by having participants who are randomly assigned to conditions overhear a discussion about some products. During the latter phase of the research session, participants could be given the opportunity to rate or select from among a list of products. In this way, the influence of the evaluative nature of WOM on consumer behavior could be determined though a comparison of participants in the PWOM and NWOM groups.

The key drawback to the experimental laboratory approach lies in the artificial nature of the research setting, which leads to questions about "ecological validity," a term that is generally used to refer to whether an experimental situation reflects the outside world (Rosnow & Rosenthal, 2005). Human experiments conducted in laboratories often bear little resemblance to the real-world settings they are intended to reflect, thereby restricting the generalizability to naturally occurring behavior. As East and Lomax (2007) have pointed out, this concern manifests itself in some notable ways for the study of WOM: (*a*) actual WOM is often solicited, and this would be difficult to induce and observe in the laboratory; (*b*) experiments (like the example mentioned above) would likely use systematically expressed PWOM and NWOM, which may not reflect the everyday pattern; (*c*) in real-life situations, the impact of WOM may not be apparent until sometime after it has been received, but in the laboratory, behavior tends to be observed in the short-term (unless follow-up sessions are scheduled); and (*d*) the measurement process in the laboratory is more conducive to assessing the attitudinal and cognitive impact of WOM rather than potentially more telling sales-related measures, such as change in the probability of purchase.

Field experiments represent one possible solution to the limited ecological validity of laboratory research. Along these lines, Ellsworth (1977) argued that experimentation in the field actually offers better prospects for revealing complex causal relationships than laboratory experimentation, where so many variables are kept constant that the complex network of interactions operating in everyday life cannot possibly be revealed. Nonetheless, experimental control and precision of measurement are often seriously diminished in field settings, and this is especially problematic for the study of WOM, which tends to be spontaneous and unpredictable. Given that field experiments can permit the measurement of sales in retail settings, the influence of WOM typically would be limited by the infallibility of recall on the part of customers (East & Lomax, 2007).

The *role-play* methodology represents a potentially useful variation of the experimental approach for studying C-to-C influence. As an investigative tool, role playing is quite flexible in terms of setting, participants, and procedure. The essence of a role-playing study is for the participant to pretend that a situation is real when in fact it is not (Geller, 1982). In one application of this approach, subjects may be asked to play an active role, from the totally improvised to one in which the experimental scenario is acted out with the aid of a script provided by the researcher. For example, to obtain greater insight into marketplace behavior, a consumer researcher may have participants play the role of a seller or customer in a simulated store setting. The person playing the role of customer may be asked to pretend that he or she is dissatisfied with a recent purchase and is trying to return it, and the researcher then can observe how the interaction plays out, perhaps by focusing on the factors that lead to a successful or unsuccessful resolution. This approach can readily be applied to the investigation of WOM and personal influence, for example, by having participants engage in a mock conversation about recent purchase choices or a simulation of advice giving.

Despite some successes at replicating the results of laboratory experiments (cf. Greenberg & Eskew, 1993) and the ethical advantages of role playing, it has drawn some criticism as a research tool (e.g., East & Lomax, 2007; Freedman, 1969; Miller, 1972). Critics contend that role-play experiments do not measure actual behavior, but rather participants' lay theories of behavior, and the expectation that role playing would replicate general relationships has not been adequately demonstrated. In the same vein, it is argued that role players often cannot duplicate the most interesting findings that come from true experiments, such as counterintuitive ones. It also has been suggested that this technique lacks the capacity to induce involvement in role players when motivational or emotional variables are studied (West & Gunn, 1978).

Retrospective Surveys

As an alternative to direct observation and measurement, researchers frequently rely on self-report approaches, such as surveys (face-to-face interviews and written question-naires) and consumer diaries, to study C-to-C influence. Such approaches consist of data collection methodologies in which people describe their own behavior or state of mind to researchers. The various self-report methodologies are conducive to both open-ended questioning and response options (which can be useful for exploratory probing of respondents' thoughts and feelings) and closed-ended ("structured") responding (which can readily be subjected to statistical analysis for hypothesis testing). As a relatively straightforward approach for gathering much useful information from large numbers of consumers in a relatively speedy fashion, it is probably safe to say that surveys represent the most popular method to study WOM and related forms of consumer influence. Researchers may choose to gather their own proprietary survey findings to test hypotheses (e.g., Bowman & Narayandas, 2001; Brown & Reingen, 1987; Reingen & Kernan, 1986; Richins, 1983) or utilize survey-based data collected for other purposes (e.g., Anderson, 1998; Van den Bulte & Lilien, 2001, 2003). As an example of the former approach, Reingen and Kernan (1986) conducted a survey investigation in an effort to map out the entire social network comprising a piano tuner's customers. Van den Bulte and Lilien pursued a similar objective through the analysis of an already existing dataset that enabled the tracking of individual physicians' discussions about medical practices with other physicians.

The attraction of survey methodologies for consumer researchers is apparent when one considers the nature of questions that are typical in WOM research, such as "What would you do if . . . ?," "Did you tell someone about X?," and "How many people did you tell?" which can readily be included among other items in a written questionnaire. This questioning approach is at the heart of the much-utilized net promoter index, which asks respondents to indicate on a 10-point scale the likelihood that they would recommend a company to others (see below). In Chapter 4, I mentioned some additional examples from my own survey questionnaire to investigate business professionals' agreement with some widespread misconceptions about WOM. Items in that survey included asking participants to indicate the category representing the last instance of WOM they could recall and to estimate the extent of its influence on their decision making. Such questioning is akin to the *critical incidents technique* (CIT), a qualitative methodology that has respondents recall in their own words previous experiences (good or bad, satisfying or dissatisfying) relevant to the topic of the investigation and then to provide specific details pertaining to each experience. The critical incidents can provide a rich set of data and concrete, relevant examples for managers.

For example, my colleague Anne-Françoise Audrain-Pontevia and I utilized the CIT to investigate commercial rumors from the perspective of marketing managers (Kimmel & Audrain-Pontevia, in press). We had managers complete a rumor questionnaire which, in part, asked them to recall specific examples of commercial rumors that reached their ear and then to respond to several closed-ended items concerning the circumstances surrounding the rumors, the severity of rumor effects, and the effectiveness of rumor control tactics. In another study using a similar approach, we identified the strategies used by managers to cope with instances of NWOM (Audrain-Pontevia & Kimmel, 2008). Both studies revealed that managers consider increasing trust in the focal product, service, or company as the most efficacious strategy for dealing with potentially damaging rumors and NWOM.

As indirect approaches to investigating consumer behavior, self-report methodologies have some inherent limitations, foremost of which is their reliance on participant recall. With the exception of consumer diaries—which require participants to keep a running descriptive record of their thoughts, experiences, and behaviors as they occur—most self-report procedures are subject to the fallibilities and biases of human memory. As East and Lomax (2007) have pointed out, the findings of a retrospective survey investigation may be skewed by retrieval bias (Tversky & Kahneman, 1973), prior expectations (Craik & Lockhart, 1972), and social desirability bias (Fisher, 1993). For example, in the aforementioned rumor study, data were derived from a critical incidents procedure dependent on participants' free recall of rumors and the circumstances surrounding rumor episodes, and thus were subject to certain potential motivational and cognitive biases. Respondents may have recalled more vivid, recent, and personally involving rumors. Negative rumors may be more memorable than positive ones (as may also be the case in studies of PWOM or NWOM) and thus overrepresented in the estimated ratio. Further, a self-serving bias could not be ruled out in the reported effectiveness of rumor-coping strategies highlighted by managerial respondents. By contrast, the direct observation approach tends to be lower in cost and eliminates reliance on recall (Godes & Mayzlin, 2004).

Concerns about privacy rights also emerge as relevant issues in the survey context, although in different ways than in field research. To what extent can survey researchers probe the private, personal lives of their subjects for research purposes, even when subjects' voluntary consent is obtained for doing so? Related and equally important issues in applied research in general involve protection of subject anonymity and response confidentiality. For a detailed discussion of these ethical issues, see Kimmel (2007).

Structured Measurement Scales

As an offshoot of the retrospective survey methodology, the use of scientifically constructed attitude and personality scales follows the self-report approach by having research participants respond to a set of prespecified, closed-ended questions or items. The items that comprise such scales are determined as a result of a rigorous selection process (see Mueller, 1986), and a participant's responses are combined to form some sort of average or summed score that reflects his or her placement on a continuum ranging from low to high or negative (unfavorable) to positive (favorable). Numerous construct measurement scales have been developed by researchers over the years to assess a wide-reaching array of personality traits (e.g., innovativeness, materialism, need for cognition, opinion leadership) and social attitudes (e.g., attitude toward advertising, private label brands, Web sites, birth control). Scales that are particularly applicable to marketing research can be readily obtained by consulting references compiled by Bearden and Netemeyer (1998) and Bruner, Hensel, and James (2005). Some examples of these scales are provided below in the section concerning means for identifying consumer influencers. As self-report measures, such scales share some of the same limitations as those described above for retrospective surveys.

Social Marketing Metrics

The preceding discussion was intended to provide guidance for researchers interested in studying the nature and dynamics of WOM and C-to-C influence. An awareness of the strengths and limitations of basic research approaches goes a long way toward making a practitioner a better consumer of research findings. Consider that a recent benchmark survey conducted by Marketing Sherpa revealed that two-thirds of the marketing professionals surveyed who claimed to have not used any form of social marketing considered themselves "very knowledgeable" or "somewhat knowledgeable" about the emerging marketing strategies (marketingsherpa.com). According to the research sponsors, "their overconfidence in unproven ability can doom social media initiatives to failure." Thus, an attentiveness to the extant research is invaluable to the success of marketing efforts.

Table 5.2 The Most Effective Social Media Tactics Are the Least Measurable

Social media tactics	Very accurately measured (%)	Very effective tactics (%)
Advertising on blogs or social networks	32	16
Online news release distribution	18	36
User reviews or ratings	15	47
Blogger or online journalist relations	11	46
Forums or discussion groups	11	42
Blogging on a company blog	9	34
Profiles on professional or social networks	7	22

Notes: The above levels of agreement regarding the measurement accuracy and campaign effectiveness for various social media tactics were obtained from a survey of 1,886 marketing practitioners conducted during December 2008 by MarketingSherpa. The results reveal that the most effective tactics tend to entail the greatest difficulty in terms of accurate measurement.

Source: MarketingSherpa Social Media Marketing and PR Benchmark Survey 2008 (MarketingSherpa, 2009).

Although it is granted that many marketing practitioners may not have the time or inclination to carry out systematic consumer behavior studies themselves, certain questions are being voiced with increasing frequency within companies, many of which reflect a common concern to demonstrate the *return on investment* (ROI)—a measure of the amount returned from each marketing dollar invested—of social marketing strategies: "How do I know if it works?" "How is it possible to define and measure social marketing success?" "Is it possible to identify consumer influencers, such as opinion leaders and mavens?" Such questions are not very surprising—indeed, one recent social media survey (prospero.com) revealed that 41% of large corporations surveyed about their social media ROI admitted that the figure was "unknown." Complicating the picture are indications that the most effective social marketing techniques are the most difficult to measure (see Table 5.2). Despite the formidable challenges posed by the aforementioned questions and their implied demands, marketing experts have begun to offer some intriguing answers related to social marketing measurement.

At the outset, it is important to point out that the benefits of social marketing efforts (see Chapters 6–8) can be assessed qualitatively as well as quantitatively, and that one type of approach should not be overused to the neglect of the other. In addition to quantitatively improving a company's bottom line (as most obviously evidenced by sales), marketing campaigns also can result in an increase in qualitative (but admittedly vague) attributes that have been notoriously difficult to measure, such as consumer loyalty, advocacy, satisfaction, feedback, authority, and influence. Marketing experts have suggested a variety of sources of indicators for monitoring and tracking the impact of a social marketing campaign, including Google Analytics, FeedBurner, social bookmarks, corporate and customer blogs, social networks (MySpace, Facebook, Bebo,

LinkedIn), authority sites (Technorati, Google), newsgroups, content communities (Flickr, YouTube, Google Video, BrightCove), and microblogging sites (Twitter, Pownce, Jaiku).

An essential key to developing useful social metrics is to reduce the content obtained from these sources into smaller chunks that can be measured and readily translated into a business context (Yongfook, 2009). An initial step in the process is to determine the relevant success metrics that correspond to marketing campaign objectives and that are available to the company given its measurement resources. The next step is to reduce qualitative outcomes into metrics that are understandable and easy to measure. For example, if a social marketing campaign objective is to increase "influence," appropriate and readily measurable metrics could be represented by the number of influential blogs linking to your campaign's Web site and the number of influential twitters retweeting your Web site. Similarly, a campaign that is oriented toward increasing "authority" might focus on metrics like page rank of your corporate blog, and its ranking relative to your competitors. When the Starbucks coffee chain launched its "My Starbucks Idea" campaign (see Chapter 6) to engage their customers and enhance their satisfaction with the firm, certain metrics were identified to provide more quantitative indicators for the campaign's more qualitative objectives. These included the success metrics of (*a*) amount of good suggestions that the company had not thought of and (*b*) amount of these suggestions the company actually implemented. Such examples provide some preliminary ideas about the kinds of social metrics that are now available to social marketers.

Share of Conversation and Related Metrics

Share of conversation (SOC) is a social metric developed by Radian6 CEO Marcel LeBrun (2009) to assess the degree to which a discussed brand is associated with the problem or category need that it was created to help consumers deal with. It evolved from a commonly used measure in the advertising industry known as "share of voice" (SOV), which represents the relative portion of advertising inventory available to a single advertiser within a defined market over a specified time period; that is, it is the firm's proportion of total promotional expenditures in the market.

One way of approximating SOV for social media would be to compare the number of online mentions (e.g., in articles, posts, videos) for a brand and its competitors. This would provide an indication as to where a brand ranks among its competitors in terms of online mentions and the margin of difference. By contrast, SOC is a metric that some find more informative for shedding light on the value of online conversations and, ultimately, WOM. An example of how this metric can be assessed is provided by the following formula, developed in reference to a popular over-the-counter pain medicine for arthritis (LeBrun, 2009):

$$\text{Share of Conversation (SOC)} = \frac{\text{Total \# of articles/posts discussing ``arthritis'' AND ``Tylenol''}}{\text{Total \# of articles/posts discussing ``arthritis''}}$$

As apparent from the example, SOC provides an indication of the online discussion about a specific brand relevant to its category need or consumer problem as a proportion of all the online discussion for that need or problem. In the context of pain medications for arthritis, SOC would consist of monitoring all the social media discussions about arthritis, taking account of what arthritis sufferers talk about and how prominent the focal brand—in this example, Tylenol—is in that conversation. In short, the measure would consider the extent to which people talk about Tylenol when they talk about arthritis. (LeBrun recommends narrowing the broader conversation as a first step, for example, by focusing on the 250 most influential Web sites.) An SOV assessment comparing Tylenol and generic aspirin may reveal that people talk about Tylenol nearly twice as much as aspirin, whereas an SOC comparison may reveal that aspirin is more frequently mentioned than Tylenol in discussions of arthritis. This would suggest that the producers of the Tylenol brand need to earn the trust of arthritis sufferers and attempt to grow its SOC. A company may attempt to do this by contributing helpful content to the Internet community (e.g., an e-book, blog post, video) so that when people discuss their malady, Tylenol will enter the conversation.

There are other measures related to online discussion that can be used in conjunction with the SOC metric, one of which is Stowe Boyd's "conversation index," which tracks the amount of conversation a blog entry generates. To understand this metric, it first is necessary to explain what is meant by a "trackback." Generally speaking, a trackback is an online feature that enables one to let other sites know that you have added a link to those sites and to know when other sites have included a link to one's own site. For example, a blog trackback is a way of informing someone that you included a link to their blog on your own blog. With this in mind, the conversation index is estimated by calculating the ratio of blog posts to number of comments plus trackbacks (i.e., conversation index = posts ÷ comments + trackbacks). In his research, Boyd (2006) found that for successful blogs, the conversation index was typically less than one, an indication that there was more conversation (as indicated by the number of comments and trackbacks offered by readers) generated by the blogs than there was number of articles posted. A useful technology for this sort of measurement approach is Trackback, a technology developed by the blogging software company Six Apart, which enables bloggers to find out the extent to which their blog postings are being cited at other blogs. This is one way of determining how infectious a blog is in spreading WOM (Corcoran et al., 2006).

The conversation index is a useful internal metric for determining success at generating conversation on one's blog in the sense of being able to monitor how the value changes over time and to compare the ratio of different posts to each other. However, there are limitations when attempting to use the conversation index as a universal measure for comparing blogs and blog posts to each other, especially due to the variation in the methods used by different blogs for treating comments and trackbacks (Zeigler, 2006).

Another potentially useful quantitative indicator, suggested by Dave Balter (2008), can be applied to shed light on the comparative worth of a WOM conversation relative to a traditional advertising impression (i.e., the delivery of a single advertising unit, such as an Internet banner):

$$(\text{\# of traditional media impressions}) \times (\text{average length of impression})$$
$$= (\text{\# of WOM communications}) \times (\text{average length of WOM communication})$$

As an example, this formula could be used to compare the cost of generating a WOM conversation (that, say, lasts 8 minutes on average) with the cost of a 30-second TV advertisement. If a marketer purchases 300 showings of a commercial on programs that typically attract 200,000 viewers (and for hypothetical purposes, we assume that all those viewers actually watch the commercial), the equation would look like this:

$$(60 \text{ million TV impressions}) \times (30 \text{ seconds})$$
$$= (\text{\# of WOM communications}) \times (480 \text{ seconds})$$

Solving for the number of WOM communications in the equation reveals that 3.75 million WOM communications would be needed to generate an impact equal to 60 million TV impressions. As Balter points out, however, although this calculation can provide a quantitative figure for marketing practitioners who need to justify their budgets, it does not shed any insight into the probable impact of the communications. It may well be the case that a strong and credible recommendation that emerges from a WOM conversation that transpires between two consumers creates significantly greater value than the passive experience of watching a thirty-second TV commercial.

An intriguing new metric for measuring the spread of WOM conversations and their outcomes, the G2X Relay Rate, has been proposed by Carl, Oles, and McGlinn (2007) as a collaboration between academic researchers and BzzAgent, a WOM-generating company that recruits consumers to participate in buzz campaigns for client companies (see Chapter 7). Whereas most of the new social metrics discussed in this chapter are limited to publicly accessible online venues, where the communication channels themselves have enhanced the feasibility of tracking digital conversations, Carl et al. recognized the need for a comprehensive WOM measurement approach that is capable of accounting for all forms of consumer conversations, regardless of medium. The G2X conversation tracking methodology is applicable to online and off-line venues, including face-to-face and phone conversations, e-mails, instant messaging, and chat rooms, and is capable of measuring WOM that is transmitted beyond the initial (i.e., Generation 1) conversational partners (hence the name G2X, for "Generation 0 to X").

In the G2X relay terminology, G0 refers to the WOM program participant (e.g., the consumer who enrolls in BzzAgent to generate the initial WOM about a client). The first generation (G1) consists of persons with whom the G0 speaks with about a product or service, and subsequent conversations initiated by the G1s are carried out with conversational partners who constitute G2, with the last WOM recipients comprising GX. The "G1 Relay Rate" refers to the number of conversational partners G0 talks to, the "G2 Relay Rate" is the number of people the G1s talk to, and so on. A series of conversations that emerge from one generation to another is considered as a "conversation thread," and the series of conversations within a thread are associated and tracked.

The G2X methodology is intended to be applicable to situations in which WOM is associated with a campaign launched by an agency, such as BzzAgent, and also can be used to track the spread of spontaneously generated WOM that is not associated with a particular WOM campaign (i.e., "everyday" WOM). At the time of this writing, the methodology's creators have only clarified how the process works for monitoring an agency campaign, which proceeds in the following way: Initially, the agency measures the WOM activity from G0 to G1, using data obtained from the reports written by program participants for each WOM incident and responses to a post-campaign follow-up survey. Additional conversations that occur beyond G1 are quantified through the use of a "conversation card" that program participants (G0s) are asked to pass along to each of their conversational partners after discussing the product or service that is the focus of the campaign. The card directs its recipients (G1s) to visit a Web site where they are invited to respond to a survey about the WOM episode and to pass the card along to a new conversational partner (G2) *if* they had an additional discussion about the brand. This process continues across each subsequent generation of conversational partners. (Each participant in the study is encouraged to participate through the offer of an incentive.)

According to Carl et al., the various surveys completed by program participants and their conversational partners capture detailed information about each WOM episode, including its timing and duration, whether a recommendation/referral or negative advice was transmitted, what was said, who said what, how the conversation was initiated, demographic information about the participants, and the like. Perhaps most importantly, the surveys also elicit from conversational partners details about "action outcomes," in the form of measures of behavioral intentions (i.e., likelihood to inquire further, use, purchase, and refer the purchase to others) and actual behaviors (i.e., inquiry, use, purchase, and recommendation behavior). As a final step, conversational partners are invited to participate in a follow-up study during which they are asked to report on any additional conversations they had over the ensuing 6-week period and the outcomes of those conversations. Built into the G2X methodology is a validation check on the self-reported data, given that program participants and their conversational partners complete separate surveys about the same WOM episode. For an application of the G2 Relay Rate methodology, see Carl et al. (2007).

Monitoring Online Activity

There are additional approaches to monitoring online activity that can provide useful social marketing and WOM metrics. I learned this firsthand as a result of the creation of my own blog about restaurants. By adding a web counter through an online monitoring service (in this case, Site Meter), in addition to obtaining an indication of the number of visits to my site each day, I was able to identify the referrals for each visit; that is, from which Web sites my visitors were arriving. Thus, at an online forum discussion about France, someone may have posted a question seeking recommendations for good restaurants in Paris where one could have a relatively inexpensive lunch during an impending trip. A visitor to the site might have been motivated to contribute to the discussion by referring the poster to my blog. This is something that would be apparent from my site monitoring information. I would recognize that someone came to my site directly from a referral that appeared in an online forum discussion about France. That kind of insight might suggest ways that I could increase traffic to my site; for example, I myself could contribute to France forum discussions, offering restaurant recommendations along with my blog's URL. Services like Google Analytics and Site Meter also provide further breakdowns about a blog's traffic, such as the proportion of visits by country, page views, time spent at the site, and so on.

The restaurant blog example provides a simple indication of how online activity can be evaluated to shed light on the connectedness of consumers and the extent and impact of WOM discussions. The available tools for monitoring online activity have continued to evolve since the early days of click-through rates for Web banners. Technorati and other authority sites serve as online search engines, rank order blogs according to their popularity, and provide services for bloggers and publishers to maximize traffic and online advertising revenue. Social bookmarketing sites like de.li.cio.us, Diigo (previously Furl), and Shadow provide indicators of collaborative information sharing online through the use of *social tagging*, the practice of adding metadata in the form of keywords to shared content. In addition to these examples, marketing experts have suggested a wide range of metrics that might be of use for assessing each emerging marketing communication approach (see Box 5.5).

Returning to the blog example, it is interesting to know how many people visit a Web site—be it a blog, a forum discussion, or a company Web site—and how they got there, but that certainly is not where the measurement process ends. A next logical consideration is what happened once they arrived at your site. This is where a key performance indicator of marketing strategy, conversion, becomes relevant (Gold, 2005). *Web site conversion* is the process of converting site visitors into prospects and customers and is obtained by considering the ratio of "completed actions" (i.e., e-mail opt-ins, producing product sales, signing up subscribers, having a particular file downloaded) to total number of Web site visitors (i.e., conversion rate = completed actions ÷ total number of visitors). This type of metric provides an evaluation of the effectiveness of a company's

---

BOX 5.5 WEB SITE AND SOCIAL MEDIA METRICS

Professional blogger Hendry Lee (2009) recommends the use of a variety of metrics for Web site tracking that can be useful to bloggers for marketing decision making. These are summarized below.

1. Really Simple Syndication (RSS) Feed Metrics

RSS comprises web feed formats for delivering regularly updated web content, such as blog entries, audio and video content, and news-related material. An RSS document, which is typically referred to as a ''feed'' or ''web feed'' includes the full or summarized text of original content, as well as metadata in the form of publishing dates and authorship. RSS feeds are available from RSS feed readers and news aggregators (e.g., AmphetaDesk, FeedReader, NewsGator, My Yahoo, Bloglines, Google Reader), which allow people to display and use the content from various sites in a time-saving fashion. RSS feeds provide consumers with an anonymous means to obtain updated content from blogs each time a new blog post appears. According to Lee, despite their anonymity, useful metrics can be obtained from RSS:

- *Subscribers/readership*—Google FeedBurner enables bloggers to track subscribers who access their RSS feed over a particular period of time, as well as aggregated subscription data from news readers. These metrics reflect content consumption activity that could be indicative of level of engagement with a blog and its influence.

- *Items use*—This metric assesses the type of content that audiences appear to most prefer. A trend toward a particular type of content would suggest an interest in future blogs on the topic in order to increase engagement.

- *Revenue*—Analytics software can be employed to track sales and other goals from RSS readers. Links can be tracked within an RSS feed via Google Analytics.

2. E-mail Marketing Metrics

These metrics can be used by bloggers who send out e-mail newsletters. The following metrics are useful for targeting and engaging prospects and customers through e-mail:

- *Sent and bounces*—To have a clear indication of the number of true blog subscribers, a comparison can be made between the number of e-mail newsletters sent (i.e., the number of presumed subscribers) and those that are returned as undelivered (''bounces''). Given that many e-mails may not reach the inbox of legitimate subscribers because of spam filtering, this measure could be combined with delivery rate, which can be obtained from an available service, such as Delivery Monitor. Optimally, a blogger would desire to have a minimal bounce rate.

- *Click-through rate*—This indicates the number of people who click on a link in the e-mail; a high rate reflects a favorable response to the message in the e-mail.

- *Unsubscription rate*—The number of people who unsubscribe to the newsletter will reflect whether you are on the right track with its message content and your approach to gaining subscribers.

3. Web Site Metrics

A number of indicators of how well a Web site (and in many cases, a blog) is being managed have been developed by marketers, some of which have been alluded to in other sections of this chapter.

(cont.)

Box 5.5 (*Continued*)

- *Number of visitors*—Generally speaking, the more traffic a Web site obtains, the more the sales and the higher the revenue.

- *Page views*—If this metric is greater than the number of visitors to the site, it indicates that people are interested in pursuing the site's content beyond the landing page. Page per visit provides a measure of how many pages, on average, each visitor sees before leaving the site and reflects the site's "stickiness."

- *Time spent on site*—This measure reflects how much time people spend engaging with a site's content, such as reading text, watching a video, etc.

- *Search engine keywords*—This metric provides an indication of which keywords people searched before reaching your site and can suggest useful directions for future content.

- *Clickstream*—This is an indication of a user's activity when he or she arrives at a Web site. In essence, it provides a virtual trail that a user leaves behind when navigating a site by revealing the sequence of clicks or page requests. (Actions are logged by the Internet Service Provider, and may also be tracked by the individual Web site, Web browser, proxy servers, and ad servers.) The insight into web users' behavior obtained from this metric can be utilized to optimize a Web site and enhance conversions and the web surfers' overall experience with the site.

marketing strategies and how satisfied people are interacting with its Web site. By continually monitoring conversion rates over subsequent time periods, marketers can obtain regular feedback regarding their traditional and nontraditional marketing efforts.

Additional insight into social media efforts can be obtained through the following measures, suggested by Macnamara (2009):

- number of unique visitors (which provides an indication of a campaign's *reach*);

- duration (length of time spent at a site sheds light on how *engaging* the content is for visitors);

- views of videos and downloads of documents (which also serve as indicators of engagement);

- return visits (a metric for assessing *frequency* and *stickiness*);

- user ratings (an indicator of *credibility* and *influence*);

- comments (conversations and chats stimulated by a blog, video, or other marketing action provide direct feedback that can serve to indicate *engagement* and *impact*);

- links to a site (also referred to as "incoming links," which reflect a site's influence and can help to identify network nodes and hubs of credibility); and

- next clicks (where site visitors go next online can provide information about future intentions—e.g., leaving a car manufacturer's site and going next to a retailer's site for that brand suggests a progression toward a purchase—and also reflects the range of information visitors are accessing and using).

Other Emerging Media Metrics

As the foregoing discussion illustrates, marketing metrics have evolved along with changes in the contemporary consumer environment. Companies have begun to combine—or in some cases, supplant—traditional means of evaluation, such as reach and frequency, demographics, and brand metrics (awareness, brand favorability, etc.) with outcome-based measures that are behavior specific and action focused (Vollmer, 2008). Accordingly, we now see a growing interest in measures of engagement (online session time, ad recall, measures of active attention to content, and traffic-to-marketer's Web site), quality and concentration of audience (WOM referrals, early adopter influence), impact on purchase behavior (repeat purchasing, online and brick-and-mortar store visits), and actual viewership (click-throughs, downloads, customer ratings). For example, the marketing consultancy firm Digital Media Communications has expertise in precisely tracking peer-to-peer sharing and online viewing of viral video clips.

In the past, rough estimates of television advertising exposure were obtained from ratings of TV program viewership. Today, it is increasingly possible to assess numbers and kinds of persons who are viewing the ads themselves, as well as the impact of the actual message on viewers' interest, attitudes, and specific actions. One syndicated data company that has pioneered some of these new measurement approaches for evaluating commercials is IAG Research, which measures the effectiveness of TV and cinema ads, product placements, and commercial sponsorships by means of an online consumer panel. IAG's system is an ambitious undertaking that goes well beyond traditional Nielsen-type measures of how many people had an opportunity to view an ad. In part, the system assesses the impact of noncommercial program engagement on ad recall and attentiveness, enabling advertisers to identify the most suitable media environments in which to place their ads.

Other firms are focusing on cross-platform metrics (i.e., measures that enable advertisers to combine and compare results for each media platform they use for a campaign) to gauge advertising effectiveness. In his 2008 book *Always On*, Christopher Vollmer provides a good sampling of some of the emerging metrics initiatives employed by media research firms as they move away from an advertising impressions mentality to approaches focused on media impact:

- The Nielsen Media Research company, famous for its TV audience measurement ratings systems, has been particularly active in responding to the new demands of the contemporary media landscape. Nielsen/NetRatings utilizes a suite of online metrics that includes total minutes, total sessions, and total page views that can be used for accurate measurement of online advertisement. Nielsen's GamePlay Metrics gathers information on the use of video games from its National People Meter sample, which is comprised of the same households that provide TV viewing data. The video game data shed light on video game usage according to game title and genre, and monitors the types of persons using specific games for different player platforms. Nielsen also has developed metric systems for blogs, digital video recorders, and outdoor advertising. For example, Nielsen Outdoor has developed GPS-enabled portable devices, so-called Npods (Nielsen personal outdoor devices), that can track each time a consumer passes an outdoor advertisement, including when each advertising exposure occurred and its duration.

- Nielsen's rival comScore has developed an online streaming monitoring system called Video Metrix that can determine which visitors to a site stay online to watch video content to its completion.
- Rentrak Corporation and Hiwire have collaborated to measure the viewing of TV content delivered via mobile phones.
- The radio tracking firm Arbitron has developed a system that combines data accrued from its Portable People Meter, shopper intercepts, and a partnership with Scarborough Research to track exposure to in-store marketing communications.

In addition to these examples, the Keller Faye Group developed the TalkTrack system, which continuously monitors marketing-relevant conversations in whatever form or context they occur, including face-to-face, telephone, and Internet (http:// www.kellerfay.com/talktrack.php). Each week, the system tracks nationally representative samples of 700 American consumers over the age of 12, resulting in measures of more than 250,000 brand conversations annually.

Sales

Traditionally, one of the most widely utilized approaches for setting marketing communication objectives has been the sales orientation. This is consistent with the view that the only reason a firm spends money on promotional efforts is to sell its product or service. If the ultimate desired effect of marketing campaigns is to contribute to a company's bottom line, then sales results indeed represent meaningful measures of a program's effectiveness. In this light, sales-related metrics for assessing a marketing effort could take the form of sales turnover, movements in market share, ROI, changes in the value of sales made after accounting for the rate of inflation, volume of product shifted relative to other periods of activity, and the like.

Despite the straightforward logic of the sales approach for determining appropriate metrics for a social marketing campaign, many critics of the approach have pointed out some key shortcomings when it is put into practice. Foremost among these is the recognition that the approach implicitly places the entire responsibility for sales performance with a marketing campaign. In fact, this is not an accurate reflection of the way business works in that sales volumes may vary for a wide variety of reasons in addition to a communication or social marketing program, including other marketing mix elements (e.g., a change in price or packaging), competitors' actions (e.g., a competitor leaves the field or raises prices), consumer needs, general economic conditions, and previous communications that have a cumulative effect (Fill, 1999). Another difficulty with the sales approach is that the impact of marketing expenditures may be delayed because consumers are not ready to enter the market. For example, a marketing campaign intended to stimulate WOM may indeed have its intended impact of increasing awareness about a new product, but consumers may not translate that awareness, and whatever corresponding interest in the product the WOM arouses, into a purchase until they are confident that the product is something they really need. This suggests that there are intangible effects (e.g., increased interest or improvement in brand image) that in the short term will not show up in sales figures. Thus, sales measures can be useful indicators of marketing impact, but they rarely in and of themselves provide a sufficient test of the success of a marketing activity.

The Net Promoter Score (NPS)

Of all the metrics put forth by social marketers in the Web 2.0 era, perhaps none has generated more excitement and controversy as Frederick Reichheld's NPS. Much attention to this concept was garnered through a December 2003 article Reichheld published in the *Harvard Business Review* entitled, "The One Number You Need to Grow." In that article, Reichheld argued that expensive, complex surveys are not required for assessing customer satisfaction and company growth; rather, these outcomes can be determined by finding out "what customers tell their friends about you." This can be accomplished by considering customers' responses on a 10-point rating scale to the simple question, "How likely is it that you would recommend [company X] to a friend or colleague?" The NPS is then calculated by subtracting the percentage of "detractors" (0 to 6 ratings, extremely unlikely to recommend), from the percentage of "promoters" (9 to 10 ratings, extremely likely to recommend) (i.e., Net Promoter = promoters − detractors). Reichheld found that companies with high loyalty and potential for growth typically achieve scores in the 0.75 to 0.80 range.

Based on data obtained from 400 companies in twelve industries by the firms Satmetrix and Bain & Co., the NPS proved more effective in predicting company growth than questions pertaining to whether the company sets the industry standard for excellence, makes it easy to do business with, and gives rise to high satisfaction with its overall performance. In certain industries, two additional questions also were found to be effective predictors of growth: (*a*) How strongly do you agree that [company X] deserves your loyalty? and (*b*) How likely is it that you will continue to purchase products/services from [company X]? Nonetheless, Reichheld concluded that the net promoter question was by far the most effective predictor across industries.

Despite its widespread adoption by some of the world's leading corporations, including Microsoft, General Electric, and American Express, the relative effectiveness of the

NPS as a stand-alone measure of satisfaction and company growth recently has come into question (see Box 5.6). Some researchers pointed out that the actual analysis on which the NPS was derived consisted of a much smaller sample than that suggested by Reich-held (Keiningham et al., 2007). A more serious problem with the index has to do with the predictive validity of responses to the hypothetical "Would you recommend..." question. The argument is that a "Yes, I would recommend" response typically tells little about actual customer WOM behavior. For example, one study of financial service and telecom companies found that only one in three customers who said they would

---

BOX 5.6 FOCUS ON RESEARCH: THE NET PROMOTER SCORE UNDER SCRUTINY

As a WOM-based measure of customer satisfaction and predictor of corporate growth, the net promoter score (NPS) has received countless accolades from a growing list of advocates and supporters, including some of the movers and shakers within the corporate world. For example, American Express CEO Ken Chenault proclaimed that "all companies should ask their customers what Fred [Reichheld] calls the ultimate question"; former GE Chairman Jack Welch dubbed the NPS "an up-and-coming management concept"; and Sage Limited's managing director Paul Stobart pointed to Reichheld's research, which showed the NPS to be "100% accurate in determining whether a company grew or shrank" (cf. Keiningham et al., 2007).

Nonetheless, the NPS does have its detractors, predominately from among marketing researchers who have submitted the index to more rigorous testing. Does the NPS truly represent "the one number you need to grow" or does it serve as yet another example of an uncritically accepted and widely applied marketing concept that practitioners have glommed onto without first subjecting it to comprehensive scientific analysis? In recent years, evidence has begun to emerge pointing to the latter. One such analysis that cast doubt on the unbridled enthusiasm lavished on the NPS by corporate executives is reported in an award-winning *Journal of Marketing* paper published by Keiningham and his colleagues (2007). In what has become an all-too familiar refrain in the Web 2.0 era, where the mad rush to alternative marketing communication techniques and magic formulas predominates, Keiningham et al.'s empirical evaluation of the NPS research was sparked by their recognition that "the evidence regarding the relationship between the Net Promoter metric and firm revenue growth . . . has not been subjected to rigorous scientific scrutiny and peer review. Indeed, no researchers have attempted to replicate the research methodology" (p. 40).

In their replication of Reichheld's research, Keiningham et al. (2007) conducted a longitudinal study involving twenty-one firms and more than 15,500 interviews in an effort to compare the initial research with other predictors of customer satisfaction, such as the American Customer Satisfaction Index, across similar industries. The replication failed to find support for the "clear superiority" of the NPS compared with traditional customer satisfaction measures when the measures were correlated with indices of company growth over a 3-year period. For two industries studied (airlines and personal computers), the traditional satisfaction measure fared even better in explaining revenue growth. In light of their research, Keingingham et al. (2007, p. 45) concluded that they "find no support for the claim that Net Promoter is the 'single most reliable indicator of a company's ability to grow'." Given that an increasing number of business executives have adopted the NPS metric under the presumption that it has been thoroughly validated by research and shown to be superior to other metrics, the question can be raised as to whether corporations are misallocating their resources toward strategies based on NPS results. This is not to suggest that the NPS is not a useful metric, only that it should be utilized as one component of a comprehensive measurement approach. According to Alan Mitchell (2008), in light of critical scrutiny of the NPS since Reichheld first brought the metric to the attention of the business community, four key lessons have emerged:

1. As pointed out above, measures that ask consumers how they *would* behave often tell us little about their *actual* behavior.

2. The NPS can be misleading when it is not submitted to appropriate examination. For example, consider the different implications of an NPS score of 40 that is derived from 70 (percentage of promoters) minus 30 (percentage of detractors) and one of 40 minus 0. Similarly, the NPS metric treats all detractors the same, whether they yield an individual score of 0 or 6, yet there obviously is a qualitative difference in how they feel about a company.

3. The NPS methodology is subject to certain practical difficulties, yielding scores that vary greatly from month to month. This volatility appears to be driven as much by market conditions, such as competitor initiatives, as by customers' actual dealings with the company.

4. Multivariate indicators nearly always perform better in predicting future performance than any single measure. Rather than following Reichheld's recommendation that the NPS can be used to the exclusion of other marketing research measures, many companies have found it useful to add NPS-type questions to their existing research battery. This has proven beneficial in turning up correlations between NPS and other scores, and avoids some of the methodological shortcomings of using NPS as one's only metric.

recommend a company actually made a recommendation, and only 13% of those referrals were acted on (cf. Mitchell, 2008). To overcome this potential problem, some WOM researchers advise the use of a more retrospectively oriented question for accurately assessing WOM behavior, such as, "How many times have you [recommended/advised against] any auto mechanic in the last six months?" (East & Lomax, 2007).

Identifying Influencers

Another area in which research and measurement serve as invaluable resources in planning, launching, and evaluating a social marketing campaign is in the identification of influential, opinion-leading consumers. A variety of approaches have been developed for accomplishing that task, ranging from self- or peer-designation to the application of sociometric methods. Some of the more widely used methodologies are described below.

Self-Designation

Perhaps the most straightforward way to identify opinion leaders is to ask consumers directly the extent to which they consider themselves as the sort of people who influence the marketplace behavior of others. For example, existing or prospective customers can be invited to complete a questionnaire that taps OL status. In the typical approach, respondents are provided with a set of statements along with a Likert rating scale (e.g., 1 = strongly disagree to 5 = strongly agree), with the overall sum of responses to the items indicative of opinion leadership status (i.e., higher scores suggest a greater proclivity to influence other consumers). Sample items appear as follows:

- Friends and neighbors frequently ask my advice about [category].
- I sometimes influence the types of [category] my friends buy.
- I tend to talk a lot about [category] to friends/neighbors.
- When asked for advice about [category], I offer a lot of information.
- I can think of at least three people whom I have spoken to about [category] in the past 6 months.

Such questionnaires are flexible enough to be studied for specific product or service categories (see Childers, 1986; Flynn, Goldsmith, & Eastman, 1994; Miled & Le Louarn, 1994). Examples of validated scales to assess OL, market mavenism (i.e., the propensity

---

BOX 5.7 SCALES FOR IDENTIFYING OPINION LEADERS AND OPINION RECEIVERS

Opinion Leadership (OL) Items:

1. My opinion on [PRODUCT CATEGORY] seems not to count with other people.
2. When they choose a [PRODUCT CATEGORY], other people do not turn to me for advice.
3. Other people [rarely] come to me for advice about choosing [PRODUCT CATEGORY].
4. People that I know pick [PRODUCT CATEGORY] based on what I have told them.
5. I often persuade others to buy the [PRODUCT CATEGORY] that I like.
6. I often influence people's opinions about [PRODUCT CATEGORY].

Opinion Seeking (OS) Items:

1. When I consider buying a [PRODUCT CATEGORY], I ask other people for advice.
2. I don't like to talk to others before I buy [PRODUCT CATEGORY].
3. I rarely ask other people what [PRODUCT CATEGORY] to buy.
4. I like to get others' opinions before I buy a [PRODUCT CATEGORY].
5. I feel more comfortable buying a [PRODUCT CATEGORY] when I have gotten other people's opinions on it.
6. When choosing [PRODUCT CATEGORY], other people's opinions are not important to me.

[All items scored on 7-point scales ranging from *strongly disagree* to *strongly agree*. Items 1 through 3 of OL require reverse scoring, and items 2, 3, and 6 of OS require reverse scoring.]

Source: Flynn, Goldsmith, and Eastman (1996).

BOX 5.8 SCALE TO IDENTIFY MARKET MAVENS

1. I like introducing new brands and products to my friends.
2. I like helping people by providing them with information about many kinds of products.
3. People ask me for information about products, places to shop, or sales.
4. If someone asked me where to get the best buy on several types of products, I could tell him or her where to shop.
5. My friends think of me as a good source of information when it comes to new products or sales.
6. Think about a person who has information about a variety of products and likes to share this information with others. This person knows about new products, sales, stores, and so on, but does not necessarily feel he or she is an expert on one particular product. How well would you say this description fits you?

[Items 1 through 5 are scored on 7-point scales ranging from *strongly disagree* to *strongly agree*. Item 6 is scored on a 7-point scale ranging from *the description does not fit me well at all* to *the description fits me very well*.]

Source: Feick and Price (1987).

---

to transmit marketplace and shopping information to others), and consumer receptivity to OL appear in Boxes 5.7–5.9.

An obvious drawback to using such self-designation measures pertains to the possibility that responses are susceptible to self-reporting biases, with some participants

---

BOX 5.9 SCALE FOR MEASURING CONSUMER SUSCEPTIBILITY TO INTERPERSONAL INFLUENCE

1. I rarely purchase the latest fashion styles until I am sure my friends approve of them.
2. It is important that others like the products and brands I buy.
3. When buying products, I generally purchase those brands my friends expect me to buy.
4. If other people can see me using a product, I often purchase the brand they expect me to buy.
5. I like to know what brands and products make good impressions on others.
6. I achieve a sense of belonging by purchasing the same products and brands that others purchase.
7. If I want to be like someone, I often try to buy the same brands that person buys.
8. I often identify with other people by purchasing the same products and brands they purchase.
9. To make sure I buy the right product or brand, I often observe what others are buying and using.
10. If I have little experience with a product, I often ask my friends about the product.
11. I often consult other people to help choose the best alternative available from a product category.
12. I frequently gather information from friends or family about a product before I buy.

[All items measured on a 7-point bipolar Agree/Disagree scale.]

Source: Bearden, Netemeyer, and Teel (1989).

---

inflating their proclivity toward influencing others and others underestimating the effect they have on others' decisions. Nonetheless, because of its ease of use (e.g., OL items can readily be included in market-research questionnaires) and the possibility of verifying opinion leaders by asking others if the person is really influential, the self-designating technique currently represents the most frequently used method for measuring OL and related constructs. The approach is apparent at Procter & Gamble's (P&G) tremor.com Web site, where a self-designation questionnaire is used to recruit teenaged opinion leaders for a product-seeding WOMM program (see Chapter 7).

Key Informant Method

An alternative approach that circumvents some of the potential biases of the self-designation method is to interview "key informants" about the persons within a social group who are most likely to be opinion leaders. Such informants need not be actual members of the groups under study, as when a professor is asked to designate the most influential students within a university class, or when salespersons are questioned about specific customers who are most likely to influence the purchase behavior of other customers (Schiffman & Kanuk, 2006). Similarly, peer nominations can be obtained from group members to identify the individual within the group that is most admired and apt to be emulated. Although questions can be raised about the objectivity of the opinion leader identification approach, it has proven useful in practice. For example, games manufacturer Hasbro used the informant method in 2001 to identify opinion leaders for its handheld electronic game P-O-X. Company researchers visited video arcades, skate parks, and playgrounds and posed the question "Who's the coolest kid you know?" to adolescent boys aged 8 to 13. The researchers then sought out the designated cool kids and asked them the same question until the resulting hierarchy of cool finally led them to someone who answered "Me!" (Marsden, 2006a). The opinion leader (referred to by the company as an "Alpha Pup") was then invited to participate in an exclusive seeding trial during which they were given ten new pre-release P-O-X units that they could share with friends (see Chapter 7).

Professional Activity

One straightforward approach to finding opinion leaders is to approach persons who are paid to give expert opinions, such as doctors, pharmacists, or scientists who have access to specialized information from technical journals and other practitioners (Solomon, 2008). Similarly, marketers can rely on the job title of target clients and customers as an indicator of OL status, based on the assumption that professional involvement with a category is predictive of a person's likelihood to influence peers via WOM. The 3M company proceeded along these lines when it identified secretaries to the company's CEOs as opinion leaders in office stationary products (Marsden, 2006*a*).

Professionals are frequently approached by marketers who recognize an opportunity for gaining consumer acceptance by encouraging the experts to recommend their offerings. This was the approach taken by Roc S.A., the European maker of hypoallergenic lotions in their efforts to break into the American skin-care market. Prior to launching a mass market advertising campaign, the French company first attempted to convince professionals about the efficacy of the product line through advertising in medical journals and free distribution to dermatologists and pharmacies.

Digital Trace

This approach involves identifying opinion leaders through an online search of category-relevant Web sites, such as blogs, web forums, and newsgroups. For example, Siemens identified opinion leaders to participate in a seeding trial for a new mobile phone by first monitoring an online user review forum. In fact, consumer forums for technological (and other) products typically have frequent posters who have advanced knowledge and expertise about a category. These persons often manage conversation threads or take the lead in providing advice and may be identified through a designation label such as "advanced user," "moderator," "distinguished member," or simply by total number of their posts. Chances are that such individuals also serve as influentials in their social world off-line.

Sociometry

Sociometric methods trace communication patterns among self-contained members of social groups or communities, such that researchers can systematically map the interactions that take place between group members (Solomon, 2008). One outcome of this approach is the identification of a referral network like that depicted in Figure 3.3. By interviewing individuals about whom they receive WOM communications from, it is possible to trace persons who represent primary sources of product-related information within the group or centralized hubs of expertise. This approach tends to be expensive, time-intensive, and limited in the sense that it requires that the group studied is an intact or self-contained one, such as a retirement community or university student residency. Relatively difficult to manage in practice, sociometric methods nonetheless can prove informative in shedding light on how WOM spreads through a community and in better understanding the role of opinion leaders within social groups.

A research approach that is an offshoot of sociometry utilizes network analysis methods to discern the kinds of social relationships that receivers of WOM have with potential communicators. This information then is used to predict the likelihood that WOM will occur. Network analysis focuses on the extent to which people are likely to serve as "connectors" (i.e., they know many people) and "hubs" (i.e., they have extensive links to numerous friends and acquaintances), and whether the connections between people are representative of "strong ties" (i.e., close relationships with friends) or "weak ties" (i.e., superficial relationships with acquaintances) (see Granovetter, 1973). Also of interest is the degree of "betweenness" that characterizes individuals within social networks, suggestive of the extent to which some people serve to span the boundaries between different groups and thereby act as bridges for information to flow from one group to the other. Such boundary spanners can be essential for the spread of WOM. If members of a particular social group (say, young skateboarders within a suburban community) are all reading the same magazines, watching the same TV programs, playing the same video games, spending time at the same fast-food restaurants, surfing similar Web sites, and so on, it becomes rather unlikely that any one member is going to bring much new information into the group that other members are not also aware of. But if one of the group members happens to still be connected with a childhood friend he met at summer camp who travels within vastly different social circles, then things can get interesting in terms of the new information that may reach the skateboarders.

Profiling Influencers

This approach to identifying opinion leaders is based on the recognition that people who play different roles in the transmission of WOM within their social networks can be segmented according to specific characteristics. You may recall the discussion in Chapter 3 that described the profiles of opinion leaders, brand advocates, and innovators. For example, we saw that opinion leaders are perceived as highly credible sources of information by their peers, are self-confident, gregarious, and heavy users of special interest media. With such profiles in hand, efforts at identifying the members of specific target groups should be beneficial in pointing out individuals who are more likely to be influential than others (see Box 5.10).

This is the logic behind the approach taken by Bradley Ferguson, founder of the research and development company Intrinzyk. Ferguson (2006) developed a segmentation profile for influencers that has proven successful in identifying consumers who cast a wider net of influence and have a greater impact on purchase decisions than other members of the general population. Based on their scores on a standardized test of personal charisma, the Affective Communication Test, and an estimate of the relative size and geographical distribution of their social networks, people are classified along

---

BOX 5.10 FOCUS ON APPLICATION: PROFILING MARKET INFLUENCERS

Several companies have developed their own approaches for generating profiles of market influencers. For example, the public relations agency Burson-Marsteller, in cooperation with NOP World (now Gfk NOP), has identified a subset of influencers referred to as *e-fluentials*. These are the 10% of the US online adult consumers who have an exponential influence on public opinion in both online and off-line spheres, generating the predominance of buzz about brands, products, and companies. Compared with other Internet users, they are more active users of e-mail, newsgroups, online bulletin boards, and listservs. Burson-Marsteller screens e-fluentials through the application of a proprietary algorithm that is based on the frequency with which Internet users engage in a variety of online activities (Cakim, 2006).

Earlier, I mentioned P&G's Tremor program, an effort by the world's largest consumer goods manufacturer to identify trendsetters. In recruiting over 280,000 influential teens (referred to by the company as "connectors"), P&G then attempted to determine the trendsetters who played a determining role in the emergence of the next hot consumer product. This effort failed, however, because such individuals were reluctant to spread the word to others because they wanted to remain different from their peers (Oetting, 2006). Instead, P&G set out to identify *trendspreaders*, consisting of teens who have a wide social circle consisting of many connections that they convey news to about products and ideas, among other content. A Tremor online questionnaire is used to recruit these individuals by asking them to convey the number of people (friends, relatives, and acquaintances) they communicate with each day, and the most sociable persons (roughly, the 10% of respondents who have on average 170 names in their address books) are invited to join the network.

The public relations firm Ketchum also attempts to identify influencers who shape the buying habits of the masses. Ketchum utilizes a methodology that combines web searches, interviews, and attempts to trace the information back to its original source. This effort revealed that the identity of influencers tends to vary according to product category; however, influencers tend to be comprised of professional experts, including financial and industry analysts, authors, reporters, academics, grassroots organizers, and advocacy groups. For example, one analysis revealed that toothpaste influence is largely spread by dental hygienists and dating experts, whereas mascara advice is conveyed by makeup artists, women's magazine writers, and optometrists (Chura, 2004).

---

two variables that have been found to be predictive of recommendation behavior and impact: their degree of charisma (expressive or reserved) and their social connectedness (social or private). Ferguson's analyses have revealed that influencers tend to have an Expressive/Social profile (i.e., high ACT scores/high social connection). They are active recommenders across diverse industries and product categories, they know on average four to five times more people than persons from the general population, and they have a greater impact on the purchase decisions of those within their social networks.

Coolhunting

Widely popularized as a contemporary marketing activity by journalist Malcolm Gladwell in a 1997 article he wrote for *The New Yorker*, coolhunting describes marketing research endeavors oriented toward the observation and prediction of ongoing and emerging cultural trends, particularly among youth culture. As described by Gladwell (1997, p. 81), coolhunting provides "a window on the world of the street":

> Ask a coolhunter where the baggy-jeans look came from, for example, and you might get any number of answers: urban black kids mimicking the jailhouse look, skateboarders looking for room to move, snowboarders trying not to look like skiers, or, alternatively, all three at once, in some grand concordance.

Marketing representatives, so-called "coolhunters," traverse inner-city neighborhoods, underground clubs, shopping malls, and other settings where young trendsetters are likely to hang out, in an effort to capture fashion and style currents that exist under the mainstream radar. Although coolhunting is mostly about the search for the next big consumer trend or fad, it is based on the identification of trendsetters through the keen observation skills of trained coolhunters. Once identified, the trendsetters can be invited to participate in focus group interviews, in an effort to obtain deep insight into their thoughts and feelings.

A Caveat: Just How Influential Are Influentials?

In his compelling and informative best-selling book *The Tipping Point*, Malcolm Gladwell presented a number of intriguing notions related to social behavior. However, the one that struck the more resounding chord among many marketers was his "law of the few," the idea that social epidemics—the widespread movement of influence through social networks—are a function of the relatively small number of people who serve as infectious agents. Gladwell (2000, p. 19) succinctly summarized this notion with his claim that behind any successful trend, "some people matter more than others." This is an idea that has long been recognized by economists, as evidenced by the 80/20 principle (also known as "Pareto's principle"), which suggests that in most situations, a small minority of people (20%) are vital in having an impact over the rest of the population. Although not originally proposed with consumers in mind, a preponderance of marketers see this notion as fundamental in understanding the dynamics of how interpersonal influence works in the consumer marketplace. In fact, some marketers suggest that an even smaller percentage of the population influences the rest, a figure that they estimate as roughly 10% (Berry & Keller, 2003; Oetting, 2006).

The impact of a small proportion of especially influential people certainly cannot be denied. For example, the results of a 2003 campaign initiated by the influencer marketing agency Ammo Marketing for Miller Genuine Draft beer revealed that over the course of the 6-month marketing program, 500 consumers who were enlisted into a marketing program to help spread the word about the beer indirectly influenced nearly 1.5 million American beer drinkers (Ferguson, 2006). The evangelists who participated in the campaign had been selected by Ammo on the basis of a lifestyle analysis that revealed them to possess the "urban mindset" that was consistent with the intended positioning of the brand for core 21- to 27-year-old drinkers. In his book, Gladwell recounted the story of the once popular casual shoe line Hush Puppies that was about to be taken off the market in the early 1990s due to declining sales. Suddenly, the shoes became enormously popular again, largely as a function of a small number of trendsetting teenagers in New York City who started wearing the shoes after coming across them in second-hand clothing stores. These cool kids served as influentials who were noticed by other young New Yorkers as well as fashion designers, and before long Hush Puppies went from passé to hip to mainstream like a rapidly spreading virus.

In light of the aforementioned examples, it seems to make sense for marketers to mount strong efforts to identify influentials like opinion leaders, innovators, and brand advocates. And there is no question that many have heard the call—estimates are that more than US$1 billion is spent each year on WOM campaigns targeting influentials, an amount that is growing by 36% per year (Thompson, 2008). However, could marketers be missing something here? Given the increasing connectedness between consumers of all ilks in the contemporary marketplace, isn't it reasonable to assume that just about anyone can serve as an influential at one time or another in certain circumstances, and that by concentrating on the 10% or 20% of opinion leaders and innovators, marketers are missing huge opportunities? According to Columbia University Professor Duncan Watts and other network-theory scientists, the answer is a resounding "yes." They argue that the proponents of the influentials theory who claim that there are consumers who are more influential than others and are disproportionately important in giving impetus to a trend fail to clarify the mechanics by which this process occurs. Indeed, when the influential assumptions have been subjected to systematic network research analysis, the supporting evidence has thus far failed to emerge. For example, Watts has carried out a series of studies utilizing a variety of research methodologies, including analyses of the patterns that emerge in the spread of e-mail messages, computer modeling of rumor spreading, virtual world computer simulations, and large-scale replications of social psychologist Stanley Milgram's small-world experiment (which led to the well-known "six degrees of separation" notion).

Although space does not permit an elaboration of each of these social network studies, some details about the small-world experiment can serve as an informative example, given the intriguing methodology designed by Milgram during the late 1960s. Milgram was interested in determining how an idea or piece of news travels through a population in his effort to shed light on the nature of the interpersonal links between people. He identified as the two most plausible possibilities that we either are connected by autonomous links with a limited number of other people or we are joined by a vast and complex interlocking web. Using the idea of a chain letter, Milgram mailed a small packet to 160 people in Omaha, Nebraska, along with the name and address of a stockbroker who lived and worked in separate cities in Massachusetts. He asked each person to put their name on the packet and then to mail it to someone they knew who would get it closer to the stockbroker, who would then try to do the same.

The idea was to get the mailing to its final destination in the fewest number of steps possible. If, for example, you lived in Omaha and had an ex-college roommate living in nearby Lincoln, Nebraska who has family in Boston, Massachusetts, you might choose to mail the packet to that person. Even though Lincoln is even somewhat further from Massachusetts than Omaha, your ex-roommate would probably stand a better chance of getting the packet to the stockbroker than you would. Once the stockbroker received the mailing, Milgram checked to see how many persons were listed on the packet to ascertain how closely connected two strangers on different sides of the country were to each other. What he learned was that only five or six steps were required for most of the mailings to reach their destination—the so-called "six degrees of separation." Significantly—and this is important in terms of the implications of Milgram's research for the influentials theory—Milgram observed that not all degrees among the six degrees of separation were equal. A large number of the letters reached the stockbroker via the same three people, suggesting that "a very small number of people are linked to everyone else in a few steps, and the rest of us are linked to the world through those special few" (Gladwell, 2000, p. 37).

Milgram's experiment stands as a fascinating example of how the world in which we live indeed is a small one, particularly in terms of the interpersonal communication of information. However, when Watts replicated the experiment on a massive scale in 2001 after having recruited 61,000 people to try to deliver e-mail messages toward eighteen targets worldwide, his results failed to find evidence of a super-connected few. Consistent with Milgram's results, the average number of connections for reaching targets was about six, but highly connected people (i.e., "hubs") did not appear to be crucial in the process. Only about 5% of the messages passed through hubs, with the rest of the messages moving from one weakly connected individual to another on their way to their final targets. Watts attributed the original findings as due to an anomaly linked to Milgram's small sample size and, because they seemed to logically make sense, researchers never questioned Milgram's results or conclusions (Thompson, 2008).

The picture that has begun to emerge from the social network research suggests that the average person is just as likely as a well-connected person to start a huge new consumer trend. According to Watts, social epidemics are the result of a critical mass of easily influenced people who adopt a brand after being exposed to a single influencing neighbor who stumbles into that role and acts as an "accidental influencer." In Watts' view, "If society is ready to embrace a trend, almost anyone can start one—and if it isn't, then almost no one can" (Thompson, 2008, p. 3). This is not to suggest that certain consumers do not have a disproportionate influence on their peers' buying behavior:

most marketers would agree that certain people do indeed have a greater impact in the marketplace than others. Although the jury is still out as to how central the role of influentials in marketing trends may be, the lesson to be taken from the debate is that the majority of consumers in the general population should not be ignored in social marketing campaigns.

Conclusion

If there is any key message to be taken from this chapter, it is that marketing practitioners no longer have any excuse to forego WOM and social marketing measurement efforts. As social marketer Martin Oetting (2006, p. 261) concluded, "...in many cases, connected marketers can now prove the effectiveness of their work—and often more thoroughly and precisely than other forms of marketing communication." The vast array of existing and emerging methodologies for tracking WOM, online and off-line consumer conversations, and the impact of social marketing campaigns suggests great opportunities for the marketing profession to respond to new marketing realities. However, this requires a shift in mentality away from the traditional marketer-to-consumer paradigm, with its focus on traditional tried-and-true advertising standards of reach (how many people in the target population that have been exposed to the marketing message at least once), frequency (average number of times each target has been exposed to the message), and brand awareness. Importantly, no research approach, methodology, or metric is without limitations, a point that Keiningham et al. (2007, p. 378) made abundantly clear in their assessment of the net promoter index:

> This is not to discount their importance, but...any single metric designed to explain customer behavior across a diverse customer base is unlikely to be an adequate gauge upon which managers can act.

As the number of research approaches and metrics for evaluating social marketing campaigns continues to grow, marketers increasingly will need guidance as to which measure is most applicable to a determination of whether a marketing action is successful or not. We are still at the stage where a standard set of metrics for evaluating the merits of the vast array of connected marketing techniques is lacking. In the view of Justin Kirby (2006*b*, p. 270),

> ...it's more than likely that there will never be one set of measurements that can be applied to all the diverse approaches being used. Instead, at the very least, a way must be found for any connected marketing campaign to be measured in terms of its impact on customer recommendation rates and the correlation between the increasing instances of these and sales.

6 Listening to and Engaging Consumers

It is probably not a bad idea to begin this first of three chapters on connected marketing approaches, methods, and techniques by reconsidering one of this book's main underlying themes, which is that the contemporary marketing environment is one in which consumers are in control. As you have read in previous chapters, consumers have co-opted products, they generate and share their own promotions, they choose the time and place for exchanges, and perhaps the most important point—and where we see the clearest link to the past—they control the dollars. It was not that long ago that marketers regularly asked their customers, "Are you connected?"—Cable TV? A computer? Internet access? Cell phone? Today, the question about connectedness has blown back into the faces of marketers. We have seen the myriad ways and extent to which consumers are connected with each other, to the point at which many no longer need marketers at all. So the relevant questions in today's marketing environment pertain to whether marketers are connected: with current and potential customers, with social media, with collaborative partners. How is it possible to get in on the consumer conversation? And what are the means by which one can leverage the conversation for corporate profit while maintaining a loyalty to the basic tenets of the marketing concept? Although you will find many suggested answers in preceding chapters, these are questions that we tackle head-on in this and the remaining chapters of this book.

In Chapter 1, I mentioned an illuminating keynote address presented by Don E. Schultz (2008) at the thirteenth International Conference on Corporate and Marketing Communications in Slovenia. During his talk, Schultz observed that "you won't find a textbook anywhere that starts with the customer, only the company." Although perhaps self-evident, his point was that it all starts with customers; that is, if consumers now are in control, and if they are the ones with the money, then everything in marketing must begin with them. Generally speaking, this is not the way marketing has operated in the past. When marketing firms have developed TV commercials, offered promotional games, devised retailer sales strategies, and the like, they have done these things so as to provide value for the media, the agency, the brand, and the firm—not the customer. This is not to say that consumers have not benefited from these activities, only that their interests have not been front and center in the minds of most marketers. In fact, until 2004, the American Marketing Association did not even offer definitions of the terms "customer" and "consumer." But change is in the air and marketers are now running to catch up with consumers—think of the film *Catch Me If You Can*. It was no accident that Schultz titled his keynote address, "On the Cusp of Communication Change." If traditional marketing has long been about talking, twenty-first century connected marketing must be, in no small part, about listening.

The Tenets of Good Conversation

If marketers are truly becoming serious about *listening to* and *engaging* current and potential customers, it is important to be clear about just what those terms entail. In a marketing sense, the terms are not really new, as marketers have long recognized the importance of gaining the attention of consumers (from the original hierarchy of effects models of the early 1900s) and generating consumer interest, involvement, and commitment (in the sense of marketing offers that have personal relevance and importance for targets). But once again, these concerns have predominately been based on a marketer-to-consumer framework. The conventional approach has been something akin to Ray Kinsella's *Field of Dreams'* baseball mantra, "If we build it, they will come"; to wit, if we produce a sexy or provocative TV ad, consumers will watch it; if we design a sleek and innovative mp3 player, consumers will desire it; if we offer a product with an attractive promotion, consumers will buy it; and so on. However, once we put consumers first, the essence of marketing communication changes. This point was made abundantly clear by one of the contemporary gurus of engagement marketing, Joseph Jaffe, author of the 2007 book, *Join the Conversation*. According to Jaffe (p. 3), in contrast to traditional *marketing communication*, which involves a one-way, unidirectional, and carefully controlled process of marketer-initiated messaging, *marketing conversation* is:

> …a two-way dialogue or a stream of messaging between two or more parties with like-minded or shared beliefs, wants, needs, passions, or interests. Conversation is not initiated by any one person, side, or organization. It is organic, nonlinear, unpredictable, and natural.

Jaffe went on to propose ten tenets of good conversation that apply to marketing conversational contexts. These tenets, which are elaborated below, provide a useful framework for clarifying the nature of listening to and engaging with consumers in the Marketing 2.0 era.

1. *Good conversation is natural (not forced).* Imagine that you were lucky enough to get your company to agree to pay for your business class seat on the tedious 5-hour flight to Reykjavik, where you are traveling to meet an important client. A nice opportunity, so you think, to prepare your thoughts about the upcoming meeting planned for the morning after your late arrival. Much to your chagrin,

however, you quickly discover that the passenger in the next seat has a proclivity toward excess chatter and immediately strives to engage you in pedantic banter, revealing personal details about himself, inquiring as to the purpose of your trip, describing his plans to bathe in the geothermal waters of the Blue Lagoon, and so on. You get the impression that your fellow passenger is talking in order to hear himself talk. It should be clear from this example what Jaffe means by good conversation being natural and not forced. It is one thing to want to engage consumers in a two-way exchange, but the point is that marketers should try to avoid talking simply for the sake of talking.

As an example of a brand story which spoke for itself without the unnecessary participation of marketing professionals, Jaffe referred to videos of the famous set of experiments spontaneously filmed by consumers (including a science teacher) to document the impressive consequences of mixing Diet Coke and Mentos candy. The videos struck a chord among countless viewers, aroused interest in the brands, and stimulated online discussions. Although it would have been possible for the Coca-Cola Company to jump on the conversational bandwagon, its participation hardly would have seemed natural. By contrast, Jaffe asks us to imagine an online posting by a blogger who describes in graphic language how she is fed up with the Apple brand, only to receive a comment to her post signed by Apple CEO Steve Jobs, who informally explains recent decisions at the company, interest in hearing consumers' comments (both good and bad), and so on. As far-fetched as that example may seem at first reading, just imagine the blogger's reaction and how easy and inexpensive (free!) it would have been to accomplish. It recalls a similar example that transpired at one of the online forums run by fans of the Boston Red Sox baseball team. One thread was brutally critical of one of the team's pitchers who at the time was not performing up to snuff. At one point in the discussion, the pitcher himself got in on the discussion, posting messages to respond to some of the fans' comments. He described his own disgust with his recent performance and his disappointment at letting his teammates down, explained his intensive approach to the game, agreed and disagreed with previous messages. Perhaps not surprisingly, the tone of that forum's discussions changed dramatically, with participants describing their new-found respect and appreciation for the pitcher who only earlier had been the target of their wrath.

2. *Good conversation is honest.* No one likes a liar, so it goes without saying that no one likes a dishonest marketer. In this era of informed skepticism, if marketers hope to join the consumer conversation, they must be willing to engage in a truly open and honest dialogue with their targets. As discussed in Chapter 2, one of the main reasons that consumers have progressively come to bypass marketers and instead seek out each other for advice and information is because of the considerable mistrust people have for traditional marketing practices. To win back consumers' trust, truth and credibility must be essential components of any

connected marketing effort. This is perhaps easier said than done. Unfortunately, for some firms, getting on the social marketing bandwagon is simply viewed as another opportunity to manipulate through the employment of new deceptive tactics that attract potential consumers to a brand.

One example of a new trend in unscrupulous marketing is seen in the emergence of fake blogs (often referred to as *flogs*). A flog is an online forum that appears to have been produced by a credible, non-biased source, but which actually originates from a company or its representative for promotional purposes. Fake blogs and fake postings on legitimate blogs are intended to generate interest in a product, service, brand, or company, and to drive traffic to a site and stimulate WOM. This is accomplished by misleading visitors into perceiving the deceptive communication as one that has been created by a satisfied or loyal customer or client who is benevolently motivated to turn others on to the focal offering by sharing honest opinions and personal experiences.

Flogs now represent a common fixture of the modern marketing landscape. Although most flogs no doubt exist under the radar, examples of this tactic that have been detected involve some of the best known consumer-oriented firms, such as McDonald's, Wal-Mart, Coca-Cola, and Vichy (see Box 6.1). In the case involving McDonald's, the fast food restaurant chain posted a fake blog in 2005 that was presented as a journal written by a fictitious couple, Mike and Liz, who claimed to have discovered in one of their meals a french fry shaped like the head of US President Abraham Lincoln. The entire flog, including posted comments, was created by McDonald's as an offshoot of an ad campaign launched during the Super Bowl, and likely was not purposely intended to mislead consumers. Nonetheless, while the TV ads were well received, the faux blog was not, having riled many legitimate bloggers within the online community. Yet, the attraction to this marketing ploy for firms is apparent when one considers that the Lincoln Fry blog initially received over two million hits before it was revealed as part of an ad campaign, with McDonald's later acknowledging that the revelation essentially revitalized the mainstream campaign (Corcoran et al., 2006).

In addition to fake blogs, comments that are posted on legitimate blogs and online forums have been surreptitiously written by professional bloggers who have been paid

---

BOX 6.1 FOCUS ON APPLICATION: WAL-MARTING ACROSS AMERICA AND VICHY'S UPLIFTING BLOG RESCUE

Wal-Mart's public relations blunder involving a fake blog provoked an enormous amount of negative buzz about the company. The fake blog, titled "Wal-Marting Across America," was created for Wal-Mart in September 2006 by the PR firm Edelman. Allegedly written by Laura and Jim, a couple who claimed to be Wal-Mart enthusiasts, the blog chronicled their journey across the United States in a recreational vehicle, visiting Wal-Mart stores along the way and interviewing exuberant and highly

(cont.)

Box 6.1 (*Continued*)

satisfied employees, ranging from store clerks to company executives. The full story of how a couple of actual Wal-Mart customers ended up fictitiously promoting the consumer-goods firm is a bit convoluted, but the upshot is that they were well paid for their involvement, with the cross-country tour having been underwritten by Working Families for Wal-Mart, a company-sponsored group organized by Edelman (see Gogoi, 2006).

The truth behind the fake blog, as well as its authors' actual identities, ultimately was revealed by skeptical critics, including a Colorado State University professor who publicly challenged the couple to acknowledge their true identities and explain who really had paid for their trip. Given the various allegations directed against Wal-Mart over the years, from exploiting foreign workers to charges that the company was actively fighting city ordinances to raise the minimum wage, the blog's overly upbeat and positive portrayal of the company and its employees raised a number of red flags. On 16 October, the fake blog promoting Wal-Mart was shut down and CEO Richard Edelman publicly apologized for the fiasco, writing on his own blog (http://www.edelman.com),

> I want to acknowledge our error in failing to be transparent about the identity of the two bloggers from the outset. This is 100% our responsibility and our error; not the client's. . . . Our commitment is to openness and engagement because trust is not negotiable and we are working to be sure that commitment is delivered in all our programs.

Only days later, Edelman revealed that his firm was behind two more flogs that also were created on behalf of Wal-Mart (Siebert, 2006).

A similar story with a more satisfying resolution is the case involving Vichy, a division of the French cosmetics firm L'Oréal. The fledgling attempt by Vichy to add blogging to its integrated marketing campaign for the launch of a new anti-aging cream (Peel Micro-abrasion) serves as another example of a fake blog that, at least initially, backfired for the company that created it. Launched in April 2005, the "Diary of My Skin" ("Journal de Ma Peau") blog presented a fake character named Claire, who used the medium as a forum to complain about her difficulties maintaining a fresh look while attending many parties and not getting enough sleep. However, it was readily clear to nearly anyone familiar with blogs that the Vichy site was more of an advertising agency creation than an actual blog: Claire looked like a professionally photographed model, comments were filtered, and the text appeared to be unspontaneous, polished, and contrived.

Given the other examples described here, it should be no surprise that within minutes of the ad agency's issuance of a press release boasting about its fictitious character blog, actual Internet bloggers began to attack the brand for its inauthenticity and creation of a false character presented as an actual consumer. The French mass media followed suit, with the marketing magazine *Stratégies* offering this assessment (Israel, 2005): "Brands that try to disguise themselves as authors are no longer credible. Reading product instructions done up like a blog is silly. Vichy continues to do top-down marketing: the exact opposite of the blogger philosophy."

Facing such scathing attacks, Vichy learned its lesson quickly. The site was relaunched as a fully functional blog, as opposed to a disguised company Web site, and the first message was the firm's apology for its misguided initial foray into the blogosphere. In order to enhance full disclosure and begin to garner trust, a photograph of the members of the Vichy team was presented, along with an invitation for bloggers to share their advice on how the Vichy blog could best be used in conjunction with their new product. Consistent with received comments, the result was an authentic and transparent blog designed to serve as an information resource for consumers. A noted French blogger with influence on cosmetics was enlisted to post on the site along with the Vichy team, and together they guided five volunteers through a 4-week cosmetics program, providing the participants with the opportunity to post unfiltered comments on the blog. In so doing, Vichy was successful in building a trusting relationship between the firm and bloggers, inviting prospective customers to try the product and comment on the experience.

According to Lynn Serfaty, a group manager for L'Oréal's Vichy brand, the blog experience taught the company some valuable lessons:

> We learned that we could talk directly to the users. They had questions for us and we had answers, so the brand didn't have to be anonymous to have status. We also learned that communication could be spontaneous and a work-in-progress. We re-adjusted as we discovered their needs and heard their questions. A perfect example was sun protection. We had a precise answer to whether you could use the product and go into the sun but bloggers asked us questions we had not previously considered: What happens if I spend a weekend in the sun? What if I live in a sunny place, and so on.

to take the side of specific companies that have come under fire in discussion threads (Upshaw, 2007). In a variation of this ploy, the marketing agency Cornerstone hired young people to log into chat rooms and pose as fans of one of their clients. Cornerstone also recruited incoming university students to throw parties for which they were offered incentives to pass out promotional material to their classmates. Various buzz management firms have paid or offered other incentives to young people for sending e-mails to their friends encouraging them to try client products. These examples are illustrative of marketing tactics that may have appeared to their designers as creative attempts to capture the attention and interest of consumers through new social media channels, but which ended up subverting those channels and running the risk of further alienating target audiences due to a lack of transparency. The backlash that occurs when these marketing tactics are revealed can be significant. For example, in addition to provoking negative online comments and unwanted publicity in the mainstream media, Coca-Cola's Zero Movement flog to promote the company's new Coke Zero diet soft drink led to the creation of an anti-Coke Zero blog called "The Zero Movement Sucks." The counter blog ridiculed the flog and called out Coke for its patronizing marketing tactics, and may have received more visits than the flog itself (Hall, 2006).

Although some of these ethically questionable marketing tactics have been defended by their designers as obvious parodies of social media trends, it would be unwise to underestimate the potential damage they can cause to the reputation of the firms involved. In the view of BzzAgent CEO Dave Balter, "Even if you're doing the right thing but you know you're going to deceive people, you have to do everything to make sure it's completely transparent, and any tactic that crosses that line you're doing a disservice to the brand [and] the consumer" (Siebert, 2006). This point was echoed by Debbie Wiel, author of *The Corporate Blogging Book*, in her response to Wal-Mart's flog: "This is so foolish on so many levels . . . everyone involved violated the basic rule: Be transparent. If you're found out, it comes back as a slap in the face" (Kramer, 2006). The following online comments by ordinary consumers also clarify why such tactics undermine the spirit of Jaffe's second tenet (Zawodny, 2005):

- Fake blogs fly in the face of why blogs are created in the first place, to create an honest, direct dialogue with customers. It shows a clear misunderstanding of the medium and will pay off with tons of negative buzz online.
- [Fake blogs] demonstrate that no one is passionate enough about the product inside the company so they had to hire an ad agency to do a fake blog to try to get bloggers to link up.

3. *Good conversation is balanced.* Jaffe's third tenet of good marketing conversation holds that conversation is not only two-sided, but balanced, in the sense that the parties operate as equal participants in the communication process. This is one way that listening and engagement obviously go hand in hand. It is one thing for marketers to set the stage so that consumers will feel compelled to talk about a product or campaign, and then to carefully monitor what is being said to make sure that the discussion is on target. But unless marketers also participate in that conversation via a two-way exchange, opportunities for active engagement will be lost.

The WOM measurement approaches and metrics surveyed in Chapter 5 suggest some of the ways that balanced, two-way exchanges between marketers and consumers can take place, whether for research and analysis purposes or for building relationships with customers and prospects. Managers have access to many of the same communication networks as consumers, which enables them to gauge what consumers are saying about products and brands. Google and blog search engines such as Technorati, Feedster, and BlogPulse are useful resources for monitoring and tracking online conversations. By regularly conducting a search of a company's name or relevant brands (followed by keywords such as "is awesome" or "sucks"), it is possible to identify indicators of important trends and effectively monitor what customers are saying. It is difficult to engage consumers on an even playing field if you do not have access to what they currently are saying about your company and its products.

Coolhunting, also introduced in Chapter 5, provides another way to tap into current buzz, which then can be used as a springboard for engaging with consumers. Again, this involves seeking out and conversing with young trendsetters in their natural habitats (e.g., urban settings, such as bars, clubs, basketball courts) to identify the latest buzz, invite reactions to new product concepts or design, and so on. Although suspicious of marketers, trendsetters will be open to those who can gain their confidence and demonstrate a genuine interest in their opinions (Kimmel, 2007b).

4. *Good conversation is open.* Openness goes hand in hand with the characteristics of good conversation already discussed—naturalness, honesty, and balance—and is

a basic prerequisite to trust. This is a lesson often learned too late by many companies in their efforts to offset false, malicious rumors (Kimmel & Audrain-Pontevia, 2010) and negative WOM (Kimmel & Audrain-Pontevia, 2008). In the case of rumors, many managers simply choose to ignore them in the hope that they will die a natural death or they may issue forceful denials, along with the threat of lawsuits against known rumor spreaders. In most cases, when such tactics are utilized by a targeted firm, they simply reinforce the perceptions held by an anxious and skeptical public that the company has something to hide. By contrast, opening channels of communication (e.g., by establishing a rumor hotline or Web page) goes a long way toward building trust in consumer–company relationships by reducing the two psychological factors that researchers have found give rise to rumors in the first place: uncertainty (i.e., how filled with questions people are about current or future events) and anxiety (i.e., how worried or concerned people are). Moreover, a set of frequently asked questions (FAQs) for the firm's Internet site can be developed based on content or themes that tend to be repeatedly received from rumor hotline users (see Box 6.2). In a broader sense, FAQs also can be beneficial in overcoming negative WOM based on inaccurate beliefs and misperceptions.

BOX 6.2 FREQUENTLY ASKED QUESTIONS (FAQS)

A growing number of Internet newsgroups and Web sites now offer listings of "Frequently Asked Questions" (FAQs), which reflect the kinds of information or clarifications that people seek about a complex issue or a particular piece of ambiguous or troubling information. FAQs and accompanying authoritative answers are usually accepted as the last word on their particular topics. These items are useful from the perspective of rumor prevention because they can serve as an effective method for identifying likely rumor content areas, as well as offering a means to reduce public uncertainties through the provision of much-needed authoritative information.

As an example, a few years ago I conducted a study on rumors related to electricity for the French national electric company (EDF). One of the company's overriding objectives was to identify the kinds of concerns and fears prevalent among the French consuming public relative to electromagnetic fields (EMFs) emanating from outdoor power plants. Company representatives conjectured that these misconceptions and fears could provide the basis for electricity-related rumors which ultimately could harm the company and exacerbate public anxieties. As a result of our search of numerous Web sites related to electricity, it was obvious that there were widespread concerns about EMFs among the consuming public. A majority of the FAQs found at those sites had to do with risks attributed to outdoor EMF sources as opposed to those emanating from domestic appliances. For example:

- How big is the cancer risk associated with living next to a power line? What is the risk of cancer in general? What is the risk of childhood leukemia?
- How close do you have to be to a power line to be considered exposed to power-frequency magnetic fields?

(cont.)

Box 6.2 (*Continued*)
- If exposure to power-frequency magnetic fields does not explain the residential and occupations studies which show increased cancer incidence, what other factors could?
- What sort of power-frequency fields are common in residences and work places?
- What is the difference between the electromagnetic (EM) energy associated with power lines and other forms of EM energy such as microwaves or X-rays?
- Is there any evidence that power-frequency fields cause any human health hazards, such as miscarriages, birth defects or Alzheimer's disease?

The electricity company intended to use these FAQs as the basis for developing materials for better informing consumers about the facts concerning electromagnetic fields (e.g., by distributing brochures responding to the kinds of questions appearing on the consulted Web sites).

Creating blogs and becoming an active participant in the blogosphere represents a fundamental new approach for connecting with consumers in an atmosphere of openness (see Box 6.3). Nonetheless, many companies still are lagging behind in this regard and are only beginning to recognize the value that can be accrued from active participation in the blogosphere. One company that *has* taken advantage of this opportunity is the US car manufacturer, General Motors, through the creation of several blogs, including the GM FYI Blog. According to Jaffe (2007), GM's efforts to engage the car-buying public through open dialogue provide an effective means for bypassing (often hostile) traditional press to communicate messages to consumers and build communities of supporters. As Andy Sernovitz (2007), author of *Word of Mouth Marketing*, noted,

> Nothing earns more credibility with bloggers than a company that is part of the blog community. Blog. Comment. Converse. Don't be a stranger. It's too late if you aren't already

---

BOX 6.3 FOCUS ON RESEARCH: WHAT DO BLOGGERS REALLY WANT?

In addition to imparting information and their opinions to the Internet public, bloggers are avid consumers and creators of online content (e.g., artwork, photos, videos, stories) and they take every opportunity to communicate with others, both online and off-line. For example 78% of American bloggers claim to send or receive instant messages in contrast to 38% of all Internet users, and 55% of French bloggers have subscriptions to more than fifty blog feeds. Bloggers are primarily motivated to share information and opinions, and the possibility of making money from their online activity tends to be a secondary interest for most. This portrait has emerged from recent studies, including a 2007 online survey of 500 randomly selected French bloggers (BuzzParadise, 2008) and a 2006 telephone survey of 233 randomly selected American bloggers (Lenhart & Fox, 2006).

These analyses have revealed that bloggers appreciate learning that a company is reading something they have written and are willing to be contacted by marketing professionals, such as by personalized e-mail. As Sernovitz (2007) points out: "Many bloggers are (pleasantly) shocked when they find out that a company is actually reading what they write. Post a note when you read something you like. Post replies and comments when you see unfair criticism." An online survey of

821 bloggers conducted by Edelman and Technorati found that although a majority of respondents said they were open to receiving contacts with companies, only 16% reported that companies attempt to interact with them in a personalized way. The poll also revealed that more than half of the bloggers surveyed write about a company or product at least once per week. Blog criticism has greater lasting power than bad press in traditional news outlets and thus can be especially harmful to a company. Corporate participation in the blogosphere provides an effective channel for establishing an open, ongoing dialogue with consumers for building trust in order to convert critics.

blogging when a negative attack happens. You can't earn respect after you need it ... you need to earn it up front, and build a storehouse of good will.

Some companies engage consumers by actively supporting brand communities. For example, Saab maintains a close relationship with brand admirers, providing direct access to the company president for comments, supporting Saab owner clubs, sponsoring annual events at which owners are invited to display their cars and attend seminars, and soliciting feedback from dedicated owners prior to car design changes. In this way, the company gains access to community information sources and thus is in a better position to identify, and perhaps affect, the information that is being relayed to and by the community (Muñiz & O'Guinn, 2005).

Recent comments by Zurich Financial CEO James J. Schiro suggest that these approaches for opening up the conversation with consumers can bring success because they are based on two fundamental ingredients: inclusion and listening (Bryant, 2009). When asked to describe the most important leadership lesson he had learned at the helm of his financial institution, Schiro responded,

> It's the ability to listen, and to make people understand that you are listening to them. Make them feel that they are making a contribution, and then you make a decision. I don't think any one individual is so brilliant that they know all of the answers. So you've got to have a sense of inclusiveness. The other most important thing is making people understand the strategy and the message, and be out front of the people so that they actually understand the mission. ... I think it is the job of leaders to eliminate uncertainty.

Schiro not only preaches the open conversation gospel, he practices what he preaches. Clearly aware that a growing number of consumers exist in a totally different communication realm than in the past, Schiro works closely with his communications staff to transmit company decisions and other messages on YouTube, a corporate blog, and through direct face-to-face interactions with customers at various service locations.

5. *Good conversation is organic.* Jaffe's main point regarding this tenet is that engagement with consumers should not operate on a fixed timeline, nor is it a temporary or onetime affair—it is ongoing, dynamic, and often spontaneous. In clarifying the difference between natural and organic, Jaffe explains that the former is the contrary of forced, manipulated, or premeditated, whereas the latter characterizes

dialogue that is productive and healthy. Perhaps it goes without saying that the organic nature of conversation is highly dependent on the extent to which the dialogue marketers establish with consumers is truly a two-way exchange. The traditional marketer-to-consumer linear approach to communication derided by Schultz (see Chapter 1) was so appealing to marketers for so many years because it was productive for companies and healthy for the advertising industry—at least in terms of profit margins. As discussed earlier, the utility of that approach has diminished in our connected marketing age.

The organic nature of marketing communication is on public view in an ongoing fashion in midtown Manhattan, New York City—in Times Square, to be exact. Long a focal point for advertisers because of the hordes of tourists and locals who pass through on a daily basis, marketers have now added staged events to their arsenal of billboards and oversized video screens. In the past few years, organizations such as Procter & Gamble, Nascar, Target, and General Electric have staged elaborate events in Times Square to capture the attention and engage passersby. For example, in its promotional ploy for Charmin bathroom tissue, P&G set up dozens of free public toilets (see Box 6.4). Target staged a stunt with the magician David Blaine, challenging him to escape from a gyroscope hung over Times Square for 2 days during the week of Thanksgiving, one of the most popular periods for tourism in New York. Spectators can experience such events firsthand and, in some cases, try out the sponsored brand. Moreover, people are motivated to capture the events to preserve as part of their vacation experience and share with friends. In the digital era, sharing the experience is easier than ever now that people are equipped with cell phones, digital cameras, and camcorders. Many consumers are no longer content simply to paste their memories in photo albums or watch a homemade video on their TV; rather, they upload them to YouTube or Facebook, add them to their blogs, Twitter friends as the experience unfolds, and so on. The reach of these new channels can be vast: at the time of this writing, videos of the Target event had been viewed nearly 75,000 times

---

BOX 6.4 FOCUS ON APPLICATION: CHARMIN BATHROOM TISSUE AND TIMES SQUARE

An annual offshoot of their enormously successful mobile marketing effort, Pottypalooza, P&G created a totally immersing brand experience with its temporary displays of public toilets in Times Square to promote Charmin bathroom tissue. The staged marketing ploy has P&G employees dressed in toilet costumes dancing and egging on passersby to try out the efficient and clean bathrooms. The stalls themselves are stocked with Charmin tissue and other Charmin products, and the Charmin song plays repeatedly through mounted speakers. The event represents an example of experiential marketing, which provides consumers with an engaging context within which they can try out a brand firsthand.

Beyond Times Square, the mobile marketing effort visits regional events across the United States where P&G's core demographic for the Charmin brand—young families with children—are likely to congregate. P&G reports that about 14% of consumers who use the portable bathroom facilities end up buying more Charmin (Pappas, 2003). The event provides a memorable experience for consumers who are motivated to share photos and videos of the event online; it effectively has generated free publicity for the brand (e.g., the Times Square bathrooms alone generated more than 100 published articles in the traditional print media); and it gets samples of the product directly into the hands of potential customers (Story, 2006). The ROI measurement for P&G's marketing event consists of a combination of indicators, including media impressions, traffic through the location and consumer feedback, and sales increase. The engaging, organic nature of the marketing effort was concisely summarized on David Polinchock's Marketing and Strategy Innovation Blog (2006):

> At the end of the day, they are creating a compelling, authentic and relevant brand experience. They're giving people something new, a way to experience the Charmin brands in a very engaging way. Plus they're delivering a very much-needed service to people visiting Times Square. It hits on every level.

at YouTube. The upshot of the growing popularity of consumer-generated photos and videos on Internet sites sparked by public marketing events is that they encourage people to do much of the work for brand owners and advertisers.

6. *Good conversation is timeless.* This tenet pertains to the lasting power of conversation that enables it to withstand the test of time, or, as Jaffe (2007, p. 130) explains, "enduring for the length of the passion the participants bring to it (and sometimes beyond)". When marketers are able to connect with consumers in an engaging way in the contemporary marketing context, conversational messages tend to possess a greater "pass-along" quality among consumers than, say, a traditional one-sided marketing communication, which is subject to arbitrary boundaries and constraints. The 2-week run in the Paris metro of a titillating billboard may create some local buzz, but is likely to fade from commuters' minds as quickly as its frayed paper begins to peel from the display mounting. However, combine it with an integrated street marketing campaign that engages consumers in a more participatory fashion and, all of a sudden, images from the campaign appear online for a worldwide audience and are talked about in multiple postings. This is exactly what happened in the case of Unilever's Axe Click campaign when the new men's deodorant was launched with the free distribution of Axe clickers (to tally the number of flirtations received) to young people on the streets of Paris and other French cities (see Chapter 8). The online images related to the street campaign are likely to continue to be available for sharing long after Axe Click paper billboards have reached the recycling plant, and for as long as the Axe clickers continue to fascinate.

7. *Good conversation is valuable.* This tenet pertains to the ability of conversation to add value to a company and its offerings, beyond merely boosting the profit margin, and more extensively than traditional marketing communication. In a broad sense, value reflects the power of marketing efforts to influence how

consumers think and feel about a company's brands. This influence is best understood through a consideration of brand equity, a concept that I covered earlier in the discussion of the consequences of WOM (see Chapter 4). Favorable conversations can enhance brand equity in a number of ways: they can work to build strong brand awareness (as long as people are talking about brands, those brands are going to stay on their minds), create brand associations (consistent with the content of the conversations), and can augment customer loyalty (by adding confidence and trust through positive referrals and recommendations from those who have experienced the brand firsthand).

Jaffe points to the Campaign for Real Beauty developed by Unilever for its Dove brand as a good example of how a marketing communication campaign can stimulate an ongoing consumer conversation in a way that successfully transforms how people think about a brand. The Dove campaign, launched in 2004, served as a fresh and original alternative to the typical commercial approach to marketing body care products. Through a series of videos and outdoor billboards, Dove generated a conversation among consumers by broadening the conception of female beauty beyond that created over several decades via mass-mediated depictions of an unrealistic ideal of attractiveness. Instead of the svelte supermodels so commonly seen in advertising, Dove's communications presented average-looking women of different shapes, sizes, races, and ages, in an effort to enhance female self-esteem. Several buzz-worthy videos, available for viewing online, represent clear indictments of the advertising industry and successfully contributed to the portrayal of Dove as the brand for all (ordinary) women.

The Dove campaign contrasts with a marketing effort created by Burger King to introduce the fast food restaurant chain's new chicken sandwich menu offering and "Have it Your Way" brand positioning. The focal point of the campaign, which also included TV commercials and print ads, was a viral Internet Web site that depicted someone dressed in an outrageous chicken suit standing in the middle of a rather seedy-looking living room. Visitors to the site (www.subservientchicken.com) are instructed to type in a command ("Get chicken just the way you like it. Type in your command here.") and then watch the chicken comply. (Designers of the site had programmed the chicken to perform over 300 different actions, including dance, lay egg, sing, touch toes, etc.) When it was launched in April 2004, only twenty people were told about it—all friends of people who worked at the Crispin Porter + Bogusky advertising firm, which had created the Web site. Additionally, some television ads flashed the web address. According to Burger King, the Web site received 15–20 million hits within 1 week, and it continues to attract numerous visits to this day.

Although the subservient chicken campaign generated plenty of buzz for the amusing Web site, it added little to brand equity in the sense of how consumers feel about the Burger King brand. Whereas Dove's campaign sparked a conversation about societal conceptions of beauty, the role of advertising in creating unattainable standards for attractiveness and body weight, and Dove's efforts to enhance self-esteem, few people ever linked the Burger King campaign to the brand or the promoted product (the chicken sandwich). Whatever conversation was stimulated by the Burger King campaign had to do with the funny Web site, but not the brand. Where's the value in that?

8. *Good conversation is heated.* It typically takes more of an effort to keep a conversation going when everyone agrees than when there is at least some disagreement, and consensus does not necessarily always translate into conversation. To say that good conversation is heated means that it provides the opportunity for a passionate exchange of views and a diversity of opinion, two important components of engagement.

To illustrate how heated conversation can promote engagement, consider once again the two examples presented in the previous section: Dove's "real beauty" campaign and Burger King's subservient chicken Web site. Imagine someone coming across one or the other of these efforts and then informing a friend about it in an e-mail. In the Dove case, we would not be surprised if that e-mail message included the question, "What do you think about what Dove is trying to say with these ads?" In the Burger King example, we are more likely to have that e-mail include the comment, "Check this out—it's super funny!" Now ask yourself, which of those e-mails is likely to generate more of an engaged discussion between sender and recipient? Similarly, imagine the successive posts on an Internet forum about either campaign. For Dove, we would not be surprised to find several pages of comments, including heated exchanges accompanied by some expletives deleted. Some people no doubt will vehemently support Dove's efforts, whereas others might challenge the "real beauty" campaign as being hypocritical and as exploitative of women as traditional ads featuring supermodels. For Burger King? Probably a few "lol"s ("laughing out loud") and "you gotta see this," some smiley faces, and some links to other similarly amusing sites (promoted by other companies).

9. *Good conversation is viral.* Marketers have long been aware that great advertising engages the consumer's mind while at the same time effectively delivering a message. People are apt to talk about something that is original—something they have not seen before and thus is talkworthy. This is the essence of what Jaffe is striving for when he suggests that good conversation is viral. Unless a marketing effort provides consumers with something worth talking about and in an engaging way, it will not move them to start a conversation with others. As Jaffe (2007, p. 137) points out, "anything that is naturally good enough will be shared." If the message is bland and mediocre, consumers are not likely to share it, assuming they attend to it at all.

One indication of the viral nature of good conversation is seen when parodies and spoofs of legitimate marketing campaigns begin to emerge. Dove's "Evolution" video, which takes us through the steps by which an ordinary-looking woman is miraculously transformed into a beautiful model through various advertising techniques (photo-shopping, air brushing, etc.), has given rise to more than one parody video (e.g., "Slob Evolution" and Foster Farms' "Transformation," both available at YouTube) that have added to the ongoing discussion about Dove's self-esteem campaign. Although such parodies mock the brand, albeit typically in a rather playful manner, their existence demonstrates how the original campaign resonated with audiences. The same has been said of Apple's famous 1984 advertisement, which was aired only once (during the 1984 Super Bowl telecast) to promote the new MacIntosh computer, but which was compelling enough to spawn several online parody versions 25 years later. Additional examples of viral marketing campaigns are discussed in Chapter 7.

10. *Good conversation is productive.* Although it may appear to be the case, productive in the sense of good conversation is not necessarily redundant with valuable. Engaging conversation can be "valuable" in the sense that it enhances how consumers think and feel about the brand concept. Productivity suggests that good conversation can result in tangible or concrete assets for a firm. Jaffe describes the case involving a South African wine company that distributed complimentary bottles of one of its brands to bloggers, who then started writing about the wine in their blogs. This simple shift in the company's approach—interacting with the blogosphere—resulted in a doubling of sales for the brand in less than 12 months. This example similarly recalls Brewtopia's viral marketing campaign (see Box 5.1), which involved consumers in all phases of the launch of the new Australian boutique beer, and Saab's open-ended dialogue with brand community members. Other demonstrations of how active, ongoing engagement with consumers can result in tangible benefits for the firm are considered later in this chapter, with a discussion of cases from Dell, Starbucks, and other firms.

Trust and the Building of Marketer—Customer Relationships

If there is a common, unwritten message running through Jaffe's ten conversational tenets, it is that marketing in the contemporary era is heavily dependent on trust. This is especially evident in the tenets suggesting that good conversation is natural, balanced, open, and honest, although an argument can be made that trust implicitly underlies each of the other tenets as well (e.g., heated conversation depends upon the encouragement of diversity of opinion and debate, which can be constructive only when it occurs within an environment of trust).

Trust also is at the core of customer relationship marketing (CRM), an approach to marketing that was discussed in Chapter 1. It is instructive to reconsider CRM and the nature of trust in marketing relationships at this juncture because of the key role that trust plays in the success of virtually any connecting marketing effort. Marketing research on business relationships has revealed that trust between partners can result in substantial benefits for the parties involved: it contributes to the level of commitment to the relationship; it serves to reduce perceived risks in an exchange situation (such as a purchase); it positively influences willingness to continue in the relationship and cooperate more closely; it can facilitate conflict resolution; and so on (e.g., Anderson & Weitz, 1989; Ganesan, 1994; Morgan & Hunt, 1994). When it comes to relationships involving services (which are distinguished by their intangible nature), trust is essential in reducing uncertainty and vulnerability among current and potential users.

According to those who have studied the concept in the context of business relationships, trust operates as a key mediating variable that is central to all relational exchanges (Morgan & Hunt, 1994). But prior to evaluating its role in connected marketing efforts, it first is helpful to be clear about how this notion is conceptualized. In terms of its relevance to business relationships, trust has been defined as "a willingness to rely on an exchange partner in whom one has confidence" (Moorman, Zaltman, & Deshpandé, 1992, p. 314). As implied by this definition, trustworthy business exchange partners are characterized by confidence, honesty, and competence (Donney & Cannon, 1997; Ganesan, 1994). The element of confidence suggests that trust, which is based on the expectation that the partner will not behave opportunistically, is comprised of a cognitive component (i.e., confidence or belief in the reliability of the partner) as well as a behavioral component, reflecting confidence in the intentions, motivations, honesty, and benevolence of the partner (Ring & Van De Van, 1992). The degree of willingness to rely on another lies at the heart of the trust concept.

In addition to these notions regarding the basic nature of the trust concept, various authors have attempted to identify the key antecedents for trust and its likely outcomes. Although there is no consensus about the specific antecedent and outcome factors, the views suggest that a number of elements have the potential to build trust in business settings, including experience with the partner, shared values, honesty, explicit guarantees, communication, desire to continue the relationship, responsiveness, clarifying exchange parameters, and the like (e.g., Geyskens et al., 1996; Morgan & Hunt, 1994). In more practical terms, marketing managers can enhance trust through truth in advertising, ethical and fair selling practices, and by ensuring the integrity of product promotions, guarantees, and promises. Similarly, a variety of outcomes of trust may be anticipated, as previously mentioned, including commitment/loyalty, expansion of the relationship, cooperation, reduced uncertainty, interdependence, and higher levels of trust.

These ideas have increasingly gained prominence in the Marketing 2.0 era as connected, skeptical consumers have concluded that the basic components of trust are more likely to be apparent in the relationships they have with each other than the relationships marketers have attempted to force on them over the years. For many firms following the tried-and-true linear model that characterizes traditional marketer-to-consumer efforts, trust typically has been relegated to a secondary role. The assumption has been that firms can gain trust if they provide their customers with high-quality offerings at attractive prices, good service, appealing loyalty schemes, post-purchase follow-ups, and the like. But as we have seen, consumers are not buying into this unidirectional form of marketing anymore. To a great extent, the current challenge for marketers is to view trust as a starting point, rather than a presumed consequence, for the business relationships they hope to establish with consumers. One way to do this is to put Jaffe's tenets of conversation into practice. Another is to assure that one's marketing efforts are ethical in nature: open, honest, and devoid of deception. Companies on the cutting edge of new marketing approaches have begun to respond to these challenges in a variety of ways, including efforts to participate in the blogosphere and by engaging with and supporting brand communities.

Participating in the Blogosphere

Active participation in the blogosphere has emerged as a representative strategy by which marketers can (re)gain the trust of consumers. I have discussed blogs in preceding chapters in various regards: as a new marketing reality, suggestive of the increasing role of consumers in the marketing process; as an example of user-generated media; as a context for learning what people are saying about your company and its brands; as a means for obtaining useful marketing metrics; and so on. Underlying the current proliferation of blogs are a variety of characteristics that make them so appealing to Internet users ("One New Blog," 2009). For example, blogs are quickly indexed by search engines; easy to update and add instantly viewable new content; easy to attract web traffic to; they rise up search engines quickly; and are relatively simple to develop and design. Perhaps most importantly, blogs embrace the conversational interactivity that is essential for marketing efforts to engage consumers. Together, these aspects of blogs suggest some clear advantages over standard Web sites for attracting web traffic and attention, and they provide a more personal and trustworthy outlet for interacting with consumer targets.

From a marketing perspective, the utility of blogs can be seen as running along a continuum anchored at one end by passive involvement (e.g., using blogs to gain brand insights by finding out what consumers are discussing) and at the other end by active involvement (e.g., interacting directly with consumer bloggers). Company-designed

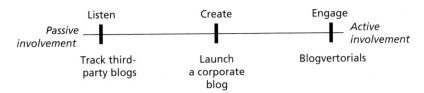

Figure 6.1 Marketing and Blog Involvement Continuum

blogs (often referred to as "brand blogs" or "corporate blogs") would fall somewhere in between these two extremes (see Figure 6.1).

One advantage to using blogs to listen to what consumers are saying about brands is that they allow one to capture consumers' attitudes and relationships with brands in a setting conducive to natural conversation (see Box 6.5). By contrast, contrived research surveys are more likely to pose questions about brands in terminology that is first and foremost on the mind of the researcher, not the consumer. Natural blog conversations can be submitted to brand analysis and comparison. For example, Latent Semantic Indexing (LSI) is one method that has been applied to the analysis of blogs to explore the connections between brands and their tangible and intangible assets. The method maps the contextual relationships between words according to common usage patterns. For example, in one study of 300 blogs that included consumer discussions of the two leading carbonated soft drinks, Coke and Pepsi, it was learned that both brands are very connected in the minds of consumers, although they are talked about quite differently (Syrett, 2005). Pepsi was found to be strongly associated with its recent promotions, with the term "Apple" ranking as most connected to Pepsi, reflecting an iTunes promotion that Pepsi had carried out with Apple around the time of the study. Additionally, the special flavors of Pepsi (Cherry and Spice) were revealed as more strongly connected with the brand than were those of Coke. The Coca-Cola brand was more clearly linked to Classic Coke than any of the various Coke flavors. Some consumers negatively associated Pepsi with weight gain concerns. In addition to other differences, the study demonstrated how blogs can be useful for assessing brand equity in terms of perceptions of such assets as quality, awareness, and brand associations.

BOX 6.5 BRAND BLOGS CAPTURE ATTENTION

Among the millions of blogs that have proliferated on the Internet are a growing number specifically dedicated to brands. For the most part, such blogs operate completely independently from the companies that own the brands, such as Coca-Cola, Netflix, the Walt Disney Company, and Starbucks. However, companies are increasingly recognizing the impact of customer-created blogs and have begun to use the blogs as an informal channel for tapping consumer opinion

(cont.)

Box 6.5 (*Continued*)

(Ralli, 2005). According to Netflix (the movie rental company) executive Ken Ross, "In addition to viewing blogs as another media channel, it allows us to keep our pulse on the marketplace." One Netflix blog (hackingnetflix.com) created by a consumer in 2005 tallies more than 100,000 readers per month, with representative postings about scratched disks or torn return envelopes generating numerous comments from readers. Such online commentary provides consumers with a sense of ownership and a stake in defining the brand's image, while at the same time serving as a potentially fruitful source of feedback for the company.

Some brand blogs offer useful information to consumers that is unavailable at the company's Web site. For example, a consumer blog about Disney (thedisneyblog.typepad.com) provides details about the weather at the company's theme parks as well as the number of accidents at the parks. A brand blog about the sports drink Gatorade (firstinthirst.typepad.com) carries both positive and negative articles culled from the Internet, as well as commentary by the blog's creator. People who type "Is Gatorade unhealthy?" into a search engine are often directed to the blog. One of the best known blogs about Starbucks (starbucksgossip.typepad.com), with 3,000 to 5,000 visitors per day, serves as a forum for lively discussions among readers who include Starbucks enthusiasts, detractors, and employees.

Companies that fail to attend to the online blog commentary are missing an important opportunity to learn how consumers really feel and what they think about brands, and stand to lose valuable insight into how products and services can be improved. Experts who follow the impact of brand blogs tend to agree that the in-depth customer feedback should be embraced by firms. As professional blogger Steve Rubel suggested, a brand blog can be viewed as a kind of "24/7 focus group that's transparent and out in the open," and it provides companies with the opportunity to find their brand ambassadors (Ralli, 2005).

Blogvertorials

Many companies have begun to move beyond the passive activity of listening to blogs by more actively attempting to engage bloggers, offering content, comments, and open access to corporate decision making. The ultimate goal of active engagement with popular, opinion-leading third-party blogs is to seek endorsements (referred to as "blogvertorials") and stimulate favorable WOM. This approach can be seen as an extension of public relations in that companies strive to develop and maintain good relations with high profile bloggers who tend to write about relevant products and services, much as marketers attempt to encourage favorable publicity from journalists, editors, and media owners (Corcoran et al., 2006). Various "blogger outreach" initiatives might be employed, such as offering bloggers inside scoops and the latest news; providing "freebies," such as samples, previews, or demos; informing bloggers about special deals; and offering exclusive interviews with representatives of the company hierarchy. In one successful effort, Nokia provided its new portable phone free to several influential bloggers in Finland and asked them to experiment with the camera function. Nokia never explicitly asked them to write about the phone on their blogs, but a majority ended up doing just that. Shortly thereafter, it was discovered that the bloggers' coverage of the new product resulted in a significant increase in traffic on the Nokia Web site (Corcoran et al., 2006).

A more troublesome example involving another Nokia cell phone was recounted by Larry Weber in his book *Marketing to the Social Web* (2007). During an interview with *Smart Money* magazine, the owner and manager of Oh Gizmo!, a blog about gadgets, innovation, and design commented that Nokia's N91 phone is "great as a music player, but it sucks as an actual phone." However, an initial review of the phone on the Oh Gizmo! blog was extremely favorable, including the comment, "Everything works as it should and works well." Once the magazine interview was published, there appeared to be an embarrassing conflict of interest, despite assurances at the blog site that although the blog's authors receive free products for review purposes, they take great care to maintain their impartiality and never "give a product a positive review when we feel it is undeserved." A follow-up review of the cell phone at Oh Gizmo! was less praiseworthy, admitting that the product was "slightly less perfect." Weber (p. 168) summarized the lessons learned from this example in the following way:

> Always be careful what you say to a reporter. And be careful what you say in your blog. The remarks may come back to bite you—once on the Web, they never go away.

We might also add that from the marketer's perspective, the same problem inherent in traditional public relations also applies to blogvertorials: once a message is picked up by the media, you lose control over it. There is no guarantee that bloggers will write favorably about your outreach initiatives, so it goes without saying that care must be taken in deciding how best to approach bloggers.

Attempts to engage with bloggers are more likely to meet with success when they are consistent with the conversational tenets discussed above, and are conducted in the spirit of transparency, openness, authenticity, and partnership. It should be obvious that bloggers are likely to be more amenable to post positive comments or reviews if they do not perceive a firm's efforts to engage as marketing ploys or veiled selling attempts. Moreover, the consequences can be profound if it is learned that brand owners have offered bribes or paid money to bloggers to induce favorable reviews. Such was the case in 2003 when the soft drink manufacturer Dr. Pepper/7 Up introduced its new milk-flavored drink, Raging Cow. The initial idea, which was a good one in a strategic sense, was to lend the product an air of hip legitimacy by reaching out to young bloggers (Bruner, 2004). The company established its own blog, invited young bloggers to be briefed about the product, and encouraged them to write about Raging Cow on their own blogs. However, difficulties arose after it was learned that the firm had specifically asked the bloggers not to mention that they had been briefed, so that it would appear that they discovered the new drink on their own and wanted to share their enthusiasm about it. This news caused a furious response within the blogging community, with many outraged bloggers calling for a boycott of Raging Cow. Despite the fact that Dr. Pepper/7 Up's effort represented one of the first corporate attempts to interact with bloggers (as part of a larger buzz campaign for the Raging Cow brand), the uproar over concerns that the company had attempted to corrupt the integrity of blogs easily could have been avoided simply by letting the product speak for itself. Chances are that some bloggers would have appreciated the product enough to enthusiastically recommend it on their blogs, without having been given the less-than-subtle nudge by the company to do so.

Corporate Blogs

Another approach to using blogs for consumer engagement is for the company itself to establish a corporate blog to promote its products and brands by regularly providing interesting news and inside information. Although this sounds relatively straightforward, it is important to bear in mind that if a firm simply goes through the motions in creating a blog because it seems to be what everyone else is doing, it is likely to end up being a waste of time. There are millions of competing blogs on the Internet, so if the corporate blog is to have any impact at all, it must constantly offer fresh, compelling, and interesting content for its intended audiences. Content must be regularly updated, preferably via the contributions of key company representatives, such as high profile directors and executives who are willing to openly share their ideas and opinions. As Corcoran et al. (2006, p. 151) advise, "The challenge is to keep readers coming back for more with fresh content that offers breaking news, insider insights, and interesting opinions." It also should be recognized that blogs are not necessarily applicable to all companies, a point emphasized by BuzzMetrics CEO Jonathan Carson ("The State of," 2004):

> Blogs are a very big deal, but they aren't necessarily the appropriate medium for every brand. If the marketing calls for connecting with various key audiences in a timely, informal and community-like manner, then a blog might be appropriate.

It is difficult to venture a guess as to which brands are or are not blog-worthy; this determination is better made by individual brand managers. Even relatively mundane products, such as candy bars, could be conducive to the establishment of a creative blog that serves to effectively provide a meeting place for updating and engaging with brand loyals. For a product like pet food, a blog would seem to be a less relevant option. Within the entertainment industry, film and music companies have found blogs to be a hugely successful means for reaching a core demographic: 18–35-year-olds who are intelligent, have money, and make many purchases online (Brown, 2006).

There are various objectives linked to listening to and engaging consumers that can be achieved from participating in the blogosphere (see Table 6.1), including generating interest (by providing content that informs and intrigues, with the potential to spread virally across other blogs and via RSS technology), driving action and sales (in that favorable blog reviews and comments can accelerate product adoption), creating good

Table 6.1 Blog Marketing Approaches and Objectives

Objective	Blogvertorials (Third-party blogs)	Corporate Blogs (Business/brand blogs)	Fake Blogs ("Flogs")
Generate interest	√	√	√
Drive action/sales	√	√	√
Create goodwill	×	√	×
Establish expertise	×	√	×
Customer dialogue	×	√	×

Source: Adapted from Corcoran et al. (2006).

will (by giving the company a human face), establishing expertise (by positioning the company as a leading authority or expert), and opening a dialogue with customers (by stimulating a two-way exchange of ideas with consumer targets that provides an alternative to traditional marketing monologue) (Corcoran et al., 2006).

Blog Marketing Ethics

As a new form of public relations marketing, blogging represents a relatively informal means of communicating with consumer targets, quickly and inexpensively. The development of traditional marketing communication approaches, such as advertising, proceeds in a rather methodical manner. For example, advertising briefs are carefully developed and reviewed, and the initial content of the message may have been changed many times prior to the ad's ultimate dissemination through a media channel. Great care is taken over the choice of words and imagery to assure that the message content conforms to legal guidelines and is unlikely to offend any particular consumer group. Blogging is an entirely different process. Blog postings may be written and instantaneously disseminated on the Internet several times a week. By the time a mistake is discovered and corrected, the blog already may have been read by thousands of site visitors and excerpts quoted across a myriad of other blogs. Thus, it is essential that organizational employees are aware of certain ethical guidelines and standards prior to posting messages on behalf of their firms.

This chapter has referred to several ways that blogs can be misused by unscrupulous and careless marketing professionals who engage in unethical practices on their blogs (e.g., the creation of flogs or bribing third-party bloggers). Given the current state of consumer connectedness and the technologies available for the rapid spread of information, unethical business practices are more likely than ever to be uncovered, resulting in serious harm to corporate reputations. As a consequence, an increasing number of firms are establishing policies for all forms of employee communication (including e-mails, verbal communication, blogging, and participation in Internet chat rooms and forums).

In his 2007 book, *The New Rules of Marketing and PR*, David Meerman Scott identified five key issues relating to proper (i.e., ethical) blogging, summarized below:

- *Transparency.* It is one thing to use a pseudonym for one's personal blog or when posting on other blogs, but it is quite another to claim to be someone who you are not. This also applies to participation on one's company blog. The message here is not to pretend to be someone you are not or to create a blog about your company without disclosing your affiliation.
- *Privacy.* It is inappropriate to communicate private information or important disclosures received by or about someone linked to the organization without first receiving permission to do so. This extends to e-mail content, SMS messages, telephone conversations, and so on.
- *Disclosure.* One must be upfront about blog content that might be construed as reflecting a conflict of interest. The Oh Gizmo! example discussed above represents a good example of what can go wrong when this principle is not adhered to. Thus, if I receive a free, tasty dessert from a restaurateur who is aware that I intend to review his establishment on my Paris restaurant blog, I should disclose that fringe benefit in my posting.
- *Truthfulness.* This pertains to a very simple rule when it comes to blogging: don't lie. As Scott explains, it is very easy (and often tempting) to make up a customer story because it makes for good blog content. I could try to impress my blog readers by claiming to have ordered the most expensive bottle of wine on the menu. But that would essentially negate the purpose of the blog in the first place, which is to provide an honest accounting of the experience.
- *Credit.* This refers to the importance of acknowledging other blogs and other sources from which you obtained content used on your own blog. It is inappropriate to cut and paste excerpts from someone else's blog without acknowledging the source and providing a link to that site. Links to other blogs provide a means of getting your own blog known and the favor is likely to be returned in kind.

These issues are clearly reflected in The Word of Mouth Marketing Association's (WOMMA) principles for ethical contact (see Box 6.6). Another useful resource for

---

BOX 6.6 WOMMA'S 10 PRINCIPLES FOR ETHICAL CONTACT BY MARKETERS

Remember: Consumers come first, honesty isn't optional, and deception is always exposed.

1. I will always be truthful and will never knowingly relay false information. I will never ask someone else to deceive bloggers for me.
2. I will fully disclose who I am and who I work for (my identity and affiliations) from the very first encounter when communicating with bloggers or commenting on blogs.

3. I will never take action contrary to the boundaries set by bloggers. I will respect all community guidelines regarding posting messages and comments.
4. I will never ask bloggers to lie for me.
5. I will use extreme care when communicating with minors or blogs intended to be read by minors.
6. I will not manipulate advertising or affiliate programs to impact blogger income.
7. I will not use automated systems for posting comments or distributing information.
8. I understand that compensating bloggers may give the appearance of a conflict of interest, and I will therefore fully disclose any and all compensation or incentives.
9. I understand that if I send bloggers products for review, they are not obligated to comment on them. Bloggers can return products at their own discretion.
10. If bloggers write about products I send them, I will proactively ask them to disclose the products' source.

Source: The Word of Mouth Marketing Association (WOMMA) Web site: http://womma.org/bloggerethics/guidelines/

corporate public discourse standards is available at the Web site of Sun Microsystems (http://www.sun.com/communities/guidelines.jsp).

Engaging with Online Networks and Communities

As with the blogging community, similar benefits can be accrued for companies when they interact with social networks (e.g., Facebook, Twitter, Internet forums). Whereas brand bloggers often enthusiastically welcome the input of brand managers, the same generally is not the case with members of social networks. Online networks provide a means for skeptical consumers to bypass marketers in the process of obtaining marketing-relevant information, so a marketing intervention within these networks may be perceived as an unwanted intrusion. Thus, marketers must walk a thin line in their efforts to engage with network participants.

In the most unobtrusive sense, the involvement of marketers in online groups, social networking sites, and Internet bulletin boards often is limited to the simple monitoring of what is being said about the company and its products. The temptation to jump in on those consumer discussions as an anonymous or disguised participant is contrary to the ethical guidelines we considered for blogs and can similarly backfire if and when one's affiliation with a firm is revealed. Acknowledging one's links to a company from the outset will bypass ethical concerns, but may be seen as invasive within the community. These limitations are likely to place the marketer between Scylla and Charybdis, face-to-face with two equally undesirable alternatives for engagement.

Reaching Out to Social Networks

To reach social network participants, some companies simply choose to rely on traditional advertising. For example, on Facebook one can purchase Facebook social ads that can reach members who share certain demographics of interest to the firm. In this case, the marketing effort is completely upfront, but in line with the linear approach to marketing that belies any real possibility of engagement. An alternative is to invite online community members to interact with brands. To facilitate this process, some companies choose to build and manage online communities that serve to connect customers. In this way, it is possible to identify and connect persons with like interests and to encourage them to share insights and serve as brand advocates. This effort could represent an initial step in building a brand community.

Marketers' opinions are mixed with regard to whether a monetary or other incentive (e.g., vouchers or entry into a prize draw) should be used to encourage people to engage with companies. However, it is generally understood that once network participants' are enticed in these ways, their mindset is shifted from a social one to a marketing-oriented one (Rhodes, 2009a). That is, they are likely to weigh how much effort they are willing to expend in their engagement with companies relative to what they are offered in exchange, an involvement that would undermine spontaneity as well as the likelihood that a long-term relationship could emerge from the transaction.

One potentially fruitful strategy for encouraging engagement is to draw from the firm's expertise so as to offer something of value to online social network and community members. Every firm has expertise in some area, and thus has something of value to share with connected consumers, brand community members, customers, and potential customers. For example, an insurance company has access to information and resources that can be of great use in assisting homeowners or for offering advice to potential home buyers. A pharmaceutical firm can share nutritional recommendations for new parents who have questions about how best to feed their babies.

By providing expertise in this way, recipients can obtain insight relative to the firm's brands, along with opportunities to directly engage in an ongoing conversation with the company. The online community experts company FreshNetworks utilizes this approach for its clients by enabling the clients to field questions from online community members. Videos, which can be provided to network users as well as uploaded to YouTube and other sites, are then created showing experts from the firm on camera directly addressing each of the questions. This is an efficient means for personalizing the conversation and for giving the firm a human face. The strategy encourages an ongoing dialogue between the company and target consumers, and is likely to provoke favorable WOM. For example, when a mother receives direct feedback from a nutritional expert speaking on behalf of a pharmaceutical firm, she is likely to share what she learned with other new mothers within her social community. Summarizing the merits of this approach, FreshNetworks's Matt Rhodes (2009a) suggests that "By answering questions from community members, you are incentivizing them within a social dynamic rather than giving them money and making their behaviors more transactional. And video brings all of this to life a lot more."

The French home improvement and gardening retailer Leroy Merlin utilizes a variation of the expert approach in efforts to engage do-it-yourselfers (DIYs). The aim of one of the company's programs is to provide the DIY community with information about products, while at the same time offering advice about home repairs and the like. One of Leroy Merlin's online tools is a company-created blog known as "le blog des passionnés" [blog enthusiasts], which divides the conversation into various subject areas to assist consumers in making their product and purchase choices.

Leroy Merlin's Web site (http://www.leroymerlin.fr) includes a link that directs visitors to a home forums page ("les forums de la maison"), sub-divided into several home improvement areas. This provides an effective means for connecting consumers with each other around the Leroy Merlin brand. The purpose of the forums is summarized by the terminology presented at the top of the forums web page: "Echangez," "Partagez," "Dialoguez" [Exchange, Share, Dialogue]. Consumer enthusiasm for these opportunities to discuss home improvement techniques, products, and repairs is evident in the Web site numbers. At the time of this writing, the number of forum posts was approaching 150,000 for approximately 35,000 different topics. In the future, Leroy Merlin could follow its American counterpart Home Depot in posting "how-to" home improvement videos on YouTube and other Web sites.

Sharing expertise across social network sites has proven to be an effective approach to engagement within business-to-business (B-to-B) contexts. A team from the business intelligence firm Information Builders used a B-to-B social network as a channel for the distribution of white papers (authoritative reports that address particular problems and offer solutions) ("How to Use," 2007). The Information Builders's approach followed five simple steps:

(1) *Spend time learning network members' interests.* This is an essential first step for obtaining a detailed understanding of the online community's makeup. For a full year prior to launching their campaign, Information Builders sponsored an e-mail discussion group in the network on the company's software at ITToolbox.com. Based on insight obtained about the network's members (e.g., the fact that they were decision makers as well as developers in charge of running IT systems), it was possible to design a white paper series that would be of specific interest and potential value to them by focusing on issues discussed at the site.

(2) *Create a mix of white paper titles.* Six white papers were developed that provided a mix of thought pieces and reports that demonstrated the company's expertise in managing tactical issues, such as software implementation.

(3) *Promote the white papers across the network.* For this step, the company made use of the profile of social network members obtained during the first step so as to efficiently target potentially receptive audiences for the white papers. The white papers were distributed through a mix of channels, including the RSS feed dedicated to Business Intelligence, weekly e-mail newsletters, and the site's blogs and discussion groups.

(4) *Customize registration page to capture lead qualification information.* Those network members who clicked on an ad or link promoting a white paper were directed to the social network's standard registration web page, where basic contact information (name, e-mail address, company name and size, job description, and whether the company had a specific project and budget) was obtained.

(5) *Add leads to CRM system for sales or marketing follow-up.* This final step was conducted using a systematic approach such that new leads who claimed to have a budget for a specific project were immediately directed to a sales team for immediate action, whereas those without budgets were added to the marketing database for a nurturing campaign.

The results of this process were impressive and exceeded expectations for generating total leads by more than 42%. The social networking audience turned out to be quite receptive to the white paper offers that were relevant to their online activities, and sales made as a result of this program delivered a 750% return on investment. Although this case concerns a B-to-B marketing focus with a specific objective (providing relevant content to a social networking community to generate sales leads), it provides an excellent example of how marketers can engage in two-way, authentic conversations with their targets. In the Information Builders' case, it is noteworthy that the company initially spent one year listening to its prospects and learning about their interests and needs through a social networking channel. In this way, the company was able to design a marketing campaign and product (i.e., a series of white papers) that began with their potential customers, rather than the other way around. In the non-business consumer context, white papers are not likely to be relevant, but the same approach could be utilized with alternative expert offers, such as FAQ documents, hosted online events, and web seminars.

Hosting Internet Events

Social networks and online communities represent ready audiences for hosting an Internet event to share expertise, new information, Q & A exchanges with customers, and the like. For example, a company executive might appear live to address concerns about a new product or to address false rumors, with audiences directed to a particular Web site (such as the company's message board) where the video event is scheduled to take place at a specified time. Afterwards, the video can be made available to registered members or else posted on sites such as YouTube and TubeMogul for open access to anyone.

Such events require careful planning to maximize the audience as well as to generate pre-event buzz (e.g., online invitations can include an "e-mail this invitation to a friend or colleague" option). A few weeks before the event is to take place, a press release can be submitted to free online press release sites, such as PRLog and PressAbout (Sielski, 2009). The event also can be publicized on the company's Web site or blog. The blog entry can be converted into an article and posted on social network sites, including Facebook, Twitter, and LinkedIn. Regular customers can be contacted and asked to inform their friends at the social networks that they participate in. If a PowerPoint presentation is included as part of the event, the slides can be posted at SlideShare.net, along with a transcript. (For additional recommendations for creating and promoting online events for engaging with social network and online community members, see Tenby, 2003.)

Engagement with Brand Communities

Another approach to engaging consumer networks is through active involvement with existing brand communities. Saab's efforts in supporting the Saab brand community was discussed earlier in this chapter. Another company that has utilized a similar strategy is Jeep, which has succeeded in interacting with and supporting its brand community for several years (McAlexander, Schouten, & Koening, 2002; Muñiz & O'Guinn, 2005). One of Jeep's cornerstone methods for leveraging its brand community is to organize jamborees akin to those pioneered by Harley Davidson—weekend events where Jeep community members gather together and bond around a program of activities involving their vehicles. In addition to teaching Jeep owners such skills as driving off-road, each so-called "Camp Jeep" is organized by the company so as to facilitate the creation of a social atmosphere built on an understanding of Jeep owners' interests, values, and lifestyles. During the weekend-long experience, participants are given fly-fishing lessons, they are offered mountain biking experiences, and can take part in a rock-climbing course. According to McAlexander and his colleagues, who have attended Camp Jeeps as participant-observers, "What this says to the owner is 'this company cares about me, they understand me and my lifestyle.' It puts individuals together with other people who feel the same way" (Society for the Advancement of Education 2003).

Company-sponsored events such as those employed by Saab and Jeep can help promote long-term relationships linking companies and consumers. Further, participants tend to emerge from the events with a stronger sense of community through the brand, which increases the likelihood that they will generate positive WOM and serve as ambassadors of the brand (Muñiz & O'Guinn, 2005). Given these desirable outcomes, from the firm's perspective there is the temptation to take steps towards actively creating communities of consumers who are loyal to a brand, and various brand community consulting companies have emerged in recent years to assist companies in that effort. However, efforts to develop brand communities can fail by forcing them to happen, largely because authentic brand communities tend to evolve spontaneously as participants begin to develop a sense of connectedness with other like-minded consumers. Muñiz and O'Guinn (2005) suggest that the best strategy is to monitor early stages of brand community growth in obvious places, such as Internet chat groups, forums, and social networking Web sites. The company can then step in and offer its resources and support, taking care not to appear as if it is imposing these things onto the community or in any way censoring community activities and discussion.

Engaging Internally or Engaging Externally?

Related to the issue of whether (and how) attempts should be made to build brand communities is the broader question of whether it is better to engage consumers within the firm's own domain, such as an online community that is created and managed by the firm, or by trying to connect with people in established social networks independent of the firm, like Facebook, MySpace, and the blogosphere. For most companies, it is logical to presume that a combination of the two approaches is likely to result in the greatest preponderance of returns, maximizing the potential for engagement among the largest possible audience. However, each of these approaches might be more appropriate for attaining different objectives and are used differently by consumers. For example, engaging people in social networks tends to be better suited for short-term campaigns intended to generate discussion and buzz, whereas one's own online community is likely to be a better place for true, personal engagement that can be nurtured over the longer term (Rhodes, 2009*b*).

Reaching consumers where they are (e.g., social networks, blogs) is a good approach for sharing marketing campaign-related content, such as videos, and for joining online discussions. This is an efficient means for gaining awareness and perhaps for stimulating buzz, especially if your shared content is interesting enough to motivate social network participants to pass it along or post it on their own Web sites. Nonetheless, what you would be achieving in this case is more likely to be engagement with the campaign than engagement with your company. The people who post and comment on your video on YouTube might care about your company, but continuing to engage with these consumers, for example, by encouraging them to go next to Facebook, or participate in a forum discussion, would be difficult. This is more manageable when you are interacting with consumers at your own online community, which offers greater control: you can compile profiling information, obtain confidential feedback in secure site areas, and continue the conversation over time.

In general, a combination of the two approaches appears to be the best strategy for firms intent on connecting with consumers via a sustainable social marketing program. A decision to concentrate on efforts to engage with one's online community members may rank as the most appropriate strategy given the firm's objectives, but that does not mean that opportunities to encourage discussion about your brands on external social networks should be ignored. In this regard, FreshNetworks recommends a "hub and spoke" approach to social media engagement. This involves engaging with consumers where they are (e.g., by providing tools and content that help amplify the WOM they create), but also creating a way to direct them back to a central space created by your firm, so that you can continue the engagement and provide a means for similarly enthusiastic consumers to connect with each other (Rhodes, 2009b). In short, the disparate social network sites (the "spokes") can be treated as gateways to an online community (the "hub"), moving consumers from a myriad of places where they connect around friends to a central space where they connect around a shared interest, topic, idea, or theme. According to FreshNetworks this model provides an effective means for moving beyond buzz to real consumer engagement.

How Companies Listen and Engage: Some Case Examples

As a growing number of companies begin to jump onto the social marketing bandwagon, they are likely to encounter some of the same difficulties currently plaguing traditional marketing efforts. Consumers may simply stop listening if the cacophony of engagement invitations grow too loud and the numerous opportunities to interact with companies begin to overwhelm. In fact, there already is some evidence that this is the case. Research conducted by the Internet Advertising Bureau revealed that nearly two-thirds of the nearly 2,000 UK adult social network users surveyed felt that they were receiving too many requests to join brand pages or install brand applications at Facebook, MySpace, Friends Reunited, and other similar sites ("Social Networkers Dislike," 2009). When asked what they disliked most about social networks, the most frequently cited response (31%) was too many invitations by companies to install applications, followed by advertising that "isn't relevant to me" (16%). Sound familiar? If these findings signal a representative trend, before long the consumer refrain, "catch me if you can," will pose a greater challenge than already is the case. This obliges marketers to try even harder to capture attention through involving, relevant, and mutually rewarding social marketing tactics.

Some companies are leading the way in the development and application of approaches for successfully listening to and engaging with consumers. Although different in scope, what their approaches have in common is the ability to elevate consumers to the role of enthusiastic marketing collaborators. We conclude this chapter by focusing on some noteworthy examples.

Dell Computer

Dell got off to a rough start in the social marketing game, but quickly got on the right track. A consideration of the series of events that elevated the company to the top tier of connected marketing players is informative. A leading seller of personal computers, Dell's new media landscape woes began in June 2005 when disgruntled customer Jeff Jarvis, the creator of *Entertainment Weekly* magazine, began posting negative comments about the firm on his blog, BuzzMachine (see Box 6.7). Jarvis appeared to have struck a chord in the blogosphere, and before long, his tirade directed at Dell evolved into the popular "Dell Hell" corner of his blog, where other dissatisfied Dell customers added their own negative commentary about the firm. Jarvis' open letter to Dell Chairman Michael Dell, which described his problems with customer service, became the third most linked-to post in the blogosphere, and traffic on his blog quickly shot up from 5,000 to 10,000 visitors per day (Gupta, 2005). It did not take long for the anti-Dell movement to balloon: Jarvis' online criticism of Dell led to the appearance of dozens of other public consumer complaints about the company's technical support.

BOX 6.7 DELL'S SOCIAL MARKETING: IT ALL STARTED WITH A POST

June 21, 2005

Dell lies. Dell sucks.

Dell lies. Dell sucks:

I just bought a new Dell laptop and paid a fortune for the four-year, in-home service.

The machine is a lemon and the service is a lie.

I'm having all kinds of trouble with the hardware: overheats, network doesn't work, maxes out on CPU usage. It's a lemon.

But what really irks me is that they say if they sent someone to my home—which I paid for—he wouldn't have the parts, so I might as well send the machine in and lose it for 7–10 days—plus the time going through this crap. So I have this new machine and paid for them to F**KING FIX IT MY HOUSE and they don't and I lose it for two weeks.

DELL SUCKS. DELL LIES. Put that in your Google and smoke it, Dell.

Posted by Jarvis at 09:48 PM| Comments (253)

Source: Mark (2008). [originally posted by Jeff Jarvis at http://www.buzzmachine.com/archives/cat/_dell.html/]

What made matters especially difficult for Dell is that the company was not prepared to handle how its customers shared their experiences online, a common problem for companies with call centers for handling customer services. If it had not been for Jarvis, some other customer is likely to have had a similar impact, spreading positive or negative WOM about Dell. As PR consultant Steve Rubel explained, "Every company is going to have evangelists and vigilantes in the blogosphere, and they need a group of people focused on influencer relations, who are kind of watching all these different conversations and figuring out how to amplify the evangelists and how to calm the vigilantes" (Gupta, 2005). The lesson that was learned by Dell in this regard, and as other companies also are quickly finding out, is that satisfied and dissatisfied customers do not operate in a vacuum and should not be treated as if they do. It is important to recognize consumers' potential for generating positive or negative content that can spread virally across the social networks within which they participate. It was Dell's misfortune that one of their dissatisfied customers happened to be Jarvis, whose influential media presence helps explain how his initial public complaints evolved so quickly into communities of dedicated Dell haters on forums such as Dell Hell.

So how did Dell respond to this wake-up call and turn things around? The company developed a four-pronged strategy, consisting of the following elements: (*a*) resolve dissatisfaction, (*b*) tell our story (e.g., the Direct2Dell blog), (*c*) join conversations (via blog posts, Twitter, YouTube, Facebook, etc.) and (*d*) share content and collect ideas (IdeaStorm, StudioDell, blogger round tables). At the outset, prior to detailing some of these elements, it is important to note that Michael Dell was astute enough to recognize that the firm's difficulties associated with customer engagement extended beyond one disgruntled consumer. This is evidenced by the following comments he made during a *Business Week* interview led by his one-time nemesis, Jeff Jarvis (2007):

> These conversations [among consumers] are going to occur whether you like it or not. Do you want to be part of that or not? My argument is you absolutely do. You can learn from them. You can improve your reaction time. And you can be a better company by listening and being involved in that conversation.

Dell put this perspective into practice 10 months after the start of the blogosphere firestorm by first addressing the issues that customers had with the firm. Picking up on Jarvis' recommendation that the company "join the conversation your customers are having without you," Dell first sent out technicians to address bloggers' complaints and solve their problems, a move that generated substantial positive buzz (Jarvis, 2007). This was quickly followed by the establishment of a corporate blog, Direct2Dell. Initially criticized for appearing too promotional, Dell quickly responded with openness and contrition by vowing to improve the blog (Gillin, 2007). The company's humble and receptive tone, along with rapid adjustments to the blog, combined to give the company a credible and human voice. Characterized under the blog's logo as a conduit for "one-2-one conversations with Dell," the blog provided the company with a means to transmit timely information to customers (e.g., an initial topic pertained to a burning battery problem) by incorporating moderated postings and reader comments. Accompanied by a useful search engine for Dell-related issues, the blog also operates as a forum that engages consumers with Dell and with each other.

If the first two elements (resolving dissatisfaction and telling the Dell story) represent the first phase of Dell's engagement strategy—containing negative customer feedback—the second phase can be characterized as that of inviting participation (i.e., sharing content and collecting ideas) (see Box 6.8). In February 2007, Michael Dell launched the centerpiece of the participation phase by introducing IdeaStorm.com, a Web site that serves as a collaborative environment by inviting consumers to tell Dell what to do. It provides an opportunity for people to suggest ideas for Dell products and services ("Post"), enables the general community to comment on and rate the ideas ("Vote"), and invites site visitors to find out how Dell has put consumer ideas into practice ("See"). IdeaStorm has operated as an effective tool for Dell in terms of product development (in this case, the product begins from the consumer side of the marketing equation) and customer relationship management. The success of IdeaStorm is evidenced by the numbers: to date, it has resulted in 11,500 ideas generated by the community, 660,000 promotions of ideas (i.e., favorable votes), 84,000 comments, and 325 ideas implemented by Dell (e.g., the decisions to sell Linux computers and reduce the promotional "bloatware" that clogs machines) (Killian, 2009). A rough breakdown of consumer-generated ideas reveals that approximately 12% received are

---

BOX 6.8 FOCUS ON APPLICATION: SUMMARY OF DELL'S ENGAGEMENT STRATEGY

Phase 1—Containing Negative Feedback

- Resolve dissatisfaction (address customer complaints)
- Corporate blog (Direct2Dell)
- One-way information push with moderated postings and comments

Phase 2—Inviting Participation

- IdeaStorm
- Product development
- Building customer relations

Phase 3—Joining the Consumer Conversation

Social media marketing efforts:
- Facebook
- Second Life
- Twitter

classified as unusable (i.e., no action needed), 4% as innovative (i.e., possible game-changing ideas), and 80% as improvements (i.e., including incremental ideas for next-generation products as well as improvements for existing products and services).

An analysis of the progress of IdeaStorm over time, however, revealed two outcomes that companies must prepare for if they choose to follow in Dell's footsteps by initiating a similar participatory mechanism: (*a*) an initially dramatic spike of ideas (e.g., Dell received about 2,000 ideas within IdeaStorm's first 2 weeks), and (*b*) the community's expectations for an immediate response to, or engagement with, their ideas. Timely feedback, clear status updates, and "thank you" mechanisms thus are essential, as well as providing a link to the company's blog. Dell now provides a means for customers to rate its products on the IdeaStorm site, and current plans for evolving IdeaStorm include its integration with social networks so as to extend the reach of the community (e.g., by encouraging friends to participate on ideas) and using the technology to address specific business needs and interest groups (e.g., soliciting ideas for the healthcare industry; partnering with the University of Texas for a competition to solicit innovative ideas that can change the world) (Killian, 2009).

As suggested in the preceding paragraph, the third phase of Dell's engagement strategy is to join the consumer conversation via the firm's increasing involvement in social media marketing efforts; that is, by interacting with consumers where they currently are spending their time. Dell's efforts in this regard thus far have focused primarily on Facebook, Twitter, and Second Life. For example, Dell uses Facebook to support a variety of social media initiatives, including a "social media for small business" Facebook fan page, "screencasts" (instructional videos on popular social media topics), and Facebook Applications (allowing users to interact with IdeaStorm, Citysearch, StormCast, etc. while on Facebook). For the virtual reality world Second Life, Dell created its own "Island" (i.e., a store), where it sells virtual computers on the island and real computers in real life. At the time of this writing, Dell had made a strong commitment to Twitter, where it had established thirty-three different sites, with all posts appearing in the name of Dell employees. For example, Dell Lounge provides cutting-edge trends in music, film, art, and technology. Other Dell topics include Dell Shares (for investors), Dell Outlet, Dell Home Offers, and Team Dell (employee Twitters). Most recently, Dell began alerting Twitter followers of Dell Outlet to sale items and offering them exclusive discounts for Dell products. Dell's Twitter approach has been praised for segmenting its different Twitter feeds into specific subjects, which is essential for such a large company with so many different lines and products. This facilitates the means by which people can locate very specific information and assistance, an important element when it comes to engaging with companies through social media.

This overview of Dell's new marketing approach reveals how substantially the company has evolved its engagement practices over a relatively short period of time. Dell has come a long way since the infamous "Dell Sucks" period and has learned some important lessons in the process; for example, when the company engages, the outcome is nearly always positive; the fact that consumers are in control should not be viewed as a threat; social media can put a human face on your company; and companies that listen, learn, and act can improve their offerings, enhance their relevance, and build loyalty and trust ("Dell Outreach," 2009).

Starbucks

Another highly successful global brand, Starbucks nonetheless has aroused the enmity of some consumers who feel threatened by the growing homogenization within the commercial marketplace and the global domination by a rapidly declining number of firms. The common refrain, "How many Starbucks is enough?" reflects how success that comes too quickly can ultimately serve to diminish brand value (see Quelch, 2008). The global recession did not help matters for Starbucks, which announced in July 2008 that it was closing 600 stores in the United States, a move that was interpreted by some as an overdue admission that there are limits to growth. Problems created by the company's growth strategy were recognized even earlier, as evidenced by this comment from a February 2007 internal memo penned by founder Howard Schultz that was leaked to the Starbucks fan site, Starbucks Gossip: "Stores no longer have the soul of the past and reflect a chain of stores vs. the warm feeling of a neighborhood store." Starbucks took several steps in an attempt to add value and restore some of the brand's earlier cachet, offering Wi-Fi service, creating and selling its own music, and putting the focus back on the coffee by revitalizing the quality of its standard beverages. However, according to marketing expert John Quelch (2008), "None of these moves addressed the fundamental problem: Starbucks is a mass brand attempting to command a premium price for an experience that is no longer special."

At this point in the book it should be evident that what was missing in Starbucks' efforts to restore its brand appeal was a focus on how the company could engage with consumers in a rapidly evolving social marketing environment. This is where Starbucks recently has made its greatest inroads in overcoming the problems associated with having become a mass brand that, in the eyes of many, "is no longer special." Starbucks' engagement campaign very closely echoes that of Dell's. Like Dell, Starbucks initially was moved to rethink its customer service approach following the appearance of a highly critical blog created by an unhappy Starbucks customer (www.starbucked.com; see Box 4.6) and other anti-Starbucks Web sites (e.g., The Delocator, which provides visitors who give their zip code a list of local, independently owned cafes as alternatives to Starbucks). This anti-Starbucks trend served, in part, as a springboard for Starbucks' foray into the social marketing arena.

As Dell had done with the creation of IdeaStorm, in March 2008 Starbucks launched its My Starbucks Idea Web site in an effort to give customers a voice by simply asking them, "What do you want?" The Web site, like that of IdeaStorm, informs consumers that they can "Help shape the future of Starbucks—with your ideas," and invites them to "share, vote, discuss, and see." The results thus far have been impressive, with consumers suggesting thousands of ideas, mainly centering on how the coffee can be improved (e.g., through better offers, more choices, bolder blends), new products that could be offered (e.g., vegan sandwiches and pastry offerings), and the desire for "freebies" (see http://mystarbucksidea.force.com/ideaHome/). Among the ideas that Starbucks has implemented include the launching of a social conversation platform, a "birthday brew" (i.e., a free drink offer on one's birthday), and the introduction of VIP cards.

My Starbucks Idea provides a means for the firm to engage with customers and prospects by giving them a role in shaping the future of the company. Not known for ever having been very open with the community, this effort also enables Starbucks to better understand customer needs and continue to innovate in ways that better serve those needs. This is particularly important for a brand that appeals to different people in different ways, and which sells things other than coffee (e.g., a cool place to hang out, a place to meet with people, free wireless Internet connections, specialty beverages, convenience, a little splurge). As David Meerman Scott (2007, p. 114) noted, "If you were marketing Starbucks, it would be your job to segment buyers and appeal to them based on their needs, not just to talk about your product." Listening to and engaging with customers clearly is essential in being able to do so successfully.

Another way that Starbucks has followed the path taken by Dell and a growing number of other companies (e.g., Nike, Honda, Motorola, Burger King) is by venturing into the social media realm. The company joined MySpace, where it offers downloads, free offers, and quirky characters as friends, and is active on Facebook, where it provides links to employee blogs and informative articles about the company (and where it has more than 1.75 million fans). More recently, Starbucks began to create sites on Twitter, including a My Starbucks Idea site, from which it sends out tweets to coffee aficionados and people who work in the coffee industry. In the future, Starbucks (and other companies) could follow another emerging tactic, which is to connect consumer collaboration efforts (e.g., My Starbucks Ideas) with widgets on white label social networking sites (Owyang, 2008). White label social networking sites provide companies with the opportunity to extend beyond the corporate Web site or proprietary platforms like LinkedIn or Facebook, by offering a framework for building an online community tailored to their needs. Such social networking platforms can be branded or changed as needed.

Starbucks' social marketing efforts have not been greeted by unanimous plaudits within the marketing community and there have been some vocal critics of the company's strategies, both new and old. For example, prior to its more recent initiatives,

Jaffe (2007) described how the company bungled some tremendous opportunities to connect with consumers. One involved Starbucks' one-named superfan, Winter, whose Web site (www.starbuckseverywhere.net) recounts his love for the brand and progress in achieving a goal: to visit every single Starbucks store in the world. To date, Winter has visited more than 9,000 Starbucks stores in 17 countries, and has increasingly drawn the attention of the mass media. What a terrific public relations opportunity for Starbucks, to have such a devoted fan whose growing celebrity revolves around their brand. However, as Jaffe noted, despite all the attention bestowed on Winter, including multiple interviews and feature stories, Starbucks has largely been absent throughout the process. Whereas Starbucks could have sent a clear message about its commitment to the community by turning Winter into an endearing spokesperson for the company, empowering him in his mission with updates about new stores and products, sponsoring his effort by contributing to his travel expenses, or inviting him to corporate headquarters for a personal tour, he was instead neglected.

Another missed opportunity involved a coupon for a free iced coffee that was distributed by e-mail to a select group of employees to pass along to consumers. As it happened, the offer was incredibly successful; however, rather than making more coupons available to desirous customers, Starbucks suspended the offer. To add insult to injury, a competing company, Caribou Coffee, publicized an offer to accept the voided Starbucks coupons. Thus, Starbucks' failure to show its commitment to consumers was Caribou's gain and serves, in Jaffe's view (2007, p. 221), as a classic example of how some marketers "want engagement and desperately look for signs of life from customers, and yet, when their customers raise their hands and reach out to them, these customers get slapped with disdain, disrespect, and disapproval."

An assessment of Starbucks' more recent engagement initiatives was conveyed by John Moore on his Brand Autopsy blog (http://brandautopsy.typepad.com). Focusing on the My Starbucks Idea Web site, Moore questioned the logic of a company with little previous social media or customer engagement experience launching such an ambitious project in its initial attempt to open up a dialogue with consumers. In his view, it would have been more reasonable had Starbucks taken a more focused approach, for example, by adding a blog-like component to its existing Web site, where customers could have been asked pointed questions about what Starbucks could do to improve its business. For instance, the decision to discontinue the oven-heated breakfast sandwiches could have been mentioned, with customers then invited to suggest what Starbucks should offer instead during the morning meal. The company's take on the suggestions then could have been added to the comments section, with updates about the most popular ideas and how the company was moving forward to implement them. According to Moore, this approach would have been more manageable than the current My Starbucks Idea Web site, which has proven somewhat unwieldy, with the same suggestions appearing repeatedly in various categories.

Both Jaffe and Moore have made some excellent points about efforts to engage that clearly are relevant not only to Starbucks, but many other companies contemplating the launch of their own social marketing programs. Nonetheless, with regard to the specific case of Starbucks, the company certainly deserves credit for rethinking its approach to customer engagement. Its recent social marketing practices demonstrate that Starbucks has made great strides in connecting with consumers and, despite some missteps along the way, is on the right track towards improving the equity of the brand.

Procter & Gamble

Innovation is the lifeblood of the marketplace, with 30% of a company's sales coming from products that are less than 4 years old (the so-called 30% rule). This has long been recognized at P&G, one of the world's leading consumer goods companies, owners of more than 300 brands in over 160 countries. Innovation has a lot to do with the long-standing success and profitability of the firm. Prior to 2000, when P&G CEO A. G. Lafley came on board, much emphasis was put into aggressive new product introductions to build up the P&G brand portfolio. Once Lafley took over, P&G began to focus on and push the company's core brands, the dozen or so top brands (e.g., Crest, Charmin, Tide, Pampers, Ariel) that accounted for more than 50% of the company's annual total sales. However, Lafley also had the acumen to acknowledge that mature markets require innovation, which remains an important focus at P&G, most recently seen in the company's movement into the health and beauty care categories, which are P&G's fastest growing segments.

With the global innovation model it developed in the 1980s, P&G established a reputation for running one of the greatest research and development operations in corporate history (Huston & Sakkab, 2006). However, as markets have changed in profound ways in recent years, it became clear that P&G's model was no longer adequate and Lafley made the decision to turn to external sources for innovation. It is in this regard that P&G has made a clear commitment to engaging with its various stake-holders. The firm's new strategy, "connect and develop," relies on technologies and networks in its search for new ideas. The approach is consistent with the mass collaboration focus embraced by the wikinomics movement (see Chapter 1), in the sense of companies tapping Web-based talent pools (so-called Ideagoras) (Tapscott & Williams, 2007). Along these lines, P&G formed an ongoing relationship with InnoCentive, Inc., a leader in open innovation sourcing, tapping the 140,000 "solvers" within InnoCentive's global network to help uncover creative solutions to some of P&G's product development challenges ("Procter & Gamble Expands," 2008). Less than 10 years ago, only 15% of P&G's product initiatives included innovation from outside the firm; by contrast, more than half of all P&G innovation now includes an external partner. At its Connect and Develop Web site (https://www.pgconnectdevelop.com), P&G invites prospective partners—including entrepreneurs, universities, research institutes, and large companies—for commercial collaborations. Links at the site are provided for the submission of innovations or simply for sharing one's thoughts. At the "share your thoughts" link, a box is provided for anyone to post a quick comment, and a feature describes how P&G has put previous thoughts into action.

One of P&G's more interesting efforts to engage with consumers is evident in its creation of BeingGirl.com, an online community for adolescent girls seeking information related to feminine care. The site provides health content, product information, and the opportunity for the teen community to interact in a secure, entertaining environment. It is no secret that the site also serves as a vehicle for the promotion of P&G brands to an impressionable market segment, in the company's efforts to capture brand loyalty among young prospective customers. Indeed, the ploy has paid off for P&G: a Forrester research analysis found that its campaign to push the Always and Tampax brands at BeingGirl.com via free sample offers resulted in a return on investment four times greater than its conventional off-line advertising campaign.

P&G has utilized various means to drive consumer traffic to the BeingGirl.com Web site, including a Web-based sweepstakes that was promoted by radio DJs and pop-up banners on other Web sites, with the prize being a free trip to an 'N Sync concert. The campaign resulted in nearly 200,000 visitor sessions at BeingGirl.com during the 4-week promotional period and 50,000 sweepstakes entries ("Radio Rules," 2001). P&G also placed digital Swapits coupons at BeingGirl.com, which could be earned and accumulated by visiting, registering, and interacting at the site. A branded auction for P&G beauty products and promotional items was then conducted at SwapItShop's

---

BOX 6.9 TOYOTA'S ENGAGEMENT WITH THE YOUTH MARKET

One of my students at ESCP Europe, Christine Lew, worked as an intern at Toyota during 2008, specifically on strategies to engage young consumers with the Toyota brand. Below, I provide her verbatim remarks from a course assignment on the Toyota program, written with fellow student Julia Mullis:

> This past summer, I worked in Toyota's Engagement Marketing Department, which seeks to interact one-on-one with the consumer. Specifically, I worked with planning and executing youth market activation sites in spaces such as The Dew Tour (platform for skateboarding and BMX biking), Motocross, and Supercross. Toyota's goal in each activation space was not merely to hang banners, but to create a dialogue with the consumer in order to transform their company's image and position it as fun, hip, and dynamic. As a specific example, Toyota created an exciting environment where kids could hang out, interact with the vehicles through fun activities, and receive small giveaways such as posters, dog tags, and key chains. In addition to this, Toyota also distributed surveys to measure the footprint (traffic, customer attitude, etc.) in the space.

> Toyota's attempt to interact with the consumer through engagement marketing shows that the company understands the importance of WOM marketing. By bypassing the traditional forms of corporate communication, they directly reached leveraged influencers by meeting consumers in their spaces in a non-obtrusive way. Establishing personal relationships with consumers, rather than shoving advertisements at them, gives Toyota credibility and trust. Toyota's engagement marketing demonstrates the strengths of a WOM campaign... availability, credibility, and experience delivery.

Web site (an online trading community for young people) so as to maintain awareness and interest in P&G brands and the BeingGirl teen community. The campaign resulted in 61,000 BeingGirl Web site visits, 600,000 auction bids, and over 26,000 items sent out during the auction (http://www.iabuk.net). For another engagement campaign targeting the youth market, see Box 6.9.

Urban Outfitters

Much of Urban Outfitters' recent advances in honing its brand image and reputation among its core audiences in a highly competitive market can be attributed to the firm's emphasis on engaging with those audiences through a variety of social marketing activities. The benefits that can be accrued from consumer engagement is openly acknowledged at the youth-oriented clothing retailer's Web site, where it is stated that the "established ability to understand our customers and connect with them on an emotional level is the reason for our success." The company claims to strive for the development of "an emotional bond with the 18 to 30 year old target customer we serve."

Urban Outfitters uses a segmentation approach in designing offerings that are perceived by target customers as creative, hip, and distinctive. This is successfully accomplished in part through direct interactions with young customers, including coolhunting (seeking out and engaging with fashion trendsetters in settings where they spend their time) and an active blogging presence. The Urban Outfitters' blog offers a focus on new fashions and accessories, contests, news about upcoming and ongoing projects, a music playlist, and links (eating, dining, photography, etc.) for various cities around the world where the firm's retail stores are located. Urban Outfitters also is committed to maintaining a major presence at the popular social networking sites, including YouTube and MySpace.

The MySpace Web site (http://www.myspace.com/urbanoutfitters) provides a forum for customer sharing and discussion, and also includes a link to Urban Outfitters' Flickr pool ("Show us how *you* wore it."), where its customers and fans post pictures of themselves wearing the brand's clothing and accessories. Consumers must join prior to posting, but the Flickr pool provides the company with a free fashion catalogue, with more than 4,000 images thus far added by nearly 1,500 members. Urban Outfitters includes some of the customer photos on a rotating basis on its various Web sites, thereby inspiring consumers to purchase and wear the company's offerings.

Conclusion

In this chapter, we have focused on a sweeping tide that is changing the nature of contemporary marketing. Businesses are quickly learning that it no longer is sufficient to do all the talking in their efforts to persuade and sell. Now, they must "join the conversation," listen to and engage with consumers, and strive to develop ongoing relationships with target audiences, by employing the same social media outlets and technologies that consumers have widely learned to use to circumvent traditional marketing appeals. As we have seen in this chapter, the list of companies that are successfully benefiting from the use of social networking media and other listening and engagement approaches continues to grow. (A wiki of many of these social media marketing applications is available at http://wiki.beingpeterkim.com/masterlist.) Although it is beyond the scope of this book to provide a comprehensive description of every noteworthy application, it is possible to discern certain commonalities that underlie their effectiveness: (*a*) they are consumer focused, in the sense of being designed primarily to serve customers, rather than the company itself; (*b*) they place the product or service at the center of each effort so that the association with the company and the brand is not lost; (*c*) they are utilities more so than marketing communications; and (*d*) they make it easier for customers to do more business with the company.

When considered in perspective, these keys to success bring us full circle in recalling the point emphasized at the outset of this chapter: everything in the new marketing landscape begins with the consumer. If there is still any doubt about this claim, consider the following blog excerpt from Adrian Ho, a founding partner of the marketing firm Zeus Jones, who offered an acutely observed commentary on social media engagement (http://www.zeusjones.com/blog/2009/the-best-social-media-marketing/):

> I think that companies make the mistake of thinking that they can behave like people on social media. The reasons that I follow or interact with people are completely different from the reasons I follow or interact with companies. I may develop a sense of friendship or community with the people behind a company's social media, but that isn't the primary reason I'll start interacting in the first place. These examples [of best social media marketing] recognise that. They understand that their company is in business to sell or do something for me and they used social media to serve me better.

7 Connected Marketing I: Word-of-Mouth Marketing Techniques

Hotmail, The Blair Witch Project, Burger King's Subservient Chicken, Dove's Evolution and "Share a Secret," Mentos/Diet Coke, Hasbro's P-O-X "Alpha Pups," Blendtec's Will It Blend, Simpsonize Yourself, Bob Dylan Facebook App, Polaroid/OutKast, USB Absinthe Spoon, Axe Click, Trivial Pursuit, P&G's Whitestrips, PowerBar, Wilkinson's Fight For Kisses, Cadbury's Dairy Milk Gorilla, Microsoft's Xbox Halo Games, Orange's "Orange Wednesdays," Virgin.net "viral e-mail," GM's "Oprah's Great Pontiac Giveaway," Harry Potter, Beanie Babies.

Needless to say, there is no shortage of examples of products or brands that have benefited from marketing campaigns intended to generate favorable buzz; some of which have been discussed in previous chapters. Most enthusiasts of alternative marketing approaches are likely to have some degree of familiarity with some, if not most, of the classic applications listed above. By their very nature, successful buzz campaigns not only get the word out about the focal product but the campaigns also get talked about in their own right (see Box 7.1). It is not surprising that the list of success stories continues to expand, if industry expenditures on alternative marketing approaches are any indication. Alternative media spending grew at a compound annual rate of 21.7% from 2002 to 2007, and it is anticipated that by 2012, one out of every four dollars spent on advertising and marketing will be allotted to alternative media ("Alternative Marketing Poised," 2008). Spending on social networks alone approached US$1 billion in 2007, a figure that is expected to rise to US$2.5 billion by 2011 ("US Online," 2007).

BOX 7.1 FOCUS ON RESEARCH: MOVIE BUZZ AND THE BOX OFFICE

The film *The Blair Witch Project* is widely cited as an iconic example of the great potential of alternative marketing efforts. The viral marketing campaign, which complemented a significantly more expensive traditional marketing push (upward of US$10 million on distribution and promotion) revolved around the US$15,000 Blair Witch Web site, which instilled mystery and intrigue that served to stimulate WOM in anticipation of the film's release in 2001 (Allard, 2006). The film's premise was that it depicted a presumably true story through the found footage of three student filmmakers who disappeared in the woods while filming their story of the Blair Witch.

(cont.)

Box 7.1 (*Continued*)

The Blair Witch Web site provided various forms of "evidence" from the missing persons' case, including sheriff's reports, photographs, and information about Blair Witch. Other documentation was published in a comic book format and posted on chat sites that appeared in the 12-month lead-up to the film's opening; before long, twenty fan sites, a mailing list, an online chat room, positive film reviews, and previews of the movie allegedly copied by a friend of someone who worked in the industry appeared on the Internet. The actual nature of this viral campaign and the extent to which the consumer-generated comments and Web sites were in actuality part of the film company's (Artisan) carefully planned viral campaign have been the subject of ensuing debates; nonetheless, the viral hype played a large part in transforming the US$30,000 film into a US$150 million blockbuster (Dobele, Toleman, & Beverland, 2005).

Over the years, the motion picture industry has reaped enormous benefits from favorable buzz surrounding new film releases, often as a result of the spread of WOM before the films make their way to cinema screens (e.g., more recently, the films *Cloverfield* and *Star Trek* followed a similar course as *Blair Witch*). Indeed, researchers have noted a definite link between patterns of WOM and movie box office revenues, although explanations for the relationship tend to vary. For example, Liu (2006) collected WOM data from the Yahoo Movies Web site for forty movies released in 2002 and found that WOM information offers significant explanatory power for both aggregate and weekly box office revenue, especially in the initial weeks following the film's opening. This explanatory power was largely attributed to the overall volume of WOM, rather than the relative proportion of positive and negative comments. The study also revealed that WOM activities were most active during the prerelease and the opening week, with persons becoming more critical during the opening week. Many persons talked about a soon-to-be-released film solely on the basis of speculation, rather than through direct experience. Liu explained his findings by suggesting that WOM in the film market primarily functions as an informative source of information that boosts consumer awareness.

Another investigation suggests a more complex dynamic underlying the relationship between online WOM and box office revenue. Duan, Gu, and Whinston (2008) obtained evidence suggesting that WOM volume was both a precursor and an outcome of box office revenue. Specifically, a movie's box office revenue and the valence of consumer WOM (positive or negative) significantly influenced the volume of subsequent WOM, which in turn leads to higher box office performance. Dellarocas, Awad Farag, and Zhang (2004) utilized a combination of metrics obtained from online consumer-generated media (e.g., movie review Web sites) and more traditional metrics to show that the early volume of online reviews can successfully serve as a proxy of early box office sales. Further, they found that the average valence of user reviews significantly predicts WOM, as well as the rate by which external publicity about a movie decreases over time.

In a follow-up study, Dellarocas and Narayan (2006) demonstrated that the propensity for a consumer to review a movie online is reflected in a U-shaped relationship with the perceived quality of the movie, such that people are more inclined to review or post ratings of films that they consider either very good or very bad. Moreover, online WOM was found to be positively related to the amount of public disagreement concerning the film's quality and the amount of formal marketing effort for the film, but negatively related to the number of theaters in which the film is released (i.e., the fewer theaters, the more online reviews). Finally, Dellarocas and Narayan also demonstrated how WOM begets more WOM, in that large numbers of previously posted reviews were found to increase subsequent moviegoers' likelihood of posting reviews for the same films. Unlike Liu, who suggested that WOM for the entertainment category of movies is linked to the desire to inform other consumers and boost awareness levels, Dellarocas and Narayan argued that their results point more to a self-enhancement motivation linked to potential social benefits accrued from conveying opinions to others.

Of course, the mere fact that a company earmarks spending for nontraditional marketing is no guarantee for success, nor can it be assumed that the return will justify the expenditure. The impact of nontraditional marketing approaches often is exaggerated, and while there is a tendency for successes to be widely reported, failures often go unnoticed by all but those who failed to reap the benefits from a campaign. For every success story, there are probably twenty or thirty failures that we do not hear about. Launching a nontraditional campaign is no simple matter: it requires clearly stated objectives, carefully identified targets, a plan for systematic implementation, available metrics for measuring its impact, and a clear justification that such a campaign is required in the first place. "Everybody else is doing it" does not necessarily mean it is right for your company or consistent with your marketing objectives.

In Chapter 6, we surveyed the various means by which businesses can get closer to their target audiences through efforts intended to listen to and actively engage with consumers. We now turn our attention to the methods that can be used to leverage this access once the consumer conversation has been joined. This first of two chapters on connected marketing approaches focuses on the means available to marketers for generating word of mouth (WOM) and marketing buzz, including the creation of brand advocates, product seeding, and brand ambassador/community programs. Chapter 8 continues our survey of connected marketing approaches with a consideration of viral campaigns and guerrilla, stealth, and live buzz marketing.

Alternative Marketing Approaches: Defined, Classified, and Deconstructed

A simple, but informative caveat that I believe I first saw in a promotion for a Word of Mouth Marketing Association (WOMMA) educational seminar observed that "there's more to word of mouth than a viral video or a Facebook application." WOM, as has been pointed out by many, is not a strategy but an outcome—an outcome that can be achieved in a variety of ways. Although we often hear mention of the term "word-of-mouth marketing" (WOMM), it is important to note at the outset of this chapter that the term typically is meant to entail a wide gamut of marketing tactics that are intended to generate enough enthusiasm among consumers that they will be moved to talk about something in the marketplace. A look at the definitions presented in Box 7.2 helps us recognize that the various forms of new marketing approaches often overlap and that the terms used to refer to them tend to be used interchangeably. One Canadian marketing services firm, Agent Wildfire (www.agentwildfire.com), distinguished between fourteen key branches of WOM, which account for 300 related marketing tactics (see Box 7.3).

BOX 7.2 DEFINITIONS

Word-of-mouth marketing (WOMM): The promotion of a company or its products and services through an initiative conceived and designed to get people talking positively about that company, product, or service.

Viral marketing: The promotion of a company or its products and services through a persuasive message designed to spread, typically online, from person to person.

Buzz marketing: The promotion of a company or its products and services through initiatives conceived and designed to get people *and the media* talking positively about that company, product, or service.

Connected marketing: Umbrella term for viral, buzz, and WOMM. Any promotional activity that uses WOM connections between people, whether digital or traditional, as communications media to stimulate demand.

Alternative marketing: Creating real emotional connections with your target market to develop WOM using the streets and the Internet via original strategies: guerrilla, buzz, viral and street marketing, interaction, and one-to-one marketing. (This term is roughly synonymous with ''connected marketing.'')

Source: Adapted from Marsden (2006*b*) and Tribeca.fr.

BOX 7.3 FOURTEEN TYPES OF WOMM

Integrated

- *Brand/customer community-building WOM*—providing a forum for key stakeholders to engage and participate in a brand through content, dialogue, activities, social connections and/or rewards.

- *Advisory panel/co-creation WOM*—the practice of inviting experts, prosumers, and innovators to collaboratively exchange ideas, develop solutions, input suggestions, and thus, endorse a wide array of company operations.

- *Influencer-driven WOM*—identifying and incubating a front row audience of opinion leaders to carry the weight of their recommendations and endorsement to their followers.

- *Product seeding/intervention WOM*—providing extremely targeted advance exposure or samples to people, typically in advance of launches, within new target audiences or as a tool for competitive conversion.

- *Referral-driven WOM*—getting an established base of advocates to recommend products and services to their trusted social circles based on brand affinity or positive experience.

- *Grassroots sponsorship/cause-driven WOM*—organizing volunteers and enthusiasts to rally around social movements and widen the circle who support and/or fund the cause.

Off-line-Dominant

- *Experiential WOM*—the creation of live, brand-relevant, immersive, and customized events focused around the lifestyle and needs of the target community who voluntarily step into your brand.

- *Buzz/guerilla WOM*—use of live events/stunts/field teams to get passersby to turn their heads and media to cover the story.

Online

- *Social media production/outreach WOM (i.e., blogs, podcasts)*—getting content and conversations developed and spread through forums, blogs, wikis, and podcasts.
- *Social network production/outreach WOM*—getting content, conversations, influencers, and traffic developed and spread through social networks; photo-, audio-, and video-sharing sites and their groups; applications; mashups; widgets; ads; and other vehicles.
- *Viral marketing/advertising WOM*—the creation of compelling, entertaining, and/or culturally important content engineered for passing along to many others.
- *User-generated content/media WOM*—generating brand-sponsored news, content, reviews, creative and other contributions through people (customers, fans, users), not company professionals.
- *Advergaming/virtual world WOM*—using multimedia forms to promote interaction and exposure between brands and users.
- *Affiliate WOM*—an explicit reward-based and reciprocal relationship between a business and third-party publishers or social media content authors.

Source: http://www.agentwildfire.com

WOM Marketing Basics

With so many nontraditional options available to marketers, it should be clear that no simple formula for launching a WOM campaign is likely to offer much utility or value to companies that differ in terms of resources, target markets, and marketing objectives. Nonetheless, the marketing literature and mass media are replete with overly simplified recommendations for launching WOMM campaigns. For example, Sernovitz (2006) promises "Word of mouth marketing in five easy steps": (*a*) identify *talkers*—people who are more likely to relay your message; (*b*) find *topics*—portable concepts for people to talk about that are simple and WOM friendly; (*c*) utilize *tools*—techniques and technology that make it easier for WOM conversations to take place; (*d*) *taking part*—participate in the conversation and engage in a genuine two-way dialogue; and (*e*) *tracking*—measure the online conversation. Although Sernovitz's "five Ts" of WOMM admittedly are overly general, they do provide a basic framework for identifying the key attributes required of any connected marketing effort. They also reflect much of the discussion in this book that precedes the current chapter: Chapters 1 and 2 highlighted emerging marketing *tools*; Chapter 3 concerned marketing targets and *talkers*; Chapter 4 dissected the WOM process, including *topical content* of buzz-worthy consumer exchanges; Chapter 5 focused on how conversations can be *tracked*; and Chapter 6 covered the various ways that marketers can *take part* in the consumer conversation. Consistent with Sernovitz's perspective, WOMMA (www.womma.org) suggests that all WOMM techniques require transparency and the opportunity for two-way dialogue in order to

- educate consumers about products and services,
- identify people most likely to share their opinions,
- provide tools that facilitate the sharing of information,
- assess how, where, and when information is shared, and
- listen and respond to supporters, detractors, and neutrals.

Most discussions of the important attributes that are required for leveraging WOM tend to emphasize the need for (*a*) a conversation-worthy idea or concept and (*b*) a great product or brand. Alluding to the first attribute, Publicis CEOs Maurice Lévy and Dan O'Donoghue (2005, p. 17) speak of "amazingly relevant" communications:

> The communication job is not to dazzle or astonish one's customers, but to make one's brands amazingly relevant to them. Rather than someone we test our supply on, the customer must be thought of as being at the heart of the development process, the brand, and the communication strategy. Testing supply has its place, but it is increasingly a small place compared to connecting in the right place.

The point is that it is not so much the marketer's job to determine what is a conversation-worthy idea or concept, but rather to identify what consumers believe is conversation-worthy. In this regard, recall our key lesson from Chapter 6: everything begins with the consumer. To a certain extent, this point also holds for the second essential attribute for leveraging WOM: a great product or brand. As noted in our discussion about the WOM process in Chapter 4, informal consumer recommendations often are sparked by especially satisfying or remarkable product experiences, a point reflected in Seth Godin's (2003, p. 3) "purple cow" notion:

> Something remarkable is worth talking about. Worth noticing. Exceptional. New. Interesting. It's a Purple Cow. Boring stuff is invisible. It's a brown cow. . . . Remarkable marketing is the art of building things worth noticing right into your product or service.

It is not surprising to learn that Apple's iPhone and amazon.com's Kindle—two popular, pioneering media devices—became instantly talk-worthy among consumers. But even the most apparently mundane products or brands can become the central focus of an ongoing conversation if those offerings are effectively brought to the attention of consumers who come to recognize their need-fulfilling potential and who see the exceptional in products that on the surface do not seem very remarkable. For example, I was initially perplexed by the following comment posted by my 22-year-old nephew on Facebook: "Today, I bought a Swiffer. My old mop is not following me around or playing love songs to get me back." He later informed me that the Swiffer—a product previously unknown to me in France—is an advanced mop that cleans surfaces like a regular mop and that the reference to his old mop was meant as an allusion to a popular TV commercial in the United States at the time. This example suggests that a traditional advertising campaign can make an everyday product like a mop "amazingly relevant" to consumers who need a practical and efficient solution to household cleaning, such as students who do not have a lot of time (or enthusiasm) to devote to cleaning up their dorm rooms or apartments. Whether or not the Facebook posting was intended as a tongue-in-cheek comment, a very ordinary product was capable of garnering enough interest to stimulate a conversation about it at a popular social media platform.

Similarly, Silverman (2005) recounted the example of another ordinary household product, the fabric softener Bounce, which became the focal product in an e-mail message that was circulating at one time on the Internet. The content of the message consisted of an excerpt that appeared in Joey Green's best-selling book, *Polish Your Furniture With Panty Hose*. It listed and described fifteen additional uses for Bounce, such as "repel mosquitoes," "eliminate static electricity from your television screen," "freshen the air in your home," "collect cat hair," and "clean baked-on food from a cooking pan." The message was sufficient to get people talking about Bounce, both online and off-line, and, in so doing, also boosted consumer awareness for the product.

Consistent with the foregoing discussion, a set of questions should be addressed prior to the decision to launch a WOMM effort (Ahari, 2007). For example, to determine whether a WOMM campaign is appropriate for the firm, one must first consider how information tends to flow in the industry. Does it diffuse in a centralized way? If so, a dramatic shift in the firm's communication strategy may be required before a WOMM campaign could become feasible. A related consideration pertains to where people get their information. If target audiences are unlikely to go online or use a mobile device, a WOMM campaign focusing on social media is likely to be irrelevant. If they are active users of new technologies, it must be determined whether they engage in social networking, the amount of time they hang out in networks online, and whether their networks are large and public or rather self-contained product or brand communities. Another question concerns how consumers interact in the focal industry. Do they tend to discuss their purchases with others? Are the purchases publicly visible? Are early adopters in the category likely to influence others? Also of relevance is whether the focal industry is a conservative one, such as a utilities company. If so, the decision must be made as to whether engaging in a nontraditional marketing campaign would damage the firm's positioning or reputation or else provide an opportunity to distinguish the company from the competition as a pioneer.

The more that is known about how targets tend to respond to marketing efforts, the better. In addition to insight into how consumers tend to interact and the nature of their traditional and nontraditional media usage habits, questions of what and who influence potential customers can provide valuable insight into whether a WOMM campaign should be launched and, if so, how. Do people tend to be turned off by traditional advertising? At what point is a nontraditional approach likely to have diminishing returns as consumers begin to perceive it as just another component of marketing overkill? Nontraditional marketing campaigns must be fresh, transparent, and honest, but they also need to avoid the tendency to overwhelm by intruding unnecessarily on consumers' lives. Marketers can circumvent common pitfalls by not solely focusing on opinion leaders and by avoiding the tendency to narrowly profile connectors. Finally, if there is no story to convey to consumers, there will be nothing for consumers to convey to one another.

The remainder of this chapter surveys some of the common types of WOM and buzz marketing, along with representative examples. My intent is not to cover all fourteen branches suggested by Agent Wildfire, but to focus on some approaches and techniques that are likely to have applicability across a variety of industries.

WOMM Techniques

The overriding objective of any application of WOMM techniques and media is to drive growth by creating a positive buzz around one's product or service. WOM that is created or encouraged as a result of specific marketing campaigns is sometimes referred to as *amplified WOM* (also "exogenous WOM"), to distinguish it from *organic WOM* (also "endogenous WOM"), which is naturally occurring, as when people become advocates because they are satisfied with a product and have a natural desire to share their enthusiasm with others. As pointed out at the WOMMA Web site (http://www.womma.org), there are some marketers who disagree with this distinction because in their view WOM is ongoing in the marketplace and, although a campaign can encourage it, WOM is the same regardless of origin. Others argue that many marketing campaigns that create or promote WOM were not intended to do so in the first place.

Although these arguments do have some merit given that WOM is a fluid form of communication, one in which the line between WOM that is marketing-induced sometimes blurs with ongoing organic WOM, some distinctions between the two forms of WOM are noteworthy. Efforts to stimulate amplified WOM are apt to be more relevant for low-engagement brands that do not tend to naturally generate consumer talk, and can be useful for spreading awareness for such brands. The duration of amplified WOM is likely to be short-term in the sense of occurring as a result of situational involvement (e.g., the prelaunch campaign for *The Blair Witch Project*). By contrast, organic WOM tends to involve high engagement brands, and is valuable in the sense of driving brand health over the longer term as a result of enduring brand involvement (e.g., as has been illustrated by the success of the iPhone and Harley-Davidson). Moreover, unlike the amplified variety, organic WOM is often experience-based and linked to set expectations, such that above expectation brand experiences will drive positive WOM (PWOM) and

BOX 7.4 FOCUS ON APPLICATION: BEATING EXPECTATIONS LEADS TO WOM

FreshDirect is an enormously successful online grocer that delivers fresh and processed foods, along with other perishable and nonperishable grocery items, to residences and offices in the New York City metropolitan area. In addition to the convenience it provides, there are other aspects of FreshDirect that make it an appealing choice for consumers. For example, it custom-prepares items for its customers through a manufacturing process called "Just In Time," which reduces waste and guarantees freshness and quality, and its offers are competitively priced in comparison to many other Manhattan markets.

Introduced to the New York market in 2002, FreshDirect quickly rose as a strong player among other grocery delivery services, which includes Whole Foods Market, a company that offers relatively inexpensive deliveries of its in-store healthy and gourmet product offerings. Both Whole Foods and FreshDirect attribute their success not to formal marketing efforts, but to WOM from customers who responded favorably to the extraordinary levels of customer service provided. This was largely a function of these firms having exceeded the expectations of customers who used their services. Early adopters raved to their friends and acquaintances who, in turn, encouraged others to try the service. In short, by exceeding expectations to such an extent, customers could not wait to share, brag, or talk about the experience with others. However, whereas Whole Foods adopted a policy of avoiding traditional marketing to spread their brand message, in recent years FreshDirect has ventured into the realm of full-scale advertising. Prior to the 2006 arrival of specialty grocer Trader Joe's in Manhattan, the decision was made by FreshDirect to counter its southern California-based competitor's bare-bones marketing approach (which involved the distribution of direct-mail flyers to residents in the neighborhood) by stressing FreshDirect's local status (Bosman, 2006). This consisted of a US$2 million television advertising campaign run on CNN, The Food Network, and local New York cable channels, with each commercial featuring a New York celebrity and including the tagline, "Our food is fresh. Our customers are spoiled." In a crowded competitive market, it stands to reason that FreshDirect could no longer depend solely on WOM. Nonetheless, there is always the threat that the local cachet that was largely developed via C-to-C influence could be lost as a result of the launch of a major media campaign. This possibility, however, was tempered by FreshDirect's strong reputation and the emphasis on the firm's local roots in the ad campaign.

below expectation experiences will drive negative WOM (NWOM). Beating expectations is a sure way to motivate customers to say good things about your offerings (see Box 7.4).

To encourage organic WOM (or advocacy), perhaps the best recommendation for marketing managers is to strive to make their brands better and different—to assure product quality and a positioning campaign that effectively differentiate the brand. In addition to improving product quality and usability, practices that tend to enhance naturally occurring WOM activity include a focus on customer satisfaction, responding to customer concerns and criticisms, opening a two-way dialogue and listening to consumers, and the application of strategies intended to build customer loyalty (see Chapter 6). By definition, amplified WOM typically requires a more direct effort to encourage or accelerate WOM, including motivating people to serve as advocates and evangelists by actively promoting a product; giving people information or products that they can share; identifying and reaching out to influential individuals and communities; and employing viral marketing strategies, such as using advertising and publicity to create a buzz or start a conversation. Some representative examples of these amplified WOM techniques are discussed below. (Viral marketing strategies are addressed in Chapter 8.)

Creating Brand Advocates and Evangelists

The notion of brand advocacy was introduced in Chapter 3. Intimately linked to brand loyalty, consumers who are favorably disposed toward a product or service often are inclined to willingly promote it to others, encouraging friends and acquaintances to—in the words of a famous Alka-Seltzer commercial—"try it, you'll like it!" Brand advocates are like religious evangelists, but rather than spreading the word about the gospel, they spread the word about marketplace offerings by enthusiastically recommending them to others. Although there is research evidence suggesting that up to 80% of customers frequently spread favorable comments about at least one brand (from 69% in North America to 90% in developing Asia), there appear to be wide variations in brand advocacy rates (Zhao, 2006). For example, according to one assessment, the global average of the percentage of people who recommended or gave advice in the preceding year ranged from 11% for CNN and 16% for Citibank to 50% for Nokia and 59% for Mercedes. Thus, referral-driven marketing techniques are sometimes required to nudge persons who have an affinity toward a product or service or who have had positive experiences with it to refer it to others within their trusted circles.

As illustrated in Figure 3.5, the goal of advocacy approaches is to convert customers who are especially satisfied with the brand and who have a strong connection and loyalty to it (i.e., brand adorers) into customers who are so satisfied with the brand experience that they are prepared to proselytize about it as brand ambassadors. Such programs also are designed to amplify the advocacy of consumers who already act as brand endorsers. There are several ways these objectives can be accomplished, including the use of branded free merchandise (such as contact cards, stationery, and stickers) for distribution and incentivized referral programs.

Personalized Branded Merchandise

One means for encouraging brand advocacy is to enable consumers to obtain free or low-cost branded merchandise to share with friends. Some common examples include sheets of personalized stickers, photo postcards, ringtones (sent to the phone to sample and share with others), and "skins" (i.e., personalized covers) for one's iPod music player or mobile phone.

Consumers can learn about such advocacy campaigns by going directly to the Web sites of their favorite brands or at centralized Web sites, such as www.icecards.com, where the details about live campaigns and available offers are provided. However, and this is where the value of such programs becomes clear, consumers are more likely to initially find out about the offers from other people who already have taken advantage of them. The process simply consists of clicking on the offer at the requisite Web site, providing the personal information that one desires to have on the merchandise (such as name, nickname, a personal photo, favorite saying or expression, lyrics to one's favorite song, etc.) and preferences for the branded material's design (such as color).

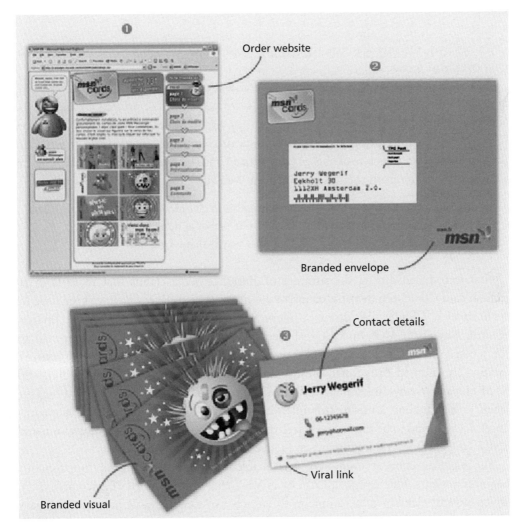

Exhibit 7.1 Icecards Example

Source: Icemedia [http://www.icemedia.nl/services/?id=11].

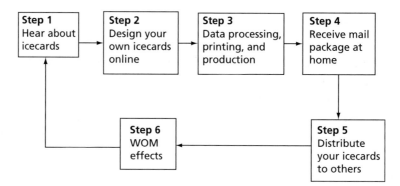

Figure 7.1 The Icecards Process

Once ordered, the merchandise then is delivered to the consumer's home within the next couple of weeks.

Icecards represent an especially innovative and successful example of this approach. Created by the Dutch firm Icemedia, icecards are personalized, printed contact cards, containing branded artwork on one side and the brand advocate's personal details on the other (see Exhibit 7.1). Sets of twenty-one cards are digitally printed and delivered to the user's home address free of charge (see Figure 7.1). The following is an example of an icecard offer, taken from the freeUKstuff.com Web site:

> Ice Cards—Get yourself some free personalised cards to give away featuring Godfather, The Game. Just choose your preferred card, add your personal details, complete your postal details, wait for the cards to arrive lol, now how easy is that—cool lol.

First introduced during the summer of 2001, Icemedia claims that more than 16 million cards have been distributed in 181 countries. To date, icecards have been used by such firms as Adidas, Vodafone, Unilever, Wilkinson, Beiersdorf, Orange, Philips, Bicardi, Universal, AXE, and L'Oréal (see http://www.icemedia.nl). A recent visit to the icecards.com Web site revealed ongoing icecard offers from Msn Lego (France), SimplyCity (United Kingdom), Sunny Delight (Spain), Yomo Desiderio (Italy), and KLM (Japan). *Icetags* are similar to icecards, but are intended as personalized luggage labels rather than as contact cards intended for distribution to friends and acquaintances. Icetags tend to be offered by travel-related companies such as lastminute.com and SNCF (the national train company in France).

The icecards concept eventually was enabled with personal photo functionality, beginning with a 2003 campaign run by NIVEA Hair Care. The NIVEA icecards offer, which was an element of a campaign to launch two new types of hair care gel, gave consumers the opportunity to design icecards with their own-styled photograph. Each icecards order earned the consumer entry in NIVEA's "Be A VJ on TMF" promotion, giving them the chance to be selected as a disc jockey on the popular TFM (Today's

Favorite Music) online radio Web site. Icecards campaigns also have been combined with sampling as part of an integrated marketing communication campaign. For example, when Axe launched its new scrub shower gel for men, Axe Snake Peel, visitors to a special campaign Web site could watch videos about the scrubbing routine and order Axe icecards. The icecards then were sent out bearing a sample of the new product, and each card could be used to obtain a €1 in-store discount for any Snake Peel purchase.

Another popular icecards campaign was developed by the sports apparel company Adidas during the 2002 World Cup football tournament in South Korea and Japan. Visitors to the Adidas Web site were offered sets of Adidas icecards as part of the "It's My Mania" campaign to promote the Adidas Predator football shoe internationally. Each icecard featured a football player wearing the new Predator shoe and bearing the "It's My Mania" slogan. Initially, a handful of e-mails were sent out to football fans inviting them to sign up for the cards, which shortly thereafter were available for ordering from the company's Web site. The e-mail campaign was extremely successful, spreading exponentially as a result of recipients forwarding the message to friends who in turn forwarded it to others. Within seven weeks, a total of 1 million Adidas icecards was sent out to fans. Follow-up research indicated that 78% of the cards were actively distributed to friends, stimulating a brand-related conversation in 65% of the cases (Marsden, 2006b). The campaign enabled Adidas to generate an extensive database of 50,000 Adidas brand advocates.

These different examples suggest some of the key advantages of the icecards method (and, by extension, other personalized branded merchandise tools). From the consumer's perspective, icecards are fun, easy, and personally relevant. The approach tends to generate an enthusiastic response: it prompts consumer action and stimulates buzz about the merchandise and the promoted brands, especially among socially active persons in the 18- to 25-years-old range. The popularity of icecards is evident in the following comment posted on a Web site providing links to free merchandise offers (www.hotukdeals.com):

> cheers man, duno why but I quite enjoyed ordering those, even got my own cool picture on them for free. . . .

From the marketer's perspective, icecards offer the identification of brand adorers and advocates through the collection of data from consumers during the ordering process. This provides companies with a database of names, addresses, and consumer insights for follow-up marketing campaigns. The creation of brand ambassadors and the viral WOM impact that results from the distribution of icecards increases awareness about the brand and helps shape a positive brand identity. Consumers can be reached in a highly targeted and controlled manner, and their response is highly measurable (e.g., number and types of icecards ordered, web traffic generated for the brand's Web site). Additionally, icecards provide marketers with opportunities to integrate online and off-line activities, combining icecards with promotional games and contests, in-store discounts, and free samples.

This distribution of branded merchandise represents a variation of *identity marketing*, which involves the use of promotional products bearing the company name and logo to create a visual identity and raise the awareness of the company and its offerings. The visual identity may be carried by the company's logos, stationery, brochures, business cards, and dress codes, as well as anything else that can be made available to consumers, such as coffee mugs, T-shirts, caps, pens and pencils, wall calendars, and so forth. In one novel approach, Freehand Advertising (http://www.freehandads.com) has representatives distribute free packets of branded notebook paper to students on American university campuses. A company's paid-for advertisement runs along the top of each sheet of paper. This approach provides a direct link to an important demographic, and Freehand claims that results indicate its effectiveness: 97% of student-recipients use the paper for taking notes in the classroom, 79% retain their notes, and students spend on average 90 minutes per day looking at the paper (the typical length of a university class). As for the potential of this tool for generating brand discussions, an estimated 25% of recipients talk about the ad during the day with their classmates.

Another variation of identity marketing involves paying young people to wear branded materials and to spend time in public settings where people are likely to congregate. For example, in 2004, Goodyear paid six young men US$30 an hour to serve as walking billboards for its Dunlop Tires brand. The "treadheads" walked the streets of Boston and visited bars, restaurants, and clubs with their hair shaved in the pattern of a tire tread and wearing T-shirts that read, "What's up with my head?" Dunkin' Donuts hired university students to place a temporary tattoo on their foreheads for US$50–100 per day while they attended campus activities. Similarly, more than 300 students sporting Reebok-branded temporary tattoos were seeded along the route of the 2003 Boston marathon, distributing free tattoos to anyone who engaged them in conversation. As in the Freehand example, this form of identity marketing generated buzz for the brand. Advocacy campaigns go a further step by personalizing the process and more fully involving consumers in conveying a firm's identity and desirability.

Incentivized WOM

The incentivized approach to brand advocacy consists of companies encouraging referrals by offering some sort of incentive or reward to people for doing so. The term "incentivized WOM" was coined by Mark Joyner in his 2005 book *The Irresistible Offer* to distinguish a type of WOM that is more greed-oriented than that motivated by the spontaneous desire to spread useful information about a product or service (so-called "inspired WOM"). Despite Joyner's contention that incentivized WOM is the less powerful variety and more apt to fail, different variations of this approach have been utilized in recent years, and research suggests that it can be a very effective strategy (Buttle, 1998; Danaher & Rust, 1996).

The classic referral program, sometimes described as a "tell-a-friend," "member-get-member," or "customer-get-customer" scheme, is exemplified by offers of monetary payment or other reward for referring a brand to another person (see Box 7.5). Some referral programs offer an incentive to both the brand advocate as well as the recipient of the referral when the latter adopts the product. This is an approach utilized by the online marketplace eBay, which invites members to introduce the service to others, with

---

BOX 7.5 FOCUS ON APPLICATION: DRIVING BRAND ADVOCACY WITH REFERRALS

Referral programs, which reward customers for promoting companies, products, or services to others, traditionally have been used as a cost-effective means for banks, service providers, and clubs to acquire new customers (Rusticus, 2006). As WOM has gained prominence in marketers' communication plans, many companies have found referrals to be a key way to spark enthusiasm and increase penetration for fledgling and existing brands. Two illustrative cases—Dove's "Share a Secret" campaign and PowerBar—demonstrate the significant power of a successfully managed referral program.

Unilever Dove's "Share a Secret" (1998)

Unilever's "Share a Secret" campaign to transform loyal users of Dove soap into active brand advocates provides a useful illustration of an elegantly simple application of the brand referral approach. As a means of recruiting new adopters to the Dove brand, Unilever invited current Dove users to mail in a proof of purchase, along with the name and address of a friend for whom they would like to pass on the "share the Dove secret" via a purchase promotion. The friend would receive a gift certificate for a pack of two free bars of Dove soap or a money-off voucher toward the in-store purchase of Dove's moisturizing body lotion. Current users were encouraged to include a personal note that would accompany the mailing to the friend. In return for providing contact details, the referrer also would receive a Dove certificate for the gift pack.

The success of the Unilever campaign exceeded company expectations, with 90% of Dove users who participated having supplied the contact details of a friend. Moreover, Dove's market share rose 10% during the promotion ("Health & Beauty," 1998). The referral program successfully utilized product trials for capturing new customers, many of whom previously had been brand switchers. Rather than simply having these prospects receive the free samples directly from the company, they instead unexpectedly received the product (or discount) as a personalized gift from a friend, thereby adding credibility and trust to the endorsement.

PowerBar (1983)

Although the phenomenal success story behind the PowerBar energy bar has a lot to do with product seeding (see pages 230–38), an important component of the launch bears a striking resemblance to the sampling tactic employed in the "Share a Secret" Dove campaign. The creation of PowerBar was conceived by marathon runner Brian Maxwell in 1983 (Rosen, 2002). Maxwell became interested in developing a new food for athletes that would be easy to digest, low in fat content, nutritious, and tasty. With the help of some friends, and after overcoming some early difficulties with the "tasty" part of the product concept, the PowerBar was born.

Given his own difficulties as a long-distance runner, Maxwell was well aware that endurance athletes are constantly on the lookout for anything that would provide a competitive edge, so he

(cont.)

Box 7.5 (*Continued*)

presumed not only that there would be a significant market for the PowerBar, but that a fertile breeding ground existed for the rapid spread of buzz about it. Nonetheless, as an entrepreneur with a limited budget, Maxwell was rather constrained in terms of a marketing approach to get the word out to attract early adopters. He met this challenge in the following way. As the product was being developed, Maxwell and his partner interviewed some 1,200 athletes in the San Francisco Bay area about their exercise regime, eating habits, and the influence of meals on their competitive performance. Once the PowerBar was available, each of the interviewees was sent a package of five free bars, a follow-up survey, and an order form for purchasing more PowerBars. This jump-started buzz about the product among athletes in the local area, and WOM grew as Maxwell handed out free bars at various sporting events. WOM was stimulated beyond the San Francisco Bay area through the use of a tactic akin to Unilever's: Maxwell's company sent invitations to existing customers offering to mail five PowerBars to anyone in the country on their behalf, along with a personal note, simply for paying the minimal US$3.00 shipping cost. It is likely that many grateful recipients contacted their friend to find out more about the energy bars, told their own friends, and so on. Only 14 years after the PowerBar creation, the company's sales surpassed the US$100 million mark; by 2000, earnings climbed to US$140 million in sales and the company was sold to Nestlè.

---

both parties receiving a US$5 voucher. Similarly, the UK financial services company Hargreaves Lansdown (HL) invited customers to add their name and postal code to a card to be passed on to a friend, enabling the latter to use the card to request further information about the company's services. If the friend invested in an HL service or placed a certificated share deal before a specified date, both the original customer and the friend received vouchers worth £500. In 1991, the US telecom company MCI introduced its "friends and family" referral program, offering a 20% discount to customers for calls to friends and family members they had referred to MCI. Those who became customers after the referral in turn were given a similar opportunity for a 20% discount if they referred their friends and family members. This approach was successful in creating a WOM-chain reaction of referrals, resulting in 10 million new customers for MCI within 2 years.

Another type of incentivized WOM approach based on financial stimulation is the affiliate or online referral program. Such programs offer anyone who runs a Web site or who otherwise is active online to recommend the company's products via the affiliate program. The way this works is that a consumer can choose to recommend a company running a referral program to others by sharing that company's referrer-personalized web links. A web link can be published on the consumer's Web site, newsletter, or blog, or it can be transmitted by e-mail or posted on Internet forums. When someone clicks on the link, the referrer is identified by the company and, should the referred visitor then make a purchase from the company, the referrer receives a commission for directing the customer to the merchant's Web site. The monetary reward typically takes the form of a prespecified amount per sale, such as a percentage of the sales or a flat-rate or multitiered payout.

The online UK-based portable media device company Advanced mp3 offers an affiliate program, which is promoted on its Web site (http://www.advancedmp3players.co.uk) as follows:

Want to increase earnings from your website? Then join Advanced MP3 Players' affiliate program and you will receive up to 4.5% commission for every purchase made by referrals from your site. Many of the transactions on Advanced MP3 Players are for high value items and the commissions will soon add up! With Advanced MP3 Players, you have the potential to offer your visitors a range of the latest and greatest MP3 players, iPods, Wireless Audio Systems, Headphones and Accessories. We take our affiliates seriously. As such, we've teamed up with three different affiliate networks to provide an efficient and reliable affiliate program. When you become part of the scheme you can rely on third party tracking, real-time reporting as well as monthly commission payments.

Joining the Advanced mp3 affiliate program is offered free of charge, and consumers can choose from among a variety of buttons, banners, and textlinks for connecting potential customers to the firm. An integrated product datafeed on all affiliate networks also is provided, thereby allowing the affiliate to incorporate product images with accompanying descriptions, pricing, and stock level information.

In essence, affiliate programs provide consumers with opportunities to host a company to increase sales. Consumers essentially act as online sellers for firms so as to receive a percentage of their sales, an approach that is consistent with a contemporary trend toward cost-per-action marketing models that focus more on return on investment (ROI) than on building consumer awareness (Oetting, 2006). The connection between affiliate referral programs and WOM was discussed in a white paper by the research and consulting firm Aberdeen Group (2003), which suggested that "Affiliates generate sales through third-party education and validation—much in the same way that word of mouth recommendations have traditionally referred business directly to movies, restaurants, merchants, doctors, lawyers and accountants." However, it should be apparent that there are clear differences between the sort of organically motivated (inspired) WOM that spreads from consumer to consumer and the incentivized referrals that are transmitted by affiliate (and related) programs. In the natural WOM situation, people are informing each other about products and services on their own volition, for the various reasons that were detailed in Chapter 4 (e.g., ego-enhancing motivations, an altruistic desire to help others, a conversation that provides the opportunity for a recommendation). By its very nature, the introduction of referral or finder fees is based on the creation of a quasi-sales situation, which is devoid of the more intimate links between consumers that are likely to add credibility and perceived legitimacy to the recommendation.

Given this distinction, it is necessary to consider to what extent the sales-related character of referral approaches undermines the communicator–recipient relationship and diminishes the overall impact of the recommendation. This is what Carl (2006b) no doubt had in mind when he investigated the contacts of agents who had been enlisted to convey WOM by the marketing agency BzzAgent (see below). His results revealed that approximately 75% of those who received advice were unconcerned about the agent's affiliation; rather, what mattered was the degree to which they trusted the agent to be honest, had their best interests at heart, and conveyed relevant and valuable information. Neither the agent's credibility nor the receiver's interest in products appeared to be affected when the agents revealed their affiliation, suggesting that an affiliate's self-serving motives for referring a product or service may have less of a negative effect on recipients than one might suspect.

Despite Carl's encouraging findings, there is a more troublesome consequence of affiliate programs that has been identified: affiliate programs can instigate questionable activities on the part of referrers and companies (Oetting, 2006). For instance, the affiliate marketing broker LinkShare, which manages over 10 million merchant–affiliate partnerships, bestows its quarterly Titanium award to the one participant in its LinkShare loyalty program who supports the most merchants and drives the greatest number of online sales for those merchants. As it turned out, several award winners later were found to have engaged in questionable tactics to amass the massive click-through numbers necessary to win the award, including manipulating search engine results, cookie stuffing (i.e., tricking affiliate software into counting buyers who had not actually clicked on an affiliate link), and the sending of spam e-mails. Such activities are contrary to the typical terms and conditions that must be agreed to prior to the registration of a potential company affiliate. For example, the Advanced mp3 conditions for affiliates read as follows:

- You agree not to solicit any services/customer/partners through spamming, indiscriminate advertising or unsolicited commercial email.
- As an alliance partner (affiliate), you are an independent contractor and not an employee of [the affiliate broker]. You are responsible for declaring your own income.
- You agree not to use [the affiliate broker] links on Websites that contain or promote any of these types of content: libellous, defamatory, obscene, pornographic, abusive, violent, bigoted, hate-oriented, illegal, cracking, hacking or warez, or that offer illegal goods or services, or link to a Website that is engaged in any of these types of activity.
- You agree not to mislead potential customers or partners in any way.

However well intended these conditions may be, there is nothing to prevent a person from agreeing to them and then engaging in the very activities they prohibit. The point is that once consumers are empowered to do the selling for companies to earn a commission, as is the case for affiliate programs, the companies lose control over their affiliates' conduct. If there is a way to cheat the system to maximize one's earnings, chances are that some participants will take advantage of the opportunity, pushing affiliate marketers to stay one step ahead of unscrupulous participants by finding ways to impose greater controls. In an interview with Trnd's Martin Oetting (2006, pp. 235–6), NOP World Consumer CEO Ed Keller observed:

> Marketers who make their marketing message available to those who seek it out, who learn from it, and then start acting on it, will be successful. And those that end up trying to penetrate paid agents into the marketplace who are saying things they don't believe, will be

looked at in the same way that people look at telemarketing today: "You're intruding on my conversation, get out of here." Right now, we are probably still too early in the process to know what crosses that boundary. But everybody in the industry needs to keep an eye on this.

Product Seeding

There is nothing inherently evil about using monetary or other incentives to motivate consumers to make favorable comments to others about one's product or service, except perhaps in the case when this is done intentionally to move poor-quality goods. But one thing to keep in mind prior to launching a referral program to stimulate WOM is that people typically will talk about good products free of charge. As Joyner (2005) concluded, "There is no substitute for an ecstatic consumer." In other words, a good product will excite consumers to spread the word on their own. This is the logic behind using *product seeding* to stimulate WOM. Product seeding is a term that has evolved from the practice of targeting selected consumers with product sampling for research purposes (so-called "seeding trials" or "marketing trials"). Seeding trials are common in the pharmaceutical industry, where new drugs are given to select physicians to use in clinical trials, a practice that has been criticized as a disguised form of marketing that is intended to get physicians in the habit of prescribing the drug (Sox & Rennie, 2008).

As a means of creating brand loyalty and advocacy, product-seeding campaigns target opinion leaders with free samples, sneak previews, or new products that have not yet appeared in the marketplace (e.g., beta versions) to obtain consumer advice about how the product should be marketed and to gain sales. As Marsden (2006*a*) points out, by getting a free product directly into influential consumers' hands and giving them a say about the way it is marketed, this approach effectively builds their support by empowering them with a sense of ownership, and thus increases the likelihood they will become WOM advocates within their social networks and accelerate sales. This certainly was the case with the PowerBar seeding campaign (see Box 7.5). The grassroots seeding effort utilized a network of 1,200 athletes who already had been engaged during the product development stage. Once they received a free package of energy bars, the wheels were set in motion for them to begin buzzing about the product.

One of the earliest examples of a successful seeding trial was carried out during the development of Post-it Notes, 3M's little sticky notepads office product. The product itself was serendipitously created following an unsuccessful effort by the company to develop a new super-sticky adhesive. Initial tests on the marketability of the slightly sticky temporary bookmarks that ultimately gave birth to Post-its proved futile, as no one could figure out how they could be used by consumers (Marsden, 2006*a*). The answer emerged when 3M carried out a seeding trial in 1977 among a sample of opinion leaders within the office supplies industry: secretaries to senior management staff at US companies. The secretaries were sent boxes of Post-it Notes from the company, and were invited to suggest possible uses for them. Before long, the Post-its started appearing on memos, drafts, desks, and correspondence, and eventually spread like wildfire across companies. This was all the evidence 3M needed to successfully launch the eventual multimillion dollar brand.

The mechanism underlying the success of the product seeding efforts of 3M and other firms appears to be linked to the fact that because participants are singled out to help a company in the development and commercialization of a product, they feel special and especially willing to help out. The psychological explanation for this process is referred to as the "Hawthorne effect," which describes the effect on participants of merely being studied for research purposes (Rosnow & Rosenthal, 2005). For example, the secretaries in 3M's seeding trials were transformed into Post-it Notes "brand champions" who felt as if they had a vested interest in the success or failure of a potentially new product. This sense of "co-ownership" of the brand clearly is missing in referral programs, where referrers typically lack the intrinsic motivation to help out because there is no sense of true engagement with the brand. As a result, an extrinsic incentive is required to prompt brand advocacy.

One way of distinguishing between WOM efforts that attempt to convert brand loyals into advocates (e.g., the icecards approach) and product seeding campaigns is to consider the different points of entry in the grapevine-harnessing process depicted in Figure 7.2, a conceptualization developed by the Gfk Roper Consulting firm (Zhao, 2006). By definition, brand loyals are already familiar with a brand, feel a strong commitment to it, and are thus primed to talk about it. As previously described, the

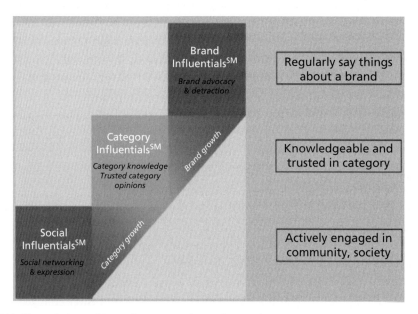

Figure 7.2 Three Points of Entry for Leveraging Influentials' WOM

Source: Gfk Roper Consulting (Zhao, 2006).

key to leveraging that loyalty is to convert these brand adorers into proselytizers who share their enthusiasm with others. As the graphic in Figure 7.2 indicates, brand influentials regularly say things about a brand; however, when advocacy programs target such consumers at the top tier of entry, the goal is to facilitate the WOM process. Having a pack of icecards at hand makes it that much easier for a brand adorer to strike up an ongoing conversation about the brand during interpersonal contacts.

When a product seeding effort like that utilized during the development of Post-its is implemented, by nature the strategy is different: the goal is to attempt to leverage WOM at the middle tier of the grapevine-harnessing hierarchy, targeting opinion leaders who are respectable, trustworthy, knowledgeable, and socially connected. When new products like Post-its are introduced to such consumers, it is not brand loyalty, but product category knowledge that is key to the development of brand advocacy. Category influentials, once given the opportunity to use the product and assess its quality as co-collaborators in the marketing process, are that much more likely to spread the word about it to others. This is what happened with the influential, upper management secretaries selected by 3M—once they discovered the value of the Post-it Notes, they became enthusiastic advocates among their peers.

The connected marketing literature is replete with examples of successful seeding campaigns. Affinitive, a company that specializes in consumer engagement marketing solutions, launched some typical product seeding and sampling campaigns (http://www.beaffinitive.com). One Affinitive campaign for Barilla Pasta was intended to strengthen the brand image and reinforce the brand's message that the making and enjoyment of meals is an art. The campaign involved sending out "Test Kitchen" packages containing product samples and information about Barilla to consumers. Recipients were encouraged to create dishes, host dinner parties, and upload photos of their dishes for others to comment on, rate, and share. Consumers provided feedback that enabled Affinitive to ascertain their pasta consumption habits and brand perception. Another Affinitive campaign was conducted in conjunction with the book publisher Random House's community-based program, Random Buzzers, which connects teen readers with the publisher and its authors. In addition to providing community members the opportunity to engage in online chats with authors and share and create content, Affinitive added a seeding component whereby participants can receive advance copies of books and book excerpts. Members then can generate buzz about the books with other passionate teen readers via social networking features.

A third example from Affinitive involved a partnership with Gillette's youth marketing agency to target male university students. The goal of the campaign was to promote the Gillette's TAG body spray brand by stimulating buzz within the students' social circles. Free TAG product samples were sent to campus fraternities and sororities, where Gillette-sponsored parties provided opportunities for consumer-generated content, such as photos, video, and text, which was then uploaded to social networking sites.

As each of these examples makes evident, a buzz-stimulating tool like product seeding typically is not used in isolation; rather, it more often than not forms part of an overall consumer engagement program. For example, getting the TAG product directly into the hands of university students added to the overall marketing engagement package intended to develop and hone a relationship between the students and the brand. In addition to the Affinitive campaign, Gillette enlisted the work of other marketing agencies to further promote the TAG brand. The Boston advertising agency Arnold Worldwide and smaller marketing firms, including Fusion 5 and AMP Insights, were tapped to engage younger male targets where they congregate, in locations such as movie theaters, beaches, and skate parks (Abelson, 2005). These young teens were asked to provide their opinions about males who wear body sprays, how they try to attract girls, how they feel about girls who take the initiative, and so on. Their responses then were applied to the development of an advertising campaign that emphasized teen fantasies, showing teenage boys attacked by scantily clad female wrestlers, female shoppers, and their girlfriend's mother. Not surprisingly, this advertising campaign turned out to be buzzworthy among members of the target audience, who revealed during the interviews their view that smelling good is an important means for attracting girls, and something that boosts their confidence with the opposite sex. Several TAG adopters later claimed to have started using the brand after hearing about it from a friend (Abelson, 2005). These connected marketing efforts by Gillette gave the company a strong footing in a highly competitive market, rising rapidly to the number two position behind Unilever's Axe brand. Axe achieved the top position among male body sprays through a variety of traditional and nontraditional marketing approaches, including a highly successful viral campaign that is detailed in Chapter 8.

Before we turn our attention to other WOM techniques, some additional applications of the seeding approach—also embedded within an integrated marketing communication strategy—bear mentioning. P&G, a company that has successfully incorporated a great deal of nontraditional marketing into its recent marketing efforts, combined Internet seeding with an incentivized WOM component to launch its benchmark tooth-whitening product, Crest Whitestrips. In a variation of product seeding, P&G's innovative Internet seeding approach relied on limited availability of the product and early adoption by opinion leaders to get the word out about the new product (Daumeyer, 2001). Starting in January 2001, Whitestrips could only be purchased in dentists' offices and online at the Whitestrips Web site. P&G then encouraged positive buzz by offering Whitestrips' purchasers money for turning friends on to the product, with each referral netting the customer US$3. Satisfied users then started telling their friends, who told their friends, and so on. In the meantime, P&G tracked who was buying the product to develop the best strategy for the eventual launch of Whitestrips in retail stores. This process lasted a period of 4 months, after which the product was made available in stores, Internet sales were shut down, and a traditional advertising campaign commenced.

P&G's seeding strategy for Whitestrips was enormously effective in creating brand evangelists who sparked interest in the new product innovation (sheets of peroxide gel worn on the teeth) and generated sales, resulting in more orders during the initial 8 weeks than the company expected to attain in 1 year. However, this success story had much to do with P&G's faith in the product at the outset, and the recognition that consumers were ready for it. Prior research conducted by the firm revealed that more than half of adult Americans desired brighter teeth, but that less than 5% had actually undergone a tooth-whitening treatment. By targeting early adopters to spread WOM for the Whitestrips kits, P&G was able to bypass reliance on a considerably more expensive mass media campaign to teach consumers about the product and stimulate interest in it. According to a P&G spokesperson for the Crest line of products, "We knew we were on to something. And we felt like the best salespeople were the users. . . . It's a jump-start. We're getting the product to people who will be the most excited and passionate about it. They become our best sales force." These comments also apply to Nokia's decision to seed the firm's new camera phone among "leading edge" Finnish bloggers who were

---

BOX 7.6 FOCUS ON APPLICATION: PRODUCT SEEDING AND TRIVIAL PURSUIT

During the early 1980s, Trivial Pursuit was an obscure Canadian board game. That was before marketing consultant Linda Pezzano designed a strategy to drum up favorable WOM, in a move that changed the nature of the way game makers do business (Martin, 1999). Pezzano launched the campaign by forwarding a series of provocative messages ("teasers") about the game to 1,800 of the top buyers who were planning to attend the 1983 New York Toy Fair, a few months prior to the event. Around the same time, she had the game sent free to some of the Hollywood celebrities whose names were mentioned among the trivial questions, including stars like Larry Hagman, Gregory Peck, and James Mason. An accompanying letter had the trivia card pertaining to the celebrity stapled to it. Some of the stars responded by sending Pezzano personal thank-you notes, which Pezzano then used in subsequent promotions. Before long, those same celebrities started to throw Trivial Pursuit parties in Hollywood which, not surprisingly, attracted a good deal of media attention. When fans heard about the Hollywood parties, they purchased the board game and began to hold their own parties. A third element of the campaign consisted of staging game-playing tournaments at various public settings, such as parks, bars, restaurants, and ski clubs—a sure way to get the game noticed and talked about.

In contrast to the traditional marketing approach used for games at the time, which largely consisted of TV ads, movie placements, and licensing agreements, the Trivial Pursuit campaign accomplished more at far less expense. By relying on a seeding approach that got the US$12 game directly into people's hands, a successful buzz campaign resulted in a Trivial Pursuit fad that spread across North America and ultimately totaled more than US$1 billion in sales—all this at a cost that was only a fraction of what a traditional mass marketing effort would have entailed. Pezzano's team also gave away free Pictionary games, a subsequent offshoot of Trivial Pursuit, to random consumers. According to Chris Byrne, one of Pezzano's assistants, "We estimated that for every complete Pictionary we gave away, we sold between 5 and 12 more. . . . She knew nobody would play a board game without getting their hands on it. She took games to the people."

encouraged to experiment with the camera function (see Chapter 6). Getting the new product directly into the hands of connected consumers resulted in a high level of interest for the product among Internet users.

One of the positive offshoots of seeding campaigns is that once the buzz begins to spread, at some point the mass media is likely to catch up with the story and publicize it to a broader audience. For example, even before Whitestrips was available in retail stores, popular magazines like *Entertainment Weekly* and *Time* ran feature stories touting the product as the next big thing in dental care, publicity that came free of charge to P&G. The role of the mass media in keeping the buzz momentum going by bringing it to the attention of a larger public cannot be overstated. In fact, this has a lot to do with the success of Trivial Pursuit, one of the most successful board games in history (see Box 7.6).

Whether a product seeding campaign effectively achieves its objectives in transforming opinion leaders into brand advocates is dependent on the nature of the product, the people, and the marketing action. In this regard, Marsden (2006) offered a ten-point checklist, which covers some of the key questions to address prior to the decision to launch a seeding campaign. Marsden's checklist is summarized below:

1. *Are we offering something new?* A seeding effort is more likely to strike a chord among opinion leaders if it offers something new and different. Products and services that have been around for some time, are generic or commodity goods, are unlikely to offer people anything that is talk-worthy and thus are poor candidates for product seeding.

2. *Are we offering something better?* Even if a seeding effort transforms participants into advocates, that advocacy is likely to be short-lived if the product is disappointing and does not provide a truly superior experience. According to Marsden, this does not mean that a seeded product has to be extraordinary or revolutionary for advocacy to lead to sales; however, a unique selling point must be evident that consumers can articulate to each other.

3. *Are we offering something that can be sampled?* This is a rather obvious question, given that seeding trials represent targeted sampling initiatives. Thus, products and services that can be provided to opinion leaders through a free sample or limited trial offer, download, or preview are obvious candidates for a seeding campaign. Higher value, low-margin products, such as some technology goods or perishable foods, will require more novel seeding approaches. Some possibilities include in-store and in-office sampling, product demonstrations at trade shows and conferences, special loans, trials using redeemable gift certificates and vouchers, and virtual online product trials and demonstrations. When DVD players first appeared in the marketplace, a number of competitive promotions were offered whereby consumers could win a free player. This got the product into consumers' living rooms, and their direct experience with the device and the

resulting WOM that experience generated greatly contributed to the rapid diffusion of the new product innovation.

4. *Have we identified our opinion-leading target buyers?* Seeding campaigns are intended to influence the influencers, so the selection of the appropriate targets who are most likely to serve as persuasive advocates is critical to the success of this marketing approach. The best candidates are persons in the target market who are likely to be responsive to trying out a product or service and who are respected, trusted, and well connected within relevant consumer networks. As Marsden suggests, the identification of such persons should be based on who is most likely to be an effective conduit of WOM in your market. The search should extend beyond the more obvious candidates—journalists, bloggers, experts, celebrities, and reviewers—to include opinion leaders among bar staff, health and fitness trainers, hairdressers, employees, satisfied clients and customers, and investors.

5. *Are we seeding to enough opinion leaders?* The more consumers selected for a seeding campaign, the more expensive that campaign will be. Nonetheless, to be effective, one must attain a critical mass of seeded influentials advocating the product or service to lead to an appreciable boost in sales. Marsden suggests as a rule of thumb that approximately 1% of the target market should be seeded, with a minimum of 250 consumers per major urban center, although this number will invariably depend on the nature and size of the market.

6. *How are we going to deliver the trial experience?* This question pertains to the logistics of how the seeding will be carried out; that is, how the product or service will be delivered to the selected participants in a cost-effective way. There are a variety of options available: sending by post or courier, hand-delivering, downloads via the Internet, or retrieval at a convenient location (shopping mall, store, hotel, etc.). Sales promotion agencies or specialist sampling companies can be contacted for advice as to the most cost-effective approaches.

7. *Does our seeding trial involve exclusive "get it first" sampling?* An essential element to a successful seeding campaign is assuring that participants have exclusive access to that which is to be sampled or trialed *before* other consumers. Such exclusivity can optimize the extent to which the selected opinion leaders engage in WOM because it enhances the value of the WOM content. Although this is easier to control during prelaunch seeding trials, targeted sampling can be combined with priority access to various services and promotions. One key is to ensure that participants get the "VIP treatment" and feel special, as important collaborators engaged in a special project with the firm. Another key is to take care to consider exactly what needs to be seeded with the product or service that will help participants spread the word, such as discounts, vouchers, promotional gifts, branded merchandise, or additional samples.

8. *"VIP vote": Are we giving seeding trial participants a say in our marketing?* This question also pertains to engaging seeding participants as true collaborators in the marketing process. Opinion leaders are not only valued to the degree to which they spread the word and stimulate sales, but also because they serve as an important source of advice and feedback about the sampled offering. One of the simplest ways to give participants a voice is to provide an online vote regarding different marketing options, such as preferred logo, advertising concept, campaign poster, promotion, distribution channel, and so on. This can be extended to providing participating opinion leaders with the opportunity to design and vote on packaging, brand name, and nature of the product or service, similar to the approach that was employed by Brewtopia in its development of Blowfly beer (see Box 5.1). According to Marsden, an effective seeding program is one that makes participants feel that they have contributed to marketing decisions without unnecessarily burdening them with work, which is why a simple vote for options is more advisable than lengthy questionnaires or interviews.

9. *Does our seeding trial offer participants an "inside scoop"?* This question can be thought of as a corollary to question 7, in that both focus on the importance of making seeded participants feel special and help create a sense of goodwill and loyalty that can increase participants' commitment to the firm. "Inside scoop" pertains to whether participants feel like insiders in the sense of knowing something important that other consumers do not. This could be something related to the firm, the industry, or the specific product or service that is the focus of the seeding campaign. A determination must be made as to what can be shared with these individuals that will reinforce their belief that they possess a special relationship with the firm, such as insider guides, brand stories, privileged access to company discussions or marketing materials, or behind-the-scenes experiences.

10. *Have we put in place a mechanism for measuring the effectiveness of our seeding trial?* As I pointed out in Chapter 5, a connected marketing effort requires that metrics are in place for assessing the effectiveness of the action taken. Because seeding typically is oriented to increasing sales, it stands to reason that sales-oriented measures are appropriate for such campaigns. For measuring off-line sales, Marsden recommends P&G's method of comparing differential sales performance between the seeding region and a control region where the campaign is not run. Various alternatives can be used for assessing the impact of the seeding campaign for online sales, such as tracking the number of sales a pass-it-on promotional discount code generates across successive waves of recipients. Non-sales measures can focus on brand awareness levels (e.g., as indicated by number of visits to a special Web site, blog, or discussion group) and amount of coverage (e.g., number of stories, column inches) in the traditional press generated by the seeding campaign.

In my view, there is another question that should be added to Marsden's list: *Is the seeding trial effort being used in isolation to market the product or service or is it integrated with other methods?* As I previously mentioned, successful brand advocacy campaigns are typically those that employ a combination of traditional and nontraditional techniques in an integrated marketing program. For example, we saw that Affinitive's TAG campaign utilized product seeding in conjunction with engaging teens in a two-way dialogue, and was followed up by traditional TV advertising. That this eleventh question is relevant to each of the WOM marketing approaches discussed in this chapter is evident in the following comments from Steve Knox, a vice president of business development for P&G's Tremor unit (Rodgers, 2004):

> Word of mouth advocacy is part of a holistic marketing plan; it is not *the* marketing plan. Unfortunately, when new things [like product seeding] come along, people start looking at them as a panacea. Of course they're not. This is a revolutionary tool that works synergistically with other media. People shouldn't consider it the only element of a marketing plan.

Brand Ambassador/Community Programs

An increasing number of WOMM efforts are intended to create and nurture brand ambassadors, often through community-wide programs. Such efforts rely heavily on the listening and engaging principles outlined in Chapter 6, in the sense that consumers are approached not as passive potential customers, but rather as long-term partners in a mutually reinforcing exchange. This approach typically incorporates some of the tools and techniques discussed above, such as product seeding and "get it first" sampling, encouraging referrals, and rewarding participants for their feedback and for spreading the word. Other elements include providing participants with behind-the-scenes and buzz-worthy information ("inside scoops") and participation in marketing decisions ("VIP votes").

Hasbro's "Operation Alpha Pups"

One example of the brand ambassador/community approach, Hasbro's Alpha Pups, was briefly introduced in Chapter 5 as an illustration of the key informant method for identifying opinion leaders. Recall that Hasbro researchers went to various settings in Chicago where adolescents congregated and asked the youngsters "Who is the coolest kid you know?" Once they ascended the hierarchy of coolness to reach those kids who answered "Me," Hasbro, with the aid of the Boston-based marketing firm Target, offered these so-called "Alpha Pups" US$30 to learn a new video game called P-O-X. By centering its marketing campaign on social influentials who had not yet developed any emotional connections with the brand, Hasbro attempted to influence WOM through entry in the bottom tier of the grapevine-harnessing process (see Figure 7.2), relying on young people who were actively engaged within their social community.

We might also imagine that group to have included opinion leaders for gaming products, situated at the middle tier of the WOM hierarchy.

Hasbro had recognized the buzz-worthy potential of P-O-X, given that the game was wireless and could be played in "stealth mode," at school or in the home essentially under the radar of any teacher or parent. For example, the game was such that kids in two separate cars at a stoplight could play against each other, and if a third car approached, another kid could get in on the action. The tactic that Hasbro used to encourage key influencers to spread the word about this new gaming innovation was ingenious, reflective of a keen understanding of the mindset of their targets. Initially, small groups of Alpha Pups were invited into a conference room and were asked to watch an impressively produced video, as company representatives and market researchers observed from behind a one-way mirror (Tierney, 2001). A deep-voiced narrator proceeded to describe how deadly extraterrestrials called P-O-X had escaped from a laboratory:

> They're already here, but we can't see them. Mankind's only hope is to enlist a secret army of the world's most skilled hand-held-game players. Their mission is to use advanced R.F. containment units to create a race of new, more powerful hybrid warriors and test them in battle against these alien infectors. A battle to save Earth is about to begin, and only he [an adolescent boy who appeared on the screen] can save us. Beware the Pox! Pox is contagious!

The participants then were informed by a hip, young Hasbro employee that as the coolest, funniest guys in their school, they had been chosen as the first P-O-X secret agents. Each was given a free P-O-X unit and the game was explained and demonstrated to them. As a result of the cleverly designed presentation, by the end of the session the Alpha Pups were pumped up and excited about the game. Before they left, they were given a package of ten additional units to distribute to their friends. This strategy was carried out with influentials aged 9 to 13 from 900 of Chicago's 1,400 schools.

Rather than choosing to launch the game with a traditional nationwide advertising blitz, Hasbro's novel marketing plan unfolded by centering on a single location, and their seeding strategy was akin to "infecting" people in a way not unlike what we might expect when an epidemic begins to spread. Prior to devising this approach, Hasbro's market researchers gauged the appeal of P-O-X by interviewing editors of game magazines and child psychologists about adolescents' concerns and interests, chatted with university students who were hardened veterans of video games, and studied customers browsing in game stores. One insight they obtained from this endeavor was that a likely appeal of the game for adolescents would be the opportunity for them to create their own world where they could make decisions for themselves—such as creating characters and battle plans—away from the influence of their parents.

Hasbro did not limit the P-O-X marketing to the seeding approach, but hoped to capitalize on the viral spread of the game with additional elements. For example, a couple of weeks after free games were distributed to the Alpha Pups, a P-O-X mobile unit began to travel through various communities letting kids sample the game firsthand, and distributed P-O-X-related merchandise, such as hats, T-shirts, and temporary tattoos. Hasbro also arranged to have P-O-X added to some in-store gaming tournaments, and radio stations gave away free units and talked up the P-O-X Web site, which ended up attracting more Internet traffic than Hasbro had ever attained. Finally, 2 months after the start of the campaign, a several million dollar national TV campaign was launched in an effort to reach a wider audience and reinforce the buzz that had been generated via the alternative marketing effort.

Although Hasbro's seeding approach was heralded by some as marketing genius, the P-O-X console itself was quickly forgotten, largely due to the strength of the competition, the appearance of other innovative games, and the fact that the novelty of P-O-X turned out to be short-lived (see Marsden's question 2). It is unclear to what extent Hasbro nurtured their relationship with the Alpha Pups beyond the P-O-X campaign, yet the potential contributions that could be gleaned from a long-term interaction with the community of influential young consumers could be extensive.

P&G's Tremor Initiative

In 2001, P&G launched its Tremor marketing unit, which represents one of the most extensive WOM initiatives based on product seeding to date. The initial program, "Tremor Teens," is comprised of a national panel of more than 280,000 US influential teens, identified by P&G as likely to serve as "trendspreaders" who frequently convey product and brand information within their extensive social networks (see Box 5.10). In an effort to convert these influentials into advocates, Tremor provides the teens with free samples, CDs, movie passes, and so on, in exchange for feedback and the opportunity to have these influential consumers lend an air of cool to the products and recommend them to their friends. Because the preponderance of P&G's products are intended for adult consumers, 80% of Tremor Teens' seeding activity is conducted for outside clients, such as consumer goods (Coca-Cola, Sony, Toyota, Hershey's, Liz Clairborne), music, and movie companies ("I Sold It," 2006). In addition to providing free products to its members, Tremor also uses coupons, discounts, and free downloads to seduce other young people into spreading the word about clients' products.

Identified by their responses to an online questionnaire as sociable and well-connected individuals who regularly communicate with others, it is not surprising that once Tremor gets a product into its teen participants' hands, word spreads rapidly. According to P&G's estimates, Tremor seeding trials have generated up to 30% increases in sales for new products (Mathew & Manda, 2005). Like Hasbro's Alpha Pups approach, Tremor's effectiveness comes from empowering participants by giving them a say about the products they sample, with opportunities for online voting and a two-way dialogue.

If there have been any glitches along the way with the program, the issue of disclosure has raised the most concern. In October 2005, a nonprofit organization filed a complaint criticizing the fact that the teen marketers are not obliged to reveal their affiliation with P&G's program. A Commercial Alert spokesperson commented that "Without such disclosure, [there is] the danger of the basic 'commercialization of human relations,' where friends treat one another as advertising pawns, undercutting social trust" (Rodgers, 2004). One father of a teenager reiterated this concern, stating the opinion that "If they're going to try to sell things to kids, they need to make it explicit that this is a selling channel." These are legitimate points, reflecting how marketing involving young consumers remains a sensitive area. Although Tremor claims that teen participants are not directly instructed to market the products they receive, it is clear that such programs require a clear set of guidelines that effectively clarify ethical conduct and limits as to how the seeded products are to be promoted.

Four years after the creation of Tremor Teens, P&G launched "Vocalpoint," another Tremor program to reach one of the company's key targets—moms. Within 1 year, 600,000 US mothers identified as having large social networks had enrolled in the WOMM program, which was modeled after the teen initiative. Participating mothers (women aged 28 to 45 and having children aged 19 or under) are provided with product samples and discount coupons, and are invited to share their opinions with P&G. The Vocalpoint moms were recruited via Internet banners posted on sites like iVillage.com, which links them to a Tremor site that provides more information about the seeding program and screens candidates with various questions. According to P&G, selected "connectors" speak on average to about twenty-five to thirty other women during a typical day, whereas for most women the number is closer to five. Each participant receives a weekly e-mail newsletter, "The Inside Track," that provides inside information about product developments and solicits recipients' opinions on a wide range of topics.

Described as "a state-of-the-art method for reaching the most influential group of shoppers in America" the Tremor program has effectively created an army of well-connected and enthusiastic accomplices for spreading WOM in a more controllable fashion than one typically can expect from a more traditional advertising campaign ("I Sold It," 2006). A case in point is the P&G dish-washing soap Dawn Direct Foam, which is advertised as the soap that breaks down and removes grease when washing dishes. Unlike other soaps, the Dawn product actually prevents oil and grease from entering the sponge, but instead are absorbed and locked into the foam itself. This is a unique selling point that is essential to convey to consumers in ads so that the brand is properly distinguished from the many competing dish-washing products on the market. However, knowing that P&G's new soap does not redeposit grease back onto one's dishes like other soaps may be an interesting piece of information for the consumer, but it is not exactly the sort of information that is likely to spark a conversation from even the most avid Dawn loyalist. Thus, the Vocalpoint campaign for the soap took a very different tack to enhance the product's buzz worthiness. Participating moms were mailed free packets of the soap that bore an image of a smiling girl on the package, along with large text that read, "Mom, can I help?" An accompanying pamphlet explained that the soap is so much fun to use that one's children will want to help out with the dishes, a point that was reinforced by including a small sponge in the shape of a child's foot in the package along with a dozen money-off coupons for the product. As Tremor VP Steve Knox explained, "We have to enable a conversation to take place. Kids not doing enough chores is a conversation taking place among moms." As a reflection of the merits of this approach, one of the Vocalpoint participants who worked at a customer service call center unaffiliated with P&G claimed to have talked about Dawn Direct Foam with about 100 of her female coworkers, many of whom had young children. But an even more compelling argument for the effectiveness of the campaign is seen in the resulting sales boost for the Dawn product. Sales in locations where the Vocalpoint effort was centered were double those of other markets that did not run the campaign ("I Sold It," 2006).

Girls Intelligence Agency

P&G is not alone in its efforts to reach out and encourage young influential consumers to serve as brand advocates. The Girls Intelligence Agency (GIA) is a marketing and research agency that engages young US females aged 8 to 29 as "secret agents" in the spread of WOM. Participants in the GIA program are prescreened to fit specific marketing-related criteria and then classified according to age, interests, and body and skin-care rituals. The girls then are invited to check in to the agency's Web site weekly where they are introduced to new products and ideas, and are asked to complete surveys, polls, and personality quizzes. In this way, GIA keeps in close contact with program participants and constantly monitors their opinions and solicits their ideas in an ongoing dialogue. With parental permission, the agency also hosts slumber parties, shopping trips, and in-room hangouts as a means to get closer to their targets and seed products for WOM advocacy.

During the numerous slumber parties that GIA organizes weekly, agents are provided with a "slumber party in a box" kit, which includes branded material with games and activities pertaining to the theme of a film or free samples of beauty care or other products. The female host invites about ten girlfriends for a sleepover, during which the girls spend several hours engaging with the GIA branded material. For the in-room hangouts, a GIA client is invited to join an informal get-together with an agent and some of her closest friends in the agent's bedroom, where the client can receive candid feedback about a product, brand, or marketing concept. The slumber parties and bedroom hangout sessions provide opportunities for marketers to obtain useful feedback about ongoing campaigns along with insight into current trends, lifestyle patterns, and motivators of the young female market. For example, prior to Capitol Records' debut of pop singing sensation Skye Sweetnam, GIA was hired to obtain feedback from tween girls as to the most appropriate look and image Sweetnam should project. Capitol used the insights gleaned from 7,000 girls at 500 slumber parties organized by GIA to reshape the singer's image, recut her debut video, and select the single from her first CD.

According to GIA's CEO Laura Groppe, the "special agents" program is designed to make the girls feel special and important, for example, by sending them "an exclusive [movie] trailer or something personal from the talent [celebrity], to make a strong emotional connection. We work with them online to plan snack and game ideas to help promote the product. If 6,000 girlfriends are partying on the same night, they can potentially spread the word of mouth to 300,000 girls" (Minow, 2004).

Tryvertising

What better way to get products directly into the hands of consumers to experience and talk about with friends than to invite people into a store and tell them to take home whatever they want, free of charge? Of course, from a business perspective, this approach does not at first glance make any sense, but few consumers likely could resist such an opportunity. As implausible as the idea may sound, it pretty much describes the concept behind Sample Lab, a members-only space that invites consumers to sample and test new products. Opened in Tokyo in July 2007 at the iconic Iceberg Building in Harajuku, Sample Lab is the brainchild of Japanese marketer Takahiro Kawanonew, who recognized that as Japanese consumers were turning off to advertising, they were turning on to a new trend in consumer behavior, often referred to as "trysuming"—the tendency to try things out prior to purchasing, especially as the number of product and brand offerings has continued to rise.

In recent years, marketers have recognized the emergence of a growing segment of consumers (dubbed "transumers") who are driven more by a desire to discover and experience products and services than to own them, a tendency to avoid boredom by following a more transient lifestyle that eschews permanent ownership and possessions. This phenomenon is seen in a predilection among some consumers to lease rather than buy, to rent clothing for onetime use, to join car-sharing clubs, to co-purchase products (e.g., a vacation home, a boat), and the surfacing of temporary "pop-up" restaurants, clubs, galleries, and shops.

The appeal of the Sample Lab concept essentially comes from giving consumers the opportunity to try out new things, be among the first to learn about new products, and, in the process, become part of a special community (Roberts, 2007). The way Sample Lab works is that consumers over the age of 15 pay a modest fee for registration and an annual membership (about US$10) to gain entrance into the lab, which opens up into an exhibition area consisting of store-like shelves stocked with a wide range of merchandise (health foods, sports drinks, office and school supplies, panty hose, barbecue sauce, mini laptops, etc.); open areas stocked with larger items, such as exercise equipment; a salon area where members can relax and chat with each other; and a powder room that provides a more private setting for women to sit and try out the latest cosmetics and facial care products. When participants find something that interests them, they can choose to purchase a full-sized version of the product in the lab or take home up to ten items per visit at no cost (excluding bigger ticket items, such as exercise machines), depending on member status. In return, members are obliged to provide feedback about the items they have sampled by completing surveys about the products.

In addition to the insights provided by collecting user feedback, which is obtained at the location or via members' cell phones, the expectation also is that members will spread plenty of WOM about the products they sampled. As one 30-year-old male member claimed, "I give some of the samples to my friends and recommend some of the products to them" (Pratt, 2008). The success of Tokyo's Sample Lab, where 40,000 Japanese consumers had purchased memberships by early 2008, prompted the opening of a second lab in Seoul, Korea, and franchise opportunities are now available for similar venues in thirty-two countries throughout Asia and Europe (http://www.samplelab-international.com).

Around the same time that the groundbreaking Sample Lab opened its doors to the public in Tokyo, several sampling salons for cosmetics also began to appear in the Japanese capital. Samples and testers previously have been offered extensively at makeup counters in department stores, but usually are accompanied by a direct sales pitch. Member-driven sampling salons, such as Club-C, allow consumers to spend as much time as they desire trying out a wide array of makeup and skin-care products, without any pressure to buy. Some salons employ a staff of knowledgeable beauty consultants, but no salespersons are apparent on-site. Products can be purchased later at retail stores or ordered online.

There is no mystery behind the success of these tryvertising initiatives—as one Sample Lab participating manufacturer claimed, "shoppers who come here get my product and really know what it's all about." With this in mind, Sony rented lab space for PlayStations with the hopes of getting the product into the hands of women, a growing demographic for the gaming industry. According to Yohko Atsuchi, who handles promotion for Sony computer entertainment in Japan, "There are a lot of people we can't reach with our regular promotional events. We thought this would be a way to access customers who normally wouldn't visit game software shops or electronics stores" (Pratt, 2008).

Traditionally, Japanese consumers have not responded very enthusiastically to well-established sales promotion appeals, such as those that promise a money-off discount or free gift with purchase. The message "act now and save 10% off the price of" likely would not be as effective an appeal as one that stressed the dependability and reliability of the company (e.g., "Our company has been in business 40 years"). Tryvertising, however, is an approach that conforms well to the Japanese desire for novelty, a high degree of curiosity about new things, and the opportunity to engage with others—characteristics shared by millions of other consumers around the world.

BzzAgents

As a Boston-based WOMM network, BzzAgent makes no secret about its ultimate objective, which is to recruit consumers who are interested in experiencing new products so as to spread WOM about them. To date, more than 600,000 volunteers have answered the call by signing up at BzzAgent's Web site (http://www.bzzagent.com) and providing information about themselves, which is then stored in the firm's database. When a company enrolls in the program, BzzAgent searches its database for agents that match the demographic and psychographic profile of target customers. The agents then receive a sample of the product for which the buzz campaign is centered and a training manual describing recommended WOM strategies appropriate for the product. Such strategies might include talking about the product with friends, chatting up salespeople at retail outlets, e-mailing or texting influential people about the product, and so on (see Box 7.7). Agents get to keep the products they promote and can earn points redeemable for extra gifts (such as books, CDs, and promotional items); however, they are required to complete detailed reports for each campaign they are enlisted to participate in. (The reports not only provide essential feedback but also help weed out people whose main interest is in receiving free products.) BzzAgent then compiles a summary report for the brand company based on the information they receive from agents working on the specific campaign. The BzzAgent Web site provides a link for volunteers to spread WOM about the agency itself by encouraging friends to join the

---

BOX 7.7 FOCUS ON APPLICATION: BRAND AMBASSADORS IN ACTION

In an in-depth article that ran in *The New York Times* about BzzAgent and similar brand ambassador marketing efforts, the BzzAgent campaign that was conducted to promote Al Fresco chicken sausage was highlighted as a benchmark example of how a well-organized WOMM effort can unfold to bring a relatively unknown product into consumers' minds and shopping carts (Walker, 2004). The campaign was run around the time of the July 4th holiday weekend in the United States, a period during which family and friends tend to get together for celebrations that often revolve around the outdoor barbecue.

Scattered throughout the country at many of these gatherings, an invited guest, friend, or relative worked undercover as a buzz agent on behalf of Al Fresco, unbeknownst to their fellow attendees. (During the early days of BzzAgent, participants were not required to disclose their affiliation with the agency.) At some point during the cookout, for example, an agent might have approached the person manning the barbecue grill, pulled out a package of Al Fresco sausages, and started chatting about how he or she happened to try out these sausages the other day and found them to be the most delicious (and healthy!) sausages around. Had the sausage-bearer been identified as an official representative of Al Fresco, we could imagine a rather obstreperous response from the chef, along the lines of, "Hey, I can't believe you're trying to sell me sausages during my weekend off when I'm trying to relax with my family!" Instead, given that the sausage-bearer was a family member or friend with no known affiliation to the company, the response is likely to have been more like "Cool, let's try them!" And before long, we would not be surprised to hear several of the other cookout guests commenting about how the sausages were a great idea at a meal that otherwise featured the same-old hamburgers and hotdogs. "Where did you buy them? I'd love to pick up a couple packages for my next barbeque!" The Al Fresco story serves as a good illustration of how brand ambassador campaigns, such as those organized by BzzAgent, tend to unfold among consumers. In the filed reports from the agents that promoted the sausages were comments such as the following:

- People could not believe they weren't pork!
- I told everyone that they were low in fat and so much better than pork sausages.
- I handed out discount coupons to several people and made sure they knew where stores carried them.
- My dad will most likely buy the garlic flavor. I'll keep you posted.

In fact, the WOM campaign conducted on behalf of Al Fresco continued beyond the July 4th weekend for an additional 3 months and involved the participation of 2,000 agents. The agents were sent coupons for free sausages to distribute to people they knew, and were provided with additional instructions about how they could promote the sausages. Here is a description from *The New York Times* article of the different tactics employed by an agent named Gabriella:

At one grocery store, Gabriella asked a manager why there was no Al Fresco sausage available. At a second store, she dropped a card touting the product into the suggestion box. At a third, she talked a stranger into buying a package. She suggested that the organizers of a neighborhood picnic serve Al Fresco. She took some to a friend's house for dinner and (she reported back) "explained to her how the sausage comes in six delicious flavors." Talking to another friend whom she had already converted into an Al Fresco customer, she noted that the product is "not just for barbecues" and would be good at breakfast too. She even wrote to a local priest known for his interest in Italian food, suggesting a recipe for Tuscan white-bean soup that included Al Fresco sausage. The priest wrote back to say he'd give it a try.

All told, the Al Fresco buzz campaign boosted sales for the chicken sausage product by 100% in some stores.

network to create buzz and "influence your favorite brands together!" Research to date suggests that participants in managed WOM programs like BzzAgent tend to generate more WOM than their peers (see Box 7.8).

Like the other brand advocate networks, BzzAgent relies on an incentivized approach to attract participants who are interested in obtaining new products to try out, while providing intangible outcomes, such as contributing to agents' feelings of being special and having one's opinions valued, as well as the understanding that one can have an impact on the success or failure of new products and brands. The power of product seeding is reflected in the findings from a 2006 study revealing that buzz members rated "experiencing new products" as the best part of participating in the program, while "earning reward-redeemable points" was ranked next to last ("BzzAgent to Expel," 2006). To sidestep the ethical concerns over disclosure, BzzAgent now requires its participants to disclose the fact that they are buzz agents.

In one campaign that BzzAgent carried out in conjunction with Arnold Worldwide for Volkswagen (VW) in 2005, VW Passat owners were sent a personalized e-mail from VW Executive Vice President Len Hunt asking them to join the Passat Alpha Driver Program, a loyalty program that invites members to spread WOM about the car in exchange for

BOX 7.8 FOCUS ON RESEARCH: THE IMPACT OF MANAGED WOM PROGRAMS

In association with the WOM marketing network BzzAgent, Marketing Professor Walter Carl compared the WOM generated by 1,000 buzz agents with a convenience sample (i.e., a nonrandom group of comparison participants conveniently available for study) by focusing on two metrics: (a) number of social interactions (i.e., any social contact) and (b) WOM episodes (i.e., interactions that included WOM about a product or service) during a 1-week period. His results, which appeared in a 2006 paper published in *Management Communication Quarterly* (Carl, 2006c), revealed that volunteers in the managed WOM program were more socially active and spread more WOM than their peers, without artificially creating it (see graph below).

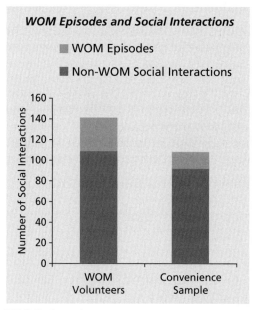

Source: McGlinn & Wylie (2006). BzzAgent, Inc.

Specifically, 29% of the interactions of WOM volunteers who had enrolled as BzzAgents included WOM content related to a product or service, compared with 14% of the interactions of participants in the convenience sample (university-educated 18- to 29-year-olds). WOM volunteers had 30% more social interactions than the non-volunteers and 97% more WOM episodes. Moreover, the WOM generated by the buzz agents was more likely to include recommendations; that is, in their everyday conversations, outside the WOM campaigns in which they participated, 71% of the WOM episodes included a recommendation, compared with 43% of their peers. When the WOM episode occurred in conjunction with a WOM program's campaign, 88% of WOM episodes involving agents included a recommendation.

These findings suggest that managed WOM programs efficiently augment organic conversations about products and brands, but do not appear to result in the artificial creation of WOM outside of specific WOM campaigns. Indeed, WOM volunteers were not found to inundate social networks with buzz about program-related products and services. Like the interactions of their peers, the WOM interactions involving buzz agents tended to be spontaneous (whether or not it was related to a managed campaign) and transmitted via face-to-face interactions. The success of formalized WOM programs requires participants to maintain the naturalness of their WOM interactions, eschewing discussions that appear artificial and forced, which likely would undermine credibility and adversely affect social relationships.

certain incentives (Spethmann, 2005). The 12-week campaign screened and accepted the membership of 5,000 Passat owners (chosen on the basis of desired demographics from the Passat database) at a dedicated Web site where they could interact with VW representatives and talk up the brand with friends. Members were given exclusive access to regularly updated photos, videos, and marketing material for the Passat, and members could earn a 24-hour test-drive with the new Passat in ten markets, before the car was available at dealerships. Special access to a webcast chat with Hunt drew 250 Alpha Driver members, a number that greatly exceeded VW's expectations. Although we might imagine that many loyal owners would have been happy to spread the word about the car on their own without an incentive, the program enabled them to earn points redeemable for options ranging from gift certificates for national retailers to iPod products. Alpha Drivers also received a special incentive to purchase or lease a 2006 Passat, and the member earning the most points won a 2-year lease for the new car.

BzzAgent continues to expand its social marketing efforts. In early 2009, the marketing network developed an alliance with the European WOM agencies Buzzador, AB, and Trnd AG, which together maintain a total of 750,000 participants with a reach of 9 million consumers. Later the same year, BzzAgent launched BzzScapes, which serves as a network of brand-centric communities that is managed by brand advocates in an effort to organize and rank all of marketers' online content, including images, videos, blogs, articles, and coupons (O'Leary, 2009). By monitoring BzzScapes, marketers will be able to use the service to find out all that people are saying about their brands online. Among the initial clients that have signed up for the service are such companies as Colgate, Ford, Procter & Gamble (P&G), and Penguin Publishing.

According to BzzAgent CEO Dave Balter, the intention behind the creation of BzzScapes was not to develop another online review vehicle, but rather to extend the relationship between marketers and brand advocates, "by empowering brand-conscious consumers to build communities around the products they love and inviting marketers to interact in a meaningful way with advocates" (O'Leary, 2009). The power of such an advocate network was pointed out by a Ford communications manager, who stated that "While we'll continue to tell people about our fuel-efficient quality vehicles, we want customers to be able to hear it directly from each other, increasing the trust and believability factor."

Conclusion

In this chapter, we have examined the new face of marketing firsthand by surveying some of the key contemporary strategies for connecting with consumers and promoting the power of WOM and brand advocacy. Although the notion of a connected marketing toolbox has been employed to highlight the various alternative marketing options available to firms

(Kirby & Marsden, 2006), it is important that managers not lose sight of the bigger picture, in terms of the need to develop ongoing collaborative relationships through approaches emphasizing listening and engagement (as described in Chapter 6). We have seen the central role that product seeding has taken in several of the WOMM techniques, which attests to the importance of having great products in the first place that are worth talking about, or at least the ability to offer attractive content when the product, service, or company is not very talk-worthy. Thus, brand managers need to look within when facing what may seem an apparently perplexing question: "Why aren't they talking about us?" Do not expect consumers to talk for the sake of talking—you must first provide them with meaningful conversational content; otherwise, efforts to encourage WOM are likely to fail, no matter which tools and techniques are employed. In this light, it is important to recall the widely cited observation that WOM is not a strategy, but an outcome.

The groundbreaking efforts to develop communities of brand advocates are likely to be joined by many other similar programs in the near future as marketers recognize the benefits that can be reaped from inviting consumer participation. As we have seen, when people who are passionate about a brand are brought together into brand ambassador programs, encouraging them to spread the word to others can prove more effective than a reliance on expensive, tried-and-true traditional marketing approaches. Consider the following comments by Jackie Huba, coauthor of *Creating Customer Evangelists* (McConnell & Huba, 2002), which speak perfectly to the central message of this chapter:

> I bought a Palm Treo from Verizon, but I couldn't figure out how to email with it. I called Verizon and spoke with three different guys, none of them could help me. So I went on the web to a place called TreoCentral.com—a self-organized community of Treo customers—and looked through the comments. I found recommendations for installing a third-party application, which I followed. And it worked! So effectively, the customers were smarter than the company. If Verizon had brought these customers in, affiliated them with their own website, or at least pointed their users to the forum, it would have provided them with a great opportunity to use a base of fans that would spread the word. But that didn't happen, so the only impression I get from them, as a customer, is that they're clueless about their own product. (Oetting, 2006, p. 255)

It is somewhat ironic that the sort of peer-to-peer buzz marketing that Huba alludes to in these remarks actually has been going on for years. As Foxton (2006) observed, organizations like Amway, Tupperware, Herbalife, and Ann Summers have long worked to create consumer brand ambassadors, if not sales representatives, out of ordinary consumers. In what may seem a somewhat archaic approach in the current era of high tech, consumers have spread the word about these firms' products during organized get-togethers with friends and neighbors, where snacks and drinks are served along with a motivational chat about the merits of the focal products. Today, the Internet has expanded the party exponentially, and the firms that can most effectively work with consumers to encourage WOM are the firms that are likely to be leaders for years to come.

8 Connected Marketing II: Viral and Live Buzz Marketing Techniques

SEX. Now that we have your attention...

It may be an age-old ploy, but marketers have long recognized that sex sells, which is an obvious reason it is so prevalent in marketing. Whether or not it has any relevance to the product or service being sold, sexual imagery is likely to capture the attention and arouse the emotions of the potential customer. At the risk of sounding redundant, it bears repeating that before marketers can hope to break through to consumers and elicit a desired response, they first must capture their targets' attention. But given the fundamental changes that have occurred in the contemporary marketplace, getting noticed has become an increasingly more difficult challenge for marketers. Sex may have long been one tried-and-true method for capturing attention, but as detailed in previous chapters, the status quo no longer holds sway in marketing. If consumers have begun to turn off to traditional marketing tactics, they may no longer be expected to turn on to an advertisement simply because it depicts a scantily clad model or insinuates sexual behavior, especially if those consumers do not bother to notice the ad at all.

If something is attention-getting, in more cases than not, it is likely to be buzzworthy, that is, a stimulant for conversation. This chapter continues our survey of contemporary nontraditional approaches for connecting with consumers by delving further into the toolbox of nontraditional approaches for engaging with consumers and stimulating word of mouth (WOM). Unlike the amplified WOM techniques described in Chapter 7, which were predominately oriented toward creating brand advocates and communities of brand ambassadors, this chapter considers innovative practices commonly labeled as "viral," "stealth," and "live buzz" marketing. These exogenous approaches typically are intended to generate buzz rather than advocacy, to attract the attention of consumer targets with content that is likely to arouse situational (i.e., short-term) involvement as opposed to enduring (i.e., long-term) involvement, and to create an effect that is more emotional and experiential in orientation than suggestive of need satisfaction. In short, our focus in this chapter is on situationally involving techniques that motivate people to talk about something they experienced in their everyday lives, online or off-line, which

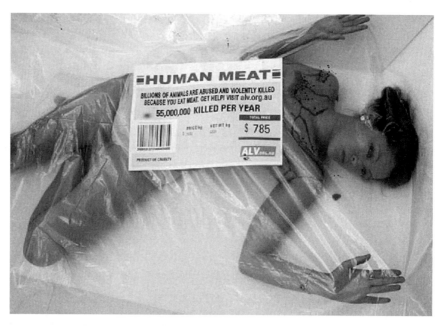

Exhibit 8.1 People for the Ethical Treatment of Animals' (PETA) Guerrilla Marketing Campaign

in one way or another incorporates a product, service, or brand. Inevitably, these methods attempt to harness WOM by entering the consumer grapevine at the bottom tier of the framework presented in Figure 7.2, capturing the attention and exploiting the connectedness of persons who are actively engaged in their community and society. Consider the following novel examples of buzzworthy alternative marketing communication approaches:

- Activists from People for the Ethical Treatment of Animals (PETA) individually displayed themselves in transparent wrapping material that made them appear as packed meat to stress their position against the killing of animals for meat. The "meat people" displays were positioned in various US urban areas heavily trafficked by pedestrians (see Exhibit 8.1).

- Traditional entertainers who pierce various body parts were hired to advertise a pharmaceutical product that promised instant pain relief. Each bore a long arrow that pierced both cheeks and had their backs painted with the brand logo and benefit. This outdoor buzz stunt was carried out in high-traffic localities of Mumbai.

- Sets of keys were left in public settings, such as bars, restaurants, stadiums, and concert halls, with a tag informing the finder not to return them because the Nissan Altima has push-button ignition. Similarly, "lost" wallets were scattered around São Paolo, Brazil; inside, a sticker advertised a local business newspaper, with the text "You found the wallet. Now find out how to fill it up. Read Caderno de Economia do Estadão."

- For a campaign conducted 1 week before a horror film festival at a local cinema in Bangalore, India, transparent sheets were slipped under university dormitory rooms to make it appear that blood had seeped through. The campaign was a huge success, with all film screenings sold out.

- A 90-second video posted at YouTube by Cadbury Dairy Milk depicted someone in a gorilla suit sitting behind a drum set as the music to a Phil Collins' hit song began playing on the soundtrack. At one point, the gorilla started drumming along with the music. The Cadbury ad, ridiculed by many as a preposterous way to advertise a chocolate bar, received 5 million views within 8 weeks and corresponded to a 7% sales increase for Dairy Milk products.

These examples give us a hint as to the range of possibilities for generating buzz that are considered in this chapter. Specifically, the chapter covers such connected marketing techniques as viral, live buzz, and stealth marketing. Along the way, I hope to debunk a widely accepted myth—that buzz, viral, street, and stealth marketing are all the same. As noted by Spheeris Associate Director Stèphane Allard (2006, p. 197), "Word of mouth marketing techniques differ and shouldn't be confused with other alternative marketing techniques. They don't serve the same objectives." Thus, our discussion will reconsider some of the definitions presented in Boxes 7.2 and 7.3, explicate the aims of the various techniques, and describe a variety of cases involving campaigns that have successfully captured attention, aroused interest, and gotten people talking about a company, product, or service.

Viral Marketing

During the 1970s, long before the notions of social media or viral marketing had entered public consciousness, Fabergé created a very successful TV ad campaign that revolved around the idea that a good product bears an infectious social quality. In this case, the product was Fabergé's Organic Shampoo. TV ads showed a young female spokesperson—most notably, the actress Heather Locklear—recommending the hair shampoo by explaining that she "told two friends about Fabergé Organic Shampoo, and they told two friends, and so on, and so on." The ad was accompanied by a terrific visual effect: as the spokesperson presented the appeal, her image multiplied exponentially on the screen, so that by the time she concluded by informing viewers that as soon as they discover the shampoo, "you'll tell two friends, and they'll tell two friends, and so on, and so on...," twenty-four small square images were apparent, clearly demonstrating the viral potential of WOM. To a great extent, this early ad illustrates what viral marketing is all about.

The Nature of Viral Marketing

According to the definition in Box 7.2, we see that viral marketing is considered as a promotional approach specifically designed in the hope that it will spread exponentially across a consumer population. More specifically, Wilson (2000) characterized *viral marketing* as descriptive of:

> ... any strategy that encourages individuals to pass on a marketing message to others, creating the potential for exponential growth in the message's exposure and influence. Like viruses, such strategies take advantage of rapid multiplication to explode the message to thousands, to millions.

In fact, the term "viral marketing" applies to a family of similar marketing strategies, and its usage in the connected marketing literature dates back to the height of the Internet bubble economy when it was more-or-less synonymous with "network-enhanced WOM" (Moore, 2003). Viral marketing has been widely distinguished from WOM marketing on the basis of whether it is occurring online. For example, continuing with Wilson's description (2000):

> Off the Internet, viral marketing has been referred to as "word-of-mouth," "creating a buzz," "leveraging the media," "network marketing." On the Internet, it is often called "viral marketing."

Thus, viral marketing typically characterizes "any marketing activity that accelerates and amplifies word of mouth *in the digital domain*" (Kirby, 2006a, p. 88, his emphasis).

Again, we see that the connected marketing terminology often tends to blur. For example, back in the early 1970s when the Fabergé shampoo ad was run, "You'll tell two friends" meant spreading the word about the product in the existing off-line modes available at that time: face-to-face, telephone, or by ordinary mail. In the contemporary era, however, the product recommendation also is likely to be incorporated online in a blog or forum discussion. The ad itself might be uploaded to YouTube or some other Internet site. In either online case, the likely impact for spreading *exponentially* would be far greater than it would be off-line, thereby resulting in a rapid *viral* effect.

Silverman (2005, p. 200) eschews the notion of "viral" marketing altogether, suggesting that it is not the proper metaphor for cases in which marketing phenomena spread. In his view:

> I believe that ideas do not spread like viruses. Viruses tend to spread with relatively low rates of contact, though pervasive contact, in a slow but very steady manner. Ideas tend to spread explosively, in a chain reaction that is more like a nuclear explosion, rather than the slow and relentless spreading of something that requires an incubation period. Either one gets the job done, but the explosion model obviously gets it done faster. Nevertheless, WOM sometimes does spread slowly. But in such cases, the slow spread reflects the likelihood that the idea is not exciting enough for it to keep going, and it usually fizzles once it gets beyond the initial

enthusiasts. Successful WOM has the characteristic that no one has heard of the product, and then suddenly, often within hours or days, everyone seems to be talking about it.

In recent years, viral applications have begun to emigrate to portable devices, which greatly enhance the explosive impact of a WOM campaign. *Mobile viral marketing* has been defined as "a concept for distribution or communication that relies on customers to transmit content via mobile communication techniques and mobile devices to other potential customers in their social sphere and to animate these contacts to also transmit the content" (Pousttchi & Wiedermann, 2007, p. 1). Based on their analyses of multiple case studies, Pousttchi and Wiedermann distinguished between two basic forms of mobile viral marketing, one in which the transmitter of WOM on a mobile device is personally implicated in the process of acquiring new customers (*active mobile viral marketing*) and the other in which the request to forward content is integrated as a component of the process, as is the case when the marketer sends an additional message (*passive mobile viral marketing*). When the active/passive characteristic is combined with the extent of network externalities (i.e., the extent to which the value of a product increases with expected number of units sold), four standard types of mobile viral marketing are identified:

1. *Motivated evangelism.* In this type, consumers play an active role in influencing others and network externalities are high. Briefly, a user must download an application and send it to others (who also must download the application) so that all can benefit from using the application. Examples include mobile messaging applications (e.g., Zlango), location-based friend finders (e.g., Mobiloco), and mobile communities (e.g., peperonity.com).

2. *Signaling use, group membership.* This type is characterized by consumers playing a passive role persuading others and high network externalities. This is the case when specific kinds of mobile network products and services, such as mobile payment procedures (i.e., the recipient of a consumer's payment could only receive the money by signing up for the mobile payment procedure) or proprietary document formats (e.g., WinZip, PDF), are required before consumers can mutually take advantage of mobile services or content. The stimulus is sent via an SMS from the company and not by a voluntary decision of the consumer.

3. *Targeted recommendation.* For this type of mobile, viral marketing consumers play an active role influencing others and network externalities are low. Such is the case when mobile users take advantage of a "send-to-a-friend" option as a result of entering the intended recipient's mobile phone number or e-mail address so that an SMS, WAP Push, or e-mail can be forwarded. Common examples include mobile ads with "send this to a friend" links, contests, and short mobile films downloaded from the mobile

Internet. Network externalities are low because there tends to be no change of benefit for customers when they forward the mobile viral content to others.

4. *Awareness, creation, benefits signaling.* This type is characterized by passive communicators and low network externalities. Such is the case when a company sends information to mobile users with little incentive to motivate consumers to pass along the content.

Although it probably is best to consider viral marketing as something that happens online, off-line examples can be noted (see Box 8.1). Consistent with his conceptualization of viral marketing as including "both systematic and unsystematic ways that your current customers acquire new customers," Chen (2008) refers to chain letters and Tupperware parties as off-line variations, which have built-in incentives (e.g., chain letters explicitly promise something in return for forwarding a letter) intended to propagate a viral process. Tupperware, Amway, and Herbalife are well-known examples of *multilevel marketing* (MLM, also known as "network" or "matrix" marketing), a form of marketing that relies on a built-in pyramidal structure in which the sales force is compensated for the direct sales of the product as well as the sales of other promoters they introduced to the company. MLM schemes, which have been widely criticized on ethical and legal grounds (e.g., Fitzpatrick & Reynolds, 1997), require that sellers recruit people to buy and sell their product, who then will recruit other people to buy and sell the product, and so on down

---

BOX 8.1 FOCUS ON APPLICATION: TRADITIONAL MEDIA AND A VIRAL MARKETING CAMPAIGN

In 1981, the French billboard contractor Avenir launched a simple application using the very outdoor medium that was the focus of the firm's promotion (Ogilvy, 1985). At the time, the billboard advertising market was rather sluggish and Avenir hoped to gain visibility, while encouraging potential clients that an outdoor campaign could be efficient, quickly adapted, and successful. Thus, on August 31, a billboard appeared in numerous locations throughout the Paris metropolitan area showing a young, attractive woman wearing a skimpy bikini and bearing the promise, "Le 2 Septembre J'enlève le haut" (On September 2, I remove the top). The message was clear to passersby: "We have a date—if you come back in two days, my bikini top will be gone." Sure enough, two days later, the billboards had been changed to show the similarly posed model wearing solely the bottom half of her bikini. Only this time, the accompanying message read, "Le 4 Septembre, j'enlève le bas" (On September 4, I remove the bottom). Once again, the promise was kept: on 4 September, the billboards now showed the young model completely naked with her back facing forward along with the statement, "Avenir—L'afficheur qui tient ses promesses" (Avenir—the poster company that keeps its promises).

Needless to say, Avenir's marketing campaign effectively captured the fancy of Parisians, and within less than a week, had spread throughout the population, with an increasing number of inhabitants searching out each successive billboard. The impact of the campaign still resonates with the French more than 25 years later, as evidenced by its reappearance, in a sense, in a Volkswagen print ad for the convertible Golf Cabriolet Coast which, along with an image of the car, was accompanied by the promise, "Demain, J' enlève le haut" (Tomorrow, I remove the top).

the line. As for WOM, Chen alludes to the idea that it is something that results organically, such as when consumers tell other consumers about a product simply because they like it. The idea that WOM is something that naturally occurs, whereas viral marketing requires more of an intervention on the part of the firm, is considered further in Box 8.2.

BOX 8.2 THE DIFFERENCES BETWEEN WOM AND VIRAL MARKETING

It is understandable that the terms "word of mouth marketing" (WOMM) and "viral marketing" are often confused or used interchangeably, given that both share the potential for driving exponential growth by leveraging consumer talk about products and services. Clearly, there is overlap in the sense that the content of both forms pertains to something in the marketplace—a product, brand, service, company, advertisement, retail setting, and so on. In one attempt to distinguish these two types of connected marketing approaches, Ellis (2008) alluded to the organic/amplified or endogenous/exogenous distinctions discussed in Chapter 7, with the former terms linked to WOM marketing and the latter referring more to viral marketing. That is, in Ellis's view, strong WOM is primarily based on a compelling consumer experience (and thus is organic or endogenous), whereas viral marketing requires an effort to "engineer" the propagation of a product or service (and in that sense is amplified or exogenous).

In this light, let's reconsider the earlier example of the Swiffer mop (see p. 217). Suppose that instead of posting some witty remarks about the product on Facebook, my nephew informed me by e-mail about the product and its super cleaning qualities. We might assume that conveying that information to me was based on his enthusiasm for the product, his desire to assist his uncle, or a combination of such motives. Unless he was being paid by the mop's manufacturer to advocate the brand to friends and family, we can label his e-mail message as an instance of natural WOM. I may follow his lead and purchase the mop, and if it turns out that I too find its cleaning power remarkable, I am likely to share that opinion with others. And so on. Eventually, more and more people will learn about the product as recommendations are communicated organically through limited networks of linked consumers. Consistent with Ellis's notions, the makers of the mop could be said to have engaged in WOM marketing in the sense of developing a terrific product that stimulated recommendations and, we might assume, by targeting early adopters and other influential consumers.

By contrast, recall that my nephew actually had posted a comment about the Swiffer mop on Facebook. At last count, he was closing in on 700 Facebook "friends." If we assume that he had uploaded the amusing Swiffer TV commercial along with his comment, chances are that many of his "friends" would have viewed the ad and passed it along to others. At the same time, other viewers of the commercial are likely to also have found it amusing and thus, like my nephew, uploaded it to Facebook, YouTube, a blog, or another Web site, thereby dramaticallyexpanding the ad's reach. Within a couple of days, thousands of consumers may have viewed the ad and begun talking about the Swiffer. This scenario gives us a clearer idea as to how a viral marketing effect evolves. Assuming that the advertising agency that created the Swiffer commercial had hopes that the ad would catch on in this way, we can say that they had engaged in viral marketing. Consistent with Ellis's distinction, the nature of the marketing effort was amplified/exogenous in the sense that the TV commercial had been designed to enhance its talkworthiness for the intended audience and was poised to incorporate a strong "pass along" quality. Had the persons who had uploaded the commercial to social network sites, blogs, and Internet forums been provided with an incentive by the makers of Swiffer for doing so, that incentivized marketing approach also would have been a component of the hoped-for viral phenomenon.

While I agree with Ellis's main distinguishing point (i.e., endogenous versus exogenous), another criterion has to do with how product-related information spreads. Viral marketing can be seen as something akin to WOM at super turbo speed—as if overnight, a message is capable of spreading rapidly across a vast and diverse consumer population, which is far more likely in the digital realm. WOM, on the other hand, may be restricted to smaller and more clearly delimited communities of consumers, and the transmission of information is likely to proceed at a more methodical pace. Unless the WOM referrals result in new users who also refer the product or service, we can imagine that the passing on of the message ultimately will die out.

These ideas about reach and spread of the message correspond to an interesting distinction offered by Seth Godin (2007), who suggested that WOM operates according to a decaying function, whereas viral marketing is characterized by a compounding function. According to Godin, with WOM marketing, a marketer might do something that stimulates a consumer to tell five or ten friends (e.g., about a great meal at a new restaurant or a lousy experience with a particular airline). This type of message transmission amplifies the marketing action over the short term and then fades, usually rather quickly. At least at the outset, viral marketing proceeds similarly—a marketer does something, a consumer tells five or ten people. However, the difference lies in what happens next. Recall Fabergé's message. Those five or ten people then tell five or ten other people, and the process repeats itself over and over again. The message spreads exponentially, like a virus spreading across a population. As Godin explains, the marketer does not have to do anything else for this effect to occur, although it may be possible to take steps to facilitate the spread of the message. However, in the majority of cases, "the marketer is out of the loop." The implications of this distinction, according to Godin, cannot be understated:

> For one thing, it means that constant harassment of the population doesn't increase the chances of something becoming viral. It means that most organizations should realize that they have a better chance with word of mouth (more likely to occur, more manageable, more flexible) and focus on that.

Hotmail: An Early Viral Marketing Success Story

Viral marketing can be said to have come into its own as a much talked-about alternative marketing strategy during the mid-1990s. It was around that time that Hunter Madsen (1996) predicted in a *Wired* magazine article that alternative marketing approaches would finally awaken the vast potential of the Internet as a "push" medium. As it happened, a team of imaginative marketers already was in the process of realizing that potential after having decided to use Hotmail to provide free e-mail accounts. According to Steve Jurvetson (1998), who was the founding venture capital investor in Hotmail, the simple idea—adding the postscript "Get your free email at [http://www.]Hotmail[.com]" to its customers' e-mails in 1996—stands as the original inspiration for viral marketing, and in the process gave rise to "six of the most powerful words in history."

The Hotmail ploy was conceived by Tim Draper, who persuaded his company to add to its Web-based e-mail a promotional element in the form of a clickable URL in every outbound message sent by a Hotmail user. As many have noted, this tactic did not require any intention on the part of the Hotmail user to recommend to the recipient to open an e-mail account—it was entirely involuntary, having originated from the firm, not the consumer. As Jurvetson (1998, his emphasis) characterized this approach, "*Every* customer becomes an *involuntary* salesperson simply by using the product. The product is fundamentally a communications product, and the marketing piggybacks on the message." Had the customer added to the end of an outgoing e-mail a postscript along the lines of, "P.S. I really recommend that you check out hotmail.com and open an account yourself—it's free and super easy to use," this endorsement would have been more in the realm of WOM, not viral marketing. (It is interesting to point out that the original Hotmail plan was for the clickable URL to be appended within the outgoing e-mail message, disguised as a P.S. That plan, which not surprisingly was very contentious within the company, ultimately was rejected (Jurvetson, 1998).) In the actual Hotmail scenario, the recommendation from a friend was implied; in fact, as described by Moore (2003, p. 350), "...the consumer 'voices' an implied endorsement of the product in the very act of consuming it."

The viral impact of Draper's Hotmail tactic by now is common knowledge. Within a period of 18 months, more than 12 million new subscribers had been recruited, at a total marketing cost of a mere US$50,000. The rapid adoption pattern approximated that of a network virus, and Hotmail rapidly became the largest e-mail provider in several countries, including Sweden and India, two countries where Hotmail did not engage in any marketing at all. According to Jurvetson (1998), "From an epidemiological perspective, it was as if Zeus sneezed over the planet." By contrast, another e-mail service at the time, Juno Online, spent US$20 on a more traditional marketing campaign, with significantly poorer results. Today, a search of "@hotmail.com" produces 261 million results.

Jumping ahead nearly one decade later to 2004 brings us to Google. At that time Google was in the process of developing the launch of its own e-mail service, Gmail, although with a different tactic than that used by Hotmail. Google's approach involved the identification and recruitment of 1,000 online opinion leaders, who were invited to try the as-yet unreleased service. In this way, Google injected an elitist aspect to the new service, which we might imagine was significantly appealing to the techies identified as influentials as well as Internet users who were not among the chosen few.

The referral aspect behind the Gmail launch required that one first received an invitation from a current user before it was possible to open a Gmail account. By initially going after influentials, interest in receiving an invitation among Internet users grew rapidly, especially once Gmail's 1,000 MB capacity was made known. As curiosity about Gmail spread, hundreds of Internet sites dedicated to the rumored e-mail service appeared and software designers unaffiliated with Google began to develop Gmail compatible software components. This combination of developments led to an epidemic of recommendations that resulted in 3 million new recruits within 3 months (Benedictus, 2007). Before long, Google had made formidable inroads in the competitive e-mail environment, and today a "gmail.com" search results in more than 193 million hits. The exponential spread of Gmail can largely be attributed to Google's savvy strategy in creating a demand for a product where no demand actually existed (at the time of Gmail's launch, there were plenty of other options for an e-mail account) and by limiting the accessibility of the service to people who received personal invitations from other users.

Practical Suggestions for Viral Marketing Campaigns

Any effort to propose a set of recommendations for launching a viral marketing campaign inevitably brings to bear a rather perplexing conundrum—that you cannot literally create a viral marketing advertisement, a viral marketing video, a viral e-mail campaign, etc. This conundrum is largely based on lazy semantics. A firm may formulate a collection of tactics at the center of a marketing campaign that is intended to have a viral impact on its target audience. What this means is that an effort has been made to "reach an acceptable level of self-sustainability through the inclusion of elements that encourage re-distribution" (Cummings, 2006). Whether that objective actually is fulfilled will depend on what happens within the consumer population. Recall Godin's comment (see Box 8.2) that once a viral tactic is deployed, the marketer is for the most part out of the loop.

For example, you can create a video that you believe will be effective in getting people talking. If it indeed satisfies that goal in that a number of consumers start commenting about the video online, linking to it, and sharing it with others through other media outlets, at some point it might be said the video is enjoying a viral effect, with talk spreading across several communication channels. But it would not be accurate to say that you *created a viral video*, only that you *created a video* that was widely popular and thereby resulted in a viral effect, as you had aimed for. If it turned out that the video was a dud that generated little if any attention among its intended audience, claiming that you created a viral video obviously would make no sense. Also making no sense is the (verbatim) assertion, "we're going to viral the campaign" (Hobson, 2009). "Viral" is not some magical ingredient that can be interjected into a marketing campaign at will. Moreover, there may be a substantial amount of online talk about the video, but the apparent buzz may not be truly viral—that is, spreading widely in an exponential fashion—but instead is limited to Twitter and YouTube commentary. Consider the following comments on Sean X. Cummings' social media blog (2006):

> I am surprised by the number of marketers I run into who say, "We've created a viral marketing program for our client." I cringe ... and wait for the, "we added a 'refer a friend' link to our email." When I explain the inaccuracy, I am not only greeted with skepticism but outright acrimony.... what the client hears when agencies [explain the true meaning of viral marketing]

is, "the internet is going to be buzzing about us because we are doing a viral marketing program!" If your program is just adding an email box and a redistribution method, it is not a viral marketing program, but it is a marketing program that uses viral marketing techniques.

With these points in mind, the following recommendations regarding the implementation of a viral marketing program must be approached cautiously—they do not constitute a magical formula but are more reflective of the sorts of things firms can do to increase the viral potential of their marketing efforts. As Kirby (2006a) noted, if we consider viral marketing broadly as comprising anything that amplifies and accelerates WOM or creates an exponential spread of a marketing message, then that would encompass a far-reaching number of approaches and techniques. In this light, many of the suggestions for connecting with consumers detailed in previous chapters are relevant to viral marketing. However, because of the intended infectious nature of the message, the risks inherent in viral marketing efforts, particularly in the digital domain, are more pronounced than for other types of WOM campaigns. Should the message be corrupted or misinterpreted, the negative fallout can be enormous. For example, Kirby (2006a) related the case involving a Carlsberg-branded text e-mail that was transmitted from contact to contact during the UEFA Euro 2004 football tournament. The understated creative theme of the message was represented by the tagline, "probably the best." Unfortunately for Carlsberg, that message was appended at some point along its viral route with the statement, "Shame their lager tastes like p*ss." Some additional examples of misguided or hijacked connected marketing campaigns are provided below (see "Live Buzz Marketing Blunders").

A good starting point for identifying some of the essential elements of a viral marketing program is to consider the successful campaign that revitalized the Honda brand in the United Kingdom (see Box 8.3). In their assessment of that campaign, Dobele, Toleman, and Beverland (2005, p. 146) identified five important viral marketing elements:

1. It built in aspects of fun and wonder into the message, providing a point of interest for consumers to engage with the brand and talk about it with others.

2. It ran the ad at the right time, gaining maximum leverage with a broad base of consumers.

3. It leveraged technology by spreading the message using multiple forms of media, including advertising and Web-based messages, enabling The Cog to cross between WOM and traditional media (the ad was often discussed on television chat shows).

4. It encouraged voluntary WOM support, thereby increasing the effectiveness of the message and the number of people who heard about it (potentially creating an audience that would then look out for the ad or search the Web for it).

5. It was tied to a visible brand that provided a real-world link between the brand message and the tangible product.

BOX 8.3 FOCUS ON APPLICATION: VIRAL MARKETING FOR HONDA UK

Around the end of the 1990s in the United Kingdom, Honda began to take strides to improve its brand image and 3% market share. It was concluded that one way to do so was to break away from the traditional formats and themes of automotive advertising at the time, which was to show sleek cars driving through idyllic settings, masterfully handling turns, braking gracefully, with a soaring soundtrack adding to the atmospheric feel of the communication. Instead, Honda decided to focus on its automotive products' precision engineering and intricate coordination of their parts by emphasizing what goes into making a Honda; in short, to communicate the message, "a car is not a car."

So as to set Honda apart from the competition as a truly special brand, it was decided that the campaign would have to go beyond simply creating a novel and innovative advertisement. Honda sought to communicate to potential customers and influencers in a way that would convert them into instruments of advocacy (Dobele, Toleman, & Beverland, 2005). Thus, the challenge was to develop a highly unique advertisement that would cut through the clutter, reach those who might influence the purchase decision (family, friends, colleagues, local car mechanics), and encourage people to talk about the brand. This challenge was met through the development of a Honda Accord ad known as "The Cog." The 2-minute video ad, which cost US$6 million dollars to shoot and took several months to complete, featured numerous individual pieces interacting like domino pieces in a Rube Goldberg-like chain reaction, beginning with an individual steel cog rolling along a board and ending with a full-sized Accord moving down a ramp and tripping a switch to release a Honda Accord banner, accompanied by the voice-over tag line, "Isn't it nice when things just work?"

The ad's initial airing on UK television was specially slotted during the broadcast of the Brazilian Formula 1 Grand Prix in 2003 so that it would reach potential influentials who would be receptive to the message illustrative of the car's flawless engineering. The ad also was made available on Honda's Web site, where it could be downloaded and watched repeatedly. Before long, "The Cog" had taken on a sort of mythological quality once it was learned that it was comprised of only one break, included no computer-generated images, and took 606 attempts to get right (Mikkelson & Mikkelson, 2006). The fact that everything seen in the video actually happened in real time exactly as it appears and without any digital tricks, enhanced its viral, pass-along quality, and people began e-mailing it to friends around the world. This viral influence contributed in no small way to Honda's record-breaking sales in the first quarter of 2004, enhancing awareness and shaping favorable attitudes toward the brand (Honda, 2004).

Although it cannot be said that any one of these elements is more crucial to a campaign oriented toward generating a viral impact than the others, the fact that the marketing action should be clearly linked to a tangible product and brand cannot be overemphasized. That is, a successful viral campaign must not only result in a viral spread of the message, but it also needs to deliver tangible benefits to the brand (Kirby, 2006a). Recall the subservient chicken Web site launched by Burger King to promote its new chicken sandwich, in which an actor dressed up in a tawdry chicken suit performs a variety of commands typed in by the site visitor (see p. 183). The point I made earlier about this campaign is that it did little to enhance the equity of the Burger King brand because it failed to make the advertised product or brand sponsor known. However, more than 5 years after its launch, the site is more popular than ever, approaching 0.5 billion hits. According to a detailed overview by Rick Webb, one of the campaign's creators, the subservient chicken has enjoyed an enormous viral impact: almost immediately after the site was launched, people began e-mailing it to their friends and it was mentioned at Boing Boing, a very popular and influential blog (Webb, 2009). The chicken campaign is discussed in numerous books, blogs, and magazine articles; has its own Wikipedia page and snopes.com urban legend page; won several advertising awards, including the prestigious Grand Clio and two Cannes Lions; received numerous homages and tributes; has attracted imitators; is studied at Harvard University and Massachusetts Institute of Technology (MIT); and has been named one of the most influential online videos of all time. Nonetheless, the campaign's impact for Burger King is far less clear.

Burger King marketing executives have characterized the subservient chicken campaign as "a success," citing its resonance as a pop culture phenomenon and the amount of Internet traffic it attracted. More pointedly in terms of sales of the TenderCrisp chicken sandwich, Burger King reported a steady sales increase of 9% per week 1 month after its debut at the chain's restaurants, the sandwich has seen "double-digit" growth of awareness, and it sells better than Burger King's original chicken sandwich (Anderson, 2005). There is no way of knowing, however, to what extent these anecdotal indicators can be attributed to the subservient chicken Web site. As evaluated by one skeptical franchise owner,

> It's difficult to show a causal relationship between sales and the advertising. [While overall] system sales are doing well, and the chicken sandwiches are selling reasonably well, ... in the long term, this thing has to evolve. I'm more of a traditionalist. I like to see the food.

Of course, similar points can be raised about Honda's Cog commercial in terms of the tenuous link between the viral effort and sales figures. One key difference, however, is the visibility of the brand and the association with a tangible product in the Honda ad, elements clearly missing in the Burger King video. The subservient chicken site does include a link for the Burger King Web site (identified as "BK TenderCrisp"), although it appears after the "Tell a Friend" link. It is easy to surmise which link likely induces more clicks. Thus, we are left with the question about the true impact of the Burger King site—when people talk about it, do they talk about the guy in the chicken suit or do they talk about the TenderCrisp chicken sandwich?

For Justin Kirby (2006a, p. 96), Digital Media Communications (DMC) Managing Director, there are three key components to any successful viral marketing campaign:

1. *Creative material*: developing and producing the viral agent that carries the message you want to spread in a digital format.

2. *Seeding*: distributing the buzz story and viral agent online in places and with people that provide the greatest potential influence and spread.

3. *Tracking*: measuring the results of the campaign to provide accountability and prove success.

Kirby emphasizes an important point regarding the seeding component, which he believes many firms assume simply entails creating entertaining material and then finding some appropriate Web sites where it can be promoted. The key, however, is not merely to aspire to spread the viral agent, but to create conversations:

> The seeding process for a viral marketing campaign is not the same as the process of online media buying; it's more like a PR process. Seeding is not just about knowing "where," i.e., finding appropriate places to locate the viral agent; it's also about knowing the "how" and the "who"—determining how the campaign can best be advocated and by who, and communicating the buzz story in the most appropriate way to each source route. (Kirby, 2006a, p. 96)

Consistent with these points, a successful viral marketing campaign requires the development of a buzzworthy story that engages people in a way that is consistent with the campaign's objectives. The story then must be incorporated within a viral agent (i.e., creative material) that is likely to spread, most likely through a digital format. Comparing once again the Honda and Burger King videos, although it can be argued that both campaigns were exceptionally creative, and thereby likely to spread exponentially online, Honda's effort excelled in the sense that its viral agent transmitted an engaging message pertinent to the brand—that all those car parts moving flawlessly in sync effectively communicate Honda's superior engineering and that, indeed, a car is not just a car. The video also included what Kirby refers to as a "wow" factor; that is, something that will prompt people to seek out and talk about. For example, "The Cog" includes a scene in which a tire rolls up a slope, as if by its own volition. This perplexing feat no doubt resulted in plenty of head scratching and bewilderment, with viewers asking, "How did they do that?" (The answer: a weight was placed in the tire so that when it was knocked the weight was displaced and, in an effort to rebalance itself, the tire moved up the slope.) As for the Burger King chicken, it is legitimate to ask, what is the brand story? If the creators of the site hoped to convey the Burger King message, "have it your way," (i.e., the chicken will do anything you want it to do) then this message perhaps is too subtle to have much impact on visitors to the site.

Another viral marketing effort that does a good job of meeting the requirements for success detailed above (i.e., a clear link to the product and the delivery of a brand-related message, packaged within a creative viral agent) is Wilkinson's 2007 "Fight for Kisses" campaign to promote a new razor for men, the Quattro Titanium. The online video trailer and advergame both focus on a common theme—that fathers feel neglected by their wives who prefer the softness of their newborn baby's skin. To win back their wives' affection, the men start shaving with the new Wilkinson razor, with the promise that it will make their skin as soft as babies. Following this development, the baby seeks revenge and begins to prepare for battle—the "fight for kisses" war thus is launched.

Wilkinson's objective with this campaign was to aspire to make some inroads into Gillette's strong market position by offering an alternative view of shaving and thereby influencing brand preferences. Rather than following the lead of its competitors by adding another traditional TV shaving commercial, Wilkinson instead developed a viral strategy to achieve two goals: (*a*) engage consumers with the brand and (*b*) highlight a benefit (smooth skin) in a new and original way ("Wilkinson," 2009). The agency that created the campaign, J. Walter Thompson in France (JWT France), developed the "baby clash" videogame, which pitted the father against the son in a humorous way, based on game references familiar to the target audience (25- to 35-year-old men), such as "Streetfighter" and "Double Dragon." The compelling scenario revolved around the razor and the "smooth skin" promise: it first was presented as a 2-minute, three-dimensional animation "teaser" trailer that mimicked those typically created to promote Hollywood movies. The trailer, which was initially posted on selected video-sharing Web sites (YouTube, Dailymotion, etc.) and influential blogs, explained the scenario and urged consumers to download the game at Wilkinson's special Web site. This step was intended to create some buzz about the campaign on the Internet. Next, a targeted media phase was launched to drive traffic to the Web site and encourage people to interact with the brand through the videogame. This included print ads in magazines, radio announcements, and the airing of a shortened version of the trailer on selected cable TV channels. Additionally, partnerships with a radio station and TV channel were created to promote a high score championship.

The results of the "Fight for Kisses" campaign to date are impressive ("Wilkinson," 2009):

- nearly 11 million Web site visitors from 220 countries (between September and December 2007);
- 400,000 downloads of the advergame;
- 6 million viewings of the trailer at video-sharing Web sites;
- 5,000 international blog mentions;
- free exposure on French TV and international radio; and
- gain of 5.4 points of market share (volume) on the disposable segment.

The Wilkinson advergame at the center of this viral game was not a mere online Flash game that likely would be played once or twice and then quickly forgotten; rather, it was an actual PC game that had to be downloaded and installed on a PC. At 100 MB, the game required a commitment and involvement on the part of the consumer. By limiting the availability of the game and the full-length trailer to the Internet, Wilkinson generated more of a viral impact, driving people to seek them out and thus feel as if they were part of the "Fight for Kisses" phenomenon. The success of the Wilkinson campaign can be attributed to a combination of elements: engagement, entertainment, brand identification and information, and creativity.

At the heart of most successful viral marketing campaigns is an engaging message that is attached to a product and likely to encourage consumers to pass it along to others. "Engaging" in this sense refers to something that can capture the imagination by being entertaining, fun, unique, or intriguing—the "wow" factor described above (see Box 8.4). But often being engaging is not enough to motivate people to take the time and effort to share something with others. Of course, sharing online is a relatively effortless activity, and in many cases, requires nothing more than typing in a friend's e-mail address. There are several reasons a site visitor may fail to do this, which can be attributed more to technology than consumer motivation. For example, the flow of Internet surfing and multitasking might influence the attentiveness of the consumer, who may come across an engaging video on YouTube, but then click away from it by moving on to other similar videos or the company's Web site. Before long, the consumer may have forgotten about sharing the original viral content with friends. Moreover, consumers have become progressively more attentive to concerns about spamming their friends' e-mail accounts. Thus, in addition to its engaging nature, a potentially viral message must be associated with a credible source (so that consumers do not feel that they are being exploited in the process), well-targeted (in the sense of making sure that influential and well-connected consumers receive it), and capable of leveraging combinations of technology (Dobele, Toleman, & Beverland, 2005).

BOX 8.4 A NOTEWORTHY VIRAL MARKETING CAMPAIGN: NINE INCH NAILS' *YEAR ZERO*

The viral marketing campaign that coincided with the 2007 release of the concept CD "Year Zero" by the rock group Nine Inch Nails (NIN) represents a perfect blending of marketing and entertainment. The campaign started with a T-shirt that included a listing of concert dates and cities. Certain letters on the T-shirt were bolded, which together formed an Internet domain name (minus the .com) for a site describing the "revolutionary drug" Parepin. In fact, this was simply the start of a cookie trail of clues and cryptically hidden Web site URLs. The Parepin site (iamtryingtobelieve.com) led to another Web site (anotherversionofthetruth.com) where one could remove a graphic image by dragging the computer mouse to reveal another image which, when clicked, directed the visitor to another site, and so on. Each successive Web site was linked in one way or another to the album's dark concept, which had to do with a dystopian view of the future reflective of general despair in the US populace ("Counting Down," 2007).

Another element of the campaign consisted of the band leaving USB flash drives in bathrooms during their concerts containing tracks from the album, which also began appearing online as another part of the puzzle. Dark, graphic images began appearing in washroom stalls at concert venues in cities such as London, Manchester, Barcelona, and Madrid. In one additional twist, the CD itself was designed in such a way that its color changed: before being played for the first time, the disk is black, but when removed it is white, and then gradually fades to gray.

The success of the overall viral marketing campaign was succinctly explained on the Adrants Web site (Natividad, 2007): "Mythology adds fuel to fan fire. . . . This is the way a viral campaign should

(cont.)

Box 8.4 (*Continued*)

be run—with a brand using multiple forms of media to play with its users and leave them things to find and chase after." According to Google software engineer Matt Cutts (2007),

> The buzz built pretty organically. USB drives were left in bathrooms at conferences and messages were hidden in conference T-shirts. It's much better to let people find you than to push too hard to get noticed. The links from the "people-find-you" approach are more organic than if someone spammed to get links to viral sites.

The integration of the marketing campaign with the brand was something that was central to the thinking of NIN band member Trent Reznor, who described the viral concept as part of the overall experience of the CD for fans:

> What you are now starting to experience IS 'year zero'. It's not some kind of gimmick to get you to buy a record—it IS the art form . . . and we're just getting started.

With regard to using combined technologies, we saw that Wilkinson did not rely solely on the Internet to inform consumers about the "Fight for Kisses" videogame, but also utilized more traditional media channels, including radio, television, and print, thereby increasing the chances of reaching a varied audience. Many companies also have begun to use SMS text messaging as a component of their viral campaigns. Text messages are cheaper than regular phone calls, require no additional software, and are especially effective in targeting young consumers. In one campaign, Heineken developed an SMS promotion associated with the British pub tradition of engaging in quiz games (Dobele, Toleman, & Beverland, 2005). Point-of-sale signs in pubs invited customers to call a number from their portable phones to receive a series of multiple-choice questions, with correct answers rewarded with food and beverage prizes. News of the promotion spread rapidly, with customers telling their friends who, in turn, also called to take the quiz in an effort to win prizes, which were awarded to 20% of the entrants. For a similar promotion, the brewer distributed scratch cards to bar patrons, asking them to text message a key word to a short code. Each time they did this, they were entered to win different prizes, and all contestants were opted in to receive a free phone application (a Heineken mobile agenda).

Over the years, Heineken has engaged consumers with other online and off-line promotional campaigns that have had viral impact. For example, cityalert.com, an online destination for urban trendsetters, collaborated with Heineken United States' interactive marketing agency Modem Mania to launch an "Own the Weekend" campaign across eight strategic urban markets. The campaign provided online event calendars, electronic newsletters, wireless alerts, and the "Top 20 Event Promoter" and "Top 20 Model" Web site boards (Hedgeman, 2004). During the summer of 2009, Heineken ran a mobile phone promotion as part of a multichannel campaign to get customers to stock up on beer for the summer. The program encouraged consumers to host a Heineken "Blok" Party for their friends. They were invited to enter a sweepstakes by sending a short text message, with two winners randomly selected to receive a free Blok Party for up to fifty guests to be held in their neighborhood, which included live entertainment, catering, and interactive leisure sports. As a Heineken representative explained,

> The Heineken 'Blok' Party program is true to our brand objective of delivering great beer and great experiences. And it offers our retail partners a unique new way to generate excitement among consumers through engaging displays and in-store merchandising materials that will help drive purchase of Heineken and Heineken Light. (Tsirulnik, 2009)

In another recent promotion, Heineken targeted young Brazilians living a dynamic, urban lifestyle by offering a free iPhone and iTouch application, consisting of the global positioning system (GPS)-enabled "Bar Finder" and the "Party Maker," the latter of which provides detailed instructions for planning a social event (Butcher, 2009). The objective of the application was to engage the youthful demographic target in an effort to have them interact with the Heineken brand. Heineken encouraged the spread of WOM by providing notes about the campaign to the mainstream press, bloggers, and consumers in their database. Within one week, the application had more than 5,000 downloads and was ranked as one of the top applications at the time. Overall, the campaign combined some of the key components of viral marketing that we previously have identified, including offering influential targets something unique and creative—the new application—as a means of engaging with the brand and sharing the experience through their social networks.

Key Components for Viral Marketing Campaigns

In his widely cited article about viral marketing, "The Six Simple Principles of Viral Marketing," e-commerce consultant Ralph Wilson (2000) identified six critical elements that can be incorporated within a viral marketing strategy. Although a strategy need not include all of these elements, the more that are evident, the more powerful the results are likely to be. In one form or another, these elements are evident in the examples already discussed in this chapter. According to Wilson, an effective viral marketing strategy:

1. *Gives away products or services.* This principle operates on the assumption that "free" captures consumers' attention perhaps more effectively than anything else. Heineken provided a cool new mobile phone application, Wilkinson offered a videogame, Hotmail enabled consumers to obtain a free e-mail service, and so on. A marketing program can provide consumers with a wide variety of free products or services, including free (but limited) software programs, widgets, wireless applications, and games. As Wilson clarifies, this approach requires a longer-term focus than many marketers typically operate by, in that providing consumers with

additional value can build a groundswell of interest that ultimately translates into greater profits in the future.

One well-known viral marketing campaign whose success is largely attributed to the astute use of a compelling incentive was carried out by the UK Internet Service Provider (ISP) Virgin.net in 2000. The campaign was launched with the sending of an e-mail offer to twenty-five persons, who were asked to forward the e-mail to a friend. For signing up to the Virgin.net database, recipients received free cinema tickets. The e-mail spread like wildfire, and within a mere 3 hours, 20,000 people had been registered, thus providing the company with an extensive consumer database (Marsden, 2006*b*).

2. *Provides for effortless transfer to others.* This principle is based on the common-sense idea that the more difficult you make it for people to pass along a message or some other marketing content, the less likely or slower it will spread. In the medical sense, viruses are easier to catch when you come into close contact with someone who already is infected; that is, viruses spread when they are easy to transmit. The same applies in the marketing context, which is why digital technology has brought viral marketing to the fore by making marketing messages (in the form of e-mails, software downloads, etc.) easier to transfer and replicate. Simple, concise messages are better; for example, the secret to Hotmail's success was a simplified six-word statement, "Get your free email at http://www.hotmail.com," that required no additional effort to spread on the part of Hotmail users.

3. *Scales easily from small to very large.* This point highlights the fact that viral influence increases exponentially from something small, just as a single match dropped in a forest ignites a fire that quickly spreads out of control. Anything that can inhibit or block the rapid growth of a phenomenon or eliminate the host will likely stop its spread. For example, if a video is deleted from online video-sharing sites, and that is the only outlet for consumers to access it, then you have a problem. Competitive activity also can pose a threat. One reason that rumors die out is that attention is diverted elsewhere, as when people lose interest in the story because it is unchanging or has become irrelevant, or because another more interesting rumor has captured people's attention (Kimmel, 2004).

4. *Exploits common motivations and behaviors.* A viral marketing message requires a fertile breeding ground in order to spread. This point once again brings us back to a recognition that message strategies need to be carefully targeted so as to reach those individuals who are most likely to be receptive to message content (e.g., consumers motivated by the desire to be cool, trendsetting, or in the know) and likely to engage in behaviors conducive to communicating, interacting, and sharing with others. It is understandable that Heineken consistently has targeted young urban consumers for its recent nontraditional marketing efforts. These are

individuals who are heavily reliant on their portable phones, heavy users of social media, and core beer drinkers.

5. *Utilizes existing communication networks.* The connectedness of consumers in the contemporary marketing environment rapidly has become a new marketing maxim. Marketers can leverage those connections to their benefit, and there is perhaps no greater necessity to do so than for viral marketing efforts, which depend on exploiting the connections that link consumers and provide built-in networks through which viral messages can spread. People who serve as network nodes, such as restaurant servers, bartenders, hairdressers, taxi drivers, and so on, can wield enormous influence through their interactions with customers. Similarly, brand community members, advocates associated with affiliate programs, and participants in social communities, such as Facebook and Twitter, already are engaged in online conversations. As Wilson suggests, if you can place your message into those existing networked communications, you increase the likelihood that it will be rapidly dispersed.

6. *Takes advantage of others' resources.* This component is a logical corollary to the preceding ones. A consideration of the case examples of viral marketing campaigns discussed previously illustrates how creative marketing plans exploit resources that already are in place to get the message disseminated. Getting a video, article, or link onto popular blogs or sharing Web sites is a sure way to get a message noticed and represents a key strategy for generating the online buzz necessary for making a viral campaign successful. For example, DuPont disseminated online a series of videos entitled "Science Stories" about the 200-year-old company's scientific contributions and ended up attracting thousands of views at a fraction of what a traditional media campaign would have cost. In so doing, the company increased awareness and shaped brand image among young consumers in unexpected ways (Flitter, 2007). One of the videos focuses on DuPont's Kevlar bulletproof vest. The 2.5-minute video is hosted somewhat tongue in cheek by an engaging young woman, and includes slow-motion footage of a bullet striking the vest, brief interviews with crime enforcement professionals whose lives were saved by the Kevlar, and an actual scene showing a policeman getting shot on the job. The video has a built-in viral feel that is likely to connect with young people who DuPont would likely find extremely difficult to reach through traditional advertising. One possible scenario suggesting the buzzworthy potential of the video series appears on the Pheedo blog (Flitter, 2007):

[The Kevlar video] has all the elements of a great viral video and residual word of mouth benefits. Imagine five teenage boys sitting around watching the latest shoot-em-up movie. One of them asks, "how does the bullet proof vest work anyway?" Another pipes up and says, "funny you should ask, I just saw this video online…"

Pheedo is an advertising service that distributes content like the DuPont videos beyond the handful of blogs and video-sharing sites that companies like DuPont typically rely on. One limitation to DuPont's campaign had to do with its scalability (Wilson's principle #3 above); that is, the viral spread of online content rarely stems from posting it on one or two popular Internet sites, such as YouTube and Boing Boing. Services like Pheedo are emerging to assist companies in spreading their content more widely through social media and e-mail.

Wilson's recommendations for an effective viral marketing campaign in large part comprise a general strategy for expanding the number of consumers that can be reached through appropriate targeting and exploitation of communication resources. Effectively complementing Wilson's perspective, Killer App's Alfa Mercado (2006) suggested several specific techniques that can be applied for a viral marketing campaign to succeed. In addition to some techniques that already have been discussed (e.g., provide free software and e-mail accounts, distribute free software, start your own affiliate program), Mercado recommends the following:

1. *Creating viral marketing awards.* Awards expand the number of creative efforts behind new marketing approaches and provide an incentive for creativity. For example, when the business school where I am employed recently changed its name and logo (from ESCP-EAP European School of Marketing to ESCP Europe), the school sponsored a "buzz marketing" competition for students to create a video that could be used to spread the word about the new name. Several creative videos were submitted (all of which were made available online), with the top three receiving monetary prizes ranging from €500 to €1,000.

2. *Providing free web space.* Companies are frantically competing to offer consumers the lowest cost on directory listings and the largest online space allotment (e.g., for blogs or personal Web sites). Consumers now are in the position of picking and choosing the best deal by picking from a host of web space providers.

3. *Creating a top 100 site.* Online users are increasingly making use of lists of Web sites relating to topics of interest. Creating a top 50 or top 100 list is an efficient way to increase one's consumer base. Amazon.com makes good use of consumers' "top" listings of music, film, and book preferences to promote offerings available for purchase at the site.

4. *Offering free banners, graphics, and templates.* Consistent with the fact that anything free will capture the attention of a great many consumers, offering creative Internet banners, useful widgets, and the like can have a significant impact in spreading a marketing phenomenon.

5. *Offering free consultation.* Free online consultation Web sites provide useful support for consumers who are searching for assistance regarding web services or

services in various fields. An increasing number of firms have added FAQs and consumer forums to their Web sites, which provide valuable channels for disseminating news and inside information regarding new products, services, and promotional campaigns.

6. *Free newsletter with bonuses.* Online shopping companies can enhance the spread of their viral marketing messages by sending out newsletters or catalogs with free online gift certificates or other incentives. This is an effective means for building a customer base and for acquiring information from consumers who sign up. The Marketing Sherpa Web site (www.marketingsherpa.com) distributes a weekly newsletter to registered members that includes free practical case studies and the weekly opportunity to win one of five copies of a new book donated by the book's author.

7. *Free screensavers, etc.* Offering Internet users' free screensavers, emoticons, or other downloadables for use on their computers serves as a way to obtain their e-mail addresses for building a customer base and for spreading viral messages.

8. *Using forums and discussion boards that use signatures.* The importance of establishing online forums and discussion boards has been emphasized previously as a means for attracting consumers who share similar interests or concerns. By obtaining their identifying signatures in the process, it is possible to discover a wide array of potential buyers from a specific market. Informative online forums are likely to be followed by a large number of participants who can be reached with a viral marketing technique.

Prior to closing this discussion, it should be noted that with the growing potential of mobile devices, researchers have begun to focus on the factors that are most commonly linked to success in mobile viral marketing campaigns. For the most part, these factors tend to overlap those already identified here, although the nature of the technology presupposes other critical elements. In their extensive case study research, Pousttchi and Widemann (2007) identified eight key success factors: (*a*) perceived usefulness by the recipient (i.e., the mobile viral content must be seen as offering a relative advantage; (*b*) reward for communicator (i.e., an extrinsic incentive for forwarding mobile viral content, such as a free, exclusive ring tone); (*c*) perceived ease of use (i.e., degree to which a mobile user believes that forwarding and receiving the viral mobile content will be effortless); (*d*) free mobile viral content (i.e., communicators do not have to pay a fee for the mobile viral content and its transmission); (*e*) initial contacts (i.e., the marketing effort requires the ability to reach "mobile viral mavens," customers who are most likely to frequently receive and send mobile viral content); (*f*) first-mover's advantage (i.e., the effort will benefit from an ability to effectively dominate a network early on so that customers do not perceive that the content can be had from other sources or competitors); (*g*) critical mass (i.e., for products and services with network externalities, there must be a minimal number of potential senders and recipients of viral mobile content for its further spread to be self-sustaining; and (*h*) scalability (i.e., the ability for the viral mobile content to accommodate success and maintain operational efficiency, as when a successful application can continue to perform well and satisfy users despite having to serve growing numbers of users). As many consumers begin to shift over to their portable devices from their PCs for online content, the means of implementing these factors will likely take greater precedence in marketers' efforts to stimulate viral effects through the mobile medium.

For a consideration of what marketers think about viral marketing campaigns, see Box 8.5.

BOX 8.5 FOCUS ON RESEARCH: WHAT MARKETERS THINK ABOUT VIRAL MARKETING

Given the increasing attention viral marketing has drawn from within the profession, it is not surprising that recent studies have focused on marketers' perceptions of viral marketing; in particular, what they want and what they expect to obtain from this non-alternative approach. For example, a 2006 study by JupiterResearch found that the most widely cited objective US advertisers who claim to engage in viral marketing hope to achieve from their efforts is to increase brand awareness (71%), followed by driving online sales (50%) and off-line sales (44%).

Marketing Sherpa's *2007 Viral Marketing Survey* to date represents one of the most extensive looks at the viral marketing landscape, based on the online questionnaire results obtained from 2,914 professional marketers ("Special Report," 2007). Some of the key findings from that study are summarized below.

- As expected, consumer marketers were found to make up the bulk of experienced viral players, although nearly half (48%) revealed that they do not have at least a "tell-a-friend" feature on their Web sites.

- Differences were apparent in what B-to-B and B-to-C marketers consider successful viral tactics. Whereas B-to-C companies were more likely to emphasize blog mentions and posting to social network sites like MySpace as central to generating attention for their viral efforts, B-to-B marketers were more focused on getting their viral campaigns mentioned in an online publication or business print publications.

- Consistent with the JupiterResearch study cited above, 80% of respondents believe that viral efforts build awareness. This belief was most apparent among "very experienced" viral marketers, who added that "growing e-mail list" and "lead generation" represent the second and third reasons, respectively, for engaging in viral marketing activity. In fact, 50% of B-to-B marketers reported focusing on lead generation (i.e., identifying and attracting potential customers), compared with 18% of consumer marketers. The results revealed that for some B-to-B companies, viral marketing has proven successful for introducing products and changing brand perception.

- Among the viral marketing tactics viewed as most successful were developing a separate presence for a campaign, such as "creating cool microsites" and online games, the latter of which were viewed as very effective for generating Web site traffic and repeat visitors. One highly successful tactic that was mentioned was book retailer Powell's use of 10-minute audio clips (*www.powells.com*) to showcase young writers at onsite blogs, which meshed well with the retailer's staff-written book-review blogs.

- Most commonly mentioned among the future plans for viral marketing campaigns within both B-to-B and B-to-C sectors were tactics that encouraged e-mail forwarding and tell-a-friend boxes, both of which entail low-cost implementation and serve as effective means for acquiring customers. The use of short videos was mentioned as being in the plans of 65% of the consumer marketing respondents.

- The most frequently cited challenge to viral marketing success is getting a core audience to push the viral process, with 62% of "somewhat" and "very" experienced respondents ranking this as their main potential threat.

Overall, what emerged from the Marketing Sherpa survey was an indication that marketing professionals who engage in the viral approach have rather tempered and pragmatic ideas about what to expect. There was little evidence of magical thinking among the respondents about the potential of viral marketing; rather, it was recognized that this marketing approach can help gain awareness, generate leads, and assist in building a customer base. Other research seems to justify this perspective. For example, the researchers behind the JupiterResearch survey concluded that viral marketing campaigns are mostly ineffective, in that only 15% of the viral campaigns carried out during the preceding year achieved the goal of prompting consumers to promote the marketer's message. As one JupiterResearch analyst noted, "viral marketers often send one campaign to all influentials. Different influential groups not only respond very differently to advertising campaigns, but also influence others in very different ways" (Luchter, 2007). As a result, marketers planned to reduce the targeting of influentials by 55% in the period subsequent to the survey. JupiterResearch President David Schatsky had this to say about targeting young people on social networking sites:

> While these sites may appear to be the most effective manner of delivering a message regardless of brand appropriateness, by failing to truly understand the audience, viral marketers stand to alienate as many consumers as they interest.

Live Buzz Marketing

Our consideration of viral marketing and buzz campaigns may leave one with the impression that alternative marketing approaches "engage" consumers only in the sense of reaching them online and inducing their incessant clicking of Web site links and forwarding of e-mails to friends. But it is again important to clarify that nontraditional marketing is not synonymous with online marketing. Certainly, the Internet is a major component of contemporary efforts to connect with consumers, will continue to operate as such, and is a major reason behind the impetus that buzz and viral marketing have gained from marketing professionals in recent years. Nonetheless, online activity is not the whole connected marketing story, and this is nowhere more apparent than in the case of live buzz marketing. Consider the example of the Axe Click marketing campaign in France.

Case Example: The Axe Click Launch in France

Unilever's Axe (known as "Lynx" in some countries) is a brand of men's body care products (deodorant, body spray, and shower gel) whose popularity in Europe, the United States, Australia, Latin America, and Southeast Asia has benefited greatly from the growing interest among men in personal hygiene products (Kimmel & Tissier-Desbordes, 1999). The Axe product line specifically targets young males aged 14–25 and is positioned as the brand that gives men "the edge in the mating game" by enhancing how they look, smell, and feel about themselves. Consistent with the Axe brand essence as one that is based on seduction and provocation, the deodorant is promoted as being an essential means for attracting potential partners—the so-called "Axe (or Lynx) effect." The brand's marketing messages use humor and irreverence to reveal how the otherwise average male can obtain sudden, incredible seductive power via the product for attracting beautiful women.

In essence, this is the brand context that effectively shaped the introduction of the new Axe Click deodorant in France during 2006. The objectives of the marketing campaign associated with the launch, in addition to gaining sales and market share, were to reinforce the Axe brand image, recruit new customers among teenage consumers, and build brand equity by enhancing awareness and conviction for Axe. It was hoped that the campaign would result in Axe Click achieving the top rank within the Axe range. The launch also was seen by Unilever as a means for breaking out of the more traditional communications approach the company previously had favored (e.g., creation of an entertaining TV ad, then a rollout to ancillary above-the-line media) by developing an unconventional communications strategy and exploiting alternative communications channels. Although past campaigns had been successful, they had become predictable at a time when other youth brands were building deeper engagement, through multimedia, experiential, idea-led campaigns (such as the popular Nike Freestyle ads). For the Axe Click launch, Unilever chose the path of teasing and live buzz marketing to start a so-called "click attitude" trend, bringing a new expression into the argot of the French teen, "je te clique" ["I'll click you"], a variation of the youthful slang, "je te kiffe" ["I've got a crush on you"].

This was accomplished via a street marketing approach that involved the distribution of free "clickers" (small hand-held devices that register counts when a button at the top is clicked) to 25,000 young people from 230 French high schools in central urban locations (Charpentier, 2006). It was suggested to the boys that they could keep a running count with the clicker each time a young girl gave off positive signals of interest (e.g., a smile, eye contact, or other flirtatious behaviors), and then compare their total with those of their friends. The clickers were given out by "Axe girls" wearing branded clothing indicating the campaign's Web site address (www.clickmore.com) and coupled with the distribution of Axe Click visit cards, also bearing the Web site address.

The provocative Web site previously had been developed as a teaser to introduce the clicker and the brand attitude. Once the clicker distribution was underway, consumers could order a free clicker at the Web site, paying only postal fees. The public and competitive usage of the clicker created something of a phenomenon at French high schools, and before long thousands of teens were visiting the Axe Click Web site to request their own. Eventually, more than 400,000 clickers were distributed.

The Axe Click campaign also included an element of event marketing with selected teens invited to attend a "click for me" evening at one of the best-known teen clubs in Paris. Invitees were given the VIP treatment, and were provided with free champagne, fruit baskets, and Axe Click T-shirts. Upon entry, the boys were asked to wear a number card so that the girls could vote for the most popular male at the party. At the end of the evening, awards were handed out, including videogame consoles and free entries for parties at fashionable Parisian night clubs. This marketing tactic proved extremely effective in triggering buzz about the Axe Click concept. The influential attendees had been treated like "stars" and subsequently engaged in much talk about the evening on high school campuses during the ensuing period, resulting in a high level of enthusiasm for the cool clicker and the "one click" craze. The live buzz marketing aspects of the campaign were reinforced through partnerships with popular French radio stations. For example, a separate Web site was established in collaboration with NRJ, the most popular broadcaster for teens, where visitors could vote for the most seductive radio host. A running count of votes was revealed by Axe clickers posted at the site and vote counts were regularly updated throughout the day. Additionally, 300 French celebrities who were recruited to endorse Axe Click were encouraged to wear the branded T-shirt and popularize the message, "j'te kiffe, j'te Click."

These various activities, which constituted the initial 1-month "teasing phase" of the Axe Click deodorant campaign (the actual product was never directly discussed), was followed by the start of a traditional advertising push featuring the actor Ben Affleck. However, this time the communications provided direct reference to the product (the "reveal" phase). The humorous campaign turned upside down the conventional tactic of relying on the movie star good looks of the celebrity to sell the product. In the ads, which ran on TV and were displayed on outdoor posters, an average looking guy is depicted as trouncing Ben Affleck in the click competition as a result of his greater seductive charms derived from the Axe Click deodorant. The ads effectively provided the link between the "click more" phenomenon and the deodorant, and at the same time reinforced the brand benefit, "Axe makes me feel, look and smell great and it helps me play on top of my game." Another aspect of the advertising campaign involved a partnership that Unilever struck with the male-oriented magazine *FHM*, which offered a free clicker with purchase of the magazine and an issue featuring an Axe Click girl on the cover. The brand used editorial advertising within the magazine, comprised of a fake, humorous article about a group of friends who were clicking experts and who offered tips on how to accumulate a high number of clicks.

Finally, 1 month later, an "amplification phase" was launched, which was intended to extend the buzz that already had evolved for the new product. A major component of this third phase, in large part designed for the purpose of gathering favorable public relations, was a "Click Dating" event that was organized in nine cafés located near high schools in several French cities. The event was staged as a seduction contest, open to 16- to 25-year-olds, challenging them to impress "Axe bombs"—models and actresses hired for the event—with their seductive qualities, with each successful action rewarded with a click. Several winners were awarded videogame consoles, but more importantly, their photos were displayed at the café and at the "Click more" Web site, providing a kind of hero status as "the best clicker in town." The event was publicized in the press, via leaflets, and at the brand Web site.

From a marketing standpoint, the Axe Click three-phase campaign was a resounding success. During the second month of the campaign alone, the "Click more" Web site received 300,000 unique visitors. By the end of the campaign, the new deodorant had obtained 10.4% penetration, the click phenomenon had permeated French teen popular culture, and the brand had risen as the top variant within the Axe range, with 1.5% of the market. Within 6 months, the Axe deodorant segment had obtained 12.5% growth when compared to figures during the previous year.

In addition to providing a context for introducing the live marketing approach, this rather extended discussion of the Axe Click campaign highlights the way an effective campaign can combine various elements of traditional and nontraditional approaches to enhance engagement with consumers, build awareness, generate excitement for a product, and evolve brand image and brand equity. The campaign's success can be traced in large part to Unilever's insight into the mindset of its target consumer segment, while successfully exploiting the power of influentials and peer-to-peer networks.

Live Buzz Marketing Defined and Classified

Of all the approaches within the connected marketing toolbox, live buzz marketing is perhaps the most difficult to pin down with a definition. According to UK marketing expert Justin Foxton (2006, p. 25), whose chapter on the topic represents a definitive overview, "if we all knew what live buzz marketing was, it would lose its power." Nonetheless, by breaking down the different components of the term, Foxton (2006, p. 26) settled on the following definition of *live buzz marketing*, which seems to be an adequate representation of what the approach entails: "A marketing technique that makes use of an actual event or performance to create word of mouth." Foxton suggests that the term "echo" can be used interchangeably with "word of mouth" in the definition and helps differentiate live buzz marketing from other buzz-generating techniques. In this context, "echo" implies that buzz is created at a specific moment by a live happening or event, and this triggers something akin to a sound wave of chatter that reverberates throughout a consumer population, repeating and imitating itself until ultimately fading away. Performers often give rise to such an echo, defined broadly to include not only actors, but average consumers who are willing to talk about something in the marketplace. In Foxton's view, all it takes is someone to generate a big enough noise to set off the echo's vibrations.

Considering these ideas about live buzz marketing with reference to the Axe Click campaign, we can recognize how Unilever enhanced the likelihood that chatter would reverberate about the new deodorant among the French teen segment by setting up several opportunities for creating a noise that would trigger a WOM echo: the on-the-street tactic of placing free clickers directly into the hands of teens at urban high schools, which triggered a wave of requests for clickers by their peers; inviting a select group of influential teens to an exclusive Axe Click party at a popular nightclub, after which they made a big deal about the special night among their friends and schoolmates; involving popular radio DJs to participate in a Click-related competition, which generated a lot of excitement among teen listeners who voted for the winner. Whatever "echo" was triggered by these events likely was maintained and perhaps enhanced by the humorous, talkworthy traditional media campaign, which featured a popular movie star who unexpectedly turns out to be the seductive loser in the ad.

Foxton (2006) distinguishes between two types of live buzz marketing, which differ on the basis of the types of individuals from whom WOM originates. *Live peer-to-peer marketing* essentially pertains to situations in which ordinary consumers serve as brand ambassadors by conveying WOM about a product, service, or brand, perhaps in exchange for product samples or loyalty points. A good illustration of live peer-to-peer marketing is found in the BzzAgent campaign for Al Fresco sausages, in which average consumers chatted up the product in non-contrived, everyday situations, such as a family barbecue (see Box 7.7). By contrast, *live performer-to-peer marketing* involves the use of trained, qualified performers who take on the role of brand ambassadors in specific settings where target consumers are likely to be found. This variety of live buzz marketing tends to be highly controlled, regulated, and measurable, and is the variation that is most likely to be thought of as synonymous with the live buzz marketing approach.

Three types of live performer-to-peer marketing techniques—secret, disclosed, and overt—differ on the basis of their potential reach and the degree of audience members' awareness that they are being targeted by a marketing effort. The potential reach of different performer-to-peer techniques is illustrated by the three tiers of awareness depicted in Figure 8.1. The top of the pyramid (high potential reach) pertains to situations in which audience members physically experience the campaign. This level

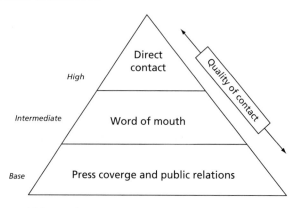

Figure 8.1 Reach Pyramid for Performer-to-Peer Live Buzz Marketing: Three tiers of awareness. Adapted from Foxton (2006, p. 28)

is characterized by the highest quality contact, but is lowest in terms of absolute number of contacts. The middle tier reflects the greater potential for reaching members of the target audience as the persons who gain direct awareness of a campaign spread WOM to other people, who in turn spread the word further. The bottom of the pyramid is where the potential is for the widest reach, as when the media begin to disseminate news about an ongoing campaign, although the marketer's control over the message is significantly reduced. Because of their uniqueness and story-telling qualities, live buzz campaigns often capture the fancy of journalists and media owners, who thus represent valuable resources for obtaining copious amounts of press coverage. In short, potential reach is an important consideration for the planning and implementation of live buzz marketing campaigns.

As different variations of live peer-to-peer marketing (e.g., brand advocacy, product seeding, brand ambassador programs) have been discussed in previous chapters, the focus below is limited to the live performer-to-peer marketing approach.

Secret Live Buzz Marketing

As the name implies, this form of performer-to-peer live buzz marketing occurs undercover, with consumers left unaware that they are being targeted as part of a clandestine marketing campaign. This approach, referred to as *stealth* or *guerrilla marketing* in its more elaborate and deceptive incarnations, typically involves the employment of product ambassadors who spread buzz about a marketplace offering without disclosing that they are doing so to satisfy marketing objectives. In practice, this is likely to entail direct one-on-one interactions with consumers. For example, at one time the makers of Dewar's Scotch whiskey hired attractive, apparently successful young men to frequent bars and restaurants and pretend to be ordinary customers who very noticeably order the whiskey and begin speaking about its merits with other patrons, perhaps offering to buy drinks for some other customers. Fully trained in Dewar's lore and tradition, these "Dewar Highlanders" offered advice to patrons and bartenders on how to enjoy whiskey and mix cocktails with Dewar's (Fitzgerald, 2002).

In 2002, as part of a US$6 million, 2-month campaign, Sony Ericsson Mobile Communications ran a controversial "Fake Tourists" summer promotion, in which sixty trained actors posed as tourists to pique interest in a new combination mobile phone and camera (Vranica, 2002). Working in teams of two or three, the fake tourists frequented major tourist attractions, such as New York's Empire State Building and Seattle's Space Needle, asking unsuspecting passersby to take their photograph with the camera. In this way, Sony Ericsson hoped to draw attention to the new product by directly engaging people with an instant product demonstration, which often sparked a conversation about the camera feature. Another clandestine stunt to promote the camera-phone involved the employment of sixty actresses and female models as "leaners" who frequented trendy lounges and bars and followed scripted scenarios designed to help them engage other patrons in conversation. In one setup, an actress's phone rang while she was in the bar and the caller's photo was seen popping up on the phone's screen. Another variation had two actresses sitting at opposite ends of a bar competing against each other with an interactive game running on the camera-phone's screen. The intent of this operation was to draw the attention of unsuspecting consumers and trick them into thinking that they had stumbled onto a hot new product, which they would then spread the word about to others.

By its very nature, stealth marketing of this sort is intrusive and deceptive, and it is not surprising that it has aroused the wrath of many critics. For example, the consumer group Commercial Alert called out Sony Ericsson's campaign, accusing the company of engaging in misleading tactics and duping unsuspecting targets. In its defence, the company and the marketing firm that created the campaign, Fathoms Communication, argued that the actors were instructed to come clean about their identity if directly asked, and that the campaign did not involve deceptive selling because the actors simply demonstrated the product, without making a direct sales pitch (Vranica, 2002). Nonetheless, such campaigns have the potential to backfire, with the possibility that negative publicity will give rise to the perception that the company is dishonest and not to be trusted.

With some creative planning, it is possible to implement less covert means to stimulate buzz in ways that are likely to bypass many of the ethical concerns that arise in reference to secretive live buzz marketing. For example, a more innocuous component of the Sony Ericsson camera-phone campaign was its "Phone Finds" tactic, in which the company placed dummy phones in various urban settings where unsuspecting consumers were likely to accidentally stumble upon them. On the phone's screen was a message that directed the finder to a special Web site where it was possible to enter a contest to win Sony Ericsson's new camera-phone. The "lost phone" technique previously was used in another intriguing marketing campaign that took place in Singapore to promote Alteco 110, a relatively unknown brand of quick-drying adhesive. It is commonplace in Singapore for people to snatch up unguarded portable phones. With that in mind, as a means of boosting consumer confidence in the Alteco 110's adhesive strength, a mock-up of a mobile phone was glued to the tops of tables at various eating and drinking establishments. Two stickers were placed next to the phone, one of which took the form of an actual-size representation of the adhesive product, and the other bearing the notice, "Yours if you can pick it up." In another variation of this approach, in place of the phone, an actual $1 coin (selected because it is easy to pick up) was bonded onto waiting benches at various bus stops along with the two stickers. Both challenges proved irresistible to many of the passersby who came into contact with either the phone or coin, and the campaign proved enormously successful in gaining awareness and building brand value for a rather mundane, everyday product. The promotion concluded with the eventual detachment of the items using a special adhesive remover from the same brand.

Some of the strengths and weaknesses of the secret live buzz marketing approach should be apparent from these examples. In Foxton's view (2006), the approach represents a way that marketers can get their messages across without irritating consumers and serves as a welcome and often appreciated alternative to traditional marketing appeals. It also provides a means for creating ideal, carefully-scripted brand ambassadors with whom consumers are likely to identify and enables the transmission of tailor-made messages most likely to strike a chord with targeted consumers. The approach is interactive and personalized, which enhances the likelihood of high-quality contacts with unsuspecting consumers. The key drawback to the approach, previously mentioned, is the possibility that the campaign may result in negative backlash when people find out that they have been duped by a surreptitious marketing ploy and when the story subsequently is conveyed by the media. Another weakness has to do with the extent to which the personalized contact inherent in the approach will generate far-reaching buzz. In Foxton's terminology, the initial interaction—that is, the noise that sets off the echo—is not very loud, and thus the extent of the echo is likely to be limited.

Disclosed Live Buzz Marketing

This form of live buzz marketing shares similarities with the secret variation, but differs in that at some point, consumers either are informed that they are being marketed to or become aware of that fact during the interaction. Thus, this approach provides the opportunity to stage a real-life scenario that engages audiences, but overcomes the potential backlash that could arise from duping the public. It allows for the element of surprise prior to having the focal product, service, or brand revealed. Disclosed live buzz marketing tactics can be applied in most public settings where consumers are likely to congregate. For example, beginning on World First Aid Day in September 2007, the Canadian Red Cross launched an innovative "street casualty" public service campaign to enhance Canadians' awareness about the importance of knowing first aid techniques and cardiopulmonary resuscitation (CPR), especially during the critical first moments after an emergency ("Know What to Do," 2007). The campaign featured realistic, life-size decals of a collapsed man or woman at the bottom of a flight of stairs in select movie theaters across Canada (see Exhibit 8.2). What appeared to be an actual person in distress from the top of the stairwell gradually came into focus as one descended, revealing that it was simply a communication ploy that had been carried out by the Red Cross. A sticker next to the body bore the awareness campaign's tagline, "Know What to Do. Learn First Aid," along with the Red Cross symbol and Web site URL where people could obtain details about first aid training. The marketing action, which captured the awareness of an estimated 7,600 people during the first 2 days alone, was an effective means for generating buzz about a topic that typically is not commonly discussed.

One of the main strengths of the disclosed live buzz marketing approach is that when its deployment is unique and creative, it is likely to generate significant press interest, and the risk that the campaign will be criticized by the media is reduced due to the fact that the marketing aspects are not kept hidden. It also is attention-getting, as audience members are captured by something so surprising or unexpected, that it is virtually impossible to ignore until what is actually going on becomes apparent to them. With regard to Foxton's echo notion, the initial noise that sets off the echo generated by disclosed live buzz marketing techniques tends to be loud and enduring, resulting in extensive WOM and high recall levels. One possible weakness of this approach is that people may experience adverse reactions to the unexpected manipulation or be annoyed by the disruption. In the case of the Red Cross campaign, seeing an apparently collapsed person in a public setting could conceivably give rise to anxiety or panic among vulnerable persons. The disclosed nature of the technique is likely to offset this possibility, and related concerns can be minimized by tailoring the scenario accordingly to the nature of the setting and likely audience.

Overt Live Buzz Marketing

The majority of one-to-one live buzz marketing efforts are overt, often involving teams of young adults who appear in conspicuous locations and attempt to engage the public through theatrical activities that prominently incorporate a product, brand, or message. With this approach, there is never any doubt as to the marketing intentions, with participants often wearing attention-getting outfits identifying a brand, and in many cases the staged events are pre-announced to the media in the hopes of gaining press coverage and a story on the local TV news.

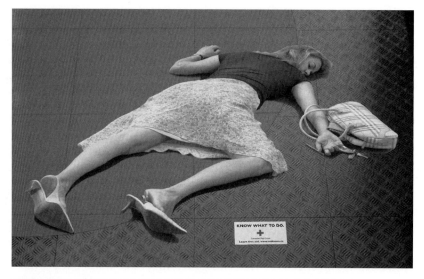

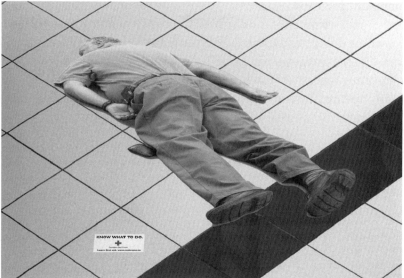

Exhibit 8.2 Canadian Red Cross "Know What to Do" Campaign, 2007
Source: http://www.adverbox.com/canadian-red-cross/.

Some of the examples discussed previously in this book can be classified as overt live buzz marketing, including the staged events that have taken place in Times Square (e.g., Procter & Gamble's (P&G) Charmin toilet tissue ploy; see Box 6.4), the employment of university students who wear and distribute branded tattoos at school events; and the PETA "meat people" display and pierced Mumbai traditional performers mentioned at the outset of this chapter. Some other examples include the following:

- The American telephone company, AT&T Corp. hired brand ambassadors to roam around high-traffic urban locations in California and New Jersey, doing random favors for passersby to promote a new AT&T local service, such as handing out dog biscuits for people walking their pet dog and providing binoculars to concertgoers (Fitzgerald, 2002).

- Hyatt Hotels arranged to have 100 bellhops in Manhattan spend the day opening doors, assisting people with their packages, and handing out hotel pillow mints and marketing brochures promoting the chain's seasonal offer for travel discounts and special deals. Additional teams of brand ambassadors drove around Manhattan, Los Angeles, and Chicago in conspicuously branded cars, stopping in high-traffic areas to dispense mints and marketing materials. Overall, Hyatt reached thousands of consumers through this relatively inexpensive marketing effort, and enjoyed free coverage on local TV and radio news and talk shows.

- At Baltimore's touristy Inner Harbor, brand ambassadors spread the word about Boost Mobile's cost-effective phone plans in an action that was carried out during the July 4, 2009 holiday weekend. The street teams attracted considerable attention by stenciling over thirty Boost Mobile logos on walkways and placing posters in high-traffic areas. A total of 6,000 promotional flyers and 500 brochures were distributed to interested passersby ("Brand Awareness," 2009).

- Designer Kenneth Cole claims to have introduced his shoe business in New York City through the use of live buzz marketing tactics. Without the resources required to enter the market in a conventional manner by setting up at the trade show at the Hilton Hotel or opening a fancy showroom nearby, he instead chose to park a 40-foot trailer truck next to the Hilton and use it as his shoes outlet. However, he quickly learned that this plan ran afoul of a city ordinance, which only allowed the distribution of parking permits to film production crews and utility companies. Cole's solution was to change his company letterhead stationary to Kenneth Cole Productions, Inc. and apply for a permit to shoot a feature-length film entitled, "The Birth of a Shoe Company" (Oetting, 2006). The day of the trade show at the Hilton, Cole's trailer was parked directly across the street prominently displaying the name of his "production company," and from time to time, models posing as "actresses" were filmed on the "set." All the while, shoes were being sold directly from the trailer, resulting in 40,000 pairs sold during the two and a half days allowed by the parking permit.

These overt live marketing examples, which represent a new kind of brand ambassador promotional approach, typically are not designed as isolated stunts, but are linked to broader brand-building efforts that serve to reinforce mainstream advertising efforts. One of the main strengths of unabashed street marketing campaigns is that consumers in general seem to appreciate receiving informative promotional messages in entertaining and innovative ways as they go about their daily activities. Such campaigns effectively cut through the marketing clutter and capture attention, and they provide interesting, conversation-worthy material that tends to be passed along to friends and family members. The campaigns can be extremely effective for generating short-term awareness boosts, significant WOM and media coverage, product sampling, and, as Kenneth Cole demonstrated, can even generate sales. According to John Palumbo, president of DVC Worldwide, which coordinated AT&T's live buzz campaign, "What we're doing with brand ambassadors actually reinforces advertising by translating the general message to the street level, helping to make a connection between people and media" (Fitzgerald, 2002).

On the downside, the cost per contact of an overt buzz campaign can become high to the extent that it incorporates sophisticated props, costumes, stages, and special lighting and sound components. It also is important to bear in mind that as the campaigns take place in public settings, passersby may have little time to pay much attention to the event: in their haste, the promoted product and brand name may be missed entirely. Marketers typically can overcome this potential drawback through the careful selection of locations and by carefully matching the creative with the environment. A more serious weakness of overt practices has to do with the difficulty of measuring their impact, especially for campaigns associated with product launches where there is no control group for comparison. In the view of one marketing consultant, "Without a clear and measurable objective to begin with, [marketers] often waste scarce marketing resources. Sure, it's creative and edgy. But so was that other product no one can remember the name of" (Fitzgerald, 2002). An additional potential weakness is relevant to each of the categories of live buzz marketing: as they gain in popularity among marketing professionals as a viable corollary to traditional marketing approaches, consumers might become overwhelmed by the proliferation of live marketing stunts and as jaded as they are now for traditional advertising.

Overall, experts tend to agree that live buzz campaigns are apt to succeed when marketers adhere to two basic guidelines: (a) keep it simple and (b) target your audience (Barnes, 2007a). Simple marketing actions can be surprisingly effective, as when company representatives directly hand out to consumers samples that can readily be used. For example, some restaurants deliver free food to talk-show radio hosts when they are on the air, and the upshot is that the businesses get plenty of free, spontaneous advertising. Reacting to the tendency for many small businesses to mistakenly believe that something small will not have much of an impact, Jonathan Fields, owner of the boutique guerrilla marketing firm Vibe Creative commented:

> If you're a yoga studio in Los Angeles, dispatching people to sit in the lotus position through the city is a waste of time because it is unlikely to drive yoga enthusiasts to your studio. But having people do it within 10 blocks of your studio is a decent idea.

Exhibit 8.3 Live Buzz Marketing: Keeping It Simple
Source: http://sandeepmakam.blogspot.com/2006/04/german-blush-teaser_08.html.

Fields' yoga example recalls an actual outdoor advertising campaign for the German lingerie store Blush. The inexpensive use of carefully placed posters by the advertising firm BBDO effectively led consumers to Blush stores by arousing their prurient curiosity (see Exhibit 8.3).

Simplicity requires that marketing tactics make a clear connection between the stunt itself and the product that is the focus of the campaign. In fact, if the product emerges as the "hero" of the live buzz effort, it is much more likely to be mentioned when people start buzzing about their encounter. For example, to emphasize the anti-dandruff benefit of its Head & Shoulders hair shampoo, P&G enlisted the cooperation of owners of some cafés in Paris to switch the salt shakers on their tables with altered replacements. The punch line was that the shakers' chrome tops had no holes. When diners attempted to use the tampered-with shakers during their meal, they were approached by a P&G representative who revealed the ploy and explained the connection to the hair shampoo.

Given that live buzz techniques often take the form of live performances, care should be taken to play to the desired audience. A successful illustration of this recommendation is apparent in an effort by the conservative, family-owned New Mexico ski resort, Taos Ski Valley, in its attempt to appeal to younger skiers (Barnes, 2007a). A local marketing agency hired by the resort came up with a simple approach, but one that was thought to have great potential with the target in question. The idea was to change the resort's logo to a cryptic symbol, arouse interest in it through a special Web site, and then to scribble the logo and the web address on Starbucks napkins and Post-It notes, which then were randomly scattered in public places across the United States. The campaign apparently succeeded: visitors to the resort's Web site increased by 44% and the resort's owners claimed to have noticed a significant increase in younger visitors to their establishment.

Live Buzz Marketing Blunders

The inherent dangers of employing outrageous, attention-getting live buzz marketing ploys to generate buzz are reflected in some noted efforts in which something went awry, leading to outcomes that were the converse of what had been anticipated. The following cases reflect how guerrilla, stealth, and street marketing campaigns can be a risky business, with the potential to run afoul of ethical and legal acceptability.

General Motors' "Oprah's Great Pontiac Giveaway"

One high-profile live buzz campaign that no doubt looked good on paper prior to its implementation was initiated by General Motors (GM) in 2004 as a means of generating WOM about the auto giant's new Pontiac G6 car. In a surprise move, GM donated 276 of the sports sedans to each member of the studio audience attending popular US talk-show host Oprah Winfrey's season premiere telecast, at a cost of US$7 million. The recipients were specially selected from among a list of people whose families and friends had written to Ms. Winfrey stating that they needed new cars, thereby imbuing the marketing effort with elements linked to aspirations and wish fulfillment. At the time, Ms. Winfrey's show had a global audience of 30 million viewers each week. At first, the stunt appeared to have been a huge success, at least in terms of the substantial amount of talk and publicity it created. According to one estimate, the event was followed by generally positive coverage in 624 news reports, including a cover story in *People Magazine*, and resulted in 242,000 visits to the G6 Web site within 24 hours of the TV broadcast (Morales, 2004). Jim Bunnell, GM's general manager for the Pontiac-GMC division, revelled in the nontraditional campaign's apparent effectiveness (cf. Oetting, 2006, p. 242):

> During the Athens Olympics, GMC ran 25 to 30 television spots for its truck products over two weeks that cost between US$7 million and US$8 million, but no one really talked

about those ads. But the same budget, spent in one day, drove a significant amount of buzz for the G6 on a daytime television show.

Alyce Lomax (2004), creator of the Motley Fool investment blog, similarly lauded the offbeat marketing approach:

> For GM, this is a pretty savvy version of product placement in a world where people can easily buzz through commercials with their digital video recorders . . . I don't know about you, but news reports describing Oprah screaming repeatedly, "Everybody gets a car!" and word that the audience "screamed, cried, and hugged each other" sounds like some pretty darn good advertising to me. That kind of unbridled joy is probably the best advertisement any company could get.

Unfortunately for GM, the apparent success of the G6 televised giveaway quickly evaporated into a cloud of negative buzz. This turn of events was prompted by widely publicized reports that the recipients of the free cars would have to pay a tax upwards of US$7,000 if they wanted to keep the gift. Although news outlets had initially characterized the giveaway as a "feel-good story," journalists subsequently enveloped the revelation about the tax in a tone of outrage, despite the recognition that even lottery winners must fork over a substantial percentage in taxes to the government. As talk about the episode turned negative, people began to assail Oprah Winfrey, accusing her of trying to unduly take the credit for donating cars to the needy, and more generally, the perception emerged that the campaign was designed to draw more attention to the marketing stunt than to the car it was supposed to sell. Indeed, although the "Oprah giveaway" resulted in plenty of buzz, both positive and negative, it did not turn out to have much of a discernable impact on actual sales of the G6 (Webster, 2005).

Aqua Teen Hunger Force Guerrilla Marketing, Boston

An example of a guerilla marketing campaign that has rapidly made its way into the annals of infamous marketing efforts that have gone wrong is one that was launched to promote the television program Aqua Teen Hunger Force in 2007 (Urbanist, 2008). A number of LED signs displaying blinking cartoon figures from the animated TV series performing an obscene gesture were mounted in a variety of high-visibility locations around the city of Boston, Massachusetts, such as bridge supports, subway stations, and public parks. However, the rudimentary magnetic devices, which were comprised of complex wiring and their own battery-packed power sources, were mistaken for possible explosive devices. The sightings of the devices caused a near-panic within the city as word quickly spread that the city was under threat. The subway system was effectively shut down, and several bridges and highways were closed; in short, during a couple of tense hours, the city was brought to a standstill as police and anti-terrorism experts located and removed the suspicious devices.

Had Aqua Force's marketing company and device designers notified police beforehand of the purpose of the marketing stunt, the media probably would have treated the campaign as an amusing story, and it is likely that considerable attention would have been generated for the TV program. As it was, those responsible for the campaign became the targets of considerable criticism, with charges that the marketing ploy was naive and its consequences poorly anticipated in the wake of ongoing anxieties about terrorism. Several critics also questioned whether the bomb scare might have been part of the campaign's designers' intentions all along as a sure way to capture the greatest amount of media coverage. Nonetheless, because of what many saw as an overreaction on the part of Boston officials, the incident probably brought more public attention and media exposure to the stunt and the TV program it promoted than was originally expected. Whether the preponderance of that publicity was positive or negative is difficult to say, although it is clear that the campaign's aftermath brought some headaches to its developers and persons associated with the Cartoon Network's TV program. No jail sentences resulted from the incident, but Turner Broadcasting was forced to issue a public apology and paid millions of dollars to city police and US Homeland Security to resolve the matter.

Sony PlayStation's Graffiti Campaign

It has long been argued by critics of outdoor advertising signage that billboards, posters, electronic signs, and so on represent a form of cultural pollution, adding to the urban blight of cities. Thus, it is no surprise that Sony's decision to promote its new Play-Station Portable gaming system before the 2005 year-end holidays through graffiti displayed on the sides of buildings in urban neighborhoods ran into difficulties almost from the outset. Intended to reinforce awareness and gain publicity, the black-on-white graffiti-like drawings, which appeared in large US cities like San Francisco, New York, and Philadelphia, depicted wide-eyed cartoon characters using the PlayStation to skateboard, hit a ball, manipulate like a puppet, and so on. Nowhere on the graffiti drawings was there any indication of the Sony or PlayStation brands or association with traditional advertising. It was hoped that the marketing action would strike a chord with urban youth and hip-hop culture.

What Sony had not anticipated, however, is that rather than being perceived by inner-city youth as a reflection of urban cool, the graffiti was viewed by savvy kids as an exploitative and transparent attempt by the company to establish street credibility so as to market a product. This led to a backlash online, with bloggers lambasting the campaign, and on the streets, where street artists began their own campaign of defacing Sony's stealth ads. For example, taglines like "Stop hawking corporate products and big business on our neighbourhood walls," "Corporate vandals not welcome," "Get out of my city," and "Fony" were spray painted on the Sony drawings. On another front, city officials argued that Sony's campaign ignored the zoning process that regulates outdoor commercial advertising in urban areas. For example, in Philadelphia, Managing Director Pedro Ramos faxed a cease-and-desist letter to Sony Computer Entertainment's US division, threatening to seek modest fines allowed by the city code or sue to recover any profit the ads produced ("PlayStation Ads," 2005). According to Ramos, "My fines aren't going to scare Sony. What will worry them is what the parents and their users will think. This really flies in the face of everything we've been trying to do with our anti-blight initiative."

The Sony example, like the other two cases described above, was a creative attempt to stimulate WOM and gain publicity through mass media outlets. On these counts, the effort assuredly succeeded, although the attention and notoriety were hardly of a positive nature. The fact that the campaign backfired in terms of the unanticipated reactions of its targets may point to a failure by the company to fully study its likely impact in advance of its launch. That point notwithstanding, one thing is clear: companies like Sony recognize the need to extend their marketing efforts beyond the tried-and-true advertising strategies of the past. In so doing, they are breaking through the clutter and having an impact.

Conclusion

So ends our two-chapter focus on some of the more promising examples of connected marketing techniques, a representative, albeit non-comprehensive overview of approaches that are pushing the envelope of marketing as we progress into the new millennium. It should be clear from the discussion that the range of nontraditional marketing techniques is only limited by the imagination and creativity of the marketers who design and employ them. Connected marketing requires thinking outside the box of traditional marketing, while adhering to some of traditional marketing's basic principles: careful targeting, understanding the needs and desires of consumers, identification of objectives, selection of appropriate metrics for measuring success, and so on.

Because many of the creative marketing techniques described here are new and somewhat untested, it is not surprising that they at times exceed the limits of propriety, ethics, legal standards, and good taste. The appropriateness of connected marketing techniques is likely to become clearer in time, with the emergence of ethical principles and legislation (Bird, 2008; Friedberg, Pfleiger, & Weisberg, 2004). However, as marketers strive to one-up the competition and break through the clutter, there no doubt will always be gray areas and differing views on the suitability of some approaches. If there is any general principle that should be emphasized in the development of a connected marketing approach it is the necessity to remain sensitive to the consumers that we serve. Rather than proceeding with an eye toward developing ingenious, undercover approaches that rely on deception, marketers should use their creativity to design approaches that are overt, informative, entertaining, likely to engage, and aimed at setting off a nuclear explosion of marketing buzz.

9 Synthesis and a Look to the Future

These are exciting times for marketers. Pessimists might characterize the current state of the profession with dire prognostications about the death of advertising, a consumer population no longer responsive to traditional marketing communication approaches, and evolving technologies that enable consumers to link with each other and tune out marketers. However, with the exception of the demise of advertising, which in all likelihood has been grossly exaggerated, the fundamental changes that are occurring in the contemporary marketing landscape should be viewed with hope rather than despair. Indeed, the challenges and opportunities within the field are boundless.

As this book has demonstrated, much progress already has been made in marketers' efforts to engage with consumers and to leverage their conversations. The various techniques that are making their way into the connected marketing toolbox continue to expand as marketers use their ingenuity to develop innovative ways to reach their targets, engage them, and stimulate word of mouth (WOM). In an effort to synthesize the various connected marketing approaches surveyed in Part II of this book, this brief concluding chapter offers five key lessons relevant to nontraditional marketing campaigns. The chapter concludes with a consideration of what marketers can expect in the coming decades.

Five Key Lessons for Connected Marketing

1. *Connections have different values.* One message of central importance that has been repeated at various junctures throughout this book is that consumer targets for a marketing campaign must be carefully identified. This message is not new; in fact, it is a long-established, basic principle of traditional marketing, and it thus should be no surprise that this book has an entire chapter devoted to a consideration of consumer targeting (Chapter 3). Of course, what *is* new is that consumers now have the technology to connect with one another with far greater facility than could have been imagined only a couple decades ago, and the resulting networks of consumer communities represent fertile opportunities for marketers who hope

to join the consumer conversation and stimulate WOM. Nonetheless, not all communities of consumers offer the same value for achieving different marketing objectives.

A useful model for illustrating the different potential values associated with varying consumer networks has been suggested by Forrester Research (see Table 9.1). According to this framework, networks differ in terms of scale (characterized by *proximity* in the table) and dynamics (characterized by *community* in the table). Generally speaking, the network with the highest potential value for connected marketing efforts is one in which the community is comprised of members who are cohesively linked with one another (i.e., "entwined") and whose connections are "intimate" rather than "public." These are individuals who stay in touch with each other on a regular basis through e-mail, phone calls, and SMS communications and whose interpersonal relationships are based on a high degree of trust. Personal recommendations and peer referrals are imbued with a high degree of credibility. Members of entwined/intimate networks are likely to pass on personal recommendations to their intimates and act on received recommendations. The Girls Intelligence Agency's organization of teen slumber parties and in-room hangouts (see pp. 242–3) is a good example of how marketers can connect with this sort of network.

Table 9.1 Connections Have Differing Relative Value for Marketing

	Community — Entwined	
	High value	**Highest value**
	Wide reach	Low reach
	Remote contact	Close contact
Public — High affinity	High affinity	**Intimate**
Proximity	**Low value**	**Medium value**
	Wide reach	Low reach
	Remote contact	Close contact
	Low affinity	Low affinity
	Loose	

The high value quadrant in Table 9.1 depicts entwined communities of consumers whose connections are more of a public nature. Such communities are characteristic of active participants in online social networks (such as people who regularly post comments on Facebook's personal "walls"), brand communities, and blogs with regular "followers" and contributors. Companies can attempt to establish an open dialogue with consumers via blogs or online engagement programs (e.g., Dell's Ideastorm and Starbucks' My Starbucks Idea) by tapping into such communities.

The medium value quadrant characterizes consumers who are linked together through loosely knit communities of friends and acquaintances. Individuals within such intimate/loose networks are likely to share content by passing it along to others online, as when forwarding a link to a humorous YouTube video to all one's e-mail contacts or posting it on one's blog. Brand advocacy and viral marketing efforts typically are oriented to tap into and influence these kinds of communities.

In Forrester's assessment, the type of consumer network that holds the lowest potential value for connected marketers is comprised of communities of consumers who are loosely connected via public forums. Persons who post comments to news stories online or periodically participate in topical, open forums (e.g., about music, sports, technology, films) represent a loosely bounded community whose members make up a wide-reaching, linked-in network. Their utility for connected marketing efforts is largely limited to viral marketing campaigns and, in some circumstances, the identification of influentials. In such forums, members typically are anonymous, identified only by user nicknames, and so recommendations have limited credibility.

Traditionally, a determination of customer value has largely focused on financial value; that is, in terms of the amount of business consumers were likely to bring to the company. In this perspective, most valuable customers would be considered those who do the preponderance of business with the enterprise relative to the costs of acquiring them, yield the highest margins, and are likely to remain loyal (Peppers & Rogers, 2004). Most marketers today are likely to share this view. Marketing vis-à-vis contemporary marketplace realities requires an approach that views consumers not as autonomous vestibules from whom one can expect to derive an adequate return on investment, but rather as active collaborators with connections to wider networks of potential long-term brand enthusiasts.

2. *Different connected marketing tools for different marketing goals.* As we have seen, engagement with consumers and the leveraging of their WOM conversations can be achieved through the use of many different tools. The choice of tools for accomplishing marketing objectives is dependent on a variety of factors, including company resources, the competitive environment, type of offering, consumer characteristics and media-usage habits, and the like. These important considerations notwithstanding, it is important to bear in mind that certain tools are more

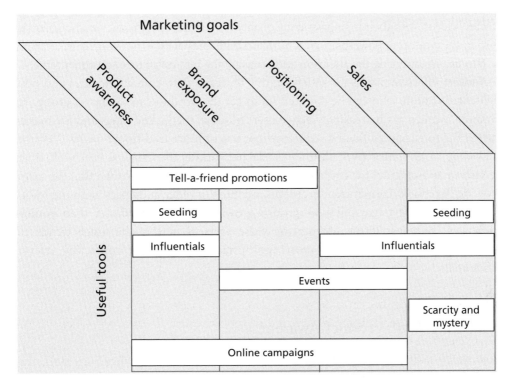

Figure 9.1 Matching Connected Marketing Approaches With Marketing Goals

Source: Oosterwijk and Loeffen (2005).

appropriate for achieving different goals and objectives (see Figure 9.1). Although the most appropriate match will have to be determined by each specific firm in many cases on the basis of trial and error and evaluation based on appropriate metrics, the following can be used as a rudimentary guide in the selection of specific connected marketing tools (cf. Oosterwijk & Loeffen, 2005).

Marketing Goal: Reaching a New Target Group

Appropriate tools: Online campaign, brand advocacy, product seeding, identifying and communicating with influentials

Marketing objectives that are oriented toward connecting with new consumer groups (e.g., the elderly, female professionals, dieters) typically can be accomplished through tools that make it possible to contact the target group directly. An online campaign can be carried out in part through links to a special company micro Web site or corporate blog that are systematically placed at Web sites frequented by the target group. Recall how DuPont effectively reached young consumers via its series of informative and entertaining "Science

Stories" videos, with their high pass-along quality (see Chapter 8). Product seeding, like that used by the creators of Powerbar to reach athletes with free packs of the energy snack, can also be effective in capturing the attention and arousing the interest of new consumer targets.

Another effective means for satisfying this objective is to contact bloggers and other influentials online who can be counted on to get the word out to the target group. For example, women are increasingly active users of social media and blogs and are making more time to engage online by reducing their use of more traditional media ("Women Who Blog," 2009). Moreover, although social networking sites, such as Facebook, might be viewed as a channel for contacting youth, recent figures have shown that the fastest growing Facebook demographic segments are those of older audiences, with the 35–49-year-old and 50–64-year-old user groups growing significantly faster than younger audiences (Burcher, 2009). Monitoring these sorts of new media usage trends can enable marketers to select the most appropriate strategies for contacting relevant influentials.

Marketing Goal: Product Awareness

Appropriate tools: Tell-a-friend promotions (e.g., brand advocacy), live buzz marketing, product seeding, identifying and communicating with influentials, online campaigns

Gaining awareness can be achieved through the implementation of a wide range of connected marketing techniques. Attention-getting strategies that are likely to be noticed by consumers and covered by media outlets, such as live buzz street campaigns and guerrilla marketing actions, represent the most obvious examples. Also effective are approaches that get the product shown to prospects by people they trust, such as influentials and friends within their social networks. Enlisting the assistance of a WOM-generating company that recruits consumers to participate in buzz campaigns represents another means for spreading awareness among specific target groups. The BzzAgent campaign to spread the word about Al Fresco chicken sausage effectively demonstrated how awareness can be gained via a more stealth-oriented approach (see Box 7.7).

Marketing Goal: Brand Exposure

Appropriate tools: Live buzz marketing, events, viral techniques, online campaigns

Live buzz marketing events can accomplish more than merely gaining product awareness. They also can effectively achieve brand exposure by stimulating WOM and acquiring free publicity. Charmin's event marketing in Times Square and Kenneth Cole's introduction of his shoe business during a New York trade show serve as good examples of how this can be accomplished. Similarly, the live buzz actions that were implemented during the launch of Axe Click, including on-the-street distribution of clickers and the invitation-only VIP nightclub event, were hugely successful in linking the marketing campaign to the Axe brand. When coupled with online support (e.g., the Axe Click web site and a radio DJ competition), the actions significantly raised the profile of the Axe brand among the target consumer audience (see Chapter 8).

Marketing Goal: Brand Positioning

Appropriate tools: Online campaign, blogging, identifying and communicating with influentials, live buzz marketing, and events

These connected marketing tools can serve to position a brand through association with the personality of the influential, the message of the online campaign, or the kind of event organized (Oosterwijk & Loeffen, 2005). Online campaigns are especially effective in positioning a brand because of the possibility of providing consumers with detailed or tailored information. A well-executed online campaign is capable of garnering high levels of exposure by drawing people to a brand's web site, and it can effectively differentiate a brand by associating it with a defining, memorable message. This was skillfully accomplished by Wilkinson, with its promotions for the Quattro Titanium razor, which incorporated engaging online videos and a downloadable adver-game to convey the message that the razor will make the skin as soft as a baby's. A live buzz event can create impressive, sticky (i.e., memorable), real-life moments for consumers through its high visibility, tailored information, and ability to have a brand stand out from the competition.

Marketing Goal: Sales

Appropriate tools: Incentivized WOM approaches (e.g., affiliate or online referral programs), seeding, contacting influentials, and scarcity

Connected marketing techniques that manage to get the product into the hands of potential customers are most likely to get the product sold. Product-seeding campaigns, such as that used by the creators of Powerbar, give consumers the opportunity to try out and experience the product first-hand, and thereby learn about its need-satisfying attributes. Offering influentials an incentive for making the product known to others within their social sphere and encouraging its purchase also can prove useful in acquiring new paying customers, assuming that the influentials have been carefully selected and are accessible. P&G's referral incentive for early adopters of the Whitestrips tooth-whitening product proved to be a critical component of the successful launch of the brand and its eventual market leadership among tooth-whitening products.

When a product is already on the market, or is an installment in a series, its scarcity can fuel desire and stimulate frenetic buying by consumers caught up in ongoing hype and rumored limited supplies. Just ask any parent of a child who is a big fan of the Harry Potter book series.

Marketing Goal: Data acquisition

Appropriate tools: Viral campaigns (e.g., product giveaways), tell-a-friend promotions (e.g., referrals), online campaigns

Any type of connected marketing tool that gets consumers to sign up at a company Web site and, in so doing, provide information about themselves (e.g., to receive a free product, a newsletter, game entry) is invaluable for the development and maintenance of an up-to-date consumer database. Heineken has developed an extensive database of young drinkers through its adroit use of competitions, giveaways (e.g., a mobile phone application), and online event calendars, electronic newsletters, and wireless alerts (see Chapter 8).

Marketing Goal: Brand Loyalty

Appropriate tools: Engagement programs, collaboration, live buzz events

Approaches that enable a company to establish an ongoing, open, collaborative dialogue with consumers are essential to gaining brand loyalty. Dell, Starbucks, P&G, and Urban Outfitters have made great strides in this direction and serve as exemplary models of how long-term relationships can be won by putting consumers' interests first (see Chapter 6). Live buzz events that attract media attention are likely to reinforce consumers' perception that their preferred brand choice is well chosen, supported by the company that owns it, and is cutting edge.

3. *No connected marketing effort stands on its own.* It is the rare connected marketing technique that can effectively achieve any of the goals described above on its own. The best results can only be attained when a systematically selected set of tools are integrated as part of an overall marketing communication campaign, which, in turn, is integrated within the context of other marketing functions (such as price, product, and place of distribution). Any firm that believes that the posting of, say, a "viral" video online constitutes a nontraditional campaign utilizing social media to achieve certain marketing goals is sorely mistaken. Without an awful lot of luck, that video, whatever its cost and whatever its impact, is destined to become lost in the void of cyberspace unless it is supported by other marketing actions. Just as

traditional advertisers have come to struggle with the vast proliferation of advertising content in physical space, online clutter has also rapidly become a growing problem for nontraditional marketing efforts to capture the hearts and minds of multitasking consumer audiences.

Consider once again the Axe Click campaign, which pulled no stops in captivating a specific consumer demographic through a combination of marketing tools. The key selling point—a brand that gives young males the edge in the dating game—was repeatedly emphasized through the implementation of a carefully integrated combination of marketing actions. Each action contributed to the spread of buzz during the three phases of the marketing campaign. Both traditional (e.g., ads featuring actor Ben Affleck and radio promotions) and nontraditional (e.g., live street marketing) methods were employed to draw more attention and give added staying power to the message. Any one of these actions alone probably would not have had much of an impact. Although the costs for the company would have significantly been reduced, the impact of a scaled-back campaign likely would have been minimal.

Despite their potential for increasing sales, connected marketing tools typically lack the ability in and of themselves to persuade people to actively go out and purchase a product (Oosterwijk & Loeffen, 2005). Other basic marketing mix elements, such as sales promotion, pricing, and distribution, are essential ingredients for translating into sales the goodwill built up by engagement or buzz efforts. Because prospects can be assumed to make use of different media, with large numbers of consumers still not connected to the Internet, multiple channel support and cross promoting will also be required for a contemporary marketing campaign to reap benefits and add to the bottom line. These points bring to mind the atypical success of a small Indian restaurant in my neighborhood, Shalimar, which opened about 5 years ago. I often kid Shalimar's owner—an astute amateur marketer if I ever met one—that I was his first customer. How did I find out about Shalimar and why did I become such a loyal patron? The answers illustrate what good marketing should be all about.

One late afternoon when I arrived home from work, I found a one-sheet, color flyer in my mailbox heralding the opening (as it happened, that same afternoon) of a new Indian restaurant just around the corner from my house. As I hadn't passed that part of my neighborhood for several weeks, the opening was completely off my radar; yet, as a fan of Indian cuisine, I immediately went to check it out. I was greeted by the owner and, as I waited for my carryout order to be prepared, he offered me an aperitif and explained his commitment to having his restaurant succeed. That commitment was evidenced by the high quality of my carryout order, and before long, my wife and I had dinner at the restaurant and have become loyal patrons ever since.

The key to Shalimar's success is high-quality cuisine at reasonable prices. That is about as buzzworthy a discovery as one can hope for when it comes to a restaurant recommendation. Along with added value (an aperitif offered before the meal, a cognac after, and a rose for the wife) and attentive service, Shalimar is always a top-of-mind choice for me when I'm searching for a convenient, satisfying dining-out experience. Shalimar's success—the restaurant always seems to be filled—can largely be attributed to traditional advertising (billboards, flyers, branded pens, etc.), a high-quality product, and reasonable pricing. The success did not require having someone dressed up as a chicken stationed outside the restaurant or the posting of a viral video on YouTube showing a Rube Goldberg chain of food ingredients transforming into a spicy Indian meal. A simple, inexpensive flyer placed in my mailbox was sufficient to arouse my interest and set me on the path to becoming a loyal, paying customer. Shalimar's owner has indeed taken the online route and set up an informative web site. Yet, any connected marketing impact for the restaurant to date has come indirectly through customer satisfaction: friends telling friends, enthusiastic bloggers (like myself) posting an online review, customer recommendations at sites like Trip Advisor, and the like. To stay ahead of the game over the longer term, Shalimar's owner in the future may have to directly tap into the connected marketing toolbox to more fully engage customers; for example, by launching a competition to devise a new menu offering, employing influential diners to make referrals, creating a Facebook page devoted to the restaurant or Indian cuisine in general, and—who knows?—perhaps even having someone dressed up like a chicken outside the restaurant taking passersby requests.

Before ending this discussion relative to the message that no connected marketing effort stands on its own, it is important to state a fact that is sometimes lost in the enthusiasm for new marketing techniques: traditional advertising is not dead. This may be stating the obvious, but all the hype about social media, viral marketing, wikinomics, guerrilla campaigns, and other trendy, nontraditional marketing developments may lead one to the perception that traditional advertising is passé and oh-so twentieth century. But have you ever noticed how many traditional advertisements—both print and video—end up creating an online buzz, attracting thousands of visits to video-sharing sites? This is because good advertising is in itself buzzworthy. And there also is evidence that traditional advertising drives consumers to nontraditional marketing outlets. Research by JupiterResearch and iProspect revealed that upward of two-thirds of consumers point to off-line channels when questioned about what influences them to conduct searches for companies, products, or services online, with television ads (37%), WOM from a friend or acquaintance (36%), and newspaper/magazine ads (30%) leading the way ("iProspect Online Channel," 2007). Moreover, the same research indicated that 38% of online search users then make a purchase after having been driven to search following exposure to some off-line channel, with print ads (30%) and WOM (30%) standing out as the most frequent drivers linked to a purchase. In this light, it is perplexing that many ads do not include relevant URLs. According to iProspect president Robert Murray, search on its own can be an effective route to sales, but "It's clear that its efficacy is multiplied when combined with offline channels. The bottom line is that integration is no longer optional." More generally, the overall message is clear: traditional (off-line) and nontraditional (online) means for reaching consumers should not be viewed as alternatives, but as mutually supportive channels.

4. *Open, honest, and ethical connections for long-term value.* Imagine that you met someone with whom you felt a very strong connection. Now think about what it really means when you say that you "connected" with that person. Your thoughts are likely to include something about feeling a high degree of comfort during the interaction; that there was an air of mutual understanding and a high degree of trust that whatever you said would be openly accepted; that you shared interests and opinions on various topics; that the interaction proved to be a pleasurable and mutually rewarding experience; and that you desired to see that person again. The relevance of this simple exercise to new marketing approaches should be obvious. Connecting with consumers can be understood as meaning all those things listed above: comfort, openness, mutual understanding, trust, pleasurable experience, and a desire to continue a relationship. Greater patience and costs are required to develop a true, long-term relationship with consumers, but the value that relationship is apt to bring to the firm and its customers can be enormous.

Now consider your reactions if you believed that the person whom you recently met had not been completely honest with you, had outright lied, or had admitted engaging in or condoning conduct that was contrary to your moral precepts. At best, you might consider your encounter a "misconnection," and although you might be willing to give the person another chance, it is likely that you would not have a very strong desire to pursue an ongoing relationship. As they say, "there are many other fish in the sea." And so it goes with marketing, where the competition in many sectors is so intense that consumers rarely are inclined to give firms a second chance. In this book, you have read about innovative connected marketing techniques that have raised ethical red flags, such as approaches that involve fake blogging, bribing third-party bloggers, undercover company representatives carrying out secret live buzz ploys, and practices that exploit the privacy rights of individuals (e.g., consumer profiling). Although such tactics may reap short-term dividends, unless conducted with extreme care and sensitivity, with the actions ultimately revealed and explained in a timely fashion, they will more likely than not backfire and drive away customers.

To illustrate how easy it is to turn off increasingly jaded consumers, consider the emergence of online instructional videos, a budding Internet niche that occupies part of the contemporary do-it-yourself movement. A growing number of online video sites, among which Howcast Media currently stands out, are joining YouTube and other established Web sites in offering short videos that provide informative and entertaining how-to content (Creswell, 2009). At the time of this writing, Howcast's library had amassed 100,000 videos, created by consumers, Howcast itself, and commercial sources, such as Popular Science, Ford, and Home Depot. In an attempt to turn a profit on the Internet, Howcast has taken the route of developing partnerships with advertisers to create instructional videos for specific products or services. The result of this approach has led to the blurring of editorial and commercial content, and thus brings to bear some of the same concerns that have been raised about the use of product placements and stealth marketing campaigns. The risk is that consumers may come to reject the approach, however innocuous it may appear at first glance. As explained by Forrester Research analyst Nick Thomas, "Users are sensitive to brands' trying to muscle into what appears to be an organic social media environment. Yes, I want to learn how to cook something, but do I necessarily want to be taught by someone who makes the ingredients?" (Creswell, 2009). In short, connected marketers must walk a fine line when attempting to become active participants in the consumer conversation. Consumers appreciate engagement, but not when it appears that a firm's primary motives are to manipulate and sell.

5. *Everything must be measured.* It has been said that whatever marketers measure is likely to improve (Keetch, 2007). The evolving array of connected marketing metrics, discussed in detail in Chapter 5, thus bodes well for future marketing efforts, assuming that firms make use of the metrics. Tracking everything that is possible relative to a marketing campaign will provide insight into which approaches work and which do not in specific situations. Of course, metrics will not be very useful unless each marketing effort is accompanied by a clear set of objectives, benchmarks, and specific goals for each stage of the marketing process. Appropriate performance indicators then can be linked to the objectives and goals so as to track the progress of a campaign and the impact of any changes in the firm's marketing approach. Performance measures also can be used to enhance a customer database, which is another essential component for companies serious about maintaining a connected marketing program over the long term.

Connecting with Consumers: What Does the Future Hold?

Predicting the future is no small task. Marketers could have hardly foreseen the dramatic changes that have taken place in the consumer marketplace in such a relatively short period of time. No one forewarned them that their models were broken or that their tried-and-true methods were rapidly becoming irrelevant. In fact, many companies continue to operate as if it were still 1960 and the digital revolution never took place, their managers befuddled when the firm's marketing efforts fall flat. If managers cannot recognize the present for what it is, how can we expect them to accurately anticipate the future? All this recalls pioneering communications theorist Marshall McLuhan's famous observation in the book *The Medium Is the Massage* (McLuhan & Flore, 1967):

> When faced with a totally new situation, we tend always to attach ourselves to the objects and to the flavor of the most recent past. We look at the present through a rearview mirror. We march backwards into the future.

In his compelling chapter, "The Twenty-First-Century Consumer Society," James Fitchett (2005) argued that caution must be exercised in attempts to forecast the future even in the short term, while wearing the blinders of the present. Rather, he suggested that a credible imagining of the marketplace of the future can only emerge when we approach the future "as a continuation of prior social trends and cultural dynamics." In Fitchett's view, it is not enough to focus solely on potential technological advances in the communications industry and their likely impact on consumers, especially without considering the broad cultural and social developments that are likely to shape the needs and behaviors of future consumer markets.

Nonetheless, in his creative imagining of the coming decades, Fitchett foresees a consumer society not unlike the one depicted in the futuristic film *Minority Report*, with marketers able to collect personal identity information via such technologies as retinal scanning as consumers wander through a shopping area, enabling a firm to beam individually customized holographic advertisements directly into the consumer's immediate vicinity. In this imagined future, consumers pass down an aisle at their local grocery store as packages call out to them. Brands that have been previously selected might ask whether the consumer was satisfied with the prior purchase and recommend the new and improved version, while competing brands suggest how they could offer greater satisfaction at a more interesting price. Parents selecting a package of breakfast cereal with high sugar content upon the urgings of their children might be confronted in the store by a holographic celebrity dentist suggesting that they also should purchase some extra dental care products if they intend to include that type of food in their children's diet.

These somewhat frightening prospects are based on presumed applications of technological advances, many of which are already being developed. They suggest approaches to connecting with consumers that re-establish the top-down, marketer-dominated models of the past. Although technology is envisioned as central to reaching individual consumers with personalized messages, such views of the future hardly portray a marketing approach that puts the consumer first. In Fitchett's view (2005, p. 47), the technologies may change the way marketers seek to communicate, but the basic marketing principles that are being applied are familiar ones:

> The principles of sales promotion, consumer behavior, and direct marketing are consistent with those that have been applied for decades. The efficiency and effectiveness of contemporary

marketing techniques may improve with future technological advances such as these, assuming that it becomes feasible to realize them, but they would only be expected to be effective so long as consumer behavior norms and communication expectations remained largely unchanged. The scenario only determines the impact of a specific technology and fails to account for other possible changes.

Among the potential changes that Fitchett had in mind is the possibility that retail formats such as shopping malls and self-service hypermarkets, themselves a relatively recent historical phenomenon, might eventually be replaced by more interactive, automated purchasing methods. As another example, consider the fact that manufacturers have begun to devise new product launches in the snack and convenience market that can compensate for the deterioration of in-home family meals. So while it may be possible to envision a future in which breakfast cereal packages call out to children in the supermarket, it may very well be that waning consumer demand for packaged cereals ultimately leads to their disappearance from the market before we ever get to the point of talking packages. In short, technology does not by itself represent a coherent vision of the future, only the means of shaping possible futures (Jacoby, 1999).

Unlike the prescient visions of some science fiction writers, such as Neal Stephenson (*Snow Crash*) and William Gibson (*Neuromancer*), it is difficult to imagine marketers in the recent past able to forecast the emergence of the Internet, with its great capacity for linking consumers, or the proliferation of portable, mobile devices to satisfy the needs of increasingly nomadic consumers. Twenty or thirty years from now we likely will be saying the same thing about developments that could not have been foreseen in our imaginings today. As many marketers finally begin to contemplate the implications of reaching consumers in the Web 2.0 era, its opportunities and challenges, the next evolutionary generations of the Internet are currently underway. Web 3.0 offers the promise of better tailoring online searching and requests specifically to users' preferences and needs, whereas a Web 4.0 could offer online users a more emotive experience through interactive rich media applications (Weber, 2007). How long before Facebook and Twitter, two centerpieces of Web 2.0, become distant memories or are transformed into something unrecognizable today?

At present, at least at a very basic level, some questions stand out relative to the developments discussed in this book:

- How fully are businesses willing to participate in collaborative efforts with consumers?
- Will consumers ultimately develop an antipathy towards social marketing efforts and start responding to them as intrusions or will they come to embrace nontraditional marketing as an acceptable alternative to traditional marketing methods?
- In what ways can traditional and nontraditional marketing approaches better coexist in more fully integrated ways?

- Will the mobile phone replace the personal computer as consumer's primary means of connecting?
- Are print newspapers and magazines destined to be replaced by the electronic format?
- How willing will consumers be to allow marketers access to personal identifying information to facilitate the marketing process and provide greater convenience and personalized communication?

In his attempt to forecast what the future holds for connected marketing, Justin Kirby (2006*b*, p. 273) offered the following ten predictions:

1. Connected marketing will become more strategic, with the focus shifting from promotion (creating remarkable campaigns) to innovation (creating remarkable products).
2. ROI metrics will be mandatory for viral, buzz, and WOM campaigns. "Advocacy rates" and "sales uplift" will become important parts of ROI metrics, displacing traditional measures such as campaign reach.
3. WOM tracking will become a key metric in brand tracking market research.
4. Buzz, viral, and word of mouth marketing will be merged into the wider marketing mix, with online viral marketing adopted and integrated within advertising, WOM within promotions, and buzz within PR.
5. Managing and avoiding *negative* WOM, online and off-line, will be an increasingly important area in connected marketing.
6. Online branded entertainment (advertainment, advergaming, alternate reality games) will be used more as key brand touch-points for entertainment brands.
7. Techniques developed in connected marketing initiatives will be adopted for change management and internal communication.
8. Techniques developed in viral, buzz, and WOM will be increasingly adopted in CRM programs as both retention and acquisition (turning buyers into advocates) tools.
9. Cell phones will develop rapidly as an important medium for spreading connected marketing promotions, such as mobile invitations, SMS barcode discounts, etc.
10. Marketers will eventually be able to locate influencers by zip/postcode, by which point they will be all chasing the same chosen few.... Should we prepare for another paradigm shift in marketing?

It is difficult to imagine anything that Kirby may have missed in his insightful set of predictions, each of which touches upon material presented in this book. Perhaps one prediction that can be added is that marketers will increasingly come to embrace the collaboration of consumers as a fundamental and essential element of the marketing mix ("People"). Consumers may now be in control, but marketers need not respond to this new marketplace reality as a threat and obstinately continue their march backwards into the future. In the optimistic scenario, marketers and consumers will coexist on an equal footing, mutually satisfying their respective needs, and embracing a future that is yet to be written.

REFERENCES

Aaker, D. (1991). *Managing brand equity: Capitalizing on the value of a brand name.* New York: The Free Press.

Abelson, J. (2005, August 7). Gillette tries to capture a whiff of teen market. *The Boston Globe.* Available: http://www.boston.com

Aberdeen Group. (2003, September). *Revisiting affiliate marketing: A new sales tier emerges in the digital commerce network.* An Executive White Paper. Available: http://aberdeen.com

Acceptable Types of Mobile Advertising According to US Mobile Phone Users. (2007, June 26). eMarketer. Available: http://www.emarketer.com

Aditya, R. N. (2001). The psychology of deception in marketing: A conceptual framework for research and practice. *Psychology & Marketing, 18,* 735–61.

Advertising Spending Worldwide, By Media. (2008, June 30). eMarketer. Available: http://www.emarketer.com

Ahari, K. (2007). Word of mouth marketing techniques WOMM. Napa Consulting Group. Available: http://www.slideshare.net

Ahluwalia, R. (2002, September). How prevalent is the negativity effect in consumer environments? *Journal of Consumer Research, 29,* 270–9.

—— Burnkrant, R. E., & Unnava, H. R. (2000). Consumer response to negative publicity. *Journal of Marketing Research, 37,* 203–14.

Allard, S. (2006). Myths and promises of buzz marketing. In J. Kirby & P. Marsden (eds.), *Connected marketing: The viral, buzz and word of mouth revolution* (pp. 197–207). Oxford, UK: Butterworth-Heinemann.

Allport, G. W. & Lepkin, M. (1945). Wartime rumors of waste and special privilege: Why some people believe them. *Journal of Abnormal and Social Psychology, 40,* 3–36.

—— & Postman, L. (1947). *The psychology of rumor.* New-York: Holt, Rinehart and Winston.

Alternative Media Poised for Strong Growth in '08, Despite Slowing Economy. (2008, March 26). Available: http://www.marketingcharts.com

American Consumers Not Connecting with 3G Mobile Phone Technology. (2006, October 25). Available: http://www.3g.co.uk

Anderson, C. (2006). *The long tail: Why the future of business is selling less of more.* New York: Hyperion.

Anderson, E. W. (1998). Customer satisfaction and word of mouth. *Journal of Service Research, 1,* 5–17.

—— & Weitz, B. (1989). Determinants of continuity in conventional industrial channel dyads. *Marketing Science, 8,* 310–23.

—— & Salisbury, L. C. (2003). The formation of market-level expectations and its covariates. *Journal of Consumer Research, 30,* 115–24.

Anderson, M. (2005, March 7). Dissecting "subservient chicken." Adweek. Available: http://www.allbusiness.com

Apple to Focus on Market Penetration Instead of Market Skimming With 3G iPhone. (2008). Available: marketing-ninja.com

ARF/AMA. (1998). 1998 *ARF/AMA Marketing research industry survey.* Available: http://www.marketing-power.com

Armour, S. (2002, February 5). Year brings hard lessons, alters priorities for many. Available: http://www. USAToday.com

Arndt, J. (1967). Role of product-related conversations in the diffusion of a new product. *Journal of Marketing Research, 4,* 291–5.

Assael, H. (1995). *Consumer behavior and marketing action.* Cincinnati, OH: South-Western.

Audrain-Pontevia, A.-F. & Kimmel, A. J. (2008). Negative word of mouth and redress strategies: An exploratory comparison of French and American managers. *Journal of Consumer Satisfaction, Dissatisfaction and Complaining Behavior, 21,* 124–36.

Bagozzi, R. P., Rosa, J. A., Celly, K. S., & Coronel, F. (1998). *Marketing management.* Upper Saddle River, NJ: Prentice Hall.

Baig, E. C. (2009, January 8). Older folks like Wii, PCs and cellphones, too. *USAToday.* Available: http://www.USAToday.com

Bailey, A. A. (2004). Thiscompanysucks.com: The use of the Internet in negative consumer-to-consumer articulations. *Journal of Marketing Communication, 10,* 169–82.

Balter, D. (2008). *The word-of-mouth manual, Vol. II.* Boston, MA: BzzAgent.

Bansal, H. S. & Voyer, P. A. (2000). Word-of-mouth processes within a services purchase decision context. *Journal of Service Research, 3,* 166–77.

Bansal, R. (2004). Urban youth—aliens! *BusinessWorld.* Available: http://www.businessworld.in

Barnes, B. (2007*a*, May 3). When guerrilla marketing backfires on a small firm. *The Wall Street Journal.* Available: http://www.startupjournal.com

—— (2007*b*, December 31). Web playgrounds of the very young. Available: http://www.nytimes.com

Barnhardt, D., Liu, Q., & Serfes, K. (2007). Product customization. *European Economic Review, 51,* 1396–422.

Beal, G. M. & Rogers, E. M. (1957). Informational success in the adoption process of new fabrics. *Journal of Home Economics 49,* 630–4.

Bearden, W. O. & Netemeyer, R. G. (1999). *Handbook of marketing scales: Multi-item measures for marketing and consumer behavior research.* Thousand Oaks, CA: Sage.

—— —— & Teel, J. (1989). Measurement of consumer susceptibility to interpersonal influence. *Journal of Consumer Research, 15,* 473–81.

—— Ingram, T. N., & DeForge, R. W. (2007). *Marketing: Principles and perspectives.* Chicago, IL: McGraw-Hill/Irwin.

Beatty, S. & Smith, S. (1987). External search effort: An investigation across several product categories. *Journal of Consumer Research, 14,* 83–95.

Beckmann, S. C. & Langer, R. (2005, September 6). Netnography: Rich insights from online research. Insights@CBS, no. 14. Available: http://frontpage.cbs.dk

Beer, R. (2002, November 1). MCBA creates interactive poster in campaign for Pretty Polly. *Campaign,* p. 8.

Benedictus, L. (2007, January 30). Psst! Have you heard? *The Guardian.* Available: http://www.guardian.co.uk

Berry, J. & Keller, E. (2003). *The influentials: One American in ten tells the other nine how to vote, where to eat, and what to buy.* New York: Free Press.

Bianco, A. (2004, July 12). The vanishing mass market. *BusinessWeek.* Available: http://www.business-week.com

Billboards Are Talking Back. (2003, August 16). Springwise. Available: http://www.springwise.com

Bird, S. (2008, June 3). New UK law criminalizes stealth marketing techniques. Available: http://www.seomoz.org

Birnbaum, M. H. (2003). Methodological and ethical issues in conducting social psychology research via the Internet. In C. Sansone, C. C. Morf, and A. T. Panter (eds.), *The Sage handbook of methods in social psychology* (pp. 45–70). Thousand Oaks, CA: Sage.

Blackshaw, P. (2006, May 21). "Intimate" vs. "incidental" word-of-mouth. Available: http://www.consumergeneratedmedia.com

Blackwell, R. D., Miniard, P. W., & Engel, J. F. (2005). *Consumer behavior*, 10th ed. Cincinnati, OH: South-Western.

Bloch, M. (2005). Marketing to seniors on the web. Available: http://www.tamingthebeast.net

Blogspotting. (2006, May 23). P&G, online, and word of mouth. Available: http://www.businessweek.com

Bone, P. F. (1992). Determinants of word-of-mouth communications during product consumption. *Advances in Consumer Research, 19*, 579–83.

—— (1995). Word-of-mouth effects on short-term and long-term product judgments. *Journal of Business Research, 32*, 213–23.

Booms, B. H. & Bitner, M. J. (1982). Marketing services by managing the environment. *Cornell Hotel and Restaurant Administration Quarterly, 23*, 35–40.

Borden, N. H. (1964). The concept of the marketing mix. *Journal of Advertising Research, 4*, 2–7.

Bosman, J. (2006, January 31). FreshDirect emphasizes its New York flavor. *The New York Times*. Available: http://www.nytimes.com

Bowman, D. & Narayandas, D. (2001). Managing customer-initiated contacts with manufacturers: The impact on share of category requirements and word-of-mouth behavior. *Journal of Marketing Research, 38*, 281–97.

Boyd, S. (2006, February 3). The social scale of social media: The conversational index. Available: http://www.stoweboyd.com

'Brain Bread' Among Novelty Products Continuing to Be Popular. (2006, June 1). Available: http://www.redorbit.com

Brand Awareness: Boost Mobile. (2009, July 13). Available: http://attackmarketing.wordpress.com

Broadband Households Number 251 Million Worldwide. (2007, March 28). eMarketer. Available: http://www.emarketer.com

Brown, J. J. & Reingen, P. H. (1987). Social ties and word-of-mouth referral behavior. *Journal of Consumer Research, 14*, 350–62.

Brown, R. & Washton, R. (2006). *The kids market in the U.S.* Available: http://www.packagedfacts.com

Brown, S. (2006). Buzz marketing: The next chapter. In J. Kirby & P. Marsden (eds.), *Connected marketing: The viral, buzz and word of mouth revolution* (pp. 208–31). Oxford, UK: Butterworth-Heinemann.

Bruner, G. C., Hensel, P. J., & James, K. E. (2005). *Marketing scales handbook, Vol. IV: Consumer behavior*. Florence, KY: South-Western.

Bruner, R. E. (2004, June 30). Raging cow: The interview. Available: http://www.businessblogconsulting.com

Bryant, A. (2009, May 11). Inclusion and listening are key to success. *International Herald Tribune*, p. 17.

Burcher, N. (2009, March 16). Facebook usage: Dominated by young audience, despite older demographics growing quickly. Available: http://www.nickburcher.com

Burt, T. & London, S. (2004, April 16). Profits in the age of an "audience of one." *The Financial Times*. Available: http://www.bain.com

Burzynski, M. H. & Bayer, J. J. (1977). The effect of positive and negative prior information on motion picture appreciation. *Journal of Social Psychology, 101*, 215–18.

Bush, A., Smith, R., & Martin, C. (1999). The influence of consumer socialization variables on attitude toward advertising: A comparison of African-Americans and Caucasians. *Journal of Advertising, 28,* 13–24.

Butcher, D. (2009, June 24). Heineken targets twenty-somethings with iPhone app. Available: http://www.mobilemarketer.com

Buttle, F. A. (1998). Word of mouth: Understanding and managing referral marketing. *Journal of Strategic Marketing, 6,* 241–54.

BuzzParadise. (2008, January). *BuzzParadise survey.* Available: http://www.slideshare.net

BzzAgent to Expel 10,000 Pests, Revamp Rewards. (2006, June 19). Available: http://www.marketingvox.com

Cakim, I. (2006). Online opinion leaders: A predictive guide for viral marketing campaigns. In J. Kirby & P. Marsden (eds.), *Connected marketing: The viral, buzz and word of mouth revolution* (pp. 107–18). Oxford, UK: Butterworth-Heinemann.

Cameron, P. (1969). Frequency and kinds of words in various social settings, or what the hell's going on? *Pacific Sociological Review, 12,* 101–4.

Carl, W. J. (2006a, May 25). Is negative WOM more frequent online than offline? Available: http://wom-study.blogspot.com

——(2006b). *To tell or not to tell? Assessing the practical effects of disclosure for word-of-mouth marketing agents and their conversational partners.* Working paper, Northeastern University, Department of Communication Studies.

——(2006c). What's all the buzz about?: Everyday communication and the relational basis of word-of-mouth and buzz marketing practices. *Management Communication Quarterly, 19,* 601–34.

——Oles, J., & McGlinn, M. (2007). Measuring the ripple: Creating the G2X relay rate and an industry standard methodology to measure the spread of word of mouth conversations and marketing-relevant outcomes. In Word of Mouth Marketing Association, *Measuring word of mouth, Vol. 3.* Bzz-Agent, Inc. and Northeastern University.

Carlson, J., Cook, S. W., & Stromberg, E. L. (1936). Sex differences in conversation. *Journal of Applied Psychology, 20,* 727–35.

Carr, N. (2008, November 7). Who killed the blogosphere? Available: http://www.roughtype.com

Charpentier, A. (2006, March 1). Unilever lance la "click attitude" [Unilever launches the "click attitude"]. *Marketing, 102,* 62.

Charlett, D., Garland, R., & Marr, N. (1995). How damaging is negative word of mouth? *Marketing Bulletin, 6,* 42–50.

Charlton, A. & Bates, C. (2000). Decline in teenage smoking with rise in mobile phone ownership: Hypothesis. *British Medical Journal, 321,* 1155.

Chen, A. (2008, March 10). *Reader question: What's the difference between "viral marketing" and "word of mouth?"* Available: http://andrewchenblog.com

Chevalier, J. A. & Mayzlin, D. (2006). The effect of word of mouth on sales: Online book reviews. *Journal of Marketing Research, 44,* 345–54.

Childers, T. L. (1986). Assessment of the psychometric properties of an opinion leadership scale. *Journal of Marketing Research, 23,* 184–8.

Chura, H. (2004, July 26). How to calculate word of mouth; Ketchum finds 200 build the buzz. *Advertising Age.*

Cisneros, O. S. (2000, August 14). Legal tips for your "sucks" site. *Wired.* Available: http://www.wired.com

Clifford, S. (2008, July 14). Product placements acquire a life of their own on shows. *The New York Times.* http://www.nytimes.com

Clifford, S. (2009, January 5). HBO is hiding little about big love. *The New York Times*. Available: http://www.nytimes.com

Cohen, N. (2007, September 3). Whiting out the ads, but at what cost? *The New York Times*. Available: http://www.nytimes.com

Coleman, J., Katz, E., & Menzel, H. (1957). The diffusion of an innovation among physicians. *Sociometry, 20*, 253–70.

Corcoran, A., Marsden, P., Zorbach, T., & Röthlingshöfer, B. (2006). Blog marketing. In J. Kirby & P. Marsden (eds.), *Connected marketing: The viral, buzz and word of mouth revolution* (pp. 148–58). Oxford, UK: Butterworth-Heinemann.

Counting Down to Year Zero. (2007, April 9). Available: http://asylum60.blogspot.com

Craik, F. I. M. & Lockhart, R. S. (1972). Levels of processing: A framework for memory research. *Journal of Verbal Learning and Verbal Behavior, 11*, 671–84.

Creswell, J. (2009, July 13). Tricks of any trade, no matter how obscure. *International Herald Tribune*, p. 14.

Cummings, S. X. (2006, December 11). Calling bull$#@! on 3 marketing strategies. Available: http://www.imediaconnection.com

Curran, S. (2007). Changing the game. In J. Kirby & P. Marsden (eds.), *Connected marketing: The viral, buzz and word of mouth revolution* (pp. 129–47). Oxford, UK: Butterworth-Heinemann.

Customer Made. (2006). Available: http://trendwatching.com

Cutts, M. (2007, March 10). Nice piece of viral marketing: NIN. Available: http://www.mattcutts.com

Danaher, P. & Rust, R. (1996). Indirect financial benefits from service quality. *Quality Management, 3*, 63–75.

Daumeyer, R. (2001, January 19). P&G's web marketing strategy shows its bite. *Business Courier*. Available: http://www.bizjournals.com

De Bruyn, A. & Lilien, G. L. (2008). A multi-stage model of word-of-mouth influence through viral marketing. *International Journal of Research in Marketing, 25*, 151–63.

Dell Outreach in the Blogosphere. (2009, April). IdeaStorm overview. Available: http://www.slideshare.net/Dell_Inc/dell-outreach-in-the-blogosphere

Decarlo, T. E., Laczniak, R. N., Motley, C.M., & Ramaswami, S. (2007). Influence of image and familiarity on consumer response to negative word-of-mouth communication about retail entities. *Journal of Marketing Theory and Practice, 15*, 41–51.

Dellarocas, C. & Narayan, R. (2006). *What motivates people to review a product online? A study of the product-specific antecedents of online movie ratings*. Working paper, Robert H. Smith School of Business, University of Maryland.

—— Awad Farag, N., & Zhang, M. (2004, December). Exploring the value of online reviews to organizations: Implications for revenue forecasting and planning. Proceedings of the 25th International Conference on Information Systems (ICIS), Washington, DC.

Dery, M. (1999). *The pyrotechnic insanitarium: American culture on the brink*. NewYork: Grove.

De Tarde, G. (1901). *L'opinion et la foule*. Paris: Felix Alcan.

Dichter, E. (1966, November–December). How WOM advertising works. *Harvard Business Review, 16*, 147–66.

Dick, A. S. & Basu, K. (1994). Customer loyalty: Toward an integrated conceptual framework. *Journal of the Academy of Marketing Science, 22*, 99–113.

Digital Marketing Services. (2004, February 11). *Casual gaming report for AOL*. Available: http://www.dmsdallas.com

Dobele, A. R. & Ward, T. (2003, December). Enhancing word-of-mouth referrals. *ANZMAC 2003 Conference Proceedings*, Adelaide, Australia.

——Toleman, D., & Beverland, M. (2005). Controlled infection! Spreading the brand message through viral marketing. *Business Horizons, 48*, 143–9.

Donney, P. M. & Cannon, J. P. (1997). An examination of the nature of trust in buyer-seller relationships. *Journal of Marketing, 61*, 35–51.

Doritos: You Create Our Super Bowl Commercial. (2006, September 14). *CNNMoney.* Available: http://money.cnn.com

Duan, W., Gu, B., Whinston, A. B. (2008). The dynamics of online word-of-mouth and product sales: An empirical investigation of the movie industry. *Journal of Retailing, 82*, 233–42.

East, R. & Lomax, W. (2007, May). *Researching word of mouth.* Paper presented at the 36th European Marketing Academy Conference, Reykjavik, Iceland.

——Hammond, K., Lomax, W., & Robinson, H. (2005). What is the effect of a recommendation? *The Marketing Review, 5*, 145–57.

————& Wright, M. (2007). The relative incidence of positive and negative word of mouth: A multi-category study. *International Journal of Research in Marketing, 24*, 175–84.

————& Lomax, W. (2008*a*). Measuring the impact of positive and negative word of mouth on brand purchase probability. *International Journal of Research in Marketing, 25*, 215–24.

——Vanhuele, M., & Wright, M. (2008*b*). *Consumer behaviour: Applications in marketing.* London: Sage.

Edelman. (2008, January 22). *2008 Edelman trust barometer.* Available: http://www.edelman.com

Elliott, S. (2006, October 9). Letting consumers control marketing: Priceless. *The New York Times.* Available: http://www.nytimes.com

Ellis, S. (2008, March 12). *The difference between word-of-mouth and viral marketing.* Available: http://startup-marketing.com

Ellsworth, P. C. (1977). From abstract ideas to concrete instances. *American Psychologist, 32*, 604–15.

Engel, J. F., Blackwell, R. D., & Miniard, P. W. (1990). *Consumer behavior,* 6th ed. Chicago, IL: Irwin.

——Kegerreis, R. J., & Blackwell, R. D. (1969). A word-of-mouth communication by the innovator. *Journal of Marketing, 33*, 15–19.

Eurobarometer 60. *Public opinion in the European Union.* Available: http://ec.europa.eu

Evans, R. (2007). Effective use of email marketing personalization. Available: http://www.opt-in-email-marketing.org

Everitt, L. (2004). Market for seniors matures in Austria. *Natural Grocery Buyer,* Summer. Available: http://www.newhope.com

Everyone Is Talking About Mobile Social Networking. (2008, May 8). eMarketer. Available: http://www.eMarketer.com

Eyram, S. (2006). The 4 P's of email marketing. Available: http://www.e-bc.ca

Feick, L. & Gierl, H. (1996). Skepticism about advertising: A comparison of East and West German consumers. *International Journal of Research in Marketing, 13*, 227–35.

——& Price, L. L. (1987). The market maven: A diffuser of marketplace information. *Journal of Marketing, 51*, 83–97.

Feldman, J. M. & Lynch, J. G. (1988). Self-generated validity and other effects of measurement on belief, attitude, intention, and behavior. *Journal of Applied Psychology, 73*, 421–35.

Feldman, S. P. & Spencer, M. C. (1965). The effect of personal influence in the selection of consumer services. In P. D. Bennett (ed.), *Fall conference of the American Marketing Association.* Chicago, IL: American Marketing Association.

Fennell, G. & Allenby, G. M. (2004). An integrated approach: Market definition, market segmentation and brand positioning create a powerful combination. *Marketing Research, 16,* 28–34.

Ferguson, B. (2006). Black buzz and red ink: The financial impact of negative consumer comments on US airlines. In J. Kirby & P. Marsden (eds.), *Connected marketing: The viral, buzz and word of mouth revolution* (pp. 185–96). Oxford, UK: Butterworth-Heinemann.

Fieseler, C., Fleck, M., & Stanoevska-Slabeva, K. (2008). An examination of the corporate social responsibility discourse in the blogosphere. In K. Podnar & Z. Jancic (eds.), *Proceedings of the 13th International Conference on Corporate and Marketing Communications* (pp. 63–9). Ljubljana, Slovenia: University of Ljubljana.

Fill, C. (1999). *Marketing communications: Contexts, contents, and strategies,* 2nd ed. Essex, UK: Pearson.

First Interactive Times Square Billboard Asks New Yorkers to Vote; Global Beauty Brand Dove Asks: "Do You Think Our Advertising Is Beautiful?" (2004, October 22). *BusinessWire.* Available: http://www.businesswire.com

Fisher, R. F. (1993). Social desirability bias and the validity of indirect questioning. *Journal of Consumer Research, 20,* 303–13.

Fitchett, J. (2005). The twenty-first-century consumer society. In A. J. Kimmel (ed.), *Marketing communication: New approaches, technologies, and styles* (pp. 42–62). Oxford, UK: Oxford University Press.

Fitzgerald, K. (2002, October 21). Use of sidewalk "brand ambassadors" increases. Available: http://www.aef.com

Fitzgerald, M. (2009, April 6). Online market research takes off. Available: http://www.btobonline.com

Fitzpatrick, R. L. & Reynolds, J. K. (1997). *False profits: Seeking financial and spiritual deliverance in multi-level marketing and pyramid schemes.* Charlotte, NC: Herald Press.

Fitzsimons, G. J. & Lehmann, D. R. (2004). When unsolicited advice yields contrary responses. *Marketing Science, 23,* 82–95.

Flitter, B. (2007, March 27). Science class with Dupont. Available: http://www.pheedo.info

Flynn, L. R., Goldsmith, R. E., & Eastman, J. K. (1996). Opinion leaders and opinion seekers: Two new measurement scales. *Journal of the Academy of Marketing Science, 24,* 137–47.

Fornell, C. & Bockstein, F. L. (1982). Two structural equation models: Lisrel and Plss applied to exit-voice theory. *Journal of Marketing Research, 19,* 440–52.

Fournier, S. (1998). Consumers and their brands: Developing relationship theory in consumer research. *The Journal of Consumer Research, 24,* 343–73.

Fox Interactive Media, Inc. (2007). *Never ending friending: A journey into social networking.* Available: http://blogs.forrester.com

Foxton, J. (2006). Live buzz marketing. In J. Kirby & P. Marsden (eds.), *Connected marketing: The viral, buzz and word of mouth revolution* (pp. 24–46). Oxford, UK: Butterworth-Heinemann.

Freedman, J. (1969). Role-playing: Psychology by consensus. *Journal of Personality and Social Psychology, 13,* 107–14.

Frenzen, J. K. & Nakamoto, K. (1993). Structure, cooperation, and the flow of market information. *Journal of Consumer Research, 20,* 360–75.

Friedberg, J., Pfleiger, A., & Weisberg, A. (2004). Undercover agency: The ethics of stealth marketing. In L. Burkhart et al. (eds.), *Confronting information ethics in the new millennium* (pp. 92–106). Boulder, CO: Ethica.

Furse, D., Punj, G., & Stewart, W. (1984). A typology of individual search strategies among purchasers of new automobiles. *Journal of Consumer Research, 10*, 417–31.

Ganesan, S. (1994). Determinants of long-term orientation in buyer-seller relationships. *Journal of Marketing, 58*, 1–19.

Gardner, W. D. (2009, July 7). Broadband to reach 640 million households by 2013. *Information Week.* Available: http://www.informationweek.com

Geller, D. M. (1982). Alternatives to deception: why, what, and how? In J. E. Sieber (ed.), *The ethics of social research: Surveys and experiments.* New York: Springer-Verlag.

Geyskens, I., Steenkamp, J.-B., Scheer, L. K., & Kumar, N. (1996). The effects of trust and interdependence on relationship commitment: A trans-Atlantic study. *International Journal of Research in Marketing, 13*, 303–17.

Gillin, P. (2007). *The new influencers.* Sanger, CA: Quill Driver Books.

Gilly, M. C., Graham, J. L., Wolfinbarger, M. F., & Yale, L. J. (1998). A dyadic study of interpersonal information search. *Journal of the Academy of Marketing Science, 26*, 83–100.

Gladwell, M. (1997, March 17). The coolhunt. *The New Yorker*, pp. 78–85.

—— (2000). *The tipping point: How little things can make a big difference.* New York: Little, Brown.

Godes, D. & Mayzlin, D. (2004). Using online conversations to study word of mouth communication. *Marketing Science, 23*, 545–60.

Godin, S. (2003). *Purple cow: Transform your business by being remarkable.* New York: Penguin Group.

—— (2007, October 17). Is viral marketing the same as word of mouth? Available: http://sethgodin. typepad.com

Gogoi, P. (2006, October 9). Wal-Mart's Jim and Laura: The real story. *Business Week.* Available: http://www. businessweek.com

Gold, K. (2005, April 9). Conversion metrics 101: Defining success at your website. Available: http:// chiefmarketer.com

Good, R. (2007, April 19). *Online virtual worlds: A mini guide.* Available: http://www.techsoup.org

Google Sites' Share of Online Video Market Expands. (2008, January 17). Available: http://www.comscore.com

Gordon, I. (1997). *Relationship marketing.* Toronto, CA: Wiley.

Granovetter, M. S. (1973). The strength of weak ties. *American Journal of Sociology, 78*, 1360–80.

Green, P. (2007, September 6). Romancing the flat pack: IKEA, repurposed. *The New York Times.* Available: http://www.nytimes.com

Greenberg, J. Eskew, D. E. (1993). The role of role playing in organizational research. *Journal of Management, 19*, 221–41.

Greenspan, R. (2004, April 2). Media multitaskers may miss messages. Available: http://www.clickz.com

Gupta, S. (2005, August 19). Jeff Jarvis vs. Dell: Blogger's complaint becomes viral nightmare. Available: http://www.mediapost.com/publications/?fa = Articles.showArticle&art_aid = 33307

Hall, S. (2006, January 11). *Coke lies, misleads with fake "Zero" blog.* Available: http://www.adrants.com

Halstead, D. (2002). Negative word of mouth: Substitute for or supplement to consumer complaints? *Journal of Consumer Satisfaction, Dissatisfaction and Complaining Behavior, 15*, 1–12.

Hanna, N. & Wosniak, R. (2001). *Consumer behavior: An applied approach.* Englewood Cliffs, NJ: Prentice Hall.

Health & Beauty Care. (1998, December 1). *Promo.* Available: http://promomagazine.com

Hearst, M. (2003, October 17). What is text mining? Available: http://people.ischool.berkeley.edu

Heath, C. (1996). Do people prefer to pass along good or bad news? Valence and relevance of news as predictors of transmission propensity. *Organizational Behavior and Human Decision Processes, 68*, 79–95.

Hedgeman, J. (2004, August 23). CityAlert.com back with Heineken USA for "Own the Weekend" campaign. Available: http://www.free-press-release.com

Herr, P. M., Kardes, F. R., & Kim, J. (1991). Effects of word-of-mouth and product-attribute information on persuasion: An accessibility-diagnosticity perspective. *Journal of Consumer Research, 17*, 454–62.

Heskett, J. L., Sasser, W. E. Jr., & Schlesinger L. A. (1997). *The service profit chain.* New York: The Free Press.

Hetherington, K. (1998). *Expressions of identity: Space, performance, politics.* Thousand Oaks, CA: Sage.

Hobson, N. (2009, March 11). Making a viral video. Available: http://www.nevillehobson.com

Hoegg, R., Martignoni, R., Meckel, M., Stanoevska-Slabeva, K. (2006). Overview of business models for Web 2.0 communities. In *Proceedings of GeNeMe* (pp. 23–37). Available: http://www.alexandria.unisg.ch

Hogart-Scott, P. & Kirby, J. (2006, October). Viral, buzz and word of mouth. *Marketing Magazine*, pp. 94–7.

Holden, W. (2007, August 13). Press release: Mobile user-generated content revenues to rise tenfold by 2012. Available: http://www.juniperresearch.com

Holmes, J. & Lett, J. (1977). Product sampling and word of mouth. *Journal of Advertising Research, 17*, 35–45.

Honda. (2004, April 8). Dramatic first quarter success puts company on course for 90,000 sales. Available: http://www.honda.co.uk

Hot Today, Not Tomorrow: Retailers Face the Terrible Teens. Knowledge@Wharton. Available: http://knowledge.wharton.upenn.edu

How Sweet It Is. (1982, July 26). *Time.* Available: http://www.time.com

How to Use Social Networking Sites for Lead Generation. (2007, September 26). Marketing Sherpa. Available: http://www.marketingsherpa.com

Huston, L. & Sakkab, N. (2006, March). Connect and develop: Inside Procter & Gamble's new model for innovation. *Harvard Business Review*, pp. 58–66.

iProspect Offline Channel Influence on Online Search Behavior Study. (2007, August). Available: http://www.iprospect.com

I Sold It Through the Grapevine. (2006, May 29). *Business Week.* Available: http://www.businessweek.com

Israel, S. (2005, June 29). Case study: The rise and fall of Vichy. Available: http://redcouch.typepad.com

Jacoby, R. (1999). *The end of utopia: Politics and culture in an age of apathy.* New York: Basic Books.

Jaffe, J. (2007). *Join the conversation: How to engage marketing-weary consumers with the power of community, dialogue, and partnership.* Hoboken, NJ: Wiley.

Jaret, J. (2006, March 23). Dear Web log: Hated the shampoo, loved the soap. *The New York Times.* Available: http://www.nytimes.com

Jarvis, J. (2007, October 17). Dell learns to listen. *Business Week.* Available: http://www.businessweek.com

Jennings, R. & Jackson, P. (2003, September). *The guide to integrated marketing success.* Available: http://www.forrester.com

Johnson, G. (2001, July 25). This summer, it's fast pitch everywhere. *The International Herald Tribune*, p. 9.

Jones, M. A. (1999). Entertaining shopping experiences: An exploratory investigation. *Journal of Retailing and Consumer Services, 6*, 129–39.

Jones, S. (2003, July 6). Let the games begin: Gaming technology and entertainment among college students. Available: http://www.pewinternet.org

Joyner, M. (2005). *The irresistible offer: How to sell your product or service in 3 seconds or less.* Hoboken, NJ: John Wiley & Sons.

Jupiter Communications. (1999). *Guerrilla marketing: Breaking through the clutter with word of mouth.* A Jupiter Communications' publication.

Jurvetson, S. (1998). What is viral marketing? Available: http://news.com.com

Kamins, M. A., Folkes, V. S., & Perner, L. (1997). Consumer responses to rumors: Good news, bad news. *Journal of Consumer Psychology, 6,* 165–87.

Karp, S. (2007, August 6). Publicis/Digitas on all-digital advertising, outsourcing, and competing with Google Yahoo Microsoft. *Publishing 2.0.* Available: http://publishing2.com

Katz, E. (1961). The social itinerary of technical changes: Two studies in the diffusion of innovation. *Human Organization 20,* 70–82.

—— & Lazarsfeld, P. F. (1955). *Personal influence.* Glencoe, IL: Free Press.

Keetch, P. (2007, October 22). The 7 keys to marketing success. Available: http://ezinearticles.com

Keiningham, T. L., Cooil, B., Andreassen, T. W., & Aksoy, L. (2007). A longitudinal examination of net promoter and firm revenue growth. *Journal of Marketing, 71,* 39–51.

Keller, E. & Berry, J. (2005, March). *The state of WOM, 2005: The consumer perspective.* Paper presented at the Word-Of-Mouth Marketing Association Summit, Chicago, IL.

—— & Fay, B. (2006). Single source WOM measurement. Available: http://cats.blogilvy.be

Kemp, M. B. (2008, May). *Social computing dresses up for marketing business—Learn from the changing marketing paradigm.* Presented at the Marketing 2.0 Conference, Paris, France.

Kiel, G. C. & Layton, R. A. (1981). Dimensions of consumer information seeking behavior. *Journal of Marketing Research, 18,* 233–9.

Killian, V. (2009, April). IdeaStorm overview. Available: http://www.slideshare.net

Kimmel, A. J. (2004). *Rumors and rumor control: A manager's guide to understanding and combatting rumors.* Mahwah, NJ: Lawrence Erlbaum.

—— (2007a). *Ethical issues in behavioral research: Basic and applied perspectives.* Malden, MA: Blackwell.

—— (2007b, June 1). Proper management: Three tips help harness consumers' growing power. *Marketing News,* p. 14.

—— (2009, April). *Beliefs and misconceptions about word of mouth in the consumer marketplace.* Paper presented at the 14th International Conference on Corporate Marketing Communication. Nicosia, Cyprus.

—— —— & Audrain-Pontevia (2010). Analysis of commercial rumors from the perspective of marketing managers: Rumor prevalence, effects, and control tactics. *Journal of Marketing Communication,* in press.

—— & Keefer, R. (1991). Psychological correlates of the transmission and acceptance of rumors about AIDS. *Journal of Applied Social Psychology, 21,* 1608–28.

—— & Tissier-Desbordes, E. (1999). Males, masculinity, and consumption: An exploratory investigation. In B. Dubois, T. M. Lowrey, L. J. Shrum, & M. Vanhuele (eds.), *European Advances in Consumer Research, 1999, Vol. 4* (pp. 243–51). Provo, UT: Association for Consumer Research.

King, S. A. (1996). Researching Internet communities: Proposed ethical guidelines for the reporting of results. *The Information Society, 12,* 119–27.

Kirby, J. (2006a). Viral marketing. In J. Kirby & P. Marsden (eds.), *Connected marketing: The viral, buzz and word of mouth revolution* (pp. 87–106). Oxford, UK: Butterworth-Heinemann.

Kirby, J. (2006*b*). Conclusion: The future of connected marketing. In J. Kirby & P. Marsden (eds.), *Connected marketing: The viral, buzz and word of mouth revolution* (pp. 267–74). Oxford, UK: Butterworth-Heinemann.

—— & Marsden, P. (eds.) (2006). *Connected marketing: The viral, buzz and word of mouth revolution.* Oxford, UK: Butterworth-Heinemann.

Klein, N. (1999). No logo: Taking aim at the brand bullies. New York: Picador.

Knapp, R. H. (1994). A psychology of rumor. *Public Opinion Quarterly, 8,* 22–7.

Know What to Do: Campaign to Convince Canadians First Aid Training Is a Smart Investment. (2007, September 5). Available: http://www.redcross.ca

Knowledge@Wharton. (2006, March 8). Beware of dissatisfied consumers: They like to blab. Available: http://knowledge.wharton.upenn.edu

Knox, S. & Walker, D. (1995). *New empirical perspectives on brand loyalty: Implications for segmentation strategy and equity.* Working paper, Cranfield School of Management.

Kotler, P. (2003). *Marketing management,* 11th ed. Upper Saddle River, NJ: Prentice-Hall.

—— Armstrong, G., Saunders, J., & Wong, V. (2002). *Principles of marketing,* 3rd European ed. Harlow, UK: Prentice-Hall/*Financial Times.*

Kozinets, R. V. (1998). On netnography: Initial reflections on consumer research investigations of cyberculture. *Association for Consumer Research, 25,* 366–71.

—— (2002). The field behind the screen: Using netnography for marketing research in online communities. *Journal of Marketing Research, 39,* 61–72.

Kramer, C. (2006, October 13). What the heck is a flog? Available: http://chriskramer.blogspot.com

Laczniak, R. N., Decarlo, T. E., & Ramaswami, S. N. (2001). Consumers' responses to negative word-of-mouth communication: An attribution theory perspective. *Journal of Consumer Psychology, 11,* 57–74.

Landis, M. H. & Burtt, H. E. (1924). A study of conversations. *Journal of Comparative Psychology, 4,* 81–9.

Langenderfer, J. & Shimp, T. A. (2001). Consumer vulnerability to scams, swindles, and fraud: A new theory of visceral influences on persuasion. *Psychology & Marketing, 18,* 763–83.

Lau, G. T. & Ng, S. (2001). Individual and situational factors influencing negative word-of-mouth behaviour. *Canadian Journal of Administrative Sciences, 18,* 163–78.

Lavidge, R. J. & Steiner, G. A. (1961). A model for predictive measurements of advertising effectiveness. *Journal of Marketing, 25,* 59–62.

Lazarsfeld, P., Berelson, B. & Gaudent, H. (1944). *The people's choice.* New York: Columbia University Press.

LeBrun, M. (2009, February 5). A social media best practice: The value of growing your share of conversation. Available: http://www.mediaphilosopher.com

Lee, H. (2009, January 31). Web site and social media metrics you should monitor. Available: http://www.problogger.net

Lenhart, A. & Fox, S. (2006). Bloggers: A portrait of the Internet's new storytellers. *Pew Internet & American Life Project.* Available: http://www.pewinternet.org

—— Madden, M., MacGill, A. R., & Smith, A. (2007, December 19). *Teens and social media.* Pew Internet and American Life Project. Available: http://www.pewinternet.org

Le Quoc, K. & Favier, J. (2008, April 25). Reaching Europeans: From creating awareness to the act of purchase. Available: http://www.forrester.com

Levin, J. & Arluke, A. (1985). An exploratory analysis of sex differences in gossip. *Sex Roles, 12,* 281–6.

Levine, M. & Pownall, S. (2004). Best practice information trends—What works? Available: http://www.roymorgan.com

Levine, R., Locke, C., Searls, D., & Weinberger, D. (2000). *The Cluetrain Manifesto: The end of business as usual.* Cambridge, MA: Perseus.

Lévy, M. & O'Donoghue, D. (2005). New trends in the promotion of companies and brands to stakeholders: A holistic approach. In A. J. Kimmel (ed.), *Marketing communication: New approaches, technologies, and styles* (pp. 11–22). Oxford, UK: Oxford University Press.

Li, C. (2007, June 21). How consumers use social networks. Available: http://www.eranium.at

—— & Bernoff, J. (2008). *Groundswell: Winning in a world transformed by social technologies.* Cambridge, MA: Harvard Business School Press.

Liu, B. (2007). *Web data mining: Exploring hyperlinks, content, and usage data.* Springer: Berlin.

Liu, Y. (2006). Word of mouth for movies: Its dynamics and impact on box office revenue. *Journal of Marketing, 70,* 74–89.

Lomax, A. (2004, September 14). Oprah's product placement. Available: http://www.fool.com

Lowrey, T. M., Shrum, L. J., & McCarty, J. A. (2005). The future of television advertising. In A. J. Kimmel (ed.), *Marketing communication: New approaches, technologies, and styles* (pp. 113–32). Oxford, UK: Oxford University Press.

Luchter, L. (2007, September 5). Viral campaigns falling short, says JupiterResearch. Online Media Daily. Available: http://www.mediapost.com

Lynch, J. G., Marmorstein, H., & Weigold, M. F. (1988). Choices from sets including remembered brands: Use of recalled attributes and prior overall evaluations. *Journal of Consumer Research, 15,* 169–84.

Macnamara, J. (2009, January 11). 10 social media metrics. Available: http://www.themeasurementstandard.com

Madansky, M. & Alban, M. (2007). Conexión cultural/connected culture: Research results on US Hispanic use of media and technology. Available: us.i1.yimg.com/us.yimg.com

Madsen, H. (1996, December). Reclaim the deadzone. The beleaguered Web banner can be zapped into an effective and eye-popping advertising shingle. But radical surgery awaits. *Wired, 4,* 206–20.

Mangold, W. G., Miller, F. & Brockway, G. R. (1999). Word-of-mouth communication in the service marketplace. *Journal of Services Marketing, 13*(1), 73–89.

Mark, D. H. (2008, September). Dell's experiment with online communities. Available: http://www.slideshare.net

Marketers Must Change How They Appeal to Consumers. (2005, April 18). BNET Business Network. Available: http://findarticles.com

Marketing Sherpa. (2009). Marketing Sherpa social media marketing and PR benchmark survey 2008. Available: http://www.marketingsherpa.com

Marsden, P. (2006*a*). Seed to spread: How seeding trials ignite epidemics of demand. In J. Kirby & P. Marsden (eds.), *Connected marketing: The viral, buzz and word of mouth revolution* (pp. 4–23). Oxford, UK: Butterworth-Heinemann.

—— (2006*b*). Introduction and summary. In J. Kirby & P. Marsden (eds.), *Connected marketing: The viral, buzz and word of mouth revolution* (pp. xv–xxxv). Oxford, UK: Butterworth-Heinemann.

Martin, D. (1999, October 28). Linda Perlozza, 54, marketer who aided "Trivial Pursuit." *The New York Times.* Available: http://www.nytimes.com

Martin, N. (2008, January 8). Study names Facebook and MySpace "types." Available: http://www.telegraph.co.uk

The Mass Market Is Dead. (2004, July). BNET Business Network. Available: http://findarticles.com

Mathew, M. & Manda, S. (2005). *P&G's tremor: Reinventing marketing by word of mouth.* ICFAI Business School Case Development Centre, Hyderabad, India.

Mathy, R. M., Kerr, D. L., and Haydin, B. M. (2003). Methodological rigor and ethical considerations in Internet-mediated research. *Psychotherapy: Theory, Research, Practice, Training, 40,* 77–85.

Maxham, J. G., III & Netemeyer, R. G. (2002). A longitudinal study of complaining customers' evaluations of multiple service failures and recovery efforts. *Journal of Marketing, 66,* 57–71.

McAlexander, J. H., Schouten, J. W., & Koenig, H. F. (2002). Building brand community. *Journal of Marketing, 66,* 38–54.

McConnell, B. & Huba, J. (2002). *Creating customer evangelists: How loyal customers become a volunteer sales force.* New York: Kaplan Business.

McGlinn, M. & Wylie, S. (2005). *The value of managed word-of-mouth programs.* BzzAgent, Inc. White Paper. Available: http://www.bima.org/whitepapers_docs/BzzAgent_The%20Value%20of%20Managed%20WOM.pdf

McGuire, W. J. (1978). An information processing model of advertising effectiveness. In H. L. Davis & A. J. Silk (eds.), *Behavioral and management science in marketing.* New York: Ronald/Wiley.

McLaren, C. (1998, Fall/Winter). "I'm with the brand": The celebrity as fan. *Stay Free,* pp. 25–8.

McLuhan, M. & Fiore, Q. (1967). *The medium is the massage.* New York: Bantam Books.

McNeal, J. U. (2007). *On becoming a consumer: Development of consumer behavior patterns in childhood.* Boston, MA: Butterworth-Heinemann.

——(1992). *Kids as customers: A handbook for marketing to children.* Lanham, MD: Lexington Books.

The Media Center. (2004, March). Simultaneous media usage briefing. Available: http://www.bigresearch.com

Mercado, A. (2006, August 8). 19 viral marketing strategies. Killer App Technologies Marketing News. Available: http://www.killerappcompany.com

Mermet, G. (1998). *Tendances: Les nouveaux consommateurs.* Paris: Larousse.

Mikkelson, B. & Mikkelson, D. P. (2006, October 10). Cog. *The New York Times* Available: http://www.snopes.com

Miled, H. B. & Le Louarn, P. (1994). Analyse comparative de deux échelles de mesure du leadership d'opinion: Validité et interpretation. [Comparative analysis of two opinion leadership scales: Validity and interpretation.] *Recherches et Applications en Marketing, 9,* 23–51.

Miller, A. G. (1972). Role playing: An alternative to deception; a review of the evidence. *American Psychologist, 27,* 623–36.

Mindlin, A. (2007, June 4). No, not everyone skips the commercials. *The New York Times.* Available: http://www.nytimes.com

——(2008a, July 21). Aah, remember your first cellphone? *The New York Times.* Available: http://www.nytimes.com

——(2008b, February 19). Word of mouth and enriching of wallet. *The New York Times.* Available: http://www.nytimes.com

Minow, N. (2004, October 7). Procter & Gamble's Tremor targets young girls and minors for viral marketing. Available: http://newmediasphere.blogs.com

Misner, I. R. (1994). *The world's best known marketing secret, building your business with word-of-mouth marketing.* Austin, TX: Bard & Stephen.

Mitchell, A. (2008, March 6). The only number you need to know does not add up to much. Available: http://www.marketingweek.co.uk

Mittal, B. & Lassar, W. M. (1998). Why do customers switch? The dynamics of satisfaction versus loyalty. *The Journal of Services Marketing, 12* 177–94.

Mizerski, R. W. (1982). An attributional explanation of the disproportionate influence of unfavorable information. *Journal of Consumer Research, 9*, 301–10.

Moore, H. T. (1922). Further data concerning sex differences. *Journal of Abnormal and Social Psychology, 17*, 210–14.

Moore, R. E. (2003). From genericide to viral marketing: On "brand." *Language & Communication, 23*, 331–57.

Moorman, C. G., Zaltman, G., & Deshpandé, R. (1992). Relationships between providers and users of marketing research: The dynamic of trust within and between organizations. *Journal of Marketing Research, 29*, 314–29.

Mootee, I. (2004). *High intensity marketing.* Canada: SA Press.

Morales, L. (2004, September 14). Oprah's fully loaded giveaway. *The Washington Post.* Available: http://www.washingtonpost.com

Morgan, G. (1988). *Riding the waves of change: Developing managerial competencies for a turbulent world.* San Francisco, CA: Jossey-Bass.

Morgan, R. M. & Hunt, S. D. (1994). The commitment-trust theory of relationship marketing. *Journal of Marketing, 58*, 20–38.

Mowen, J. C. (1995). *Consumer behavior,* 4th ed. Englewood Cliffs, NJ: Prentice-Hall.

Moynihan, R. (2008). Key opinion leaders: Independent experts or drug representatives in disguise? *BMJ, 336*, 1402–3.

MS Celebrates Worldwide Halo 3 Success. (2007, October 4). Kikizo. Available: http://games.kikizo.com

Mueller, D. J. (1986). *Measuring social attitudes: A handbook for researchers and practitioners.* New York: Teacher's College Press.

Mulhall, L. (2006). Brewing buzz. In J. Kirby & P. Marsden (eds.), *Connected Marketing: The viral, buzz and word of mouth revolution* (pp. 59–70). Oxford, UK: Butterworth-Heinemann.

Muñiz, A. M., Jr. & O'Guinn, T. C. (2001). Brand community. *Journal of Consumer Research, 27*, 412–31.

—— —— (2005). Marketing communications in a world of consumption and brand communities. In A. J. Kimmel (ed.), *Marketing communication: New approaches, technologies, and* styles (pp. 63–85). Oxford, UK: Oxford University Press.

Murphy, X. (2005, September 1). 4 common errors marketers make when targeting people of Caribbean heritage. Available: http://www.jamaicans.com

My Starbucks Idea. (2008). Available: http://mystarbucksidea.force.com/ideaHome/

Natividad, A. (2007, February 16). NIN builds album hype with somber world forecasts. Available: http://www.adrants.com

Naylor, G. & Kleiser, S. B. (2000). Negative versus positive word-of-mouth: An exception to the rule. *Journal of Satisfaction, Dissatisfaction and Complaining Behavior, 13*, 26–36.

Newman, J. X. & Staelin, R. (1972). Pre-purchase information seeking for new cars and major household appliances. *Journal of Marketing Research, 9*, 249–57.

Nosek, B. A., Banaji, M. R., and Greenwald, A. G. (2002). E-research: Ethics, security, design, and control in psychological research on the Internet. *Journal of Social Issues, 58*, 161–76.

O'Connor, J. & Galvin, E. (2001). *Marketing in the digital age,* 2nd ed. Harlow, UK: Pearson Education.

Oetting, M. (2006). How to manage connected marketing. In J. Kirby & P. Marsden (eds.), *Connected marketing: The viral, buzz and word of mouth revolution* (pp. 232–66). Oxford, UK: Butterworth-Heinemann.

Ogilvy, D. (1985). *Ogilvy on advertising*. New York: Vintage.

O'Leary, N. (2009, May 18). BzzAgent goes social with BzzScapes. *Adweek*. Available: http://www.adweek.com

One New Blog Created Every Second Means Your's Is Irrelevant Unless. (2009, April 27). Available: http://www.articlesbase.com

Onishi, N. (2006, September 4). In a graying Japan, lower shelves and wider aisles. *The New York Times*. Available: http://travel2.nytimes.com

On the Tips of Their Tongues. (2006, November 23). *The New York Times*. Available: http://www.nytimes.com

Oosterwijk, L. & Loeffen, A. (2005). *How to use buzz marketing effectively?* Unpublished manuscript, Mälardalen International Master Academy. Available: http://www.eki.mdh.se

O'Reilly, T. (2005, September 30). *What is Web 2.0? Design patterns and business models for the next generation of software*. Available: http://www.oreillynet.com

Owyang, J. (2008, March 20). *Where customers submit, discuss, and vote ideas: "My Starbucks Ideas."* Available: http://www.web-strategist.com

Pappas, C. (2003, June). The rolling thrones: How Charmin uses bathroom humor to increase sales 14 percent. Available: http://www.exhibitoronline.com

Peppers, D. & Rogers, M. (2004). *Managing customer relationships: A strategic framework*. New York: Wiley.

Perera, P. (2006). Segmentation of consumer markets and effective marketing. *CIM Marketing Canada, 2*, 1–3.

Peterson, R. A. & Wilson, W. R. (1992). Measuring customer satisfaction: Fact or artifact? *Journal of the Academy of Marketing Science, 20*, 61–71.

Pezzo, M. V. & Beckstead, J. W. (2006). A multilevel analysis of rumor transmission: Effects of anxiety and belief in two field experiments. *Basic and Applied Social Psychology, 28*, 91–100.

Pfanner, E. (2008, July 21). Reading device enlisted to help French papers. *The New York Times*, p. C6.

Pine, B. J., II & Gilmore, J. H. (2000). *Markets of one: Creating customer-unique value through mass customization*. Boston, MA: Harvard Business School Press.

PlayStation Ads, Disguised as Graffiti, Spark Controversy. (2005, December 29). *USA Today*. Available: http://www.usatoday.com

Polinchock, D. (2006, November 26). Charmin bathrooms in Times Square. Available: http://blog.future-lab.net

Pousttchi, K. & Wiedermann, D. G. (2007). *Success factors in mobile viral marketing: A multi-case study approach*. Proceedings of the 6th International Conference on Mobile Business, pp. 1–8.

Pratt, S. (2008, March 27). A trip to the Sample Lab. PBS transcript. Available: http://www.pbs.org

Procter & Gamble Expands Its Utilization of Innocentive.com's Open Innovation Marketplace. (2008, April 22). Available: http://www.marketwire.com

"Push Marketing Versus Pull Marketing." (14 August, 2006). Available: www.morebusiness.com

Quelch, J. (2008, July 2). How Starbucks' growth destroyed brand value. *Harvard Business Review*. Available: http://blogs.hbr.org

Radio Rules with Female Teens. (2001, Fall). Available: http://www.aef.com

Rainie, L. (2007, January 31). *28% of online Americans have used the Internet to tag content*. Available: http://technorati.com

Ralli, T. (2005, October 24). Brand blogs capture the attention of some companies. *The New York Times*, p. C6.

Redman, R. (14 November, 2003). Steve Jobs: CEO, Apple. *CRN*. Available: http://www.crn.com.

Reichheld, F. F. (1996). Learning from customer defections. *Harvard Business Review, 74*, 56–61.

—— (2003, Nov.–Dec.). The one number you need to grow. *Harvard Business Review, 81*, pp. 1–11.

—— & Sasser, W. E. (1990). Zero defections: Quality comes to services. *Harvard Business Review, 68*, 105–11.

Reingen, P. & Kernan, J. (1986). Analysis of referral networks in marketing: Methods and illustration. *Journal of Marketing Research, 23*, 370–80.

Rhodes, M. (2009*a*, April 3). Using experts to get real engagement in online communities. Available: http://blog.freshnetworks.com

—— (2009*b*, May 12). Build your own community or go where people are? Do both. Available: http://blog.freshnetworks.com

Richins, M. L. (1983). Negative word-of-mouth by dissatisfied consumers: A pilot study. *Journal of Marketing, 4*, 68–78.

—— (1984). Word-of-mouth communication as negative information. In T. C. Kinnear (ed.), *Advances in consumer research* (pp. 697–702). Provo, UT: Association for Consumer Research.

Ring, P. S. & Van De Van, A. H. (1992). Structuring cooperative relationships between organizations. *Strategic Management Journal, 13*, 483–98.

RNCOS Releases a New Report—3G Market Forecast to 2010. (2008, July 16). Available: http://www.free-press-release.com

Roberts, K. (2007, August 31). Sampling Japanese style. Available: http://krconnect.blogspot.com

Rodgers, Z. (2004, May 28). Marketers pay their way to the youth market. *ClickZ*. Available: http://www.clickz.com

Rogers, E. & Shoemaker, F. F. (1971). *Communication of innovations: A cross-cultural approach*. New York: Free Press.

Rosen, E. (2002). *The anatomy of buzz: How to create word-of-mouth marketing*. New York: Doubleday/Currency.

Rosnow, R. L. & Kimmel, A. J. (1999). Rumors. In A. E. Kazdin (ed.), *Encyclopedia of psychology, Vol. 7* (pp. 122–3). New York: Oxford University Press & American Psychological Association.

—— & Rosenthal, R. (2005). *Beginning behavioral research: A conceptual primer*, 5th ed. Upper Saddle River, NJ: Pearson.

—— Yost, J. H., & Esposito, J. L. (1986). Belief in rumor and likelihood of rumor transmission. *Language and Communication, 6*, 189–94.

Ruebhausen, O. M. & Brim, O. G., Jr. (1966). Privacy and behavioral research. *American Psychologist, 21*, 423–37.

Rusticus, S. (2006). Creating brand advocates. In J. Kirby & P. Marsden (eds.), *Connected marketing: The viral, buzz and word of mouth revolution* (pp. 47–58). Oxford, UK: Butterworth-Heinemann.

Ryu, G. & Feick, L. (2007). A penny for your thoughts: Referral reward programs and referral likelihood. *Journal of Marketing, 71*, 84–94.

San-Galli, N., Krouglikoff, A., & Kimmel, A. J. (2005). *Actimel case study*. ESCP-EAP Marketing Department, Paris, France.

San Miguel, R. (2008, August 13). Facebook stands atop social networking world. *TechNewsWorld*. Available: http://www.technewsworld.com

Schiffman, L. G. & Kanuk, L. L. (2006). *Consumer behavior*, 9th ed. Englewood Cliffs, NJ: Prentice-Hall.

Schlosser, E. (2001). *Fast food nation.* Boston, MA: Houghton-Mifflin.

Schmitt, E. (2004). *Left brain marketing.* Available: http://www.oblique.com.au

Schroeder, S. D. (2000, October 13). Choosing the right segmentation approach. *DMNews.* Available: http://www.dmnews.com

Schultz, D. E. (2008). *Caught on the cusp of communication change.* Keynote address presented at the 13th International Conference on Corporate and Marketing Communications, University of Ljubljana, Slovenia.

Scott, D. M. (2007). *The new rules of marketing & PR.* Hoboken, NJ: John Wiley.

Seelye, K. Q. (2006, October 31). Newspaper circulation falls sharply. *The New York Times.* Available: http://www.nytimes.com

Sernovitz, A. (2006, January 17). Word of mouth marketing in five easy steps. Available: http://www.marketingprofs.com

——(2007, July 23). Dealing with detractors: Responding to negative word of mouth. Available: http://www.newcommreview.com

Sharf, B. F. (1999). Beyond netiquette: The ethics of doing naturalistic discourse research on the Internet. In S. Jones (ed.), *Doing Internet research: Critical issues and methods for examining the Net* (pp. 243–56). Thousand Oaks, CA: Sage.

Shapiro, C. (2006). Can scent sell? A growing number of retailers seem to think so. Available: www.scentair.com

Shavitt, S., Lowrey, P., & Haefner, J. (1998). Public attitudes toward advertising: More favorable than you might think. *Journal of Advertising Research, 38,* 7–22.

Sherman, E. & Topol, M. T. (1999). Anticipating the impact of new technologies on retailing. *Journal of Retailing and Consumer Services, 3,* 107–11.

Sheth, J. N. (1971). Word of mouth in low-risk innovations. *Journal of Advertising Research 113,* 15–18.

Siebert, T. (2006, October 20). Edelman reveals two more Wal-Mart 'flogs.' Available: http://www.mediapost.com

Siegel, L. (2006, May 15). Keller Fay's Talk Track reveals consumer word of mouth. Available: http://www.kellerfay.com

Sielski, K. (2009, April 2). Five simple steps for real-time lead generation via social marketing sites. Available: http://www.articlesbase.com

Sifry, D. (2005, August). *State of the blogosphere, August 2005, part 1: Blog growth.* Available: http://technorati.com

Silverman, G. (2001). *The secrets of word-of-mouth marketing: How to trigger exponential sales through runaway word of mouth.* New York: AMACOM.

——(2005). Word of mouth: The oldest, newest marketing medium. In A. J. Kimmel (ed.), *Marketing communication: New approaches, technologies, and styles* (pp. 193–209). Oxford, UK: Oxford University Press.

6 Unique Web Communities That You Won't Forget. (2007, November 22). Available: http://www.makeuseof.com

Smith, A. (2008, July 22). *New numbers for blogging and blog readership.* Available: http://www.pewinternet.org

Smith, W. (1956). Product differentiation and market segmentation as alternative marketing strategies. *Journal of Marketing, 21,* 3–8.

Smith, R. E. & Vogt, C. A. (1995). The effects of integrating advertising and negative word-of-mouth communications on message processing and response. *Journal of Consumer Psychology, 4,* 133–51.

Social Media Marketing Still Lacks Strong Metrics. (2008, March 31). Available: http://www.marketingcharts.com

Social Network User Demographics. (2009, January 27). eMarketer. Available: http://www.emarketer.com

Social Networkers Dislike Constant Invites. (2009, April 21). Available: http://www.iabuk.net

Social Networking Goes Global. (2007, July 31). Available: http://www.comscore.com

Society for the Advancement of Education. (2003, December). *Companies building "brand communities."* Available: http://findarticles.com

Solomon, M. (2008). *Consumer behavior: Buying, having, and being*, 8th ed. Upper Saddle River, NJ: Prentice-Hall.

Sox, H. C. & Rennie, D. (2008). Seeding trials: Just say "no." *Annals of Internal Medicine, 149*, 279–80.

Special Report: Viral Marketing 2007. (2007, April 18). *Marketing Sherpa.* Available: http://www.marketingsherpa.com

Spethmann, B. (2005, September 14). VW offers perks in exchange for brand ambassadors. *Promo.* Available: http://promomagazine.com

Stanley, T. L. (1995, October 23). Kiddie cars. *Brandweek, 36.*

The State of Viral Marketing, Part 1. (2004, November). Available: http://www.avantmarketer.com

Stern, B. B. & Gould, S. J. (1988). The consumer as financial opinion leader. *Journal of Retail Banking, 10*, 43–52.

Stevens, J. (2008, May). *How to generate marketing value and brand evangelists from social network communities.* Paper presented at the Marketing 2.0 conference, Paris, France.

Stevenson, S. (2007, May 30). How Pond's infiltrated *The Starter Wife* writer's room. *Slate.* Available: http://www.slate.com

Stoke, S. M. & West, E. D. (1931). Sex differences in conversational interests. *Journal of Social Psychology, 2*, 120–26.

Stone, B. (2008, July 24). New tools from Facebook extends its web presence. *The New York Times.* Available: http://www.nytimes.com

Story, L. (2006, December 11). Times Sq. ads spread via tourists' cameras. *The New York Times.* Available: http://www.nytimes.com

Strong, E. K. (1925). *The psychology of selling life insurance.* New York: McGraw-Hill.

Study Reveals Ineffective Word-of-Mouth Metrics. (2006, January 20). *Daily Research News.* Available: http://www.mrweb.com

Summers, J. O. (1970). The identity of women's clothing fashion opinion leaders. *Journal of Marketing Research, 7*, 178–85.

Swan, J. E. & Oliver, R. L. (1989). Postpurchase communications by consumers. *Journal of Retailing, 65*, 516–33.

Syrett, M. (2005, April 26). Exploring blogs for brand insights. Available: https://www.marketingprofs.com

Tanikawa, M. (2004, October 23). The unleashing of the pet industry. *International Herald Tribune*, pp. 16–17.

Tapscott, D. & Williams, A. D. (2006). *Wikinomics: How mass collaboration changes everything.* New York: Portfolio.

—— —— (2007, February 15). Ideagora, a market place for minds. *Business Week.* Available: http://www.businessweek.com

TARP/Technical Assistance Research Program. (1981). *Measuring the grapevine: Consumer response and word-of-mouth.* The Coca-Cola Co., Atlanta, GA.

Taylor, J. (2007, December 12). Gen Y's influence on household purchases. *Millennial Marketer*. Available: http://www.millennialmarketer.com

Technographics Insight: Different Video Game Console Brands Find Different Niches. (2008, June 26). Forrester Research. Available: http://www.forrester.com

Technorati. (2008). *State of the blogosphere 2008*. Available: http://technorati.com

Tenby, S. (2003, December 8). Hosting online events. Available: http://www.techsoup.org

Terra Briefs. (2008, June). *Be a smart marketer: True representation of the Hispanic online audience – Solved!* Available: http://www.terra.com

Thompson, T. (2008, January 28). Is the tipping point toast? Available: http://www.fastcompany.com

3 Billion Mobile Subscriptions. (2007, July 2). Available: http://www.mobilemonday.net

Tierney, J. (2001, August 5). Here come the alpha pups. *The New York Times*. Available: http://www.nytimes.com

Top Trends in Social Media and Business. (2008, January 9). Available: http://www.marketingservicestalk.com

Trott, P. (2008). *Innovation management & new product development*, 4th ed. Upper Saddle River, NJ: Prentice-Hall.

Tsirulnik, G. (2009, June 10). Heineken taps mobile for multichannel promotion. Available: http://www.mobilemarketer.com

TV Viewing and Internet Use Are Complementary. (2008, October 31). Available: http://www.nielsen.com

Tversky, A. & Kahneman, D. (1973). Availability: A heuristic for judging frequency and probability. *Cognitive Psychology, 5*, 207–32.

UK Kids and Teens Communicate Nonstop. (2008, November 10). eMarketer. Available: http://www.emarketer.com

Upshaw, L. (2007, July 30). Integrity in marketing is not optional. *Advertising Age*. Available: http://adage.com

Urbanist. (2008, May 6). 5 great examples of guerrilla marketing gone wrong. Available: http://weburbanist.com

US Advertising Spending Growth, By Media. (2008, June 10). eMarketer. Available: http://www.emarketer.com/

US Online Social Network Advertising Spending, 2006–2011. (2007, May 5). eMarketer. Available: http://www.emarketer.com/

Van den Bulte, C. & Lilien, G. (2003). *Two-stage partial observability models of innovation adoption*. Working paper, Wharton School of Business, Philadelphia, PA.

——— (2001). *Medical Innovation* revisited: Social contagion versus marketing effort. *American Journal of Sociology, 106*, 1409–35.

Venkatraman, M. P. (1989). Opinion leaders, adopters, and communicative adopters: A role analysis. *Psychology & Marketing, 6*, 51–68.

Viscarolasaga, E. (2008, February 18). Mobile phone startups are chasing the consumer. *The Journal of New England Technology*. Available: http://www.masshightech.com

Vollmer, C. (2008). *Always on: Advertising, marketing, and media in an era of consumer control*. New York: McGraw-Hill.

Vranica, S. (2002, July 31). Sony Ericsson campaign uses actors to push camera-phone in real life. *The Wall Street Journal*. Available: http://online.wsj.com

Walker, R. (2004, December 5). The hidden (in plain sight) persuaders. *The New York Times*. Available: http://www.nytimes.com

Wangenheim, F. (2005). Postswitching negative word of mouth. *Journal of Service Research, 8*, 67–78.

——— & Bayon, R. (2004). Satisfaction, loyalty and word of mouth within the customer base of a utility provider: Differences between stayers, switchers and referral switchers. *Journal of Consumer Behaviour, 3*, 211–20.

Webb, R. (2009, April 6). Happy 5th birthday, subservient chicken. Barbarian Blog. Available: http://www.barbariangroup.com

Weber, L. (2007). *Marketing to the social web.* Hoboken, NJ: John Wiley.

Webster, S. A. (2005, March 22). "Oprah" buzz works no magic for Pontiac G6. *Detroit Free Press*, p. C2.

Weiman, G. (1982). On the importance of marginality: One more step into the two-step flow of communication. *American Sociological Review, 47*, 764–73.

Wells, M. (2004, February 2). Kid nabbing. *Forbes.* Available: http://tinyurl.com/cuh3a.

West, S. G. & Gunn, S. P. (1978). Some issues of ethics and social psychology. *American Psychologist, 33*, 30–8.

Westbrook, R. A., (1987). Product/consumption based affective responses and postpurchase processes. *Journal of Marketing Research, 24*, 258–70.

Where Do Social Media Passions Intersect With Advertising Effectiveness? (2007, May 24). Available: http://lsvp.wordpress.com

Whiteley, R. & Hessan, D. (1996). Customer centered growth: Five proven strategies for building competitive advantage. Menlo Park, CA: Addison-Wesley.

Why Word of Mouth Rules! (2008). *The Influencers.* Available: http://www.theinfluencers.ca

Whyte, W. H., Jr. (1954, November). The web of word of mouth. *Fortune*, pp. 140–3.

Wilkinson "Fight for Kisses" Media Solution. (2009). Available: http://www.coloribus.com

Wilson, R. F. (2000, February 1). The six simple principles of viral marketing. *Web Marketing Today.* Available: http://www.wilsonweb.com

Wilson, W. R. & Peterson, R. A. (1989). Some limits on the potency of word-of-mouth information. *Advances in Consumer Research, 16*, 23–9.

Wojnicki, A. (2006, June 7). PWOM vs. NWOM: More on the debate. Available: http://www.womma.org

Women Who Blog. (2009, June 5). eMarketer. Available: http://www.emarketer.com

Word of Mouth Marketing Association (WOMMA). (2005, July 12). *WOMMA Terminology Framework.* Available: http://www.womma.org

World Internet Users. (2009, March). Internet world stats. Available: http://www.internetworldstats.com

Yale, L. J. (1987). *An empirical study of word of mouth behaviors: Antecedents, processes and outcomes.* Working paper, Graduate School of Management, University of California-Irvine.

Yankelovich Partners, Inc. (2005, April 18). 2005 marketing receptivity study. Available: http://www.yankelovich.com

Yongfook. (2009, March 17). Social media ROI: Measuring the unmeasurable? Available: http://zygote.-egg-co.com

Zawodny, J. (2005, February 7). McDonald's fake blog. Available: http://jeremy.zawodny.com

Zeigler, T. (2006, March 14). Weighing in on the conversation index. Available: http://www.bivingsreport.com

Zeithaml, V. A. & Bitner, M. J. (1996). *Services marketing.* New York: McGraw-Hill.

Zhao, X. (2006). Global word of mouth. Paper presented at WOMBAT2 conference, San Francisco, June 20–1. Available: http://cats.blogilvy.be

INDEX